100 Years of the F.A. Cup

Double delight. *Above:* Tottenham's team of 1961 run the lap of honour, with Blanchflower and Norman holding the Cup over Dyson's head.
Below: Frank McLintock holds the Cup aloft to celebrate Arsenal's victory of 1971.

100 Years of the F.A. Cup

The Official Centenary History

by

TONY PAWSON

WILLIAM HEINEMANN LTD
Official Publishers to The Football Association

Distributed by
PAN BOOKS LTD, 33 TOTHILL STREET, LONDON, SW1

William Heinemann Ltd

15 Queen St, Mayfair, London WIX 8BE

LONDON   MELBOURNE   TORONTO
JOHANNESBURG   AUCKLAND

First published 1972

© Copyright The Football Association 1972

SBN 0 330 23274 6

Printed in Great Britain

Contents

APPENDICES

Author's Acknowledgements

My grateful thanks to Mr Denis Follows and his staff for all the help I received. This cannot have been easy during the problems of The Football Association's move from 22 to 16 Lancaster Gate but I was given unfailing assistance particularly by Mr J. Carvosso and Mr M. McNamara.

Geoffrey Green's expert knowledge was also invaluable and I am much indebted to him and to Brian Glanville and Eric Todd for their ready assistance.

Arthur Rowe and Joe Mercer were as helpful and knowledgeable as when they coached me in my playing days. Bill Slater and Tom Finney, who used to give me lessons on the field, were just as patient and kindly in guiding me in this work.

Of the many managers who gave me their views I was particularly grateful to Don Revie, Sir Matt Busby, Ron Greenwood, and Bill Nicholson who all spared me time at inconvenience to themselves.

Of the players, Danny Blanchflower and Trevor Bailey readily contributed to the book, while Jimmy Dimmock was particularly helpful in conveying to me the feel of football in the 1920s.

The Royal Engineers gave me much information on the early years and I am indebted to Brigadier Lacey and Lt-Col Stear.

To Dr J. Loughrey I am indebted for the detailed statistical tables in the Appendices and for assistance with the proofs. Mr D. Hillman also gave invaluable help with the research.

In the rush to meet my deadline I was particularly grateful for the expert typing of Marguerite Rogers, the proof reading of Paul Pollock and the tolerance of my wife and family.

The following books and newspapers have been of special help and I am grateful for the use of extracts from them:

Football from the Goalmouth, ed. Roy Peskett (Sporting Handbooks, 1948)
'The Cup' 50 Years of English Football, D. Mackenzie (Wyman, 1933)
History of Queen's Park F.C., Richard Robinson (Nisbet, 1920)
Association Football, John Goodall (Blackwood, 1898)
Cliff Bastin Remembers, Brian Glanville (Ettrick, 1950)
The History of the Tottenham F.C. 1882–1946, G. Wagstaffe Simmons (Tottenham Hotspur F. & A. C. 1947)
A History of the Corinthian F.C., F. N. S. Creek (Longmans, 1933)
The Times, Sunday Times, Observer, Guardian, Sunday Pictorial, Sunday Mirror.

Mr H. E. Bates has kindly allowed me to use his account of the 1953 Cup-Final written for the *F.A. Book for Boys* (Heinemann).

Other books I have found of great assistance are:

The Official History of the F.A. Cup, Geoffrey Green (Heinemann, 1959)

Association Football and the Men Who Made It, Alfred Gibson and William Pickford (Caxton, 1906)

The Real Football, J. H. Catton (Sands, 1900)

The 100 Years Story of the Nottingham Forest F.C., ed. J. H. Turner (Nottingham Forest F.C., 1905)

The Book of Football (Amalgamated Press, 1906)

Football Through the Ages, Percy M. Young (Methuen, 1957)

Famous Footballers, C. W. Alcock and Rowland Hill (Hudson & Kearns and the *News of the World*, 1896)

Manchester City, Meredith to Mercer, Eric Thornton (Hale, 1969)

Leeds United and Don Revie, Eric Thornton (Hale, 1970)

Manchester United, Percy M. Young (Heinemann, 1960)

West Bromwich Albion, Peter Morris (Heinemann, 1965)

Aston Villa, Peter Morris (Naldrett, 1960)

Football in Merseyside, Percy M. Young (Stanley Paul, 1963)

The Wolves, Percy M. Young (Stanley Paul, 1959)

The Stanley Matthews Story, Stanley Matthews (Oldbourne, 1960)

The Newcastle United F.C. Story, John Gibson (Pelham, 1961)

Bolton Wanderers, Percy M. Young (Stanley Paul, 1961)

Soccer in the Blood, Billy Walker (Stanley Paul, 1960)

Hotbed of Soccer, Arthur Appleton (Hart-Davis, 1960)

Gunners on Target, Geoffrey Mowbray (Stanley Paul, 1961)

Cup-Final Story 1946–65, David Prole (Hale, 1966)

A Lifetime in Football, Charles Buchan (Phoenix House, 1955)

The Footballers' Companion, Brian Glanville (Eyre & Spottiswoode, 1962)

The History of the Amateur Football Alliance, W. E. Greenland (Standard Printing & Publishing Co., 1965)

Spurs, A History of the Tottenham Hotspur F.C., Julian Holland (Phoenix House, 1956)

Spurs – The Double, Julian Holland (Heinemann, 1961)

The West Ham United Football Book, Dennis Irving (Stanley Paul, 1968)

Forward Arsenal, Bernard Joy (Phoenix House, 1952)

The Romance of the Wednesday 1867–1926, Richard A. Sparling (Sheffield Wednesday F.C., 1926)

Going for Goal, Peter McParland (Souvenir, 1900)

40 Years in Football, Ivan Sharpe (Hutchinson, 1952)

Don Davies – an Old International, J. Cox (Stanley Paul, 1962)

People in Sport, Brian Glanville (Secker & Warburg, 1967)

Postscript

The F.A. Challenge Cup's centenary season 1971/1972 was quick to prove that there is always something new in this traditional competition. On November 20th, 1971, Ted MacDougall of Bournemouth scored a record nine goals in the 11–0 defeat of Margate. On the same day two Amateur sides, Oxford City and Alvechurch, shared a goal-less draw in their *fourth* replay in the fourth qualifying round. Only four other Cup-ties had gone to five matches: Arsenal v. New Brompton in 1899, Barrow v. Gillingham and Leyton v. Ilford in 1924 and, the longest in playing time, Stoke City v. Bury in January 1955.

Alvechurch won the sixth game on Monday, November 22nd, to end the Cup's record marathon. Two days later they were knocked out, beaten 4–2 by Fourth Division, Aldershot. It was a tribute to their fitness that they could still give a League side a hard game.

1

The Birth of the Cup

There has never been any necessity to define 'the Cup'. For everyone in England that brief reference automatically implies The Football Association Challenge Cup. Its astonishing popularity has fathered a host of imitators, each drawing on the sure recipe for success. The World Cup, the European Cups, the U.E.F.A. Cup, the League Cup, the Texaco Cup, the Amateur Cup, the Women's Football Association Mitre Challenge Trophy, there is room for them all and each develops its own fascination. A hundred years from its modest beginnings the Challenge Cup still reigns supreme, more vigorous and popular than ever, more firmly rooted in the fibre of the country. It is at once modern and traditional, a part of our social history and our culture that is undated and timeless in its appeal.

Our pioneering past has shaped many parts of the globe, but from all our traditions the Cup now has as great an impact as any. For it was the Cup that stimulated the astounding growth of Association Football that has such an effect on the lives and imagination of nations throughout the continents.

Compare the story of association football with that of cricket or rugby. In the 19th century cricket had all the advantages. Squire and labourer were nurtured on it and there was a deep love of the game in all classes. Yet now interest is less intense and widespread. Only as cricket began to lose some of its appeal did the legislators institute a knock-out competition and the Gillette Cup, started in 1963, has already brought a new dimension to the game. Rugby administrators regarded Cup competition and professionalism as the ultimate evil. So despite the support of so many schools the game has always been limited in its appeal and has inevitably split between the amateurs of the Union and the professionals of the League. Association football reversed the process. Within eight years of its formation The Football Association started the Cup Competition to give impetus to the spread of the game. It was the stone that started an avalanche and led to the rise of professionalism, the development of the League system and an undreamed of advance in the game's popularity. The Cup was the catalyst that changed the whole concept of association football and made it truly the game of the people throughout the world. You can admire it for so firing the imagination or curse it for bringing in its train the problems of sportsmanship and crowd control. But you cannot ignore its vast appeal.

An insignificant atom can generate an uncontrollable force. So it was, that a quiet meeting of a small committee launched fifteen Clubs into a competition that was to change a way of life. The scene was a small, oak-panelled room at the *Sportsman*

1

Major Sir Francis Marindin, RE, KCMG, President of the F.A. 1874–90.

office, London: the date July 20, 1871, eight years after the formation of The Football Association. There sat seven men, dressed in the height of fashion as befitted their place in society. The talk was of the events of the day: the siege of Paris by the troops from Versailles; the proposal before Parliament to abolish the system of purchasing commissions in the Army; the serious illness of Edward, Prince of Wales; the decision of King William of Prussia to assume the title of German Emperor. Soon their conversation drifted to the exploits of their football clubs, for each was a member of one or other of the best-known teams of that period.

Charles Alcock of the Wanderers was tall and athletic, and about thirty years of age. Near him sat A. Stair of the Upton Park Club, Honorary Treasurer to the F.A. Committee; C. W. Stephenson, of Westminster School; J. H. Giffard, of the Civil Service Club; D. Allport, of the Crystal Palace Football Club; M. P. Betts, of Harrow; and an officer of the Royal Engineers, Captain Francis Marindin.

After the formal business had been dealt with, C. W. Alcock proposed the competition. 'That it is desirable that a Challenge Cup should be established in connection with the Association, for which all clubs belonging to the Association should be invited to compete'. The idea was received at once with general favour, and finally approved at a subsequent meeting held on October 16, 1871, which was attended by representatives of eleven clubs as well as by the F.A. Committee.

Because most of the fixture cards for that season had already been completed the northern clubs were absent, but fifteen teams in all entered, and of these only two – Queen's Park, Glasgow, and Donington Grammar School – came from north of Hertfordshire. Hitchin, Royal Engineers, Reigate Priory, Maidenhead, and Great Marlow were all outside the Metropolitan radius, but the other eight entries – Wanderers, Harrow Chequers, Barnes, Civil Service, Crystal Palace, Upton Park, Clapham Rovers, and Hampstead Heathens – were all within easy reach of the City and came fairly under the heading of London Clubs. Here they were, the fifteen original entries for a competition which nowadays attracts over 400 clubs.

2

The Celebrated Wanderers

Six teams dominate the first ten years of the Cup. In order of appearance and importance the first of the leading actors to take the stage must be the Wanderers. 'The Celebrated Wanderers' as Major Marindin always referred to them are inseparably linked with the Cup. Their early history is the Cup's early history. Both the Wanderers Club and the F.A. Challenge Cup were conceived by C. W. Alcock and five times in the first seven years they carried off the trophy – 'the insignificant pot' that excited ever-growing interest. Charles Alcock himself had the satisfaction of leading Wanderers to victory in that first Final at the Oval in 1872.

Association football sprang from the Public Schools where football was regarded as much as a character-forming exercise as a sport. The tough breed of Empire builders was brought up on physical challenge and fortitude as the game's main characteristics, with less emphasis on the grace and skills of the sport. In the great debate that launched Association Football and split off the Rugby code, hacking was a fiercer cause of controversy than handling. Hotly defending this somewhat barbarous practice Campbell had declared 'hacking is the true football game and if it were done away with all the courage and pluck of the game would be at an end'. 'Putting the boot in' was quite respectable before the Association code.

Football indeed had violence in its pedigree. The antiquarian Stubbs wrote 'concerning football playing I protest unto you it may rather be called a friendly kind of fighting than recreation'. But that was mild compared with the comment on apprentices' football in the Elizabethan Age 'A bloody murthering practice, rather than a fellowly sport or pastime'. In 1608 Leet records contain the entry 'That whereas there hath been heretofore great disorder in our toune of Manchester and the inhabitants thereof greatly wronged and charged with the makings and amendinges of their glasse windows broken yearlye and spoyled by a company of lewd and disordered p'sons usinge that unlawfull exercise of playinge with the ffoteball in ye streets of said toune breaking many mens windows and glasse at their plesures and other great inormyties.'

Even that toughest of English soldier statesman, Oliver Cromwell, found football too tough for his liking. In a reminiscence concerning the Reverend John Wheelwright's less saintly days at University it is recorded that 'Cromwell declared unto the gentlemen about him that he had been more afraid of this gentleman (Wheelwright) at football than of anything else since in the field, as he was infallibly sure of being tripped up by him'.

Nineteenth century public school football was hard indeed by our standards,

C. W. Alcock, Secretary of the F.A. 1870–95.

though more refined than its primitive versions. Courage was still at a premium and the Association code of 1863 did nothing to justify Campbell's fear that the game would go soft.

Bodily challenge was still the essence of its appeal, and the idea that the professional game is now harsh and ruthless would have made the early giants laugh. It was nothing for a finalist to play on with a broken collar bone and in 1878 J. Kirkpatrick even continued to keep goal with a broken arm. This was particularly courageous when goalkeepers could be charged for the fun of it regardless of where the ball was. Indeed one of the earliest tactical ploys was for one forward to fell the goalkeeper while another was shooting.

It was Harrow more than any other school that was excited by the pure sporting aspects of the game. Dribbling was the art that enthused them and kept them playing after they had left school. Old Harrovians were instrumental in getting the dribbling code accepted and in forming three of the earliest football organisations – Sheffield, Harrow Chequers and Forest. It was the last of these teams that developed into the Wanderers.

Forest is usually regarded as 'the first football club of modern times' and was

5

certainly the first to make any impact on the South. All its members were old Harrovians and their home ground where they 'erected their posts' in 1859 was at Snaresbrook close to Epping Forest. For five years their ground and their success remained constant though their rules were as varied as their opponents until they became one of the founder members of the Football Association in 1863. Their love of the dribbling game was ably defended by their Secretary, J. F. Alcock, who devoted much of his energy to preserving the rule against hacking that had split association and rugby factions. While his elder brother fought the administrative battle Charles Alcock developed the Forest Club. He was described as 'a man of fine and commanding presence, who had a happy knack of being able to persuade others to his way; he may not have been the most machine-like of officials, but he was essentially a leader'. How fortunate that he was not a meticulous rules and red tape man or he would have lacked the perception from which was born the Wanderers and the Cup. He enlarged the membership of Forest by no longer confining it to old Harrovians and he abandoned Snaresbrook in favour of convenient grounds in various parts of London. Some of the older members declared it impractical to have 'an organisation of ex-public schoolboys wandering from place to place'. As so often, opposition hardened resolve giving the Club new impetus and a new name – 'The Wanderers'.

Football was still 'rather a recreation and a means of exercise for a few public schoolboys than a truly National sport.' But two things were to change this. The first was the attraction of the game and in particular of the skill of dribbling. For Alcock this was the game's highest achievement. In the 1873 Football Annual he wrote 'A really good player will never lose sight of the ball, at the same time keeping his attention employed in spying out the gaps in the enemy's ranks which may give him a favourable chance of arriving at the coveted goal. To see some players guide and steer a ball through a circle of opposing legs twisting and turning as occasion demands is a sight not to be forgotten.'

Modern tactics and talents have inverted those early principles. Association football is now a passing not a dribbling game. And that greatest of all dribblers, Stanley Matthews, never needed to look at the ball. Instinct and touch kept it under complete control while his eyes and mind were free to spot the weakness and plan the move. The priorities in the game have changed, but the speed and skill of the accomplished dribbler is still its most spectacular art and the quickest way to the crowd's affection. Then as now it was dribbling that caught the imagination. But it was the second factor, the Cup, that was decisive in developing a game that fascinated the country and then the World.

Again, it was C. W. Alcock who took the lead. The Wanderers became strongly represented on football's governing body and by 1871 Alcock was Secretary of the F.A. – the first of the four powerful characters who guided the Association through the next hundred years. In that year Charles Alcock was 29. Born at Sunderland and educated at Harrow he combined the best qualities of the rugged North and the smooth South and was ideally suited to spread the game. There were still only

30 clubs belonging to the Association and Alcock was determined to improve this. So he tabled the resolution to start a Cup Competition that he rightly believed would fire interest in the game. We have seen how readily the idea was accepted. Fittingly, it was Wanderers who won that first competition and Charles Alcock who captained them to 1–0 victory over the Royal Engineers at the Oval. The catholic composition of the Wanderers' team was now such that they had six future internationals in their side and their best players were T. C. Hooman of Charterhouse and R. W. S. Vidal, 'the prince of dribblers', from Westminster. Edward Bowen in goal was little tested but at the age of 36 he was still an outstanding goalkeeper – no mean achievement in the days when training was unknown and goalkeepers were fair game for the heaviest of charges. M. P. Betts scored the winning goal that day playing for the Wanderers under the assumed name of A. H. Chequer. Betts made no attempt to conceal the fact that he was a Harrow Chequer from the Club which had scratched to the Wanderers in the first round. Clearly rules about transfers and being Cup-tied were more elastic in those early days!

The Wanderers were aided on their way to the Final by their power in committee as well as on the field. In the quarter-final they drew 0–0 with Crystal Palace and progressed under Rule 8 of the Competition which stated: 'In the case of a drawn match the Clubs shall be drawn in the next round or compete again at the discretion of the Committee'. This was, however, a sensible decision to send Wanderers into one semi-final against Queen's Park, Glasgow, and Crystal Palace into the other against the Royal Engineers, who would otherwise have had a bye into the Final. It would seem fairly simple to start with 15 Clubs and have no byes after the first round. But in 1871 nothing was simple in starting a National Competition. Queen's Park from Glasgow could not afford to travel frequently to the South and they were put straight into the semi-final, which upset the pairings. Again, Wanderers were held to a goal-less draw, but Queen's Park could not afford to travel back to London so they withdrew, letting Wanderers through to the Final. This caused great disappointment in London where their first match had been described as 'the most remarkable event in modern football'. But as yet neither the honour nor the rewards of medals of 'trifling value' were sufficient to justify the expenditure on a second trip to the capital. It was to be a long time before the rewards for individuals were to be counted in thousands and for Clubs in tens of thousands.

Betting was so much the fashion of the day that, at this time, the M.C.C.'s cricket laws contained a section regulating it. So it was hardly surprising that there should, from the start, be betting on the results of Cup games and, after their fortunate progress to the Final, the Wanderers were listed at 7–4 against. But, in the event, Lieutenant Cresswell had his collarbone broken after ten minutes and, though he continued playing, the Royal Engineers were too handicapped for anything but a courageous rearguard. Once Betts had scored from an acute angle after Vidal's long dribble had made the opening, the Engineers did well to keep their margin of defeat to this single goal.

For Charles Alcock this was his last appearance in the Final, as injury robbed

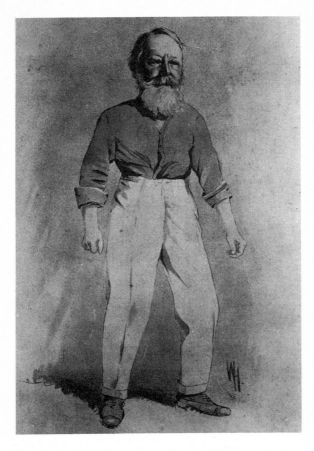

Lord Kinnaird, President of the F.A., played in nine Cup-Finals and won five Cup winners' medals.

him of further Cup medals. He was also forced to withdraw from two International against Scotland, the second time after he had been seriously hurt in a match at the Oval between Old Etonians and Old Harrovians. But in his final season 1874–5 he achieved his ultimate ambition and played for England against Scotland. Now age and injury forced him to give up the game, which continued to benefit from his passionate enthusiasm as he devoted all his time to furthering the interest of the Football Association. For a time his club, too, continued to prosper.

The Wanderers had won again in 1873, the only year in which there was a genuine 'challenge' for the Challenge Cup. As holders they were exempted to the Final, 'challenging' Oxford University, the winners of the knock-out rounds. They also had the right to choose the ground and, with their customary random selection, they picked Lillie Bridge, now covered by the railway lines at West Brompton. Battersea Park would have been a more natural choice, but this was the favourite ground of Vidal, now playing for the University. He was the most feared man in a talented Oxford side, but on the day the Prince of Dribblers gave no trouble. He was subdued by Spondee Howell whose 'great feet recalled the metrical figure to the imaginative'. At this stage of the game strength was still of more importance than speed or skill. Howell had it and so did Lord Kinnaird, the formidable figure who dominated so many finals. Not only did Kinnaird score a decisive goal 'threading a way between the forest of Oxford legs' to shoot through the posts, he also gave his team virile and flamboyant leadership – a striking sight with his flowing red beard, his long white trousers, the orange, violet, and black jersey of the Wanderers, and a blue-and-white quartered cricket cap. C. H. Wollaston also scored, but it was the colourful Kinnaird who played the main part in preventing a double success for the dark blues on Boat Race day.

The Boat Race indeed was still much more of an occasion than the Cup-Final and kick-off times were arranged so as not to interfere with seeing it.

Kinnaird was soon to leave the Wanderers, his electric personality revitalising the Old Etonians. This was a loss that could not easily be made good. True the Wanderers still had a galaxy of Internationals, but many had divided loyalties. Kenyon-Slaney, a Captain in the Household Brigade and later a Member of Parliament, was a high-scoring centre-forward who also went back to the Old Etonians. Two internationals, R. W. S. Vidal and F. H. Birley, preferred to play for Oxford University during the next two seasons and helped to defeat Wanderers 1–0 and 2–1 in the quarter-finals.

Not until 1876 did Wanderers reach the Final again and once more they won, defeating Old Etonians 3–0 in a replay after a goal-less draw. T. B. Hughes hit two of the goals and Wollaston scored the third. This was also the third of his Cup-winning appearances and clearly Wollaston was one of England's finest forwards. Between 1874 and 1880 he was capped five times against Scotland.

This Final was also notable for the appearance of Frederick and Hubert Heron the only two brothers to play together in an international and in a Cup-winning side. They were selected against Scotland for the game on March 4, a fortnight before the Wanderers won at the Oval. Hubert was the cleverer player, his only fault an insidious individualism inspired by his compulsive love of dribbling. Pickford notes that 'he had a reputation that even in those days extended as far as Scotland where, in one of the English matches, the Scottish right-half devoted the whole afternoon to knocking him over as the only way to stop him'. Who says that the game has got rougher?

In one of the matches between Wanderers and Old Etonians, Alcock tried out a peculiar charge of his own on the amiable giant, 'Quintus' Lubbock. 'By Heaven' roared the normally placid Lubbock 'if you do that again I'll hack off your legs'. Such little differences of opinion were settled as usual without the intervention of the referee for there was no ill-will behind the friendly rivalry.

In the 1876 Final five former Wanderers – Kinnaird, Hogg, Kenyon-Slaney, Bonsor and Lubbock – all appeared for the Old Etonians. This was a portent of the drift back to Old Boys' sides that was to destroy the Wanderers. But they won again the next year, their vast superiority over Oxford being confirmed only by two goals in extra time. The following year they took the Cup for the third successive time. After a bye in the semi-final – an absurd concept in modern times – they met the Royal Engineers who had defeated Old Harrovians. Lord Kinnaird was back captaining the side and he swept the Wanderers to a 3–1 victory.

Wanderers' success was largely due to their magnificent forward line, which had included Wollaston, Kennick, Edwards, Wylie, Hubert Heron, and Wace, the last three also playing together against Scotland.

The 1878 Final was their third successive win and the zenith of their power and fame. The Cup could have been theirs to keep, but Alcock thoughtfully saved his own Committee additional expense by returning the trophy to the Association on the condition that it was never to be won outright by any Club.

No doubt the Wanderers expected to win it often enough again. But, surprisingly, the old soldiers of the game were about to fade away. As Gibson and Pickford record in their invaluable *History of Association Football*, the Club which had borne such a great share of the hard work of founding the game was on the eve of dissolution. Composed as it was of a collection of members of other Clubs it found increasing difficulty in securing players.

'Old School Clubs' were being formed in growing numbers and it became almost mandatory in the etiquette of the day for a player leaving school or University to offer himself to his Old Boys Club.

In September Kinnaird, and other leading players, resigned from the Wanderers to play for the Old Etonians. A few days later the two Clubs were drawn together in the First Round. The Wanderers, without time to build a new team, were also wedded to out-of-date tactics. Shearman records that 'Passing-on completely superseded dribbling about the same time the great provincial centres came to the front, about 1878 or 1879.' But the Wanderers were still influenced by Alcock's conception of dribbling as the supreme skill. While they could field eleven brilliant individuals, they had continued to be successful. But now they were savaged 7–2 by an Old Etonian side of superior talent and teamwork. The combination of ball-control, long passing, and snap shooting destroyed the Wanderers and they never recovered from the defeat.

Left without Cup fixtures they tried to play a friendly match against Clapham Rovers under floodlight – but the game had to be abandoned early. Next season they hinted at a revival with an early win over the Old Carthusians. But in the third round they once again faced the Old Etonians and once more they went down. This time the score was 3–1. Though the game was more evenly balanced the result was disastrous. It hastened the movement of players from the Club and in 1880 – the year the Universities withdrew from the Competition – the 'celebrated Wanderers' suffered the indignity of having to scratch. This was the death blow and the Club drifted quietly to dissolution. The Wanderers' Cup record – five Finals and five wins – was a guarantee of immortality and a reminder of the deeds of the spirited and carefree players who launched the Cup with such fine flair and enthusiasm.

3

Other Early Giants

Apart from the Wanderers, the Royal Engineers of Chatham were the most consistent team in the early years. Having lost that first Final at the Oval and again in 1874 they won the Cup at last in 1875. Why was the Army interested in football and what was so special about the Sappers?

The public school background of many of the officers explains their enthusiasm for Association Football. Success, however, was rooted in the character of an individual and the traditions of Chatham. In the 60 years since an Establishment, now the Royal School of Military Engineering, had been set up for them at Chatham for instruction in the duties of 'sapping, mining, and other Field Works' the Sappers had built a reputation for mental and physical fitness. By 1875 Sir George Trevelyan could write 'The Royal Engineers – the select of the select, everyone of whom before he obtains his commission runs the gauntlet of an almost endless series of intellectual contests for years together – could turn out the best football eleven in the Kingdom and within the last twelve months gained a success at cricket absolutely unprecedented in the annals of the game. The match in question was against an eleven of I. Zingari. Eight wickets of the Royal Engineers fell for an average of more than ninety runs a wicket, and this stupendous score was made against good bowling and excellent fielding.'

The Establishment at Chatham was formed in 1812 in response to an urgent request by the Duke of Wellington, who was concerned at the losses suffered by the best of his officers and men in siege operations.

The first Director of the Establishment, Major Pasley, was a man of remarkable talent who organised a revolutionary system of practical instruction. At the time few soldiers could read or write and it was considered that to educate the soldier or the N.C.O. to carry out fieldworks on their own might make them conceited and insubordinate. Pasley encouraged the adventurous spirit and a readiness to take risks. Rochester Bridge then had many narrow spans and at certain times the tide rushing between the piers made navigation hazardous – an ideal situation in Pasley's view for realistic pontoon training. The demonstrations of siege operations on the Great Lines at Chatham were described by Charles Dickens in his *Pickwick Papers*. Pasley, who was represented as the dashing Captain Bulder, greatly impressed Mr Pickwick as did the 'astounding evolutions' carried out that day.

With such a Director the Engineer officers were encouraged to be versatile and to take part in sport. In the early days it was shooting or hunting with the neighbouring pack of foxhounds, with sailing as a summer diversion. Soon cricket and

11

The Royal Engineers team of 1872 with eight of the
players who took part in the first Cup-Final at the Oval.
Major Marindin is in the centre of the back row.

then Association Football became equally popular sports. The man to develop
football was Major F. A. Marindin, the Brigade Major at Chatham from 1866 to
1874. He was one of the three central characters in the development of the Cup and
the game.

In this cynical age it is customary to pick on the foibles and follies of the Victorian era and to ignore their extraordinary talent, vigour, and achievement. It
was a time when a young subaltern might suddenly find himself in charge of territory twice the size of Britain and make as good a job of running it as can the United
Nations of today with all their experience and resource. Never was this resilience,
confidence, and ability more apparent than in the Royal Engineers. The School of
Military Engineering at Chatham's Brompton Barracks made them the technocrats
of their day at a time when there were no technical colleges outside the Army.

In the year that the Cup competition began their diverse activities ranged from
designing the Albert Hall to the development of the 'steam sapper', a traction

12

engine which pulled a train of vehicles across country and was the forerunner of the Army's mechanical transport. Marindin himself was fully imbued with this professional skill and personal resource. His successful service career culminated in his becoming Inspector of Railways for England and he was also responsible for setting up the electric lighting system for London. For his great public services here and in India he was awarded the K.C.M.G. in Queen Victoria's Jubilee Year.

Such was the distinguished man who also played so prominent a part in the development of the Challenge Cup and of Association Football. From 1874 to 1890 he was President of the Football Association giving to the game the status and backing that guided and encouraged its explosive growth. It was his self-sacrifice that absorbed without turmoil the new professionalism which the Rugby Footballers so strongly rejected. And it was the presence of men like Sir Francis Marindin, Lord Kinnaird, and Charles Alcock which helped overcome the sneers that Rugby might be a hooligan's game played by gentlemen, but association football was a gentleman's game played by hooligans.

His enthusiasm had soon built up a formidable football team at Chatham and in 1869 the Royal Engineers joined The Football Association. Two years later Marindin was a member of that select Committee which initiated the Cup. Twice he led his team into the Final though he was absent from the winning side of 1875. Thereafter he played little though occasionally turning out for the Old Etonians of whose Club he was President. Yet he holds unchallenged one Cup record: he refereed eight Finals between 1880 and 1890. A. Stair, C. J. Hughes, and J. Lewis come closest to him each officiating on a mere three occasions. His constant selection for this controversial job underlined his great reputation. Rarely was his judgement and impartiality challenged. Queen's Park, Glasgow, were angered by having two of their goals disallowed in the 1884 Final. Scots may still aver that he cost their Club the English Challenge Cup, but as he disallowed a Rovers' goal as well it is probable that he was more expert than the players in interpreting the Offside Law. Certainly contemporaries were astounded that his ruling or fairness should be queried.

Marindin's Engineers from Chatham were without doubt the best team in the country during those first four seasons of the Cup. All their matches were against leading Clubs such as the Wanderers or the Universities or the Gitanos, and their playing record is remarkable:

	Played	Won	Lost	Drawn	Goals For	Against
1871–2	21	16	1	4	59	3
1872–3	20	19	1	0	74	2
1873–4	25	22	1	2	70	8
1874–5	20	17	0	3	41	8
Total	86	74	3	9	244	21

An impression of football at Kennington Oval in the early days
when the cross-bar was a tape.

244 goals for and only 21 against! Only three matches lost in four years and two of those were the Cup Finals of 1872 and 1874!

The Wanderers could gather a side of more talented individuals, but the fitness and team spirit of the Sappers made them the most formidable and consistent opponents. From their style of play we can get a good picture of the tactics and formation in these early games. Their line-up was the fashionable one of a goal-keeper, one back, two half-backs and seven forwards, three in the centre and two on either wing.

Lieutenant Ruck recalled that 'the centres were selected for weight, strength, and charging powers as well as their talent as dribblers, the game being perhaps a bit strenuous and many goals got for the R. E. by hustling goalkeepers through their own goals all ends up. The keynote of Royal Engineers football was combination not individuality and that was the great advantage they possessed over their opponents. The *esprit de corps* which was so marked in their professional capacity permeated their games.'

Lord Kinnaird confirmed this with his comment: 'The Sappers had discovered a new development of the game due to greater combination.'

They were the first to appreciate that football was essentially a team game and a passing game. This was not just in their realisation that 'passing-on' was as im-

14

portant as dribbling. It was seen also in their 'backing-up' of the player with the ball.

The Sheffield Association, who had many splendid games with them despite the initial difference in their rules, noted their ability to be all up in attack or back in defence. They were fit and fast enough to have the whole team covering the goal-keeper one moment, then surging upfield the next. This must have been an even more effective tactic in the days of long dribbles and short passes than when the Russians re-introduced it so successfully just after the Second World War.

The frequent reference in Royal Engineers match reports to the umpires' and referees' job being a sinecure indicates their sporting approach to the game. But in those days hard knocks were readily given without offence taken and the normally accepted principle – on which University matches were still refereed until the 'thir-ties – was that gentlemen did not foul intentionally so there were no fouls. This happy view of human nature has changed somewhat, but clearly the Royal Engi-neers, for all their sportsmanship, were no suitable opponents for the squeamish. The definition of 'fair' left plenty of scope as is indicated in one match account of 1873 after they had been kept waiting for late opponents. 'Our fellows being by this time fairly well disgusted began to peg into them pretty sharp and "little George" very soon sent a man to grass with a sweet though fair hack which was heard all over the ground. The individual was afterwards seen standing in goal on one leg like a stork.'

It was perhaps surprising that the Royal Engineers had to wait until 1875 to win the Cup. In that first Final at the Oval they were unlucky to have one of their best players severely injured near the start and this clearly prevented them achieving their usual devastating finish based on greater fitness.

In 1874 they also fell below their best form when the talented Oxford side defeated them. But the next season was their year of triumph. Sadly Major Marin-din was not to lead them to victory at the Oval. Not, as one story had it, because he withdrew from the Final rather than play against his fellow Old Etonians. That would have been in keeping with the tradition of some of the teams, but nothing would have undermined a Sapper's loyalty to his Corps. In fact Marindin was posted away from Chatham before the season and so could take no part. Major Merriman took over as captain providing positive leadership and competent goal-keeping. In so far as the team had a star player it was Lieutenant P. G. Von Donop, who, like Vidal, was christened by some papers 'Prince of Dribblers'. 'I shall never forget the extraordinary manner in which he seemed to pivot round the opposing player and then finish off by a most accurate shot' wrote Lieutenant Ruck whose own style was more direct and physical. Renny-Tailyour was another fine forward, a centre with the happy knack of scoring goals and the peculiar distinction of play-ing for England at Rugby and Association Football. Goodwyn and Onslow were rated exceptionally fine backs with the long kick that was the prime skill require-ment. Lieutenant Sim was another unusual player, reputedly the first to develop heading which has become such an important part of the game, but had no place in its original concept.

15

The Royal Engineers team went through the season without defeat, but they were given a hard fight for the Cup. Oxford and Cambridge contested the semi-finals so strongly that the Engineers and Old Etonians had little to spare in winning through. In the Final with the Old Etonians, the first game at the Oval was drawn after extra time. There is a full account of this match in a later chapter, but it was mainly remarkable for the handicap imposed on the Engineers by the existing rule that ends were changed after scoring a goal. This led to their playing against a gale for most of the ninety minutes and the unfair disadvantage they suffered caused the present rule to be introduced. Several leading Old Etonians were unable to take part in the replay, but surprisingly the Royal Engineers had some difficulty in winning.

Once more in 1878 the Royal Engineers of Chatham reached the Final, but it was difficult for them to maintain such high standards indefinitely. Lieutenant Ruck noted that 'a sympathetic Commandant and a sporting Brigade Major could at that time do much to retain at Chatham the services of a good cricketer or football player by posting him to H.M.S. Hood for submarine mining duties.' Such tactics have aided many service units, but the Sappers' resources could not keep pace with the development of the game and of professionalism. However, in 1908 they did add to their football honours the Amateur Cup which had been started soon after the Professionals began to dominate the Challenge Cup.

But the high point of the Sappers' sporting record is that season of 1875. The exhilaration and fellowship of these early Cup Games is well summed up by two reactions to their victory. The Chatham Commandant was unable to be present at the replayed Final because of official duties. Word of the victory was passed to him on the parade ground and General Galwey 'in defiance of all rules and regulations threw his cap in the air.' Charles Alcock's reaction was equally happy. Writing as Secretary of the F.A. in the *Football Annual* he commented: 'No one who is any way identified with the Association game but feels a certain amount of pride that the Cup at last adorns the mess at Chatham, a fitting guerdon for the best football players who ever kicked a ball and a suitable ornament for the table of the jolliest fellows who ever undertook the onerous duties of host.'

There is a pleasant tailpiece to the R.E.'s association with the Challenge Cup. The Army F.A. requested that their band should play at the 1972 Cup-Final in honour of the Corps' past exploits on the field.

An Army band is always colourful and when the Cup started the R.E.'s uniform was particularly striking. The Prince Consort himself designed it for the amalgamated Corps Regimental Brass and Reed Band. The uniform consisted of a black bearskin head-dress, white tunic with bright blue facings and ornate gold trappings and scarlet trousers. This had been changed to more practical scarlet tunic and black trousers when three years later the R.E. had their name forever inscribed in the records of the Cup.

One of the Royal Engineers' keenest opponents was Oxford University with whom they had many a closely matched contest. The University Association Foot-

16

ball Club had been founded on November 29, 1871 and limited at that time to 40 resident members.

Another rule accepted that the Club play 'according to the "Association Rules"' omitting in Rule 6 the words – 'unless there are at least three of his opponents between him and the goal.' However, the University was keen to enter the Cup and they soon agreed to accept the Offside Rule as it stood which was a necessary condition of entering the competition.

Inevitably Oxford had a number of the best footballers from the Public Schools in its team and with players such as Wollaston, Vidal, Birley, and Ottaway was bound to make an impact. Indeed they were the team to win the qualifying competition to 'challenge' the Wanderers in 1873, surviving on the way a very hard game with the Royal Engineers.

But in their own view they were out of condition and not at full strength when they took on the Wanderers at Lillie Bridge to lose by two goals.

Once Kinnaird had run right through them to score, Oxford dispensed with a goalkeeper 'all efforts being directed to accomplish the down-fall of the Wanderers goal'. Instead this allowed Wollaston to score a second with a long shot.

Nepean and Patton were absent from an Oxford team that never found its true form. But next year they had their revenge in the third round, proving too good for Wanderers and sweeping on to the Final. And this time they won at the Oval defeating the Royal Engineers.

The newspaper report indicates that there was no doubt of their superiority on the day:

'The final tie for the Challenge Cup was played on Saturday at Kennington Oval in the presence of upwards of 2,000 spectators. The well-known ability of both teams and the fact of its being the last tie caused the match to be looked forward to with great interest. The Wanderers held the Cup for two years, but were defeated this season in the third round by Oxford. The ground was in good condition and the weather fine. At 3.15 the Engineers having lost the toss kicked off from the Gasometer end against a fair wind. The Sappers at first carried the ball into the Oxonian territory, but Birley kicked it to Ottaway who, with Vidal, made an attempt to reach their opponents' goal, but were well crossed by Van Donop, who effected a fine run along the side of the ground, but Ottaway again made away with the ball. The Engineers were now unfortunate in twice violating the rule as to "hands" and very soon after kicked the ball behind which gave the Dark Blues the advantage of a corner-kick and, after a loose bully in front of the Engineers' goal, Mackarness sent the ball under the tape. Ends being changed the Engineers again threatened the Oxonian goal, but it was not long ere Ottaway, Maddison, and Vidal rushed away with the ball and Patton kicked the second goal for the Varsity. Ends were again reversed and Digby once or twice conducted the ball nearly the whole length of the ground, but was well received by Mackarness and Birley and the Engineers were compelled to act on the

17

defensive for some time; they made one or two good attempts to score, however, the ball going a very little over the tape and Renny-Tailyour made a shot at the goal the ball rebounding off one of the posts. Towards the end some very determined play was shown by both sides, but neither was able to effect a goal. At 4.45 time was called, Oxonians being victorious by two goals to nothing. Oxford brought a very strong team – Birley, Vidal, Rawson, Patton and Ottaway especially distinguishing themselves. The Engineers scarcely played up to their usual form.'

The next season it was to be the Engineers who carried off the Cup and again their match with Oxford was fiercely contested. This was the semi-final tie and the first game was drawn 1–1. The replay was won by the Engineers with a goal so close to time that no one was sure if it counted. What sensational reporting that would evoke now, what a strain it would put on spectators' nerves. But the Oxford minute book records the game without undue emotion and with welcome brevity:

'The next match was played on the same ground (The Oval) and after an equally well-contested game the Engineers won by one goal. The luck was quite against Oxford as twice the ball hit the tape once in the opinion of everyone going beneath it. In addition the goal was got *2 seconds* before time and so great was the excitement that it was quite uncertain whether the player who took the ball was in play or not. However, as stated Renny-Tailyour put the ball through the Oxford goal just as the umpires were calling time and so after a most pleasant game the R.E. at last turned the tables on their old friends and afterwards succeeded in winning the Cup.'

Twice more Oxford were to reach the Final losing narrowly to Wanderers and Clapham Rovers.

Against Wanderers ill-luck pursued them as Todd was badly hurt early on and retired to goal. They took the lead however when 'Waddington by a wonderful shot scored a goal for us, Kinnaird stepping back with the ball in his hands'. Goal hardly seemed the best place for Kinnaird's versatile talents, but he was not further tested. In the second half Oxford 'fell to pieces' and the Wanderers scored twice to win.

In the 1880 Final they were beaten by the only goal and that was their farewell to the competition.

Lloyd Jones scored for Clapham Rovers to 'vociferous cheers' after a good run by Sparks. The applause for Clapham Rovers play indicated 'that they were the popular party, the plucky manner in which they have fought for the Cup since its inception and the hard luck they have had on more than one occasion justifying the feeling in their favour'.

Next season the Oxford players voted by a large majority to withdraw from the Cup and Cambridge did the same. Perhaps the growth of the competition put too great a demand on their time. Perhaps travelling expenses were too big a drain on the Club's small resources with the minutes recording that such payments must never reduce the balance below £15. More likely it was disenchantment with the increasing competitiveness and more professional approach. In any event their exit was well-timed for the Cup was soon to be a hopeless quest for the part-time amateur.

4

The Scots and the Professors

Queen's Park, Glasgow, was a surprising side to find in the original fifteen entrants and we can now trace the Scottish involvement with the English Challenge Cup. The 'Queen's Park Football Club' was formed on July 9, 1867. With a fine disregard of superstition it was decided to elect thirteen members of Committee and the Club was launched, with Mr Mungo Ritchie as President.

The members' interest in football had been stirred when a small group of athletic Scotsmen moved to the Queen's Park recreation ground to get more room for practising hammer throwing, tossing the caber, or putting the ball. Since they exercised close to a football pitch used by a Branch of the Y.M.C.A., they tried out a game with the youngsters. This they so enjoyed that they began to play among themselves, purchasing a ball after a sixpence-a-head collection. This soon had to be repeated when the ball burst. Perhaps they can be classed as the first of the 'tanner fitba' players, the later Scottish term for those who learn juggling skills with cheap balls.

The connection with the Y.M.C.A. was brief, and within seven years the Club Secretary was telling the Annual Meeting: 'The muscular christianity to which we owe our existence – for we were evolved (that's the scientific term!) from the Young Men's Christian Association – was not always in favour!'

At first there was only a hazy idea of the right rules for the game and they wrote to Mr Lillywhite in London for advice. James Lillywhite, the former Nottinghamshire cricketer, had become the leading purveyor of sports equipment and information. He sent them the *Rules of the Field* which were the current Association Rules.

On November 3, a letter was published in the Glasgow Herald:

ENGLAND versus SCOTLAND

Sir, – Will you allow me a few lines in your paper to notify Scottish players that a match under the above title will take place in London on Saturday, 19th instant according to the rules of the Football Association? It is the object of the Committee to select best elevens at their disposal in the two countries and I cannot but think the appearance of some of the more prominent celebrities of football on the Northern side of the Tweed would do much to disseminate a healthy feeling of good fellowship among the contestants and tend to promote to a still greater degree the extension of the game.

In Scotland, once essentially the land of football, there should still be a spark left of the old fire and I confidently appeal to Scotsmen to aid to their utmost the efforts of the Committee to confer success on what London fondly hopes to

20

found, an annual trial of skill between the champions of England and Scotland. Messrs. A. F. Kinnaird, 2 Pall Mall, East London, and J. Kirkpatrick, Admiralty, Somerset House, London, will be glad to receive the names of any Scottish player who will take part against England in the match in question. I am, etc.

Charles W. Alcock
Hon. Secretary of Football Association.
West Dulwich, Surrey. 1st November 1870.

A Scottish team selected in London was hardly calculated to satisfy Scottish aspirations. However, Queen's Park decided to nominate Mr Robert Smith who had just moved to London and was also a playing member of South Norwood. Scotland's team in that first game was selected from J. Kirkpatrick (Civil Service), A. F. Kinnaird (Old Etonians), G. E. W. Crawford (Harrow School), H. W. Primrose (Civil Service), C. E. Nepean (University College, Oxford), Quintin Hogg (Wanderers), G. F. Congreve (Old Rugbeians), R. Smith (Queen's Park), G. G. Kennedy (Wanderers), T. F. Inglis (Charterhouse), F. Chappell (Oxford), A. K. Smith (Oxford) and W. H. Gladstone, M.P. (Old Etonians). That team fairly sums up the social status of the game at the time, but was hardly representative of Scotland. The first match was won 1–0 by England, the second on February 28, 1871, drawn 1–1.

Robert Smith reported in detail on the strange features of the English game, particularly the entire prohibition of the use of the hands; and the fact that while the ball was in play the practice was to run or dribble with the feet, instead of indulging in high or long kicks. He was warmly thanked for the information and his 'able and spirited play on behalf of Queen's Park and Scotland at both Association matches'.

Scotland did not recognise these games as Internationals and the first official fixture was in 1872 with Queen's Park providing the whole Scottish team and making all the arrangements. This was a 0–0 draw and it is interesting to note that the feature of the English play that astounded the Scots was the clever dribbling, particularly of C. J. Ottaway. Later it was the Scots who were to maintain Alcock's tradition of clever dribbling and close passing.

But C. W. Alcock's letter did more than start an interest in Internationals. It brought to the notice of Queen's Park that there was a body called The Football Association and they promptly decided to join. They were therefore among those who were informed of the decision to start the Cup competition. When Queen's Park heard about the proposal for the English Challenge Cup they were immediately interested and sent a guinea towards the purchase of the Cup. As this was about one sixth of their total funds at the time it might appear an unusually generous gesture. In fact they had received a letter from Mr Alfred Stair, Treasurer of The Football Association, intimating that the minimum subscription was one guinea. The Club was keen to take part, but concerned about the problems of travel and expense. They therefore sent the minimum subscription until more was known and instructed Mr Gardner and Mr Wotherspoon to forward suggestions to the F.A. that would place Queen's Park on an equal footing with other Clubs. It was in part their representations that led to Queen's Park being exempt until the semi-final. Arrangements were also made that the Final should be played the following day *if* Queen's Park won, so that only one journey to London would be necessary.

Queen's Park were later to refer to the Cup as the 'blessed pot' though it is uncertain whether this was out of respect for its success or exasperation at the problems it caused them. But their first match in the competition went off smoothly and happily and their Club Secretary, Mr A. Rae, minuted this report:

'The last of the three outside matches – and indeed the most important in the history of the Club – was the contest with the London Wanderers for the Association Silver Challenge Cup. In the fourth tie the Royal Engineers were drawn against Crystal Palace and the Wanderers against the Queen's Park. According to the rules of the competition, the Final and immediately preceding ties were to be played in London. It was in the faith that arrangements had been made with the two other contending Clubs that their tie should be played off before ours with the Wanderers so that in the event of Wanderers so suffering defeat from us we should be able to play the final tie on the following day that the London trip was decided upon.

'The funds which had been collected for the projected Border match were diverted to the London match and eleven men chosen, two resident in London (the brothers Smith), to represent the Club. The match was played at Kennington Oval on the afternoon of Monday, March 4th, at 3.30 p.m. The day was fine and very favourable to the game. The turnout of spectators was large. The Wanderers having won the toss Queen's Park kicked off. After playing an hour and a half, the game, very much to the astonishment of the Londoners, who expected to carry it without much effort, ended in a draw. The result was very creditable to the Queen's Park team. The team against whom they contended had no fewer than eight of the picked "International" players of England and Scotland (that is, Scots picked by Londoners for the sham International games). The long railway journey was against our players and Mr Edmiston, one of our best men, was most unfortunately quite disabled almost at the outset. The game was pretty equal and very hard although the Queen's Park lost more chances at goal than their opponents.

'The match had created considerable interest both in England and Scotland and was perhaps the most prominent event in the annals of modern football. Few clubs in Scotland play the Association rules and this difficulty precludes to a great extent the arrangement of outside matches.'

There was no replay as Queen's Park could not afford to stay.

Not until 1883–4 did Queen's Park play again in the English Cup because of the expense and difficulty of games in London. By then they were still in effect the national team of Scotland with pride and prestige at stake. The start was satisfying enough with Crewe Alexandra trounced 10–0 and Manchester beaten 15–0 at Titwood Park. Aston Villa were beaten 6–1 'unable to break through the magnificent back play of the Queen's Park team than whom there are not a better four in the world'. W. Arnott and A. H. Holm, the backs, together with C. Campbell and J. J. Gow, the half-backs, were Queen's Park's strength and helped them to a narrow win over Old Westminsters. In the semi-final they were matched against the holders Blackburn Olympic at Nottingham on March 1. In their Jubilee History the game is thus described:

'Imagine fifteen thousand spectators, ninety-nine out of every hundred of whom were supporters of the English team. It was a damper for the young players; the strongest nerves would be severely tried under such circumstances. Olympic put in a lot of rough work, by which they had won the Cup from the Old Etonians the previous year. It was of little avail against Queen's Park. The battle raged with great fierceness and intense excitement prevailed. The score at half-time stood 1–0 in favour of the Queen's Park. Very soon after crossing, the Doctor (Smith) lowered the Olympic colours for the second time. Watt came along with a third. There was a strong suspicion that the Blackburnites around the ropes wished to burst up the game, but the encroachers were kept back and the game, which had been stopped, was resumed. Dr. Smith a few minutes from the close ran the ball from his own end and flashed through a fourth goal. The Olympic could do nothing against the splendid back play of the Scots.'

The Final was a sad disappointment for Queen's Park and not for the last time different interpretations of the Rules were to cause much resentment. For the Scots had two goals disallowed – for offside – before Blackburn Rovers scored their two. And though Christie got one back the defeat was regarded as unfair and humiliating. Major Marindin was as impartial as ever being just as strict in disallowing for offside a goal by Rovers. But the decisions niggled Queen's Park not so much because they lost as because the goals were regarded as perfectly fair under Queen's Park's usual interpretation of the rules. The bitterness was still reflected in their Jubilee History which records:

'The Queen's Park, as holders of the Scottish Cup, threw into the scale the Championship of Scotland when it entered the contest for the Championship of England. The Rovers having defeated the Scots by 2–1 established their right to be considered themselves champions of the United Kingdom. It is true the Queen's Park were refereed out of the game by Major Marindin whose views of the 'off-side' rule were peculiar and vain, but this was not the fault of the Rovers. It is no use now criticising Major Marindin. He no doubt acted honestly according to his lights; but the Queen's Park was never convinced, nor the Scottish public either, that victory ought not to have been gained by 3–2 as the goals disallowed the Queen's Park, from a Scottish interpretation of the rules, were legitimate. The Club took the reverse very sorely to heart and contemplated washing its hands of the English Association and the Cup with all its disappointments and annoyances . . . The appeals against Queen's Park were so persistent that the team got afraid to kick the ball when at all near goal. Major Marindin acted a most extraordinary part. On the Sunday after the match he came to the hotel and told the team they had the ball through the Rovers posts a foot and did not claim, and also that the first goal scored by the Rovers was distinctly off-side, but no appeal was made. Arnott emphatically stated that he appealed loudly, but no notice was taken. The Major ought to have kept the information to himself and not thus increased the chagrin of the Queen's Park. On his own showing the Scots won by 3–1. The Queen's Park counted in the other two goals disallowed and asserted they gained the day 5–1.'

The mathematics of defeat are always sad and the 3–1 calculation erroneous enough to show that temper was clouding judgement. But Queen's Park recovered their poise to enter again next year, overwhelming Old Wykehamists 7–0 in the early rounds. But the Cup of bitterness for them was still to provide 'annoyances and disappointments'. The annoyance came in the third round of the second series of games necessitated by the growing number of entries. In the game against Notts County 'The absence of arrangements to shepherd a record crowd at Trent Bridge caused serious inconvenience and annoyance to Queen's Park. It is unnecessary to enter into details of the play which were interesting and exciting, so much so that the crowd after half-an-hour's play broke the ropes and flowed over the line seriously hampering the players, especially Gillespie in goal and impeding him in his attempt to save the first goal. After half-time when the Queen's Park was ahead by 2–1 so much did the spectators encroach on the field that the Queen's Park captain entered a protest at the game being considered final. Players, referee, and policemen and others spent twenty minutes in partially clearing the field of play and the game having been set in motion Notts County effected a draw 2–2.'

The referee, Mr Pierce Dix, ordered the teams to play an extra half-hour, but the Queen's Park unanimously refused to do so.

A replay was ordered at Derby, rather than Glasgow and the expense of this added to the sense of frustration. However, so great was Queen's Park's popularity and such crowds did they draw that they made £219. 8s. 7d. profit from their matches. Twenty thousand came to the game at Derby and soon that fine all-round sportsman, William Gunn, won the ball from a corner to give Notts the lead. But 'Gow was in grand fettle and his attentions to the "Great Gunn" were touching.' With Gunn subdued Queen's Park scored twice, Watt 'sending the leather whizzing through the Notts goal' and then Moore 'gave Arnott a nice clean shot which he judged to a nicety, and the great back, with a strong drive obtained unexpectedly what proved to be the winning point of a hard game.'

But Queen's Park were far from finished with Nottingham. In the semi-final they were drawn against Forest and the game at Derby ended in a draw. 'Widdowson and Leighton dribbled the ball down the left-wing for Danks to score for the Forest after 28 minutes play. Campbell was given a throw-in and handing the ball to Allan, that player passed to Anderson, who with a beautiful shot equalised.'

This time the replay was in Scotland at Merchiston Castle School ground in Edinburgh. An own goal soon put Forest behind and two more for Sellar clinched matters. Now came the great disappointment. Queen's Park hoped for their revenge against Blackburn Rovers whom they met once more in the Final. But they were without Harrower and Christie and only Sellar played in his best form. A long shot from that great half-back, Jim Forrest, put them behind in the first period and Brown scored another in the second to defeat them 2–0. They generously recorded: 'This victory was fairly gained. On this occasion no goals were disallowed, nor could the Scots complain of the officials. They were beaten fairly and all felt the better team had won.' It was Blackburn's sharp-shooting that upset the Scots and caused them such disappointment.

Sadly, that was their last chance of taking the Cup. Next year they scratched to South Shore (Blackpool) in the second round. And in 1886 Preston North End beat them 3–0 at Glasgow. The result and the scenes that followed were equally disastrous. Already the Scottish F.A. was getting restive at the English competition being played in Scotland.

In the First Round of 1886–7 there were seven Scottish Clubs in the draw:

Third Lanark	v.	High Walton
Darwen	v.	Heart of Midlothian
Renton	v.	Accrington Stanley
Queen's Park	v.	Preston North End
Everton	v.	Glasgow Rangers
Darwen Old Wanderers	v.	Cowlairs
Blackburn Olympic	v.	Partick Thistle

Glasgow Rangers reached the semi-final, but the Preston North End game with Queen's Park added injury to insult. In the Queen's Park view:

'The Preston team, one of the best exponents of the dribbling art, played an extremely rough and "dirty" game. Fouls were repeatedly given against them for tripping and charging behind, inexcusable acts for which there was no necessity as they secured the victory 3–0. This rough play culminated in an act of treachery on the part of Ross junior, one of eight professionals in the North End team. The scene which took place at the close of the game baffles description and one the like of which had never been witnessed in any game in Scotland. The act which aroused the passion of the mob was perpetrated on Harrower, the Queen's Park centre. About five minutes from the close Harrower, who had played grandly up to this point, fastened on the ball. Ross junior, was behind him and this player, instead of tackling his man in front, charged him low down from behind, causing Harrower to fall backwards on his left shoulder. So forcible was

25

the fall that he lay stunned while the spectators yelled and howled in a perfect frenzy of righteous anger.'

Ross had to be rescued from the crowd by the Queen's Park players and then tried to slip out of the ground with C. Campbell. Though he had disguised himself in a long ulster and a hat he was soon recognised and had to fight his way back to the pavilion. Finally, Sandy Maxwell, the groundsman, sneaked him out of a back window and up the Mount Florida slopes to safety.

This further irritated the Scottish F.A. On May 10, 1887 a new rule was introduced on the motion of Mr Richard Browne (Queen's Park), President of the Scottish F.A. 'That clubs belonging to this Association shall not be members of any other Association.' So ended Scotland's participation in the English Challenge Cup and it was sad that Queen's Park, who had done so much to foster interest in it, should never have been rewarded with the 'blessed pot' that their talents so clearly deserved.

Queen's Park has never abandoned its amateur philosophy, but from other Scottish Clubs players were drifting South in search of football and jobs.

Darwen was the first team to make a serious challenge to the supremacy of the 'Old Boy and Officers Mess' sides and was probably the first English Club to employ professionals. It was in 1878–79 that Darwen reached the quarter-final to be drawn against the Old Etonians. A local subscription had to be raised to send Darwen to play at the Oval and in London the challenge of a Northern team of Mill workers was not taken as too serious a threat. A walk-over was expected and appeared all too likely at half-time when the Old Etonians led 4–0. A fifth goal early in the second half seemed so conclusive that the Etonians eased off.

They had under-estimated the skills of the two Scottish 'professors' in Darwen's team. Jimmie Love and Fergie Suter had been 'attracted' to Darwen after playing there for the Glasgow Club, Partick. Their clever ball control and skilful close passing techniques were new and alien to the Southern game. Under their urgent prompting Darwen drove forward in determined quest for the goal that would let them go out with honour and return home with heads held high. Such was their elation when they did score that suddenly the whole course of the game was changed. The Old Etonian defence disintegrated under the repeated attacks and in the last quarter of an hour the 'Darreners' snatched four more goals to level the score. With jubilant confidence they challenged the Old Etonians to 'finish the game' there and then, but the invitation was hastily declined by their exhausted and dejected opponents.

Under the rules of those days the replay three weeks later, was again at the Oval and another public subscription had to be launched. Such was the interest and excitement that £175 was raised with Old Etonians contributing £5, and the Football Association £10. Again the match was drawn 2–2 and the fascinating contest was only resolved at the third attempt. At last Darwen was overwhelmed 6–2. But their spirited challenge was the herald of a new era with footballing skill passing

The Darwen team of 1879 was the first to challenge the supremacy of the
Old Boy teams. In the front is Fergie Suter, probably the first of the 'professionals'.

from the public schools and the army to the masses and the professional. Association football was about to become a truly National game.

In theory all teams were still amateur and payment was not allowed. But Jimmie Love and Fergie Suter had clearly had some inducement to transfer to Darwen. Local Lancashire rivals began to query the propriety of playing the two Scottish 'professors'. Mr Hindle, Darwen's Secretary, always strongly denied that Love and Suter were paid to play and no evidence was ever produced to contradict him. He never denied, however, that the jobs which Love and Suter held in Darwen – far more remunerative than they had had in Scotland – were a reward for their services to the local Club. They can therefore be regarded as the first of the Scottish professionals who began to infiltrate into English football. Many of the Scottish playing contacts had been with Lancashire and it was Lancashire that was soon to dominate the Cup and play the leading part in developing professional football.

Fergie Suter was later to gain three Cup Winner's medals with Blackburn Rovers and it was in part his transfer of allegiance that brought Rovers into prominence. Blackburn indeed was soon to be the leading team in the Cup and their local matches with Darwen were always fierce and heated affairs.

On November 27, 1880 their game ended in a near riot which was reported at great length in the *Darwen News*.

'The rivalry between the two Clubs was very great last season, but is now doubled in intensity for various reasons. Last season the Rovers defeated Darwen in their English Cup Tie, but they were afterwards defeated by Darwen in

27

the Final tie for the Lancashire Cup. Saturday's match was the first between these two Clubs this season and there was a great deal of betting as to the result. During the year both Clubs have undergone considerable changes which is commonly supposed to incline in favour of Blackburn. When the season commenced it was found that Suter who last season captained Darwen had gone over to Rovers who were also joined by Douglas, from Glasgow, the latter having been a Scotch international player. Notwithstanding these reverses Darwen abated not one jot of heart and hope, but went into the contest confident of victory.'

A crowd of over 10,000 had paid £255 to watch at Blackburn's Alexandra Meadows. Against the wind Darwen more than held their own and the reporter recorded that the rowdy Blackburn public were prepared to put a stop to the match 'whenever they saw Darwen gaining the upper hand'. They did indeed encroach on the pitch after Darwen scored. 'This occurred at the "sixpenny end" and considering all the circumstances was not much to be wondered at, but the conduct of the spectators at the shilling or grandstand side was more reprehensible.'

The match was level at half-time, but then 'Suter charged Marshall by a jump that is prohibited in the Lancashire rules. Marshall said something. Suter raised his arm and clenched his fist after which Marshall got hold of Suter round the waist and turned him head downwards and let him go quietly to the ground. No blows were struck, no fight took place, but immediately the crowd closed in and the game was stopped amid cheering, hooting and shouting on the part of the now disorderly mass of spectators.'

Clearly the rivalry between these two teams was anything but friendly and the incident underlined the intensity of feeling that the Cup competition had helped to excite. Professionalism and betting added a keener edge to the game's challenge.

Darwen was the catalyst for the change and the Club has a distinctive role in the history of the game. Their Minutes only go back to the year that the Cup started, but Darwen was playing football in the 1840s. In one match against neighbouring Turton, tempers became so inflamed that the match was abandoned. Blows were exchanged, the blood began to flow and the Darwen team made off across the moors pursued by the locals. Somewhat battered they retreated back to 'Peaceful Valley' in which Darwen lies.

Once they had begun to make a mark in the Cup, Darwen remained for many years one of the leading Lancashire teams. Two seasons after their great struggle with the Old Etonians they reached the semi-final after beating Romford by a startling 15–0 in the quarter-final. In the same year, they became the first team to win the Lancashire Senior Cup Competition and one of their players, T. Marshall, was capped for England. When the First Division of the Football League was started in 1888 Darwen failed by a single vote to be elected as a founder member, losing out to Accrington Stanley.

Nothing daunted, they gained admission to the Second Division when it was founded and at once won promotion. But soon they were to be swallowed up by the colossus of their own creation. As professionalism spread, the large cities with their great popular support became too rich and powerful for the small town teams. By the turn of the century Darwen had dropped out of the League and through the Lancashire League to the Lancashire Combination. Yet they were still to make some impact on the Cup. In 1902 they played Woolwich Arsenal at the Anchor Ground in Darwen after disposing of Blackpool, Southport Central, and Nelson. As usual a battle between the giants and the gnomes attracted a large crowd with horse lorries drawn up round the touchlines as makeshift stands. There was to be no upset of form for Woolwich Arsenal won 2–0. But perhaps Darwen's most remarkable match was also against Arsenal in the third round at Highbury in 1932.

No other Lancashire Combination side has ever progressed so far in the Cup and for two seasons Darwen were enjoying remarkable success after engaging 'Joe' Smith as player-coach. The former Bolton and England centre-forward revitalised their team and prepared himself to become one of the outstanding Football Managers. In the first year he led them to victory in the Combination League Championship and Cup and in the East Lancashire Charity Cup. George Shaw, their outside-left, recalls playing seven games in eight days for a wage of thirty shillings as their success congested their fixture list. The combination Championship and Cup were retained the next season, although Joe Smith had moved on to manage Reading before his long and successful career in charge of Blackpool. But Darwen also fought their way into the third round of the F.A. Cup beating Burscough, Lytham, Dick Kerrs, Prescot Cables, Peterborough, and Chester, the top of the Third Division (North). That string of names is a fair indication of the catholic composition of the Cup with all the small teams hoping for what Darwen achieved – a match with the Arsenal at Highbury.

Once Darwen had been a power in the Competition, but now they were a very small David against a very mighty Goliath, for Arsenal were at the height of their power with the finest forward line in the land. The Cup cannot always work miracles and Darwen were to find just how good that attack was. George Shaw remembers the brief moment of hope as Robinson on the right sold Hapgood a dummy in the game's opening move, then curled his centre across goal. Preedy or Shaw could have nodded it in, but each left it to the other. Thereafter the confusion was all in the Darwen penalty-area. By the interval Arsenal were leading 8–0 – 'eit nowt, just like Gandhi's breakfast' was the wry comment in Darwen's dressing room. Centre-half, Crompton, had struggled unavailingly in the mud as the play swirled swiftly past him.

'Well tried' they said to him consolingly at half-time. 'I came down by train and I feel as if I had just run all the way back to Darwen' was the depressed reply. Bastin 4, Jack 3, Hulme 2, Lambert 2, was the goal tally with Alex James making the openings. Then at last Bob Dale scored from a corner to give Darwen their moment of joy. A meaningless gesture? Quite the reverse for it brought the loudest cheer of the day. 'The roar that rolled from the terraces could be heard over all North London. The metropolis knew that Darwen had come to Town.'

Only in the Cup can 11–1 defeat feel like triumph and the day remains a proud and happy memory. For that is how George Shaw and his friends recall it, while the Darwen *Golden Jubilee Handbook* enthuses: 'Our side's achievement in reaching the third round was remarkable as we are the only Lancashire Combination Club to have progressed so far.' In those early years Darwen gave the Cup a push that was to shove it for ever beyond their reach, but they could still share in the excitement and the glory.

5

The Old Boys' Clubs

The developments that Darwen had inspired were soon to overwhelm the Old Boys' Clubs, but not before two had moments of glory. Outstanding were the Old Etonians who became the leading side in the land once the Wanderers had left the scene. How the game had changed by the time they celebrated their centenary with a dinner at Quaglinos on November 15, 1965. By then standards of football were no longer those that had made them the major power in the early days of the Club Competition. The height of their ambition was now the Arthur Dunn trophy (initiated for public schools' football by an early Etonian International, A. T. B. Dunn).

Of all the schools whose various codes of play were combined into the original 'Association' rules, Eton, Harrow, and Charterhouse were to make the most significant contribution to the competition. Harrow was the source of the Wanderers and must take some credit for their success. But it was the Old Etonians who played in six finals and won the Trophy twice. And from the Old Etonians came the game's most flamboyant player and able administrator. The Hon. A. F. Kinnaird bestrode the early years. By modern standards he may have been a little eccentric, but he personified the boundless enthusiasm and the sheer joy in the game of those early amateurs. It is common enough to see players leaping in exuberance or hugging each other as the vital goal is scored. It took Lord Kinnaird to celebrate victory over Blackburn Rovers in 1882 by standing on his head in front of the pavilion to the equivalent of a standing ovation from his fellow Etonians. His sturdy figure, flowing beard, and magnetic attraction for the good story make him football's equivalent of W. G. Grace (who refereed football and took a part in converting Gloucestershire to the Association game).

The two had much in common, the aura that surrounded them building on fact and myth to make legend. If some of the stories of Kinnaird are suspect, in sum they give a fair picture of the man and his impact on his day.

It is said that his energetic play worried his wife who once warned him that he might break a leg. 'Perhaps, but it won't be mine!' was the ebullient reply. It was the same when Alcock asked him before one game if he would rather it was played fair, or that hacking was allowed. 'Oh, let's have hacking' was the delighted cry. But there was plenty of skill to back the energy and enthusiasm. How otherwise could he have won the Final for the Wanderers by 'threading his way through a maze of legs'? How won five Cup Winner's medals with Wanderers and Old Etonians (a total to be equalled by Wollaston and Forrest, but never surpassed)?

No one else has ever played in *nine* Finals. It was he who arranged the Club's earliest games in 1865 and he was President of the F.A. from 1890 to 1923. Indeed a giant of a man bringing to the game a vast enjoyment. He was capable of sparking off and then controlling the explosive expansion of football, giving it zest, character and status. Of all the game's personalities perhaps to him alone can be applied that over-worked phrase 'we shall never see his like again'.

Major Marindin, too, was an Old Etonian and a President of their Club, though it was as a sapper that he made his major contribution. So the Old Etonians would have their place in football history even if they had achieved nothing on the field. But in those early years they were one of the four dominant teams and their record would have been even more impressive had they not given such assistance to the Wanderers. Their high spirits found expression in the 'fancy kicking' that so startled some opponents. For they were apt to spring into the air to volley the ball. But perhaps their carefree attitude to the game is best illustrated by two Finals in which the Cup eluded them. Extra time was not compulsory yet they readily agreed to it against the Royal Engineers though they were a man short with Ottaway injured. And when at last a Northern team won they were just as generous to Blackburn Olympic. To save them another journey to London they agreed to go on with one man off the field and two others injured. That was the right way for them to leave the scene, playing fair and giving generous tribute to Olympic.

The gates were small enough in those days, but the Old Etonians never received a farthing from them, for two-thirds went to the Surrey C.C.C. and one-third to the F.A. And though they once declined to continue into extra time with Darwen's Mill workers they were prepared to contribute to the cost of the return match. It was third time lucky when Old Etonians first took the Cup in 1879 defeating a Clapham Rovers side with such fine players as J. F. M. Prinsep and N. C. Bailey, who was to captain England. N. C. Bailey and Clapham Rovers set the precedent for a Cup tradition, when they came back to win at the Oval the season after their defeat. But J. F. M. Prinsep had to wait two years to get his revenge for he transferred his allegiance to the Old Carthusians.

Old Carthusians were the only other Old Boys team to win the Cup with Parry and Prinsep gaining International honours as well. Indeed they maintained their form longer than the Etonians and by 1887 those fine backs, the Walters brothers, were still good enough to get them through to the quarter-finals of a competition dominated by professionals.

This was the last time an Amateur team had a real chance of winning the Cup as they came close to overcoming the great Preston North End side in the quarter-final.

A. M. and P. M. Walters were a formidable pair at back, both hard and rough in a gentlemanly way. A. M. was short and square with shoulders like the West door of a Cathedral. The two were automatic choices for England, their playing careers ending tragically when they gave up the game to please their father after their younger brother had been killed while playing. W. N. Cobbold and A. Amos were also in the side bringing their tally of internationals to four. Early in the game C. A. Smith, better known as Aubrey Smith the actor and cricketer, had the goal at his mercy when he was tripped from behind. According to a contemporary account:

'The play then became decidedly rough. Half-time came with no score to either side. In a few minutes Cobbold sent a wonderful shot through the Preston goal. Immediately afterwards he was badly lamed, but the splendid play of the two backs kept the Northerners well out of the Carthusian goal. Just before time a foul was given against a Carthusian back; most spectators thought it should have been given to the other side and that a Preston man had tried "jumping". But the foul was given against the Carthusians, and the ball headed through goal off the free-kick. This made the score one all at the end of ninety minutes. An extra half-hour had to be played; the Carthusians were now one man short and Preston got the winning goal. This was the last great struggle of an old boys' club for the Association Cup. C. Wreford Brown was in goal on this occasion . . . He may well have been very undecided as to what was his place, for he was within three seasons, a forward, a goalkeeper, and a centre-half.'

The Old Carthusians were later to win the Amateur Cup sharing with the Royal Engineers the distinction of being the only teams to win both trophies.

Few of the other Old Boy sides achieved much. Old Wykehamists had four Internationals in F. H. Birley, F. J. Green, L. S. Howell, and W. Lindsay, who all gained winner's medals with the Wanderers. But when the Old Wykehamists entered the competition their side scratched in the first two seasons, then twice reached the fourth round only to lose 9–1 to Blackburn Olympic and 7–0 to Queen's Park. After such daunting experiences they retired to concentrate on their own form of football which is still played on narrow grounds hemmed in by canvas netting.

Old Westminsters were more successful – three times reaching the quarter-final and giving Queen's Park a hard fight in 1884.

But the point of no return for the Old Boy teams was really that moment of extra time in 1882 when little Costley on Blackburn Olympic's left wing drove the winning goal past the Old Etonians' goalkeeper, Rawlinson.

6

The Decline of the Amateur

Blackburn Olympic's victory ended the era of amateur domination of the Cup and it was appropriate that they should have beaten Old Etonians in the Final. For this team more than any other symbolised the public school and upper class spirit of those early years. Darwen had been the first team to challenge this supremacy and to widen the concept of football. Perhaps more than any other games it was their three-match duel with the Old Etonians that first excited national interest and encouraged the rise of professionalism.

As the Cup began to capture the imagination of the country it became a prize to be coveted. And covetousness was soon backed by money. The motives were laudable enough. Civic pride or club spirit roused the aspirations and sharpened the determination. At first this was expressed in a willingness to practise more and train harder. Then came the thought – if only we had a better centre-half or a better centre-forward or whatever. And in those days five shillings a week might be sufficient attraction to win a club a footballer of outstanding talent. To add to the local potential, a number of skilful Scots were moving south and were ready enough to join a team for a good job. Queen's Park, Glasgow, to this day amateur in practice and principle, commented scornfully on the conversion of labourers into tobacconists. By a strange irony the Scots were to make an official complaint when England first introduced a professional into their team – that outstanding wing-half Jim Forrest who did so much to make Blackburn Rovers the dominant side of the next three seasons. The complaint had no basis in the rules of Internationals which were intended to allow each country to field its strongest possible side. But it was typical of the annoyance that the early professionalism aroused – a compound of natural irritation at an unfair advantage and an expression of the sharp class distinctions of Victorian days.

Neither Darwen nor Blackburn Olympic was officially a professional team, but the running now passed to Blackburn Rovers who won the Cup in three successive years 1884–86. Their success opened the first gap in standards between the genuine amateur and the practiced 'professor'. For Blackburn Rovers was indeed a professional side in every respect, though not at first admitting to it. The speed with which the professional took over was the only surprise for never again was an amateur side to make a real mark on the competition. By 1886 there were only four amateur teams in the 5th round: Brentwood, Old Carthusians, Old Westminsters, and Swifts. Old Westminsters survived to the sixth round to be overwhelmed 6–0 by West Bromwich Albion. Swifts alone were good enough to reach the semi-final.

34

There they lost narrowly to Blackburn Rovers, going down 1–2 in a game played at Derby. Next season Old Westminsters and Old Carthusians survived until the quarter-final and old Carthusians were there again in 1888. But that was the last time an amateur side had a credible chance of winning the Cup.

Inevitably the rise of professionalism put strains on The Football Association. Inevitably there was strong opposition to recognising payment as a respectable development and to admitting professionals to an Association dominated by amateur thinking and officials wedded to amateur concepts. But the F.A. administrators were broadminded enough to overcome their prejudice and the transition was achieved with less disturbance and dissension than had attended the original arguments over a common code of playing rules.

The Cup had changed the pattern of football and the decisions of the administrators – so obvious now, so difficult at the time – ensured the dynamic growth of the game.

Recognition of professionalism quickly stifled the chances of amateur teams in the Cup, but never extinguished their contribution to this unique competition. Indeed the newly formed Corinthian Football Club might still have dominated the Cup, but for its Rule 7 which stated: 'The Club shall not compete for any Challenge Cup or any prizes of any description whatsoever.' The Corinthians were the quintessence of aristocratic amateurism. The Club had been formed at a meeting on October, 1882 in a small gaslit room in a building in Paternoster Row with late arrivals sitting on boxes. The meeting was called by N. L. 'Pa' Jackson, Assistant Secretary of the F.A. This elegant and commanding man was disconcerted by the continual defeats the English side was suffering at the hands of the Scots who had beaten them six times in the last seven encounters. The reason he rightly attributed to better teamwork, rather than individual skill and to the fact that the Scottish team practised together in contrast to England's casual and carefree approach. He hoped to encourage the leading amateurs to play together in friendly matches so that they understood and learnt from each other's styles. Many of the leading players attended the meeting and there was enthusiastic acceptance of the idea with the first game against St Thomas's Hospital ending in a 2–1 win to launch the new Club.

But enthusiasm was not so easily sustained as the requirements of the Corinthians' friendly matches clashed with those of their own Clubs. The history of the Corinthians refers to the early problems of getting a full side to turn out – the very problem that had destroyed the Wanderers – and recalls the quote of a later captain. Asked how his side was doing he replied: 'Not so badly considering our team usually consists of seven men, three telegrams, and one apologetic letter that arrives next morning.' Still, in the first full season they won ten matches and lost ten.

Then 'Pa' Jackson took over the running of the Club and its great days began. On December 1884 they fielded their strongest side against the Cup winners Blackburn Rovers and trounced them 8–1. The team was M. J. Randall (goal); A. Watson and W. F. Beardshaw (backs); A. Amos, C. Holden-White and F. E.

35

Saunders (half-backs); F. W. Pawson, B. W. Spilsbury, Dr J. Smith, W. N. Cobbold and T. Lindley (forwards). The half-back line was quite outstanding making it easy for the powerful forwards with two unusually gifted players in their line. W. N. Cobbold was rated the best forward in England at this period – yet another to be christened 'Prince of Dribblers'. No doubt he had some similarities to the unchallenged wizard of the dribble, Stanley Matthews. For he had a peculiar shuffling run and disliked heading the ball. Nor was Cobbold the most aggressive of players. With his legs swathed in rubber bandages and wearing ankle guards he was careful to avoid getting hurt. But he was too fast and elusive for the robust tacklers of the day and his shooting was unusually accurate, precision rather than power being the feature of his play. Tinsley Lindley was a formidable partner, a dangerous winger who was to captain Nottingham Forest and England. Pronouncing his name was also regarded as a suitable test of sobriety at celebration dinners!

Preston North End narrowly defeated the Corinthians in the next game and indeed usually got the better of them in an exciting series of matches. This was no freak of form for proud Preston was the first club to take full advantage of the legalisation of payment. Already Preston were taking over from Blackburn Rovers as the outstanding team in the country but no sooner had they achieved the double than they were heavily defeated by the Corinthians. The successes of the Corinthians indicated that there was less prejudice than might appear in amateurs still dominating the England side, while professionals dominated the Cup. As late as 1894 the whole England team that won 5–1 against Wales was made up of Corinthians. The 1886 team against Scotland was in relative terms one of the best England has fielded and there was no real quarrel with the selection of nine Corinthians and two Blackburn Rovers players. For these Corinthians included such giants of their time as the Walters brothers at back with N. C. Bailey and R. T. Squire at half-back.

A further service the Corinthians rendered the game in 1887. That was Queen Victoria's Jubilee Year and a 'Jubilee Festival' was arranged at the Oval with the Corinthians playing Preston North End and Lancashire playing a rugby match with Middlesex. The 1–1 draw fairly represented the still even balance between the best of the professionals and the best of the amateurs and at the end of the day the Prince of Wales, later King Edward VII, accepted the Presidency of both the Rugby Union and The Football Association. Royal patronage marked the final acceptance of the game as a National sport and a part of the social future of the country.

A true measure of what the Corinthians might have achieved was seen in the institution of the Sheriff of London's Shield Competition. This was designed to raise money for charity and over ten years collected more than £3,000. This feature encouraged the Corinthians to accept the concept of the leading amateur team playing the leading professional team for the shield. Their Rule 7 was amended to read: 'In the event of a Cup Competition being started in which one amateur and one professional club compete the committee shall have power to enter the Club for such competition.' The Cup winners always represented the professionals and in nine of the ten years the competition lasted the Corinthians represented the amateurs. On the other occasion their old rivals, Queen's Park, Glasgow, with whom they battled annually, took their place and shared the trophy with the cup winners. That was in the second year of the competition. In the opening competition of 1898 the shield was also shared after Corinthians had fought two drawn games with Sheffield United. But it was Corinthians who were to be the first winners defeating Aston Villa 2–1 in 1900.

During the period 1883–90, 52 out of the 88 international caps against Scotland had been awarded to Corinthians. But by the turn of the century the genuine gap in class was appearing between individuals as well as between teams. The fully-trained and dedicated professional was beginning to be a cut above the more care-free if no less dedicated amateur. And from 1900 onwards the Corinthians began to struggle to give a worthy challenge to the Cup winners. Indeed by 1902 there was adverse comment on their quality and it was recorded that the crowd were laughing at the 'aimless manoeuvring of the Corinthian forwards'. But there was no laughing in 1904. Bury came to the Shield match as holders of the Cup won by the largest margin of all time 6–0. Within a quarter-of-an-hour they were two goals up and looked to be heading for another record win in the Shield Competition. A record indeed it was, but an unexpected one. For Corinthian forwards recaptured their old brilliance and thrashed Bury 10–3. The jeers changed to excited applause as the crowd revelled in the traditional dash and sweeping rushes of the Corinthian forwards. Bury who had gone through the Cup without conceding a goal had to confess themselves baffled by the speed and originality of the moves that led to S. H. Harris scoring five goals and G. S. Harris scoring three; with S. H. Day contributing a couple.

That amazing result was typical of Cup football for it was against all the form of the time and against the steady evolution of professionals into a higher species of player. That first decade of the 20th century was the watershed in which the amateur went over the hill leaving the peaks to the professionals. It was in 1894 that the trend was officially recognised with the initiation of the separate Amateur Cup Competition won by Old Carthusians in that first Final at Richmond.

Thirteen years later the pressures were such that there was an internal 'split' with the Amateur Football Association, now the Amateur Football Alliance, separating from The Football Association. It is no part of this history to explore the reasons and the rights and wrongs of that old quarrel, except insofar as the Challenge Cup was affected. The basis of the grievance was set out in a letter which stated 'it is well known that for some years past amateurs interested in association football have been dissatisfied with the policy of The Football Association. Amateurs have no objection to professional Clubs or Professional players as such and are indeed quite ready to play with, or against, them, but they do claim that amateur sport should not be controlled or administered by those whose chief aim and interest is to engage the services of the most skilful players with the sole object of obtaining the most lucrative gates. A large body of amateurs has accordingly insisted on the right of belonging to and being governed by a District Association from which the professional element is entirely excluded . . . but the Football Association, at their General Meeting on May 31st, decided to compel the remaining Amateur Associations to admit professional Clubs to membership. The Committee of the Amateur Football Federation . . . have accordingly resolved to form a separate Association confined to amateur Clubs.'

The breakaway was supported by most of the leading amateurs because of the determination of the F.A. officials to oppose their desire for separate administration. The breach was never fully healed until the more sympathetic days of Stanley Rous as Secretary of The Football Association and close friend of the A.F.A. Its immediate effect was that members of the new Association were debarred from playing against Clubs affiliated to the F.A. and this hastened the elimination of amateurs as a collective force in the Cup.

Individuals still made their mark notably the Rev. K. R. G. Hunt, who was right-half for Wolverhampton Wanderers in their Cup Victory of 1908. An old Oxford blue and a Corinthian, he made a significant contribution to the defeat of Newcastle by scoring the first goal. Newcastle were probably the best team of that day having narrowly failed to achieve the double in 1905. when Villa beat them in the Final. In 1907 they had experienced one of those misfortunes which the Cup so artfully contrives having been defeated at home in the first round by Crystal Palace – a team close to the bottom of the Southern League. They wiped out the unpleasant memory by winning the League again that year and in 1908 they were back in the final, firm favourites against Wolverhampton Wanderers. But the Crystal Palace ground had as paralysing an effect on them as the team. The very name seemed to shatter their nerves and they were quite unable to win a final there. This time it was Hunt and the Wolves right winger, Harrison, who destroyed them. Kenneth Hunt in an interview after the game said 'of the football seen Newcastle had about ninety per cent, but the ten per cent for which Wolves were responsible plus their dash and direct methods, proved sufficient to undo the Tynesiders'. The newspaper headlines read:

HARE AND TORTOISE
A NEW VERSION OF AN OLD PROVERB
How Pretty Football Failed to Win the Cup

Not for the last time speed and strength triumphed over skill as Hunt brought to Wolves something of the swashbuckling spirit of the amateur game. He and Hedley scored in the five minutes before the interval and Harrison settled the issue with a decisive goal after Howie had won one back. It was a happy hunting day for the 'Hs': there were only four on the field and each scored a goal in one of those coincidences that so abound in this competition.

But the Corinthians were not content to leave it to individuals to carry the amateur flag. With the Sheriff's Shield as a precedent and well-wishers urging them on they finally decided to enter the Challenge Cup. It was a bold decision twenty

38

The Corinthians forced a second replay with Brighton and Hove
Albion at Stamford Bridge in January 1923.

years too late for success. Rule 7 was amended finally to read: 'The Club shall only compete for Cups and prizes upon such special occasions as may be determined by the Committee.'

Election to the Corinthians was confined by unwritten law to old boys of Public Schools and to members of a University, though a few exceptions were allowed. It was hardly to be expected that these would now hold their own with the pick of the professionals, but in 1922 arrangements were made to enter the Cup. The Corinthians' early games had been played at the Oval, or West Kensington, or Richmond. Then in 1895 Queen's Club at West Kensington had become their headquarters. Now they moved to Crystal Palace playing their first friendly match there against Tottenham Hotspur on September 11, 1922. Exemption had been given to the first round of the Cup and they were drawn against Brighton and Hove Albion. What a tussle that was! The first game was drawn 1–1 and so was the replay. A crowd of 20,000 had watched each of those matches, full of fine football and fluctuating fortune. The second replay was watched by 45,000, but the earlier contests had drained the players. This is the account of the game in *The History of the Corinthian F.C.* by F. N. S. Creek.

39

Corinthians, 1923–24: *standing:* A. H. Phillips, J. R. B. Moulsdale, B. Howard-Baker, L. B. Blaxland, K. E. Hegan; *seated:* F. W. H. Nicholas, C. T. Ashton, J. S. F. Morrison, A. G. Bower, A. G. Doggart, F. N. S. Creek.

'For this match, the third against Brighton within ten days, the Corinthians received a great welcome from the large crowd, whose hopes of seeing another stirring game were, however, hardly realised. The match, in fact, seemed rather tame and uninteresting after the previous two; and, although the pace was fast, weak finishing by both sides tended to lessen the enthusiasm. For once Hegan was not at his best, and the Corinthians' short-passing game was not very successful against some keen and robust tackling. Doggart and Ashton each got in hard shots during the first half, but in both cases they went straight to the goal-keeper. Blaxland played a very sound game at wing-half, and Hunter was again a great spoiler in the middle of the field. There was no score until a quarter of an hour from time, when a good movement on the Brighton left wing led to a hard shot, which hit an upright, and from the rebound, the only goal of the match was scored. The game then became more exciting as the Corinthians fought for an equaliser, and Doggart was almost through when he was badly fouled on the edge of the penalty area; but Brighton packed their goal too well for the Corinthians to have any chance of scoring from the free-kick. Bower was once again a tower of strength at back, Baker was sound all through the match, and Hunter and Blaxland were fine defensive halves.'

The first success the Corinthians had was in the following year against their old victims Blackburn Rovers. Once more it was like a stoat with a rabbit, as described in F. N. S. Creek's book:

'The meeting of these old rivals was one of the features of the first round when Corinthians won 1–0. The ground was soft, and the Corinthians had the advantage of a fairly stiff breeze in the first half. Hegan was soon prominent, and hit the upright with a glorious cross-shot before he gave Doggart the ball 25 yards from goal. Doggart dribbled a few yards, appeared to lose control temporarily, and then suddenly drove a low shot into the corner of the net. This was after fifteen minutes' play, and both Phillips and Creek missed narrowly soon afterwards. For the remainder of the first half play was even, with Baker and Ashton in turn making fine saves for the Corinthians. In the second half the Rovers had more of the game, but the magnificent wing-half play of Moulsdale and Blaxland caused them to bunch too much down the middle of the field. This played into the hands of such sturdy defenders as Morrison, Bower and Ashton. In the last fleeting minutes of a thrilling struggle, the Rovers tried desperately to save the match, and Baker had to make a brilliant save from a free-kick taken on the edge of the penalty-area before the Corinthians won their first Cup-tie by 1 goal to nil.'

In the second round they crashed 0–5 to West Bromwich Albion and they were never to get beyond this hurdle. There were, however, two other victories to cheer them. Walsall was defeated 4–0 on their own ground only six years before their own remarkable victory over Arsenal.

In 1929 Norwich were also overrun, crushed 5–0 on their home pitch. That was one of the Corinthians' most attractive displays despite their winger, Jenkins, being badly injured at the start. Graham Doggart, later to be Chairman of The Football Association, was in wonderful form. A brilliant dribbler he scored the third goal after a run that was rated the finest individual effort in the history of the Corinthians' Cup Ties.

But their outstanding performances were a draw against Manchester City and a splendid match with Newcastle. In 1927 Newcastle were League leaders when the match was played and 56,000 watched an absorbing game. Until 14 minutes from the end Corinthians clung tenaciously to a single-goal lead. A long, sweeping pass

41

from Norman Creek sent Hegan slipping past his back for Ashton to hit home the centre.

Try as Newcastle would, not all the wiles of Hughie Gallacher could make any impression on H. Chadder, A. G. Bower, or B. Howard-Baker. Then a free-kick glanced into the net off a full-back's shoulder. With one man off the field and two more injured the Corinthians were overwhelmed in the final minutes, two more goals giving welcome relief to Newcastle.

Even more exciting was their match with Manchester, as recorded in *The History of the Corinthian F.C.*

'Although the team had never before played together as a side, the Corinthians began at a tremendous pace, and it was not long before Creek scored as a result of a fine combined movement in which Hegan and Jenkins were prominent. Manchester City equalised a minute before half-time, immediately after Baker had made a magnificent save. Gradually the professionals improved, and when, with only a quarter of an hour left for play, they scored from a centre taken on the full volley, the Corinthians looked a beaten team. But the last fifteen minutes were crammed with excitement. Hegan, taking a long pass from Ashton in mid-stride, ran almost up to the goal-line, and lifted the ball over the goal-keeper's head into the net. The cheers had barely subsided when he made another electrifying run, put across a perfect centre, and Creek made no mistake with his shot. With only three minutes to go, Baker caught a centre, took two steps, ran into Bower, took two more steps, cleared – and was penalised for "carrying". The free kick was taken six yards from the near upright, with both teams swarming round the goal mouth, and from the ensuing melee the ball was forced into the net for the equalising goal of a thrilling match. There was hardly a minute in the whole game when one goal or the other did not seem to be in danger. For once the Corinthian defence was not so good as the forwards, whose display in the earlier and later portions of the game was worthy of the great traditions of the Club, while Hegan stood out as the finest player on the field. The team was: B. Howard-Baker (goal); A. G. Bower, A. E. Knight (backs); C. B. G. Hunter, C. T. Ashton, F. H. Ewer (half-backs); R. G. C. Jenkins, A. H. Chadder, F. N. S. Creek, F. Hartley, K. E. Hegan (forwards).'

In eighteen Cup games the Corinthians only won three matches, though usually giving their opponents a game challenge. As they summed it up there were only two respects in which their play had been proved inferior. There was a lack of skill in heading – not one of their 23 goals had yet been headed home – and they could never match the remarkable agility and competence of the professional goal-keepers. These weaknesses and a lack of thrust in the forward line, prevented them making a decisive impact on the Cup. At least they showed that the best of amateur teams was still capable of giving any professional side a hard fight. Like the Wanderers the Corinthians finally faded away ceasing to be a unique or powerful force after their merger with the Casuals just before the War.

Pegasus, the combined Oxford and Cambridge side, inherited something of the Corinthian spirit winning the Amateur Cup at Wembley in 1951 and 1953 before crowds as large and enthusiastic as at the Challenge Cup-Final itself. But despite all the advice to try for that prize as well, they recognised that the gap in standards had now grown too great to be bridged.

Yet there have been three outstanding performances by Amateur Clubs in the years since the war. Walthamstow Avenue surprised the football world in the Cup season 1952–53. Stockport County were beaten 2–1 in the third round and Walthamstow were then drawn against Manchester United. On any ground that was in prospect hardly a match to trouble the punters and at Old Trafford a cricket score seemed the inevitable outcome. But Walthamstow Avenue had an experienced side with several gifted players. There was Saunders, a forceful hard-tackling half-back, who was later to captain Chelsea to victory in the League. And on the wing was Trevor Bailey, that all-round sportsmen who delighted in any fight against the odds. With a gale making a mock of delicate football, Manchester United came close to defeat before their own crowd. Trevor Bailey recounts his still vivid impression of the two games that tested the great United side close to destruction.

'In 1952 we had won the Amateur Cup at Wembley in front of a capacity crowd and in the following season embarked on a remarkable F.A. Cup run in which we managed to knock out two Third Division teams before being drawn away to Manchester United in the fourth round.

'Not surprisingly, the outcome was considered such a certainty that the match was not included in the Pools and Bookmakers were prepared to offer seventy-five to one against, and throw in the draw for good measure. I only wish that I had been less of a realist than one of my colleagues and had a flutter on the outcome because to everyone's amazement, including our own, we managed to achieve a draw. It must rank as one of the most improbable results of modern times in this great competition.

'The game was fought in a minor hurricane and, as a result of some quite superb 'keeping, a packed defence, and a certain amount of good fortune, we came in at half-time only one down with the happy knowledge that we would have the tornado behind us in the second session. This considerable advantage enabled us to attack and in the seventieth minute Jim Lewis, who was certainly the finest amateur centre-forward of that period, calmly picked his spot and levelled the scores. From that moment on it was anybody's game and if Manchester United did not exactly panic, their players were visibly and understandably rattled by this totally unexpected turn of events.

'For financial, and safety reasons – our home ground could only hold about 12,000 spectators – it was decided to stage the replay at Highbury on a Wednesday afternoon. The decision was more than justified as over 50,000 turned up to see this amateur club who had managed to hold First Division, Manchester United.

'Although we were unable to repeat the performance (miracles do not happen

43

twice) we were certainly not disgraced, eventually losing by five goals to two. However, I have often wondered what would have occurred if my shot had gone in, instead of rebounding off the underside of the cross bar and thence directly upfield for United to notch the fifth goal which put the result beyond doubt.'

Equally unusual was Tooting and Mitcham's performance against Nottingham Forest in the 1958–59 season. This was the year that Forest won the Cup and the nearest they came to defeat was in the third round against the amateurs. Again, the winter weather helped to eliminate the difference in skills. It was a game I had gone to watch in the knowledge that nothing is impossible in the Cup. And on the frosty ground Tooting and Mitcham's greater dash and determination seemed to have won them the match until a harsh penalty saved Forest late in the game. Or that was how it seemed to me at the time when I wrote for the *Observer*:

'Deservedly leading by two goals at half-time, Tooting and Mitcham were denied victory only by two farcical incidents. The first an error by their goalkeeper, the second an unnecessary penalty. This was the best performance by an amateur team in the F.A. Cup since Walthamstow Avenue drew on Manchester United's ground six years ago. The ground conditions gave them their chance, but there was no denying the skill and courage with which they took it.

'But it was luck that decided the game and for Tooting's left-half, Murphy, there was a harsh lesson in swift changes of footballing fortune.

'Shortly before the interval Murphy scored Tooting's second goal as he ran on to a loose ball to drive home a tremendous left-foot shot from 25 yards. But in the second half ecstasy turned to despair first as his gentle back pass bounced over the hands of Secker, a goalkeeper grown too confident to keep his eyes on the ball or his body behind it, then as a shot was driven against him and the referee awarded a penalty from which Gray scored. He could be blamed for neither of these goals for the pass was sensible and true and the penalty unfortunate. The ball seemed to strike him near the shoulder and there was no indication of intent to handle.

'It was the long ball quickly chased that brought the errors and the opportunities and in the first half Tooting alone exploited them.

'Soon after the start Holden's long pass down the centre should have been cut off, but with Thomson leaving the Forest goal as hesitantly and awkwardly as a novice skater testing the ice, Hasty reached the ball first to lob it over his head and against the bar. Shortly another hopeful kick by Holden set Thomson an identical problem. This time he advanced far enough to kick the ball against his centre-half leaving Grainger free to follow the rebound and push it into the empty net.

'It was clear by now that the difficulty of making an accurate pass and the pause necessary to control a ball had so reduced Forest's game that Tooting's fitness and determination enabled them to intercept most of their moves. Burkitt alone was complete master of the icy conditions playing with all his

44

usual poise. Despite the flow of passes, Forest's forwards were rarely dangerous except for the occasional thrust from Wilson and some elusive dribbling by Imlach. Then came Murphy's thunderbolt to send Tooting further ahead and put them for a time in complete command.

'Their confidence however was their undoing. In the second half they started to play as close as Forest as if to try and beat them at their own game. The tactics that had been so successful in the first half were never repeated and the Forest defence, slow and clumsy in the turn, was never tested again.

'Soon came Secker's sad lapse to offset some competent saves by this reserve goalkeeper; as Nottingham's pressure steadily mounted, their calm and steady play making the occasional opening. Imlach, Wilson, and Quigley all missed from close range before the penalty gave them an equalising goal that was beginning to seem beyond them.'

Nottingham Forest won the replay 3–0 without any further fears and that was a truer reflection of comparative ability. It was Sutton United in 1970 who perfectly illustrated the present relationship of the leading amateurs to the country's best. Their reward for reaching the third round was a home tie with Leeds United. For them this was a great occasion with their supporters determined to enjoy the day, rather than cherishing hopes of victory. The game unfolded without causing us any tremors in the Press seats. In the *Observer* I recorded:

'The weather was too mild, the pitch too good, to give Sutton any hope of containing Leeds. . . . When an amateur team clashes with a First Division side only the elements can upset the natural logic of events. Left to rely solely on their footballing skills Sutton at least forced Leeds to exert themselves and on occasion disconcerted the formidable defence.

'This was an achievement in which they could take pride. Faulkner had an impressive game at centre-half dominating the air and defeating Leeds' early tactic of the high ball lobbed to their tall strikers.

'But on the ground Allan Clarke was too sharp for them, snapping up four goals while Lorimer collected a couple.

'Sutton once hit the bar when Pritchard's stinging shot surprised Harvey and they were always eager to attack. It was typical that the sixth and final goal should come as they were driving upfield. Lorimer dispossessed Faulkner and Clarke, racing into the gap, took his smooth pass to slide the ball home. The precision of the move was a measure of the difference between the teams.'

Leeds departed with kindly compliments not neglecting to pick up on the way, Faulkner, the outstanding Sutton player.

But if the hope of an amateur team reaching the Final had long since passed individuals could still attain that ultimate soccer distinction. After Hunt's triumph with Wolverhampton, J. F. Mitchell was another to play in the Final, a bespectacled goalkeeper who was to be part of the one dramatic moment of the 1922 match, the last at Stamford Bridge. A rugged formless game was decided as Billy Smith, Huddersfield and England's outside-left, set off on a long dribble. The cheers and the tension mounted as he reached the penalty-area. Then Hamilton, Preston's right-back, caught up with him from behind, his tackle sending Smith sprawling. At once the referee pointed to the spot and despite the violent protests Mitchell was left to face Smith over twelve yards of mud and an ocean of silence. The rules then allowed him to move and he jumped up and down on his line to distract the kicker. But to no avail for the ball slammed past him for the decisive goal. Sixteen years later these two teams were to meet again and in another ill-tempered featureless match it was to be Preston who evened the account with Mutch's last-minute penalty. In all the pressure of Wembley nerves who can explain that no penalty-kick has failed however tense the situation?

Not until 1946 was another amateur to reach this stage and again the loser's medal was his reward. Arthur Turner, a 22-year-old R.A.F. officer, was centre-forward for Charlton Athletic in the first post-war Final. But it was another Turner, Charlton's half-back, who made the major contribution to a colourful and exciting game, ideally in tune with the carefree mood of a people released from War and seeking escape from its remaining austerities. After 80 minutes of fruitless play, Turner scored twice in a minute, turning a low centre into his own net then driving a free-kick into the defensive wall to bobble over the line as Doherty's leg deflected it past the stranded Woodley. But it was Derby's centre-forward, the burly Stamps, who won the game in extra time while Arthur Turner was powerless against Leuty, the game's outstanding defender.

The following year it was disappointment again for an amateur. Kippax, was on the wing for Burnley, a handsome dashing player who brought some colour to their dour, destructive style. But against Charlton he could make no headway, no impression on the game that was won by Duffy's fierce shot. Selected to play against France in a full International Kippax had to withdraw and never got another chance of a cap.

Bill Slater is the last man to play in the Cup-Final as an amateur. Still at University he was brought into Blackpool's side in 1951 when Brown was injured. In the early minutes of the game his shot grazed a post, but as Newcastle and Milburn took charge there was little he could do to turn the tide. He had to leave early from the dinner for Blackpool's defeated team to report back to University. Huddled unnoticed in the corner of a second class carriage he was surrounded by Tynesiders celebrating their win.

Bill Slater personifies changing attitudes to the game and the way in which amateurs now merge with professionals. For he was to return to Wembley in 1960 to take the Cup as Wolverhampton Wanderers' Professional captain.

How it would have surprised Lord Kinnaird to see a member of the staff of Birmingham University leading out one of the most dedicated professional teams of modern times. But for Slater it was a sensible step when soccer has an appeal that embraces graduate and artisan, a status that commands as much or more respect

46

than other professions. The only difference that payment made to his approach was to bring a greater sense of responsibility and greater pressures to play hard and achieve results.

A diffident man off the field, when he first approached Stanley Cullis he told that formidable Manager of Wolverhampton Wanderers that all he wanted was a game of football. 'I am quite happy to play in any of your reserve teams' he said. 'If the reserves are good enough for you, you aren't going to be good enough for me or Wolverhampton' was the forceful rejoinder.

Slater in fact was good enough for England and good enough to be voted Player of the Year before Wolves won that Final. Admirably consistent and unflappably calm, Slater's talents were best expressed as a wing-half where his cool interception and perceptive distribution were used to best advantage. Like Billy Wright, whom he succeeded as captain, he also played inside or centre-half, but there the similarity ended. Wright's outstanding characteristics were terrier-like energy, tremendous power in the tackle, and the spring in his feet that made him dominant in the air for all his lack of inches. Only in conscientiousness and consistency were the two alike.

The steady increase in the pressures and challenge of the Cup are well expressed by Slater's experience.

Coming unexpectedly into that 1951 Final he was relaxed enough to enjoy the game despite the result. Afterwards the Blackpool players wished him to share in the proceeds of a fund-raising brochure they had organised and it was eventually ruled that this would not infringe his amateur status. His share of the proceeds turned out to be £2. 5s. 0d!

Before the 1960 Final the pressures of speeches, interviews, and chairing the players' fund-raising committee generated great nervous strain. The night before the Final he shared a room with young Stobart to give confidence to an inexperienced player coming in unexpectedly as he had done nine years before. But it was Stobart's cheerful chatter that calmed him.

The game itself was marred for Slater by the accident to Whelan, carried off before half-time. So flat did the victory seem against ten men that he, like the authorities, became converted to the need for substitutes.

Part-time training would have been a problem had he had to fit in with a more complex tactical plan than that of Wolves. Even so being part-time had its difficulties. For one key game a plane was chartered to fly him after work to an evening match at Sheffield. But the Auster pilot could not locate the landing strip and when Wolves kicked off Slater was busy hitch-hiking from Worksop.[1]

He is the last of the long line of amateurs to have a decisive influence on the Cup but, as his career showed, the distinction had become more of an irrelevance.

[1] When the plane came down unheralded at the R.A.F. Aerodrome there, it had been surrounded by firetenders, ambulances, and angry officers!

7

Lancashire Leads

The first decade of the Cup had belonged to the Southern Amateur and the elite of the Public Schools and Universities. But football's origins were in the working class and once the Cup had fired their imagination it was only a question of time until they made it their own.

The year that Lancashire took over was 1883 and it was Blackburn Olympic who finally brought the Cup North, defeating the Old Etonians in extra time. In theory they too were amateurs but with imported players in their team there is little doubt that some of their side were paid in cash or kind. But it was still a memorable achievement and a memorable game.

This is how it was described in *The Only Authentic Record of the Cup* edited by D. MacKenzie in 1932.

'Aristocrats *versus* Artisans would have suitably titled this memorable encounter between teams from the historical playing fields of old Eton and a nondescript eleven of working men from Blackburn.

'That the southern team of famous amateur cracks would have their colours lowered by such a combination was a thing unthinkable – but the unexpected happened.

'The Olympic eleven, composed mostly of spinners, cotton operatives, and players of humble origin, gave such an exhibition of football as had never been seen in London before. The welding together of short passes, and dribbling with occasional long passing from wing to wing, utterly demoralised their opponents, and their tactics simply wore the Etonians off their legs. Charging from behind, pushing with hands, and in some cases even holding were frequent incidents in a game where appeals were continuous, but apart from these lapses, the Olympic adoption of the Scotch system of play left their opponents guessing, and before they had time to size up the "new model" the first triumph of Lancashire in the final was assured.

'On the call of time, each side had scored one goal, but the Old Etonians agreed to continue for an extra half hour. During this period, Dewhurst, on the right wing, sent one of his long high passes to little Costley on the left wing, the latter making no mistake and notching the winning point.

'The scenes which followed this match at the Oval were hitherto without parallel in the football world, and when "Captain" Warburton (a master plumber) was handed the Cup by Major Marindin, the then President of the Association. Excitement quite carried the provincials away.'

48

So Olympic achieved what Blackburn Rovers had narrowly failed to accomplish the year before. This was the more remarkable when one recalls that association football was relatively new to Blackburn.

It had been introduced ten years before by Mr John Lewis, later to be President of the Lancashire F.A., Vice-President of the F.A., and a Senior Vice-President of the Football League. When he moved to the town from Market Drayton he found that, as in most of East Lancashire, the Harrow game – a mixture of Association and Rugby rules – was the popular sport.

At a meeting in the St Leger Hotel in November 1872 attended by seventeen people, Lewis launched the Rovers as Blackburn's first association football Club. Thomas Greenwood was elected captain, giving the Club the backing of a family as prominent in the civic and business life of the town as in sport. Another Greenwood, D. H., was to prove a full-back of outstanding ability and win caps against Scotland and Ireland. The Greenwoods also preserved the close link with their old school, Malvern, and the Club's colours were derived from Malvern's quartered shirt with blue substituted for green. D. H. Greenwood recalled that the earliest tactical instruction he received in a house game was 'go for the man and never mind the ball!' But this was not passed on to the Rovers.

Jack and Fred Hargreaves, sons of Blackburn's Coroner, soon joined the new Club and both were to win International honours. Jack was regarded as one of the best wing forwards of his day.

Another local recruit was 'Monkey' Hornby, the brilliant athlete better known as a Rugby International and outstanding Test Cricketer. He joined the team for the opening match on their new Alexandra Meadows ground in which visiting Partick were beaten 2–1.

To the local talent were soon added some itinerant Scots as the rivalry with Darwen grew sharper. It was indeed a surprise that it should be Olympic rather than Darwen or Rovers who first brought the Cup North. Whatever Olympic's actual status there was a professional thoroughness in their preparation for the game against the Old Etonians. Employers were asked to give their players Saturday mornings off and such was the excitement that all agreed to a concession quite out of keeping with the current industrial tradition. A raffle was run in the town and the proceeds used to take the team to Blackpool for a week's training that paid such good dividends.

More significantly two of the team, Jack Hunter and George Wilson, had joined the Club in 1882 from Sheffield Zulus. The Zulus had been giving exhibition matches with players theatrically attired and money charged at the gate. This had led to trouble with the Sheffield Association and it is a reasonable assumption that Hunter and Wilson would have wanted a price for joining Olympic. Whatever the inducement, Jack Hunter, who captained England, was certainly a bargain. He was the man of the match in the decisive game with the Old Etonians.

Blackburn was to stay in command for three more years but it was now the Rovers who took up the running. Three times in succession they carried off the

Cup and that was a record never again to be equalled. The Wanderers had achieved it as Major Marindin reminded their Captain, Jimmy Brown, when he handed him the Challenge Cup. 'But it was a very different game then, Major' was the pointed reply. Indeed it was! Whether their players were paid or not Blackburn had changed the concepts and standards with the competition growing ever keener. That year 130 clubs had entered, a striking contrast to the initial 15 or the 43 when Wanderers last won the Cup.

Fergie Suter was prominent in the Rovers side taking part in four Finals for them. With players like that in their team their amateurism was bound to be suspect. For The Football Association, strongly backed by the Birmingham and Sheffield Associations, was out to kill the practice of payment. Accrington Stanley were the first team to be penalised, excluded from the competition on the same day they had beaten Park Road 3–2 in a Cup Tie.

It was a time for plain speaking and the matter came to a head on January 19, 1884. Preston North End drew with Upton Park, who immediately lodged a complaint that their players were paid. Major Suddell, Preston's Chairman, surprised the F.A. when he admitted the payments and argued that this was a necessary and justifiable development.

Preston were disqualified, but their stand gave power to the campaign to legalise professionalism. Charles Alcock was broad-minded enough to be impressed by Major Sudell's argument and the thought that this was an inevitable development which should be controlled rather than fought.

At the F.A.'s General Meeting Alcock proposed 'that professionalism be legalised, the details to be submitted to a Special General Meeting of the Association'. This was seconded by N. C. Bailey, one of the outstanding players of the old school, of Southern Amateurs. But if the South were amenable the Sheffield and Birmingham Associations were implacable. 'If you cannot beat them, join them' had no place in their philosophy. J. C. Clegg and C. Crump led the opposition that rejected the proposal and went on to tighten the screw. In June 1884 a new ruling prohibited expense payments for lost wages to apply to more than one day per week and, worse still for the North, barred any imported player, or any but Englishmen from playing with English Clubs in the Cup. This brought the Northern Clubs into open revolt and at meetings in Blackburn and Manchester it was proposed to form a new British Football Association.

As proposal and counter proposal led the F.A. into one blind alley after another the provincial clubs were in confusion and conflict. For a year the battle raged. On one side were ranged many of those who had established the game in the South and were broad-minded enough to see Professionalism as a necessary further step. They gave firm support to the Northern contingent ably led by Mr R. P. Gregson, Secretary of Lancashire, and a talented administrator.

Finally professionalism was legalised at a Special General Meeting of the F.A. on July 20, 1885. This was on a motion proposed by Dr E. S. Morley of Blackburn, famous for his cigars, velvet coats, strong convictions, and blunt speech. Some limitations were still enforced such as the ruling 'Professionals shall be allowed to compete in all Cups provided they qualify as follows: In Cup matches by birth or residence for two (2) years past within six (6) miles of the ground or head-quarters of the Club for which they play.'

But the Northern Clubs had most of what they wanted and were well satisfied.

Blackburn meanwhile were busily cementing Lancashire's lead, getting on with the game while the arguments raged.

In winning the Final of 1884 they had defeated a Queen's Park side with ten internationals and, to show the 2–1 victory was no fluke, they improved on their performance, beating Queen's Park 2–0 in the next year's Final. Once more it was carnival in Blackburn with Olympic joining the victory procession in a Wagonette as the Rovers' honoured guests.

The shield presented to
Blackburn Rovers in 1886
for their third
consecutive victory.

When Blackburn Rovers completed their hat-trick by beating West Bromwich Albion in 1886 Alcock's recent rule prevented the Rovers winning the Cup out-right. But the F.A. presented them with a silver shield 'in commemoration of their winning the Challenge Cup three years in succession viz. 1884, 1885, and 1886.'

The Rovers continued to make their mark on the competition and soon came close to repeating their three successive wins. In 1890 they were again in the Final with three survivors from the teams that had won such renown – Forrest, Loft-house, and Walton. Their opponents were Sheffield Wednesday in the first Cup-Final clash between red rose and white. More than 20,000 people surged into the Oval and it was fortunate that the military were allowed free entrance for soon soldiers in their scarlet jackets were being called to help control the crowd. Such was the excitement that *The Times* recorded: 'The Cup Final has now assumed the dignity and importance of an International match.'

But the new status of the game brought greater pressures and perhaps for the

51

first time nerves were to play a decisive part. Rovers had seen it all before, but for Wednesday it was a new and demanding experience. A Blackburn reporter saw Mr R. P. Gregson coming from the dressing rooms and asked who was going to win. 'Sheffield are beaten now!' said Gregson 'The Wednesday are down in the dumps. They are as quiet as mice. They have not a word to say. They look frightened. But the Rovers are singing and whistling and carrying on like a lot of kittens. Unless I am very much mistaken they will win easily.' Gregson was not mistaken for Blackburn won by a record 6–1. Townley became the first to score three goals in a Final, his second a magnificent shot from near the corner-flag. Walton, Jack Southworth, and Lofthouse also scored while Mumford at last turned the ball home on one of the rare occasions that Wednesday could get past Forbes.

Mr T. B. Mitchell a native of Dumfries was now Blackburn's Secretary and kept them well supplied with leading Scottish players. His successful scouting raids made him so unpopular north of the border that he had to go in disguise and on one occasion was chased through hedge and ditch ruining his clothes. Forbes, Brandon, Dewar, Campbell, Gow, Anderson, and Marshall were all acquired by him to maintain Rovers' high standards.

The team was good enough to win again the next year defeating Notts County who were in the Final for the first time. Nerves may have played a part again for Notts County had just beaten Rovers 7–1 in a League match. True, Blackburn were not then at full strength and their outspoken Chairman, Dr Morley, had complained that 'they had played like old women in clogs'. It was, however, generally predicted that Notts County would win until an anxious, hesitant start saw them three goals down at half-time. Dewar, Southworth, and Townley had settled the game by then though Notts were more like themselves after the interval with Oswald scoring twenty minutes from the end.

Rovers' five wins had now brought them level with the Wanderers. It was to be another 37 years before they fought their way back to this last stage of the competition and took the Cup for the sixth time.

Though they remained successful Cup-fighters, often reaching the semi-final, they were never again to enjoy such sustained success as in the years that belonged to James Forrest. Like Lord Kinnaird and C. H. R. Wollaston he gained five Cup Winners' medals and with the competition growing ever more demanding no one else was to achieve that distinction. Forrest was an outstanding wing-half, capped twelve times for England, a durable player of supreme quality. But Blackburn had possessed other remarkable players, none more distinctive than 'Herby' Arthur, who kept goal in three of their successful Finals. He joined the Club as a right-half then volunteered to keep goal in a second eleven match and found his true vocation. An imperturbable individualist he once came out alone to face Burnley in a League match when the rest of the Rovers' side was sheltering in the dressing room frozen by the driving snow and piqued at being three down. J. C. Clegg, the referee, ordered the game to go on, but Arthur at once claimed for off-side. He then took so long over the kick that Mr Clegg finally abandoned the game in bewilderment.

Jimmy Brown, a bustling centre forward who scored the wonderful individual goal against West Bromwich in the replayed Final of 1886 was the most dashing of their forwards. But Harry Campbell who, with McCallum of Renton, had formed one of the greatest wings in Scottish history, was perhaps the cleverest. So good was his passing that it was said any player who could not shine when Campbell partnered him ought to seek other means of livelihood.

Yet all the great players of Rovers' early years were no match for one who never won a medal. In 1896 Robert Crompton was signed 'a very promising youth who has played for the Trinity Club'. He was to win 42 caps with England, the finest right-back of his time. But the Cup is no respecter of persons and this honour was always to elude him in the 24 years of his playing career.

For much of the Cup's history Blackburn Rovers have remained a powerful name in football, though they have slipped sadly at present. Their last victory was in 1928, won as often, against the odds. Huddersfield were the favourites, but for less than a minute. Hardly had the game started than Blackburn's forwards swept up-field for Roscamp to lob the ball just under the bar. Mercer the goalkeeper jumped to catch the ball spinning and swirling in the breeze. But Roscamp had been racing up as if this was some 'up and under' kick at rugby and now he struck swift as a cobra. Mercer was sent flying and the ball bundled into the net – a goal in less than sixty seconds. It is so difficult to make a fair shoulder charge on a goalkeeper as he gathers the ball that there must be an element of doubt about this goal – as about Lofthouse's charge on Gregg in 1958, but the referee's decision was accepted readily enough and Wembley rang with the cheers.

In the hush before the game began a little Blackburn supporter had rung a vast bell shouting 'Each time ah ring t'bell Blackbourn'll score'. They had answered him at once, but success went to his head as the bell rang out frenziedly throughout the match. But there was nothing excitable about Blackburn's play, only a relentless determination that wore down Huddersfield's famous forward line.

Before half-time McLean sent a shot arrowing into the net to put them further ahead. Alex Jackson narrowed the gap with a shot that bounced down off the underside of the bar. It was for this that he had been moved into the centre for the second half, but not even his restless energy could find another opening. Huddersfield had spent themselves and Roscamp settled any argument with a final decisive thrust.

More than thirty years were to pass before Rovers came back to Wembley and now the magic had gone. While they supplied the neat approach work it was Wolves who came driving through to take three goals off a Rovers side that lacked their determination and teamwork. On the very morning of the match Dougan had asked for a transfer and he played as if his mind was already elsewhere. It was a sad final curtain call for a team that had held the centre of the stage so effectively for so long. Only Aston Villa has beaten and only Newcastle equalled these six Cup wins of the Rovers.

Preston North End might well have rivalled them for Major Sudell soon achieved

53

his object of building up a formidable team. The 'Invincibles' became their nickname, but in the Cup they were surprisingly vulnerable. 'Proud' Preston was their other title so perhaps a fall was inevitable. Certainly they went out of their way to tempt the fates. The story went that they were so confident of victory in their 1888 Final that they wished to be photographed with the Cup before the game. Had they not beaten Hyde by an unbelievable 26–0, the competition's most pitiable massacre? Was a local Staffordshire side with a wage bill of £5 10s. per week likely to upset their high paid 'professors'? 'Had you not better win it first?' was Major Marindin's brusque retort and West Bromwich Albion echoed the query. Bewitched by Billy Bassett, Preston faltered to defeat.

Yet such was their drawing power that the Oval had to be closed when the crowd reached 17,000. And there was no denying the attraction or effectiveness of their Scottish style.

The next season was their year of triumph, unmatched and now unmatchable. For they went through their League programme of 22 matches without losing one and lifted the Challenge Cup without conceding a goal.

John Goodall, the outstanding forward in their devastating line thus describes the power of their play. The team was 'the best combination I have ever seen, it was not that the opposition they met was weak, as is supposed now, but that their own football was brilliant and that the players were splendidly matched for each other's style'. Goodall was no thoughtless boaster, but a student of the game whose reflective comments were shrewd and restrained. And the evidence indicates that this was a fair judgement of Preston.

Yet it was not until 1922 that they were back in the Final and a further 16 years before they won again. Neither of these games, a rough duet with Huddersfield resolved each time by a penalty, brought much credit to them. More in keeping with their style of play were the exciting Finals of 1954 and 1964. But for all their fine football they lost each time, no new tale in the story of the Cup. And perhaps it was an apt comment on their days of greatness for sometimes they were too clever for their own good. It was the down-to-earth teams like Albion who were to have the more consistent record.

Preston were not just a good team in those early years; they also played the game with a splendid spirit. Inevitably football has had its rough passages with passions stirred on the field and in the crowd. Enough examples of this have been quoted already. But the game is also full of generous enthusiasm and players imbued with sportsmanship.

John Goodall was one of these, his equable temperament an example to all. His philosophy of the game is just as valid today:

'One great point in football that cannot be too strongly urged is the maintenance of good temper. I do not say this merely because of the desire to keep the game pure and honourable, but because an even temper is essential to good play. There is no game which is more calculated to rouse the evil passions, and therefore a great deal of restraint and self-control are absolutely necessary. A player must not regard it as a personal insult if the ball is taken from him, or if he is the victim of a charge which, if heavy, is nevertheless legal. One might just as well expect a batsman to cherish a bitter hatred for the fieldsman who has just caught him brilliantly.

'The enemies of football argue that the game rouses the combative instinct in one; the friends reply that therefore there is all the more reason why the game should be played, because a golden attribute is the quality of curbing one's temper, and long experience of football tends to this.'

Preston were always at their best when they remembered his precepts.

Lancashire papers that some years before gave full accounts of Rugby matches, but ignored games under the other code, were soon forced to change their coverage by the success of Preston and Blackburn. The interest and excitement inspired by their deeds in the Cup also helped to set new standards for neighbouring teams. Rivalry was sharpened and the quality heightened by the Lancashire F.A. Cup which added the yeast of competition to the stodgy fare of friendly fixtures.

One of the teams that rose to the top was Bolton Wanderers, a Club that had developed out of Christ Church F.C. In April 1886 they beat Blackburn in the Final of the Lancashire Cup when Hewitson scored 'a splendid goal that it would have been impossible for anyone to stop'. The year before they had beaten Black-burn 5–1 in the semi-final only to be disqualified when Rovers complained that five of their players did not have the necessary two-year residential qualification.

These two matches against the most successful team in England were clear evidence of Bolton's potential. But they were hardly the most consistent of sides, losing 12–1 to Preston the following season. Not until 1890 could they achieve anything of note in the Challenge Cup and by then they had established a reputation for eccentricity. The previous season their second round match against West Manchester had been abandoned because it became too dark to see what was happening. Bolton won the replay 9–0, but were then heavily defeated in Belfast by the newly formed Linfield Athletic.

Little wonder that when their Cup run began with a win over the current Irish champions Wolverhampton's *Express and Star* reported:

'"The Bolton Wanderers are a funny lot and their latest freak is to beat a strong Irish Club, Belfast Distillery, by 10 goals to 2." The third goal was certainly freakish as the visiting goal-keeper caught the ball and fell to the ground where-upon "all the Wanderers attempted to roll him through the posts . . . More than half the players were struggling in the mud, but eventually the Wanderers managed to drag custodian, backs and the others through the coveted space."

Non-league Sheffield United were now defeated 13–0 by more normal tactics; then Preston were beaten at Deepdale in a stirring rally after two goals had been conceded in eight minutes. So to the semi-final against Sheffield Wednesday whose defeat of Notts County had been as much a triumph of litigation as of soccer.

Manchester City F.C., winners of the F.A. Cup in 1904; *back row:* J. Parlby, C. H. Waterhouse, E. Hulton (Chairman), J. E. Chapman, G. Madders; *second row:* T. E. Maley (Secretary and Manager), J. Hillman, C. Livingstone, J. McMahon, T. Hynds, W. Gillespie, L. W. Furness, J. Broad (Trainer); *third row:* F. Booth, S. Frost, W. Meredith (Captain), S. Ashworth; *front row:* A. Turnbull, H. Burgess.

Twice the match had had to be replayed because of protests. The semi-final was played in a rainstorm and Bolton had enough chances to win. But it was Wednesday who sneaked through 2–1. Four times the ball was in the net and each time the goal was disputed – but only Bolton's would-be equaliser disallowed. The Bolton supporters commented sourly 'Sheffield Wednesday will not now be required to protest themselves into the Final'.

The teams were to meet again in the semi-final four years later and this time the score was reversed. Two goals by Bentley and the stout defence of Sutcliffe, Somerville, and Jones saw Wanderers through to their first Final. But as the paper had said Bolton were a funny lot and went poorly prepared into the match with Notts County. Logan followed Townley's early example in scoring a hat-trick and only inspired goalkeeping by Sutcliffe confined Notts County to four goals.

The *Football Field* commented:

'The poor Wanderers are catching it pretty hot on every side. Neither the Committee nor the players are spared and we must loyally say some of the remarks passed on the latter are totally unjustifiable. We are convinced the men honestly did their best to win, but the other side were in superior condition to the Wanderers.

'Say what we will when we find five men in the team labouring under a disadvantage it makes a bit of a difference. Paton, as everybody knows, was swathed in bandages, Gardiner (who replaced the injured Turner) was not trained, Bentley was ill, Somerville had been seriously troubled with his face for two or three days before the match and Hughes got hurt five minutes after the start. Add to this the fact that the men were fagged and jaded after their Easter gruellings and had not been afforded the opportunity to train properly, and the defeat does not look so black.'

Certainly it did not look black in Birmingham where there was smug satisfaction that 'At any rate the old pot has not gone to Lancashire'. Success always invites envy, but in fact it was to be another ten years before there was the first all-Lancashire Final. Again, Bolton Wanderers were to pick up the losers' medals defeated by a single goal from Manchester City's Meredith. But for a Second Division team they gave a courageous display in happy contrast to the debacle of 1894.

One of the men to build up Bolton had been J. T. Bentley, a Secretary of strong character and varied talent. He was a successful player and referee, a President and formidable champion of the League against any encroachment by the F.A., an England selector and a journalist. He was a practical, down-to-earth character who had no love of fancy words or frivolous action. His shrewd judgement and concise style were apparent in his contribution to the *Football Field* and as editor of the *Athletic News*. He set a new fashion in reporting, aiming to be informative and interesting, rather than flowery, to underestimate, rather than to gush. 'He is to the point with the pen as with the tongue, and calls a football "the ball". Such things as "inflated spheres", "tergumentary cylinders" and "the leather globe" he leaves to others. A champion of his day is to him a "good player" or a "sound one". He does not deal in superlatives.'

Who better to give an account of that 1904 Final though perhaps his Bolton sympathies show through:

'Another Cup Final has been played and won, and for the first time the great trophy of the year has gone to Manchester. It could not have been sent to a more enthusiastic football district, unless it had found its way to the opposing town, only ten miles away.

'We had typical cup final weather – fair and bright, and there was a much better crowd than most people anticipated, over 62,000 being present. They were mostly in favour of Bolton, probably owing to them being considered the weaker side. At any rate, anything the Boltonians did was heartily cheered and better play on the part of Manchester was received in comparative silence. Yes, there is little question about it – Bolton were the popular side, and had the Cup been taken to Bolton, the victory would have been most popular.

'There was no mistaking the feeling of the crowd from the time the teams came out of the pavilion to the final whistle sounding, and the Hon Alfred Lyttleton, in his admirable little speech, opened in capital fashion by expressing sympathy with the Wanderers.

'With the single exception of Boyd, the Bolton half-back, the teams turned out at full strength, all the Manchester injured players being able to take part in the game, which was not a very good one, but better than the majority of finals. It was always interesting, for both sides fought most strenuously.

'In the first half Manchester had a lot the best of it, and more than deserved

57

the single goal but to my mind the goal – that all-important goal – ought not to have been allowed. From the pavilion we had a splendid view, and Meredith seemed to be waiting behind Struthers and quite a couple of yards offside. The majority about me favoured this view, but such a good judge as John Lewis agreed with the decision of the referee, who personally had not the slightest doubt about the matter. But to me it seemed a clear case of offside, and it is a pity that the result should have been decided by what at the best must be considered a doubtful point. On the play it was well earned, but seeing Meredith, as I can still see him, standing, and then making a dart for the ball well behind Struthers, I cannot but think it hard lines on the Wanderers to lose the match by a goal which was open to so much question. But on the play the City fully deserved to lead by that odd goal.'

WANDERERS' FINE DASH

'Immediately on resuming the Wanderers set about their work as if they meant business, and if the City deserved the goal they had secured the Wanderers were certainly entitled to an equalising point. They showed splendid dash, and for twenty minutes played the game they did against Southampton, Sheffield United and Derby County, with the exception that they seldom shot. Indeed, all through the shooting on both sides was poor, and the only decent shot on the part of the Wanderers in the first half was that by Taylor, who, after a careful run, gave Hillman a thorough teaser from long range.

'During the first half-hour after the interval the Bolton men were simply "all over" their opponents, and had they followed up their energetic work by having a drive for goal the Cup would not have been located in Manchester for the next twelve months, for the City backs were by no means faultless, and afforded every opportunity for scoring. Then for ten minutes the City seemed to realize that it was time they did something, and the Boltonians had an anxious time of it, for Manchester attacked in fine style, and but for sound defence must have added to their score.

'Then, to their credit be it said, Bolton came over once more, and their opponents were sorely tried during the last five minutes. White sent in a shot which only missed by inches – but miss it did, and Manchester City won by 1 goal to 0.

'Leaving out the doubtful character of the goal which settled matters, Manchester were the better team, but this superiority was by no means pronounced, and had Bolton displayed the form shown in the previous round they would have won, for Manchester City did not play their usual game. Possibly it was because the Wanderers' dogged persistency did not allow them to do so, and for this the Bolton men must be given every credit.

'There was supposed to be a shining star on each side – the extreme right-wing – but Meredith did little or nothing for a man of his reputation except scoring the goal, and Stokes did less.'

Birmingham Gazette, April 25, 1904.

Billy Meredith scores the winning goal for Manchester City
at the first all-Lancashire Final in 1904.

This was not the greatest match for that wonderful winger whose chewed quill toothpick 'kept me feet moving and me mouth dry'. It would be a pity if Meredith were to be dismissed with such modest commendation. A further tribute to his skill came from another Lancastrian writer, Don Davies, 'Old International' of *The Guardian* who was as precise and entertaining with words as Meredith with the ball.

'Billy Meredith, football genius, began his career in first-class football in 1894 and played regularly for 31 years. Altogether he scored 470 goals in no fewer than 1,363 matches and played 51 times for Wales in International matches. To commemorate his 50th appearance for his country against Scotland on February 26, 1920, he was presented with a silver centrepiece before the start of the game. In popularity, eminence, and mastery of his art, Meredith was the Lloyd George of Welsh football. The parallel is by no means perfect, but it was curious how many points of resemblance could be traced. Both men had a following not far short of the entire Welsh nation; both were hailed by friends as the highest product of Welsh genius and by opponents as the lowest form of Welsh cunning. Both found it necessary to leave Wales to find adequate scope for their talents, yet both returned repeatedly in their hey-day to pay off debts in their heart-felt gratitude.

'Round about 1894, when Meredith was a youth, the newly formed Manchester City Football Club sent a deputation to Chirk, North Wales, with orders

59

to bring him back. This mission was fulfilled but not without some hair-raising experiences. The angry townsfolk, roused by the thought of a local genius being sold for alien gold, seized one of the deputation and threw him into a nearby horse trough. It is safe to assume that the sight of the stripling for whom he had suffered did little to warm this gentleman's damp spirits on the journey home in the train. There sat Meredith, no doubt silent, with close-cropped hair, face pale and cadaverous, a slender frame, all skin and bone, and a queer pair of legs, rather like outsize calipers. Yet, in later years, when these same caliper legs and body of thistle-down lightness vaulted airily over countless vicious tackles, when this same Welshman, quill in mouth and with grim sardonic smile, became a terror wherever his long raking stride and neat precise centring were to be seen, then, no doubt, the assaulted scout would regard his baptism from a less distasteful angle. In retrospect it would become a privilege.

'Those ninety minutes of consummate ball control and trickery every Saturday afternoon, to the roars of an adoring multitude, were Meredith's one means of communion with his fellow men. For the rest he was as silent as a Trappist. Like Alan Morton of Scotland, he was constantly toying with the ball, spinning it, trapping it, juggling with it, until his feet developed the tactile sensitiveness of an ordinary person's hands. His mind persistently dwelt on the problems of the game. Nothing was too small to escape him. Take corner kicks in wet weather, for example. He placed the ball with laces underneath, to raise it a little from the mud, elementary, of course, but such things count. When a penalty rule was enforced, allowing a goalkeeper to advance to the six-yard line, Meredith killed it by walking to the ball and hooking it, gently but irretrievably, over the goalkeeper's head.

'Unlike some eminent isolationists, Meredith was a great collaborator. He lived and prospered in what might be called the great "Triangular Period", when "insider", "outsider" and wing-half worked and manoeuvred as one. Great triangles at once rise to the mind. Cuggy, Mordue and Buchan; Boyd, White and McEwan; then Duckworth, Meredith and Halse. Both for Manchester City and Manchester United, Meredith coached and produced superb wing-halves, for without their collusion the famous Meredithian back-heel, the game's most joyous red herring, would have lost the effect it had. "Old Skin" as he was affectionately called by his team-mates, tasted all that football had to offer in the way of Cup medals and International honours. When his playing days were over, he observed the conventions and "took a pub". The story goes that during the Manchester blitz a bomb exploded at the back of the pub and a shower of Welsh International caps descended on the neighbourhood. They took some time to collect again, for there were 51 of them.'

Manchester's wild celebrations of their first win suddenly turned to dust and ashes. From ecstasy to agony is a commonplace of the competition, but this contrast was cruel. One day there was Meredith carrying the Cup in triumph through the packed streets; then the whole team was debarred from further service with the Club. An F.A. investigation found that illegal bonus payments had been made to players; the Secretary and some Directors were suspended; Manchester United gathered a rich harvest that was to include Meredith while City faced a new season with a playing staff whose first and second teams conceded 27 goals in the opening days of the season.

Manchester City was as quick to recover from the blow as United from the disastrous air crash in later years. The City's enthusiasm for soccer demanded success and over the years both Clubs were to achieve it in full measure. So too were Bolton Wanderers whose wayward beginnings were forgotten in the 'twenties when they built their reputation as the most formidable of Cup fighters.

But Manchester City's win over them had a symbolic significance. For all the contribution that Bolton, Blackburn, Preston, and Bury had made, or Blackpool and Burnley were yet to make, the advantages were with the great cities. In 1971 it is sad to see all of these Clubs struggling in the Lower Divisions, unlikely to have much hope of a Trophy that last went outside the First Division in 1931.

In these days of £100 per week wages, of £180,000 transfers and of £12,000 bonuses to sweeten the Arsenal double, only the big cities can pay the price of continuing success.

But while Manchester and Liverpool remain so dedicated to football, Lancashire remains a prime and powerful force in the Cup and in every other competition. Clubs from the County have won 28 of the 88 Finals and that gives the red rose a proud pre-eminence.

8

Midland Mastery: Aston Villa – The Cup's Leading Team

Next in time and ultimate success are the Midland teams. But while Lancashire can field a full eleven of Clubs that have won the Cup, the Midland challenge is less widely spread.

Four Clubs have made the main contribution and if we look at their records we see they have maintained their form over a span of years. Aston Villa, Wolverhampton Wanderers, West Bromwich Albion, and Nottingham Forest have won the Cup 18 times between them and only Villa is currently in soccer's shadow.

Yet Aston Villa is the competition's most successful team, seven times triumphant. And this was the Club that first destroyed Lancashire's mastery.

It was in 1887 that Aston Villa achieved their ambition and it was neighbouring West Bromwich Albion whom they beat 2–0 in the Final. This was a far cry from their first halting appearance in the 1879 Cup season when they scratched in the second round, rather than face Oxford University.

On the way to the Oval they survived a marathon tie with another midland team. It needed three replays before they at last got the better of Wolverhampton Wanderers. Darwen gave them another scare in the sixth round, coming back from a three-goal deficit at half-time to score twice and do everything but equalise. Villa were so sure of themselves at the interval that they accepted champagne proffered in a loving cup by the President of Moseley Football Club. By the end of the game it was a case of 'God pardon us, nor harden us, we did not see too clear', as Villa staggered to undeserved victory.

This story intrigues me, but I doubt if the champagne alone was responsible for the sudden swing in the game. In an Amateur Cup-Final, when suffering from a high temperature, I was given both champagne and brandy at half-time and the only effect was a marked improvement in body swerve.

What was seen as a fortunate recovery from folly was followed by a classically perfect game against Scotland's best. In the semi-final at Crewe, Glasgow Rangers were defeated 3–1. Villa had absorbed the Scottish tradition of 'real fitba' and the game was a splendid spectacle of clever footwork, of neat passing, and subtle dribbling. Rangers were effectively a full Scottish International side, but Villa outpaced and out-thought them.

West Bromwich Albion had reached the Final the year before, becoming the first

Midland Club to achieve this distinction. Blackburn had defeated them then, but this year they were the favourites.

Their semi-final win over Preston had been as notable as Villa's and the Birmingham Press was divided in its loyalty. The *Birmingham Daily Post* backed Villa to win and by reflex action their rivals, *Avis' Gazette*, predicted success for Albion. Albion indeed were confident enough to plan their route back with the Cup – mapping out a victory tour that took in South Wales and reached West Bromwich without going through Birmingham!

They had completed special training at Ascot race-course and their high hopes were not unjustified. But there is little justice about the Cup. The day, April 2, saw a somewhat fortunate win for Villa in the first all-Midland Final.

Albion controlled the match in the first half and only Coulton and Simmonds gave good cover to goalkeeper Warner, who was in splendid form, repeatedly foiling the attempts to charge him over his goal line. The giant, Bob Roberts, sporting the long cricket flannels he always wore, was a more famous name in Albion's goal – but it was he who committed the fatal mistakes that swung the game.

Aston Villa had come back into the game once they accepted that centre-half Perry was in confident control of their captain, Archie Hunter. Their normal tactics were to feed the ball to Hunter but now they switched their attack to the wings. Soon Dennis Hodgetts broke clear and Roberts made no attempt to save, assuming he was offside. But Major Marindin's imperious finger pointed to the centre and the strong protests had no hope of success with that experienced referee.

Two minutes from time Archie Hunter at last broke free picking up a loose backpass before colliding with Roberts. Lying on the ground Hunter still stabbed the ball over the line to settle the issue.

'Brummagem' in 1874 was typical of an industrial city with hundreds of chimney stacks and furnaces blackening the town. As 'growlers' bumped along the cobbled streets, sport flourished on its outskirts bringing lively enjoyment to a dreary environment.

It was then that members of the Villa Cross (Aston) Wesleyan Chapel founded the Aston Villa Football Club. Once more muscular christianity was to be closely allied with football. In view of such early associations it was perhaps surprising that many clerics should later revile the game. But the growth of professionalism and the turbulence of crowd behaviour were unnatural evils in a number of churchmen's eyes and their attacks delayed the game's social acceptance throughout the country.

One other thread runs through the early pattern – the Scottish influence. Nowhere was it stronger than in Birmingham. Two Scots brought Association Football to the City. Another Scot, George Ramsay, built the Villa and it was William McGregor who helped the Club and founded the Football League. George Ramsay joined the Club by chance after talking his way into a practice game in Aston Park. This dapper 21-year-old dazzled his clumsy companions with his sleight-of-foot and delicate ball control. And since he was soon to stamp his personality on the

Club it was hardly surprising that he should instil into Villa the Scottish tradition of clever ball play. The members were so intrigued by his magical skills as he waltzed around opponents in his small polo cap and the long pants he had designed himself that he was soon elected captain.

Now, by another lucky chance they acquired Archie Hunter, the finest captain in their history. He was looking for Calthorpe F.C. when he came to Birmingham from Ayr, but could not find their ground. Then he heard of Ramsay and promptly signed on with Villa. What a capture that was, for Hunter was an inspired player and a forceful leader. He was a skilful dribbler, one of the earliest to shield the ball with his body, but it was his dash and the power of his shot that endeared him to the crowds. Since his employer did not like football he played at first under an assumed name, but later his popularity was such that Villa hired a special train to take him to Nottingham when he could not get away with the rest of the team. He and Ramsay launched Villa on the spectacular career that was to bring a record number of Cup victories, the double in 1897 and the heartaches to which all football clubs are heir. For triumph is never pure and perpetual.

Like most football clubs Villa are used to a struggle. In the early days at the Perry Bar ground their supporters came armed with turves and insults to exchange with rival followers.

Success did not come easily to the 'Perry Pets'. Their first impact in the Cup was in 1880 when they beat those powerful sides, Forest and County, on their own grounds at Nottingham. But the fall came swiftly when they crashed at home to the Stafford Railway Works Club from Wolverhampton.

In 1882–83 they made good progress again until they met Notts County in the 4th round. Three goals down at the interval Villa fought back to level the scores until that great cricketer and sportsman William Gunn ran clean through their defence to score the winner. Even then a certain equaliser was saved when a Notts defender fisted the ball away, protected by the lack of a penalty-kick rule.

Friendly matches and a 6–1 defeat in the Cup by Queen's Park, Glasgow, gave Villa the chance to study Scottish tactics and converted them to the *two* full-back system. But it was not until that season of 1886–87 that they really savoured the sweet scent of success in the Cup. A rollicking start with victories of 13–0 over Wednesbury Old Athletic and 6–1 over Derby Midland preceded an interminable battle of replays with Wolves spread over seven weeks. That was a gruelling prelude to the final triumph over West Bromwich Albion at the Oval.

Next season they were drawn against Preston's Invincibles in the fifth round with a record gate of 27,000 pouring into Perry Bar. With the jostling crowd twice breaking on to the pitch, mounted police and a few Hussars from the neighbouring barracks had such difficulty in establishing control that the game was abandoned with Preston leading 3–1. The Clubs fixed a replay date but The Football Association disqualified Villa and ordered the result to stand. That was the season that one of their Committee men, William McGregor, launched the League because Villa's supporters were tiring of one-sided friendly games with local teams.

In the Cup-Final of 1887 West Bromwich attack as Bayliss heads for goal.
Note the umpire by the far post, the lack of a goal net, and the look of
Kennington Oval.

But by 1890 Villa were faring so badly in League and Cup that Mr F. W. Rinder
forced the committee to resign and was himself elected Financial Secretary. With
his energetic guidance Villa entered their golden era. 1892 was the decisive year
when three remarkable players joined the Club. There was John Devey, an inside-
forward who was only kept from a string of International caps by John Goodall of
Preston and Steve Bloomer of Derby – two of the game's immortals. Devey first
played for the Club at baseball, but was to be a captain in the Archie Hunter mould
and later a Director of the Club, a rare transition. His right-wing partner, Charlie
Athersmith, was the fleetest of players, a dashing wingman of the Joe Hulme type.
He was to win twelve International caps and in 1897 gained every honour open to
a player – caps against Scotland, Wales, and Ireland, and League, and Cup winners'
medals. The third was craggy James Cowan, a centre-half of steely determination
and dominating presence. His personality made a great impact on the crowds who
loved his one sign of weakness. In those days of attacking centre-halves his shooting was wildly inaccurate. 'There goes Cowan's skyscraper,' was the cheerful cry
as he sent the ball soaring over the goal.

65

These fine players took them through to the Oval and so confident were the Club's supporters of beating Albion that one wrote to the local paper 'it is a sheer waste of time and money for the Villa to have to travel down to London to play'. They did indeed waste their time for the Cup, as always, tripped up the over-confident with the outsider romping home. Villa had thrashed Albion 5–0 and 3–1 in the League, but at the Oval young Billy Bassett and Albion's strong wing-halves won the match by a clear three goals. A shirt-sleeved crowd of 25,000 watched on a day of sunshine and memory. For this had been announced as the last Final at the Oval with the authorities fearing damage from the ever-growing multitude of spectators.

Back in Birmingham there was bitterness and disbelief. One Birmingham tradesman had exhibited a dead throstle (Albion were called the 'throstles' or the 'baggies') in his window. When news of the defeat came in, this was swiftly replaced with a lively replica of the bird standing on John Devey and tearing the Cup from his hands. Another shopkeeper was not so well prepared with no substitute for his display of coffins for Albion's use. Instead the blinds of the shop were hurriedly pulled down! Disappointed followers in Birmingham knew little of the wizardry of Billy Bassett on the wing, or the new triangular moves between him, his inside McLeod and his half-back. They looked for some comforting explanation of disaster. The unfair choice of scape-goat was goalkeeper Jimmy Waring. Deciding he had sold the match they smashed all the windows of his public house.

The Villa management were more realistic in their assessment, at once arranging a transfer of the Albion wing-halves, Reynolds and Groves, who had so upset their calculations. It was an astute move for Reynolds was to play a leading part in Villa's victories of 1895 and 1897 – the first a return contest with his old club Albion. That wonderful match against Everton, which clinched the double for Villa, is described in full in a later chapter and this was the peak of the Club's achievements.

But it was no sudden flash of inspiration. Villa's victories have been evenly spaced over the years. They won again in 1905, in 1913 (their fame attracting the record gate of 120,081 to Crystal Palace for a game against Sunderland) and in 1920. The lean years thereafter were ended with Peter McParland's match when his forceful play was the centre of all the action, the controversy, and the goals.

In that 1957 game they were surprising victors in the Cup Final over a Manchester United side crippled by injury. Yet the swings of the game have buffeted Villa cruelly in recent years. On an April evening two years later, under the floodlights at the Hawthorns and with only two minutes of the game remaining, Allen scored the goal that sent them sliding into the Second Division. West Bromwich Albion, whose history is so interwoven with theirs, had given the push from which they have still to recover.

The claret and blue shirts no longer intimidate, but nothing can tarnish their proud record in the Cup. Their distinctive style of clever ball play and attacking football made Villa over the years the most attractive as well as the most successful of teams. It had the advantage, too, of giving scope to individuality – and the Club

This was the programme for the last Cup-Final played at Kennington Oval, March 12, 1892.

This print of Sunderland playing Aston Villa gives an impression of the style of two teams who met in the semi-final of 1895.

The 1957 Final: McParland scores the second goal for Aston Villa beating substitute goalkeeper Jackie Blanchflower.

Harry Hampton (*fourth from right*) scored both goals when Aston Villa beat Newcastle United in 1905.

had the players of character and flair to take advantage. There was Athersmith's legendary game playing with an umbrella in pouring rain. There was Cowan sneaking off under pretence of an injured back to train for and win the Powderhall sprint in 12½ seconds. He returned £80 richer, but faced a fine and suspension when his ploy was discovered – though the suspension was soon lifted and Mr Rinder enjoyed the joke at the Club's expense. There was Pongo Waring – dashing centre-forward – who scored 49 of that record 128 First Division goals in the season 1930–1. There was 'Happy' Harry Hampton, the first Clown Prince of Soccer, whose two goals won the 1905 Final.

Sadly in modern times the Club could give no scope to that player of infinite flair and individuality, Danny Blanchflower. But its day will come again and football will be the more colourful if it can recapture its golden past.

9

Midland Mastery: The Supporting Cast

It was not Villa alone that led the Midland challenge, tilting the balance of power from Blackburn's Rovers and Preston's Invincibles. West Bromwich also came to the fore with a rush, surprising many with their instant success.

From the Black Country was to be mined a rich seam of soccer talent and the homespun West Bromwich Albion Club has a right to be regarded as the most 'English' of the successful Cup fighters.

In some senses their record is even more impressive than Villa's for over the years they have had a greater consistency with success extending into today's fiercer challenge. They have stayed better than Villa and they reached the Final a year earlier.

A group of young men from the spring-making factory of George Salter and Co. started the side together with some lads from Christ Church School. Association football was unknown in West Bromwich so for their first ball they had to walk to neighbouring Wednesbury, home of the 'Old Athletic', then one of the strongest sides in the Midlands.

Appropriately they called themselves the West Bromwich Strollers in that first year before the Albion district of the town caught their fancy. Their first goalposts were pieces of wood about two inches square 'fixed in the ground in as upright a position as the wind would allow'. An old piece of rope was the crossbar and 2d. per week the subscription. But only four years later the Staffordshire Cup was theirs at the first time of trying and in the season they had lost only five of 39 games.

The Club's annual report was bold enough to finish with the prophetic words 'We hope the time is not far distant when even the English Cup will find a home in West Bromwich for what Club has better material to work on than in our players – so young and yet so skilful?' Entering the competition the next season they were chastened by a first round defeat from Wednesbury Old Athletic.

But the following year 1885 they reached the 6th round to give the great Blackburn Rovers team a hard fight. In 1886 they went two better, overwhelming the Small Heath Alliance (later to become Birmingham City) in the semi-final and drawing with Blackburn Rovers at the Oval. The replay was at Derby, the first Final to be decided outside London, and the redoubtable Rovers were two goals too good.

So, the following season, were Aston Villa when Albion bounced straight back to the Final. For the third successive year they fought their way back to the Oval and now they were up against the pride of Preston who had 43 consecutive victories to their credit and a Cup tally of 50 goals to two in six matches! That traditional story of Preston asking to be photographed with the Cup before the game may well be myth, but they had grounds enough for such confidence.

Albion's mood was expressed clearly enough in their Cup match bills headed 'Death or Glory'. They had no fears of Preston's imported professors.

As we have seen it was to be third time lucky for the 'English' team.

And that summed up the Albion and established an Albion tradition. In that first Final nine of their side were West Bromwich born and the other two came from close by. There is the other story, probably true, that Major Marindin came to their dressing room after they again beat Preston in the following season's semi-final and asked: 'Are you all Englishmen?' When this was confirmed he complimented them on their play and presented the ball.

Major Marindin had no liking for the importation of Scottish players, nor had Albion. In the early part of the next century the Club policy banned such imports from Scotland for nearly thirty years.

Albion was launched as a local team and there has always been a family atmosphere about the Club. When they won the Final at last it was young 'Billy' Bassett, only eighteen-years old and playing at inside to allow 'Spry' Woodhall to stay on the wing, who destroyed Preston with his speed and his passing. He made the goals for the captain, Jim Bayliss, and for Woodhall. Over his 13 years with Albion he was to establish himself as a legendary figure in the game and win sixteen International caps. When, soon after his retirement, the Club was neglected, heavily in debt, and facing extinction, it was to Billy Bassett that the supporters turned. He was brought in as Director, elected Chairman within three years, and guided their affairs until 1937. He died just before a semi-final game with Preston North End and the F.A. felt that some special tribute should be paid, though the Club looked only for a simple silence of respect. In the event 'Abide with Me' was sung – and what more appropriate tribute could there be to a man who had so often made Cup history? But for the Albion team, who had lost their father-figure, the deep emotion of the moment and of the singing left them so drained that they were three goals down within twenty minutes.

A local journalist, Ellery W. Jephcott, whose son was to play for the Club, thus described Bassett:

'Being only 5 feet 5½ inches in height and weighing but 10 stone he had to depend entirely upon speed and skill for his success against burly opponents who were allowed far more latitude in using their weight than is the case today. He was, however, exceptionally fast with the ball – which is different from mere running ability – knew exactly when to centre and could place the ball in the goalmouth with uncanny accuracy. Moreover he possessed in the fullest degree

71

what is known as the "big match temperament". The greater the occasion the better he played.

Billy Bassett was used to being close marked. His reputation was such that when he played in Germany the wing-half followed him even when he went outside the touchline, or round behind the net to see what would happen. As he recorded, "still my Teutonic friend never left me. Had I gone up in a balloon I think I should have found him treading on my toes along the Milky Way"'.

Bassett's long connection with the Club was in keeping with the family spirit of Albion.

It was also typical of this spirit that Fred Everiss, who took over as Secretary at 19, should have stayed 52 years in the post and that his son, Alan, should later succeed him.

Albion had other talented players in those early days who had already taken them to two Finals before Bassett added the decisive extra touch of class. There was Jimmy Bayliss, captain and forceful centre-forward, whose reported death was prematurely confirmed by Albion in 1897 so that Birmingham newspapers paid fitting tribute to him before the mistake was discovered. For many years he was able to treasure a pocket book of reports labelled 'My Obituary'. There was Bob Roberts, so proud of his International cap that he always kept goal in it. He was a formidable fourteen stone, a great asset in those days when lesser goalkeepers could be sent flying over their line or be pinned to a post while the forwards scored.

We have seen Albion get the best of Villa in that last Final at the Oval, largely because their wing-halves, John Reynolds and Willie Groves, were so much the masters of Harry Devey and John Baird. Both Reynolds and Groves were 'imports' – Groves a centre-forward from Celtic converted by Albion to wing-half, Reynolds, an Irish Internationational from Distillery, who later discovered he was English born and won eight further caps with England. Both were acquired by Villa, though they were fined £25 for approaching Groves without Albion's consent. Their fickleness helped to confirm Albion's distaste for expensive outsiders. Reynolds in particular was suspected of 'playing for his transfer' and received a sharp letter. 'The directors are extremely dissatisfied with your play in the last few matches and in consequence have instructed me to inform you of their decision to fine you £1 per week until your form improves'.

So Reynolds slipped away to Villa and helped beat Albion in a remarkable game at Crystal Palace decided by the quickest goal in the history of the Finals. That was in 1895. The only goal of the match was scored so fast that few in the vast crowd saw exactly what happened. From the kick-off Athersmith streaked away down the right and Bob Chatt met his centre to be credited with the goal. But the players best placed to see said that 'Kicker' Reader booted out Chatt's shot only for the ball to hit Jack Devey, Villa's centre-forward, and rebound into the net. Anyway it was a goal with less than thirty seconds gone, and despite a wonderful display by Bassett it was enough to win the Cup. Albion's fighting spirit was personified by centre-half Higgins who was so badly cut in a clash of heads that he finished the game swathed in bandages. Colonel North, the 'nitrate King', was much impressed by his courage and gave him £5.

After Bassett, Pennington was perhaps the Club's finest player, but like so many of the most talented footballers, he never gained the coveted winners' medal.

Jesse Pennington and Bob Crompton of Blackburn were perhaps the greatest pair of backs that England had, but neither played in a winning Cup side. How close Pennington came in 1912! Barnsley had slogged their way to the Final through an endless series of dogged replays as if foreshadowing the war of attrition that was soon to engulf Europe. Again, it was a drawn game at Crystal Palace and there were still no goals after full time in the replay at Bramall Lane. Then in the final two minutes of extra time, Tuffnell broke clear with Pennington snapping at his heels. It would have been easy to trip him up, but that was not Pennington's way. He and Albion were noted for their sportsmanship and he let Tuffnell run on to score.

That was typical of Pennington. He was once offered £55 to ensure a match was drawn or lost. Instead he showed the letter to the Directors and the 'nobbler' was trapped and sentenced to five months at Stafford Assizes.

There are some teams for whom the Cup seems to have a special stimulus, as for Newcastle in the 'fifties or Tottenham Hotspur in the 'sixties. Over the years it has been just such a catalyst for Albion transforming their teams to greatness. Five times they have won the Cup, but only once the First Division Championship.

That was in the first season after the Great War when they were nine points clear of Burnley with Chelsea trailing further behind. Appropriately one of their team had signed his forms in the trenches – little Tommy Magee, the 'pocket Hercules' of a wing-half who stood only 5 feet 3½ inches at 18 but was to play for England.

When they won the Cup in 1931 Albion also won promotion from the Second Division, as runners up. This is the only time that a Club has achieved this particular double, though Huddersfield Town, Burnley and West Ham have all gained promotion and been beaten finalists in the same season.

Billy 'Ginger' Richardson had just joined the Club and it was his goalscoring skill that gave them the decisive thrust. Swift off the mark and deadly near the goal he was to score 228 League and Cup goals with another 100 in War-time games in a career that extended over fifteen years. W. G. Richardson was signed for £1000 from Hartlepools on the advice of Jesse Pennington. The 'G' in his initials was an invention of Albion's to distinguish him from their centre-half, the other Billy Richardson. If the mythical 'G' was meant to stand for 'goals' he was rightly christened. For in the Final he got two past Harry Hibbs, the decisive one coming within seconds of Birmingham equalising. Straight from the kick-off Glidden, Richardson, and Carter swept through the centre without a Birmingham man touching the ball, except for Hibbs' fingertips as Richardson's shot slid past him. The Birmingham supporters were so busy celebrating their own goal that many of them never saw the move. Richardson was nearly as surprised, 'I can only remember seeing myself in front of Hibbs and tapping the ball past him' he said. The game

73

had been played in a continuous downpour, but so absorbed in the battle was little Magee that he suddenly asked 'Has it been raining?' as the Albion players went up to the Royal Box.

Albion's Cup run had started with a swaying struggle against Charlton, decided only at the third attempt and by the eleventh goal. And it was Charlton that they beat 3–2 in their last League game to make sure of winning promotion. Again it was Richardson who scored the winning goal as he had done against Everton two days earlier. In the space of a week he had scored four of the most important goals in the Club's history. But as next season he was to snatch four in five minutes against West Ham there was nothing exceptional in that!

In 1935 Albion were back at Wembley for an exhilarating Final against Sheffield Wednesday with quick-silver shifts in the play and the fortunes. It was anybody's match after Albion had twice come from behind to level the scores. For once W. G. Richardson missed an easy goal and in the closing minutes Rimmer put two past Albion's Pearson. As the final thrust went home, the dejected goalkeeper booted the ball back into his own net. Only thirty seconds were left, but W. G. Richardson came sprinting back to snatch the ball and dash for the centre-circle still desperately eager to retrieve his error.

Nineteen years later, Vic Buckingham, a Manager full of ideas and enthusiasm came as close as could be to adding the double to Albion's records. He had already coached the Oxford and Cambridge team, Pegasus, to win the Amateur Cup and now he adapted for West Bromwich the 'push and run' method that had been so successfully taught to Tottenham Hotspur by Arthur Rowe. With Nicholls and Allen as lethal strikers and Barlow, a powerful attacking wing-half, he went beyond the 'make it simple, make it quick' of Spurs. There were well-rehearsed moves from dead ball situations like the goal that finally defeated Newcastle in the fifth round as Allen ran to meet Lee's low corner and volleyed it into the net. There were long passes to vary the clever close play. Above all there was the instinctive understanding of Nicholls' response to Allen's through balls, often hit with his back to the goal.

Certainly the pupil's team defeated the master, as West Bromwich hit home three against Tottenham in the sixth round. It was harder going in the semi-final against Port Vale. The Third Division team had conceded only 21 goals in 46 matches.

Once Albert Leake had scrambled a goal the odds were in Port Vale's favour. They were still ahead at the interval with Allen and Nicholls searching in vain for space in the packed penalty-area. Then came a fortunate relief for Albion as Dudley's centre floated over King into the net. And at the end a penalty by Allen sent West Bromwich to Wembley. The League title then looked theirs but in the long wait for the Final everything went wrong.

Goalkeeper Heath was so badly injured he never played again and other casualties mounted with each game. In a disastrous finish only three points came from seven games leaving Wolves the clear winners. Even Villa, struggling to avoid relegation, beat Albion 6–1. What a preparation for the Final! But somehow confi-

74

dence returned on the day with Preston beaten in the closing minutes by Griffin's goal. Albion's captain, Len Millard, had the taxing task of containing Tom Finney, now a greater player than Matthews. Most footballers have some opponent they particularly fear and Finney the left-footed winger playing on the right, was Millard's tormentor 'I *never* can play Finney . . . he can go either side of you so easily'. That had been his worry, but this time he played him coolly enough, with other defenders briefed to assist.

Preston were in the habit of working the ball out to Finney, their captain, and afterwards he recognised that he should have changed their tactics. Angus Morrison on the left wing was causing Albion great anxiety, but was never brought into the game enough to be decisive. So the Cup went to West Bromwich and Finney was left without a winners' medal.

For many of us Tom Finney was the epitome of the great footballer, modest, courageous, sporting, and with breathtaking skills. He was a beautiful mover, a good header of the ball, shrewd in his distribution, and confident in his control. More direct than Matthews he was sharper in his finishing and the argument is endless as to which of these two was the more accomplished. Staffordshire apart, there was no little disappointment that Finney had not emulated Matthews' triumph of the year before.

There has recently been established a Soccer Hall of Fame in Newman Street in London, a kind of animated Madame Tussaud's of the game. Initially there were twelve players and administrators selected by a distinguished panel as the immortals of soccer. Inevitably Tom Finney was one of them.

A fine team had got the better of an outstanding individual and again it was Albion's combined strength that took them to victory in 1968. Yet the main memory of the match is of Astle. He had scored in every round and he took the one chance Everton allowed him. That forceful shot sweeping into the net wide of West was seen over and over again at the start of a T.V. programme. Few goals can stand that amount of repetition. Yet this was so decisively taken that the interest never failed.

On the long hard road to the Final the most remarkable performance was at Anfield. It was practically illegal for a team to survive there in the League let alone the Cup. Yet Albion, held at home, contrived to keep at bay Shankly's determined team and their fervent supporters on the Kop.

Sixteen times semi-finalists, ten times Finalists, five times winners, West Bromwich Albion indeed made their mark.

Between 1886 and 1898, of the 26 finalists 16 were Midland teams. For Villa and Albion had strong support from Wolverhampton and Nottingham.

Wolverhampton Wanderers was another Staffordshire Club to typify that close association of town and team that has been a feature of English life. The Cup is the proper starting point of the consuming interest in football which brings fulfilment for millions. Accepting the philosophy that 'that action is best which procures the greatest happiness for the greatest number' it may well have done more for the

In Memoriam of
⚜ Everton Football Team ⚜

Who departed from the Cup Competition through a severe attack of Wolves.

And whose hopes were interred at the Football Cemetery, the same day.

They came in all their glory,
From that noted Toffy Town,
To fight the famous 'Wolves'
A team of English renown

The 'Toffy's' came on boldly,
'Their victory for to seek ;
But now they go home gravely
O'er their troubles for to weep,

Farewell, farewell dear old Everton,
No more for the Pot you will dribble ;
You have lost it to-day through difficult play
And we'll shout farewell for ever and ever.

'Funeral Cards' were popular comment on the losers, like this one recording Everton's defeat in 1893.

social life of the country than any politician or civic leader. The more sensible of these indeed have always maintained close links with the sport that is so much a part of people's lives. And from the early days the Town of Wolverhampton took pride in its team. By March 27, 1893 the Mayor was remarking to his Town Council that the previous year he was in the South of France and one morning when bringing in the coffee the waiter spoke to him of the Wolverhampton Wanderers, observing they were doing very well.

Local support burgeoning into world wide interest is indeed the history of Wolves, with the Cup a golden strand even in the black years. They too were a home-spun side with little enthusiasm for the imported professors. In the *Football Who's Who* of 1904 J. J. Bentley recorded: 'Wolverhampton Wanderers is another Club which relies greatly upon local talent and it is very seldom indeed you hear of the Wolves thinking of engaging a Scotsman . . . Last season they commenced with eight Staffordshire born men and three from the adjoining county of Shropshire. The Wolves may not possess the most scientific team in the League, but they always place a trusty, go-ahead eleven in the field. I should say they look after locals better than any Club in England'. And the locals repaid them from the first with some striking performances. The start of the Wolverhampton Wanderers Cricket and Football Club – its first title in 1881 – demonstrates the diverse support for the game. The Club developed from the St Luke's Church School and was fostered by two young pupil teachers, Jack Baynton and Jack Brodie. Jeremiah Mason, publican of the King's Arms, and his son, Charles, were closely concerned with the team

Wolverhampton Wanderers, F.A. Cup winners of 1893:
Baugh, Allen,
Topham, Malpas, Rose, Swift, Kinsey,
Wykes, Butcher, Wood, Griffin.

and the school. The first treasurer was Levi Johnson, Councillor and Publican of the Ring O'Bells which provided dressing room accommodation. His financial skill was of special value in that first year when total gate receipts were £80 and the cash in hand at the end of the season £1 0s. 0d. Fifty-six years later Johnson was still on the Council and still helping the Club.

School, Church, Inn, and Council have given solid support to so many Clubs and all combined to give Wolverhampton their start.

When Wolverhampton Wanderers began their long career they were not yet the town's premier team. The Stafford Road Railway Works team had already made a name for itself and was contemptuous of the newcomer, declining to play the up-start team. When public opinion forced an encounter Stafford Road put out a weak team and were defeated. But in 1884 their full side including International Jim Whitehead was trounced 5–1 in front of 7,000 spectators. Wolves had arrived and they pressed home the point two years later by defeating Stafford Road 4–2 in the Cup after being two down at half-time. Powerful recovery late in the game was to remain a feature of Wolves' play.

77

The following year Wolverhampton's name became known throughout the land after a long-drawn contest with Villa, the eventual winners of the Cup. This third round tie needed three games to settle.

At Dudley there was a 1–1 draw after the teams had protested about the state of the ice-sheeted ground. Tickets had been sold in advance and reduced to 4d. while carriages had been admitted through a 'private gate' at a shilling for two-wheelers and 2s. 6d. for four-wheelers. The replay surprisingly was also at Dudley Road and again the goals were shared – six of them this time. So to Perry Bar with special trains running from London and Wolverhampton. So great was the interest that the gate was around 10,000 and included Mr George Kynock M.P. for Aston. Politics and sport were already interwoven and no doubt the local M.P. was delighted to patronise Villa's 2–0 victory.

It was in 1889 that Wolves fought their way to their first Final only to become the foil for Preston's remarkable feat. But four years later they were back again waiting to know their opponents from an endless semi-final between Everton and Preston. Their form in the League had been so disappointing that the team committee temporarily resigned after a 10–1 defeat by Newton Heath (later Manchester United). In the middle of their long drawn battle with Preston, Everton came to Molineux and won 4–2 with eight reserves in the side.

But such omens mean nothing in the Cup. With some gay and dashing players in the forward line like Dick Topham, still up at Oxford University, and young Joe Butcher, Wolves were quite capable of raising their game.

The Final had moved from the Oval to Manchester's Fallowfield ground. The new organisers were quite unprepared for the crowd of nearly 50,000. The record receipts of £2,559 were pleasant enough, but with barriers shattered and the crowd on the fringes of the pitch, the match itself was in question.

The referee, C. J. Hughes, kept his own counsel as to whether it would be counted a Cup-tie or a friendly. It was anything but friendly on the field, the fierce game rivalling the commotion in the crowd where an 'Everton fire balloon ignited and nearly set the canopy of the stand ablaze'. After an Everton goal had been disallowed Allen scored the decisive one midway through the second half. The Wolves' wing-half scored with a long, high kick that 'descended as a dropping shot towards goal. It was brilliant sunshine, and as the Everton goalkeeper looked for the ball the sun dazzled his sight so that the ball fell beside him into the net.'

Such was the confusion at the end that the officials were loathe to hand over the Cup without Lord Kinnaird's sanction – and he had gone home! However, it was soon with the Wolves' players and well filled with champagne.

Wolverhampton received only £10 from the gate (which was not divided among the Clubs, but kept by the F.A.) and had to make do with the honour.

It needed another good Cup run in 1896 to avert financial difficulty. Derby County were defeated in the semi-final for all the efforts of the great Steve Bloomer. But having defeated more highly-placed teams in all the earlier rounds, Wolves found Sheffield Wednesday too much for them in the final.

Sheffield's strength was in Crawshaw, a centre-half who admirably fitted the fluid attacking pattern of the day, and Spiksley, a swift and opportunist winger. It was Spiksley's two goals that gave Sheffield their first win after the disappointments of that thrashing by Blackburn Rovers in 1890 and in the semi-finals of 1894 and 1895.

Wolves went down to the Second Division in 1905 and seemed to have found their right level until that great Cup run of 1907–08 which ended in triumph over Newcastle, leaders of the First Division.

They had trained hard; 'The usual regime of health – giving country walks and lung-expanding exercises' had been indulged in. By all, that is except for Kenneth Hunt, who was at Oxford on weekdays immersed in the Early Fathers, and for the other amateur, B. O. Corbett.

Glossop were easily disposed of, but Bradford City forced a replay before Hedley's goal finished them. 'Now we are ready for the other B's – they of Bury' was the local view. A right one too for 27,121 saw Wolves win 2–0.

Swindon, another railway town team, gave them a hard fight. But with their captain, Wooldridge, off injured Hunt gave a remarkable display, taking over so well 'that there were times when he appeared to be playing all Swindon himself'. And in the last two minutes Harrison and Hedley scored decisive goals. So the excitement and the gates mounted as Stoke succumbed 1–0 to their 'aggressive' play. 'Still onward. Black-and-gold in the Ascendant' were the headlines as they moved on to the semi-final and 2–0 victory over old rivals Southampton.

Faced with the great Newcastle side Kenneth Hunt was asked by a reporter how Wolves could deal with them 'We shall hustle them off their game' he said and as we have seen that was precisely what Wolves did.

The Lord Mayor of London presented the Cup, commenting on the Englishness of the winners and commending 'so healthy a game as football which must benefit the body and also the mind.'

It is customary to lament the interference of politics in sport. But so great was the joy in Wolverhampton that sport for once interfered with politics. An election was scheduled for the night of the team's triumphant return and *The Times* lamented 'It is feared that public meetings fixed for tonight will be deserted as the Wolverhampton Wanderers team come home at half-past 7 o'clock with the Association Cup. Arrangements were made for an enthusiastic welcome and a parade of the town with Cup, brass bands, and banners. It is expected that for two hours the town will be given up to demonstration.' And so indeed it was with the crush so great that there was no chance to stop for the cakes and cocoa that Hunt's father had prepared at St. Mark's Vicarage.

The hustings became very much a second eleven fixture with the Liberal candidate, Thorne, beating the Unionist, Amery, by a mere eight votes. But Wolves may have helped Mr Thorne to his narrow majority for there was a stirring exhortation on his behalf worth at least eight votes 'Emulate the Wolves. Get to work at once. Poll early. Gain goals. Score your majority before half-time and then work

79

unceasingly to increase your lead until the whistle goes for full-time.' Those were the tactics that brought the Cup to Wolverhampton and Thorne to Westminster.

Not until 1921 were Wolves back in the Final following a fine win over Cardiff. Before King George V they were held to a draw at Liverpool, but won decisively in the replayed semi-final at Manchester. So to Stamford Bridge and defeat by Dimmock's goal. 'Our play is plain and straightforward. It is fast and resolute and it is marked by a boldness that commands respect.' Thus did centre-forward George Edmonds describe their style in the *Sporting Star* and it was not quite good enough for the great Tottenham team.

Excuses could be found in the pouring rain, in the omission of the Wolverhampton coat of arms from the clean shirts at half-time, in the absence through injury of the 'auburn-haired little warrior, Baugh' whose family already had a collection of winners' medals. But in truth Woodward's hesitation and Dimmock's fierce shot produced the fair result.

Wolves now slid into the Third Division (North), the darkest days for a town so dedicated to football. But solid support and intense local interest helped their steady revival.

Soon Wolves began the climb back and by 1927 were playing well enough to reach the sixth round, going down by the odd goal to Arsenal at Highbury. 'We should have reached the Final if we could have bought a centre-half,' noted the Manager. But the Directors apparently felt that it was also time to acquire a new Manager. Soon they had appointed Major F. S. Buckley, a man of Herbert Chapman's calibre, and within a few years they also had in Stanley Cullis, the best centre-half in the country.

Major Buckley was one of the most colourful and successful of Managers. He had been a talented centre-half, first with Aston Villa and then with Derby. An international Cap against Ireland was a reward for his strong and competent play. Major Buckley's army career had begun at the age of sixteen and it had been while serving in Ireland that his football skill was first spotted. In the First World War he achieved the rank of Major when serving with the 'footballers Battalion', the 17th Middlesex Regiment. Afterwards he had managed Norwich City and Blackpool before leaving to take charge of a team that was in depressing trouble financially and on the field. Buckley was one of the first Managers to run a Club as an efficient business with a cultivated flair for publicity. His restless energy and enquiring mind led to constant change and experiment, not all of it successful. In his second year Wolves were knocked out of the Cup by the Midland League team, Mansfield, whose special training diet of fresh milk and eggs had cost precisely nineteen shillings! 'Kick and rush aptly describes the style of play adopted by both sides' was the newspaper comment.

Under Buckley's influence Wolves steadily became more scientific and more successful, though retaining the zest and vigour for which they had always been noted. By 1932 Buckley had the Club out of the red and back in the First Division, where they remained for 32 years. Only Arsenal and Chelsea have outstayed them.

Their lasting power on the field was also to become proverbial for they specialised in the dramatic recovery and the late win. Their play was not always pleasing to the critics and indeed in 1937 the F.A. wrote to Major Buckley, 'In view of the numerous reports of misconduct by players at Wolverhampton Wanderers Club during the past two seasons, the F.A. Council, meeting in London today, decided that the application of the Club for permission to play matches on the continent during the coming season be not granted'.

Stanley Cullis was by now making a name for himself as a superlative centre-half imbued with unusual perception and courage. At his instigation the players sent their own reply, 'We should like to state that, far from advocating the rough play we are accused of, Major Buckley is constantly reminding us of the importance of playing good, clean, and honest football'.

The side was now confident enough to take risks in going for goals, their success in League and Cup a blow at more negative theories. In 1939 they could well have won both, but had the frustration of being runners-up in League and Cup in the same season, like Huddersfield and Arsenal before them.

The 1939 Final was one of those surprising upsets of form. Few teams have been so fancied to win as Wolves or so written off as Portsmouth. The technological age was arriving and Buckley's much publicised glandular treatment and his 'therapeutic diathermy machine' were expected to give his players extra stamina to add to their extra skill.

But it was Portsmouth's Manager, Jack Tinn, whose famous white spats proved a more powerful talisman than any scientific gimmick. At the critical moment Wolves' courage failed them and there was no sign of the incisive forward play that gave them five goals against Grimsby in the semi-final. Worrall's wing play and the lucky sixpence in his boot made sure that the Pompey chimes would swell in triumph round Wembley's twin towers.

Before the Final Mr Montague Lyons K.C., M.P. for East Leicester had addressed a question to the Minister of Health asking whether 'his attention has been directed to statements that gland extracts from animals are being administered to football players . . . whether he will order an investigation into these allegations and whether he regards this practice as desirable in the interests of National health'. Neither the extracts nor a psychologist could bring Wolves the Cup. But the Major's enthusiasm had brought new interest to soccer with his early promotion of youngsters – his cubs were particularly effective forerunners of the Busby babes – and his readiness to experiment with new methods and new tactics.

In the long run it was Buckley's sure eye for ability that gave Wolverhampton the firm base for success. At that 1939 Cup-Final a young lad, William Ambrose Wright, was looking after the kit for Wolves.

The players' strip and the Club's future were in safe hands for no footballer in the history of the game has given more effective service to Club and country. At inside-forward or wing-half Wright was to prove tirelessly efficient, utterly dependable. And despite his lack of inches he was to become an even better centre-half in the Cullis tradition of technical excellence and terrier-like determination. It was typical that he should be able to match strong, tall players such as John Charles in the air. For Billy Wright always had this gift of rising above himself. Only once was he to be in a winning Cup side, taking Wolves to their win over Second Division Leicester in 1949.

But in the late 'forties and the 'fifties Wolverhampton were the country's most consistent team along with Manchester United. Cullis now was Manager, bringing the same qualities of attack and determination that had made him so feared on the field. The combination of his fire, Wright's consistency, flying wingers, and long passes kept Wolves near the top of the League. More than that, it brought heart back to English football with some telling blows against the leading foreign sides after Hungary had shattered our confidence.

Another win in 1960, this time under Slater, emphasised that Wolverhampton are never a side to be taken lightly in the Cup.

Nottingham Forest have no such splendid record of sustained performance, but they were the earliest of the Midland teams to have any success in the competition. Indeed, they reached the semi-final in their first season of entry (1878–79) – the only Club, apart from Swifts, to have achieved this. They beat Notts County in the first round and the powerful Sheffield Club with the Cleggs and the Barbers in its team. So to the Oval and victories over the Old Harrovians – ('They had to play during a considerable portion of the game with only 10 men, but they showed up well' said the *Sportsman*) and Oxford University ('a well-earned victory won by spirited and unselfish play' reported *The Daily Telegraph*). But with S. W. Widdowson injured by half-time they lost 2–1 to Old Etonians in the semi-final, Widdowson finishing the match before being confined to bed for some days.

Next season they reached the semi-final once again, but Oxford's backs and goalkeeper were in fine form and the University won by the only goal. During these two seasons some of the papers described Forest as the *best* team in England, but they were apt to have as many *bests* as they had *Princes of dribblers*.

Forest, however, had gained a reputation in a very short space of time and we have seen how hard they were soon to hunt the Queen's Park team when they reached the semi-final for the third time. The Club had been in existence since 1865, three years later than neighbouring Notts County. Football had taken over in Nottingham from the local game of 'Shinney' and one of its founders recalled, 'the first set of players who came out were regarded as a company of harmless lunatics who amused themselves by kicking one another's shins'.

The first act of the little group of sportsmen who formed the Forest Club after a meeting at the Clinton Arms was to send one of their number to purchase red flannel caps. This he did from a shopkeeper named Daft – a suitable action by men thought mad as hatters. The cap was then the distinctive feature of soccer kit and red became Forest's distinctive colour. Soon a Nottingham newspaper could report:

'The hold of association football is beginning to earn the affections of people who are nothing if not lovers of sport. The wonder would be if the game did not win adherents among the general public as well as athletes seeing what a noble pastime it is.

'What pluck and determination, what powers of endurance and what strategy is used in the exercise of football.'

Not until 1898 was Forest to win the Cup defeating Derby County 3–1 in the Final. Capes opened the scoring with a brilliant ground shot that clean beat goalkeeper Fryer after 19 minutes. The great Steve Bloomer headed an equalising goal, but before half-time Capes again steered home a close shot. The second half was fiercely contested, but four minutes from the end the captain, McPherson, tackled a defender then shot while lying full length on the ground. Once more Fryer was beaten and it remained only for Lord Roseberry to present the Cup and congratulate McPherson on so gallantly winning the trophy.

The newspapers made the Forest back, Adam Scott, the hero of the game with Arthur Capes and McPherson also praised for their part in upsetting the highly-fancied Derby team. The paper also commented: 'Few clubs by their long association with the game and its most treasured traditions have better deserved or earned the distinction and we venture to think that the success of the "Reds" will be heartily and encouragingly welcomed'. That was a fair statement for Forest had played a major part in the development of the game. As a happy coincidence the day they won the Cup was Sam Widdowson's fiftieth birthday.

They were the first to introduce the referee's whistle, experimenting with it in 1878 when playing Sheffield Norfolk. After a successful trial the whistle took the place of the white flag used earlier.

Forest were also the first to develop the system of two backs, three half-backs, and five forwards which is still the basis for showing team formation on the programmes. The earliest line-up had been 7–2–1 and on occasions that is the way the game is played now except that the 7 are defenders and not attackers.

Football shin guards were also a Forest invention devised by Widdowson in 1874. Sam Weller Widdowson was indeed a Dickensian character in the richness of his sporting enthusiasm and his appetite for life. A burly centre-forward, he played with fearsome vigour, intimidating the less robust. But he was also ingenious and inventive. These were the days when hacking was common and once Widdowson started to protect his leg with a shin guard the custom soon spread. It needed a player with his reputation for courage to achieve such ready acceptance for a lesser man would have risked being branded as effeminate in those tough times. He was also the strategist who devised the tactical formation that lasted so long.

Another stalwart of the early days was Dr Tinsley Lindley who played for Forest as well as the Corinthians. He was another individualist so fleet of foot that he rarely if ever wore boots, preferring to play in walking shoes so as not to reduce his speed. Lindley was a doctor of Law, but was not above breaking the rules on occasion. In the early days of the League he turned out for Notts County on one occasion with the result that they were fined £5 and one point. Lindley's advocacy restored the lost point though the fine was increased.

Sixty-one years were to pass before Forest reached the Final again. Once more they carried the day playing for the first twenty minutes some of the finest football seen at Wembley. Even though Dwight then broke a leg they were too far ahead in goals and class for Luton to catch them. Dwight indeed had few moments of anxiety as he watched the closing stages on the hospital television.

Their record was not so impressive as Villa's or Albion's or Wolverhampton's, but together with Notts County, the first second division side to win the Cup in 1894, they ensured that Nottingham made its full contribution to the period of Midland mastery in the 'nineties.

10

The Cup comes South

Professionalism had been slow to catch on in the South and, once Warburton had borne the Cup away in triumph to Blackburn, eighteen years passed before London could do more than admire the trophy on Cup-Final day.

Then came Tottenham Hotspur's remarkable win in 1901, the ultimate act of giant-killing unrivalled in the 100 years of the competition. This is the only time since the League was formed that a non-League side has won the Trophy and it was little wonder that 110,820 should crowd into Crystal Palace for the Final. But for Payne's boots it might have been a different story.

Tottenham had started playing on the Marshes in 1882, the name Hotspur taken from a cricket club. Once more there had been support from the Y.M.C.A. with Mr Ripsher lending them the premises for a meeting and becoming President when the Club was in difficulty after only a year. The Club was amateur in outlook and the games happy-go-lucky. One against Brownlow Rovers was reported as abandoned because the ball burst ten minutes from time and no replacement was available. It was also recorded that Evelyn were defeated by five goals and one disputed goal to one. Reports of that day often logged the disputed goals though those unfinished arguments did not appear to affect the results.

The rules of the Club included: 'That the uniform of the Club be navy blue, with scarlet shield on left side of jersey, with the letter "H" thereon, and every member is requested to wear same in matches.' In this smart kit they improved their play sufficiently to enter the London Football Association Cup in 1885. They won their first game against St Albans 5–2, but were crushed by the Casuals that year and Upton Park the next. Still their progress was steady and they were soon giving F. W. Beardsley a trying time in the Royal Arsenal goal, or hunting Millwall Athletic hard in the fifth round of the London Cup. As many as 4,000 spectators were attracted to watch some of their games and when The Football Association started the Amateur Cup in 1893 they entered for it.

Interchange of players was frequent in those days and a game was offered to Ernie Payne, who had been turning out for Fulham, but wanted a move. All Payne's kit was at Fulham, but it had disappeared when he went to collect it. So he arrived without any and while Tottenham could provide the shorts, knickers and stockings they had to give him ten shillings to buy the boots. At once Fulham charged them with poaching and professionalism. The Council of the London F.A. dismissed the first charge, but ruled: 'The ten shillings given to Payne to buy the boots was an unfair inducement offered to him to play for Tottenham Hotspur.'

Their ground was closed for a fortnight and the peculiar ruling attracted sympathy and support for the Club. It also turned their thoughts towards professionalism and by 1896 they had joined the Southern League and were recruiting players for £1 per week.

The Southern League was founded in 1894 following a circular sent out the previous year by Woolwich Arsenal:

'My directors are of opinion that the time has arrived when some effort should be made to improve the game of football in the South of England, so that Southern clubs might approach the standard of efficiency attained by many of those in the Northern and Midland counties.

'They think this can be done by the strongest clubs in the South forming themselves into a combination or League, and feel sure this joint action would give a great impetus to the game, and at the same time cause the public to take a keener interest in the matches played.

'We intend calling a meeting of representatives of Southern clubs interested in the movement to discuss the matter. Should your committee take a favourable view of it, we shall be pleased if they will appoint a representative to attend the meeting.

'The clubs I have written to are Chatham, Millwall, Old Westminsters, Casuals, Crusaders, London Caledonians, Old Carthusians, Old Etonians and Clapton.'

Arsenal were elected to the Second Division of the Football League before any action could be taken. Millwall carried on their work calling an inaugural meeting. With Mr Henderson, the Millwall Secretary, filling the same role for the new League, Clapton, Ilford, the Royal Ordnance Factories, Swindon Town, Reading, Southampton St Mary's (later to become Southampton) and Luton Town were elected to the First Division of the Southern League and a Second Division was also formed.

Within a few years Pickford and Gibson were to record that the Southern League was 'as entirely professional as the Football League itself, but it began mildly enough'. But not so mildly that it did not soon make an impact on the Cup. Southampton St Mary's was quick to emerge as the dominant team heading the table in the year that Spurs joined and finished fourth. And in 1900 Southampton reached the Final of the F.A. Challenge Cup only to lose by four goals to Bury whose record in Cup Finals is:

Played	Won	Goals For	Against
2	2	10	0

Their 6–0 defeat of Derby County in their only other Final remains a record as does their overall goal average for the Finals. Certainly Southampton could not hold them and Bury had a much easier passage than in the semi-final. There they had come within a minute of defeat before a replay was won by a last desperate

A section of the crowd, estimated to be over 110,000
at Crystal Palace for the 1901 Cup-Final.

effort from Pray and McLuckie – whose names no doubt aptly summed up the team's feelings at the time.

Southampton had pointed the way and now Spurs went one better. They had headed the Southern League for the first time in 1900 – a brief interlude in Southampton's supremacy – and their team was strong enough to challenge all comers.

It would be pleasant to record that Tottenham's triumph in the Cup was achieved by Londoners. In fact none of their team was born nearer to the Seven Sisters Road than Grantham. There were five Scots, two Welshmen, and an Irish outside-left. In those do-it-yourself days John Cameron was Manager, Secretary, and inside-left. The other key figure was centre-forward Alexander Brown – 'Alexander the Great' to the fans. He had played for Preston and Portsmouth and was commented on as 'extraordinarily effective with his head and many of his goals have come from the manner in which he rather hits a ball with his pate than guides it between the posts. Brown is more skilful in seizing openings made by others than in creating them himself'. How fortunate! For of the 20 goals Spurs scored in the Cup games Brown collected 15, including all four against West Bromwich Albion in the semi-final, both goals in the drawn Final, and the last decisive goal in the replay. No wonder he was called 'Alexander the Great'. The *Sporting Life* account was less ecstatic. 'Brown may not be an ideal centre, but he has a keen eye to the main chance, and he discriminates nicely as to when to score with the head and when with the foot.'

Tottenham had no easy road to the Final. They were nearly beaten at home in the first round by Preston, only a remarkable diving header by Brown saving them with nine minutes to go. Having won the replay at Deepdale they had to meet Bury, the Cup holders. The 'Shakers' might have overawed many teams and nearly overran Spurs in the first 20 minutes – but again Brown was equal to the challenge with two fine goals.

You need luck as well as skill to win the Cup and Tottenham had their good fortune at Reading. In the closing moments of an untidy, vigorous game, with the scores still level, Tait fisted away a shot that had beaten Clawley, the Tottenham goalkeeper. The referee was unsighted and the linesman unhelpful to Reading's vociferous appeal. A goal kick was given and 'what yells and boos there were for the referee'.

Thereafter progress was smooth and sweet until the vast crowd spilled into Crystal Palace to see the match against Sheffield United; nearly all of them came to cheer the South and the underdogs. This memorable match was worthy of the occasion, being rated 'well above average of Cup-Finals, fast and ably contested'.

The first half had been fast and fluctuating, a twenty-yard shot by Priest beating Clawley in the Spurs goal after eleven minutes. Tottenham levelled the scores before half-time when Brown headed a free-kick past the giant Foulke.

Five minutes into the second half a sweet Spurs' move ended with 'a rasping shot from Brown billowing the net'. With the cheers still rolling over the ground Lipsham brought Clawley to a diving save. The goalkeeper fumbled the ball and Ben-

88

nett charged in to force it behind. The linesman signalled a corner, but to the surprise of Spurs and the fury of their supporters the referee gave a goal, judging that the ball had earlier crossed the goal line. In the opinion of most spectators it was an injustice to Tottenham – but who can be certain and how many impartial viewers were there?

This was the moment that 'Nudger' Needham, Sheffield's captain and a half-back of infinite flair, might so easily have taken charge of the game. But Tottenham held on gamely and were glad to draw.

The replay was at Bolton and again Spurs fell behind, Needham and Lipsham setting up a goal for Priest shortly before the interval.

As the teams came out again the shouts of 'Good Old Spurs' and 'Up the South' proved more effective than cries of 'Give us more goals', or 'Take the Cup to Yorkshire again'.

Cameron and Smith put Tottenham ahead and Brown settled the match, heading home powerfully from a corner. When J. L. Jones, the Tottenham captain, received the Cup from Lord Kinnaird his brief speech had no hope of being heard over the ecstatic cheering.

At the 1901 celebration dinner Tottenham decked the Cup handles with blue and white ribbons, a custom that has now become part of the presentation ceremony.

Mr Charles Crump, the able Vice-President of the F.A., who had refereed the match that first took the Cup north, underlined that it was meant to have a wandering life. And wander it did the following year, when the holders went out in the first round and the beaten finalists came back to win. The lore of the competition approves of both events, but Spurs were far from humiliated.

In the first round they were drawn against Southampton and the two most powerful Southern teams battled it out over three games. The second replay was at Reading with the snow driving down and the lines picked out in a blue compound from a lawn tennis marker. Southampton squeezed home by the odd goal and went on to their second Final.

With Sheffield United back at Crystal Palace there were three unusual players striving for a medal. Southampton now had at back C. B. Fry, the most remarkable athlete of his generation. Test cricketer, holder of the world record long jump, scholar, and football player extraordinary, nothing seemed beyond his grasp. The one weakness of his game was the usual amateur's fault of heading with hunched shoulders. Aiming as always at perfection he eliminated the fault by constant practice. But the winner's medal was to elude him going instead to the Sheffield team and Billy Foulke 6 feet 2½ inches tall and 21 stone in weight. Today he could only be a figure of fun and it is amusing to match him in the mind with Bonetti's lithe agility. But the goalkeepers then were anchored to their line and he was impervious to charging and difficult to pass.

Ernest Needham, the Sheffield United captain, was one of the great individualists whose style lesser players copied at their peril. An intelligent, adventurous half-back his instinctive understanding of the game meant that he rarely played himself into

89

Cartoonist Frank Gillett sketched this series of
cameos of the 1902 Cup-Final.

90

trouble when he drove forward in attack. As danger threatened Needham suddenly reappeared where he was most wanted. Very fast and very wiry, he was proof that football reverses the old adage that the 'good big 'un is usually better than the good little 'un'.

Exceptional fitness was demanded of wing-halves and it was here that the difference between the professional and amateur was most noticeable. No one was more energetic than Needham and in defence he was tenacious as a lamprey.

Southampton saved themselves at Crystal Palace with a disputed goal scored almost on time. There may have been some justice in Sheffield's protests for *The Daily Telegraph* reported: 'Wood knew he was off-side and said so.' This equalised the goal scored earlier by Alf Common, later to achieve fame as the first man to cost £1,000 in transfer fee.

It had been a harsh, undistinguished game and for the replay United had to substitute Barnes for the injured Bennett. There was a different atmosphere and quality in the deciding match.

The Times recorded: 'A week's quiet rest had certainly had a subduing influence and the teams showed that even with such a prize at stake good football can be played without sacrificing either robustness or pace.'

Once more Southampton fought back from a goal down, but this time Barnes settled the match when he scored from Common's pass. Poor Southampton! So near again, but they couldn't keep the Cup in the South.

11

The Open Championship: Yorkshire, the North East, and Liverpool

With the Southern League developing professionalism in the South the competition was no longer monopolised by relatively few Clubs. Records were harder earned and just to win was achievement enough.

The Yorkshire influence on the competition was steadily increasing and it was natural that Sheffield should come to the fore. The City had been one of the first to be captivated by association football and had been a powerful force in developing the game. By 1857 Nathaniel Creswick and William Prest had founded the Sheffield Club with a Committee of leading citizens. They laid down eleven rules for the game, their laws being influenced by Harrow, Rugby, Winchester, and Cambridge.

When The Football Association was formed six years later the Sheffield Secretary William Chesterman, wrote asking for the Club to be enrolled and making sensible suggestions for amending the rules including the use of a cross-bar. There was no agreement to their proposals and, as other Sheffield Clubs started, such as Wednesday in 1867, the Sheffield Association was formed with its own distinctive code. For many years they were to preserve the special features of their game though this did not prevent matches being played with other Associations.

The spread and strength of football in Sheffield was evident enough in a 6–0 win over London at Bramall Lane in November 1877 and a charity game in aid of the 'Sheffield Football Players Accident Society' on January 20, 1878. It was in that year that this progressive Association arranged its first match under floodlight. As the *Sheffield Independent* described it:

'The match was announced to commence at half-past seven o'clock and considerably before that hour the roads to Bramall Lane were completely besieged ... Behind each goal was placed a portable engine each of which drove two Siemens' dynamo machines – one for each light. The illuminating power equalled 8000 standard candles and the cost per hour for each light was about $3\frac{1}{2}d$.'

As in any big town football was both a unifying and a divisive force. The common front against outsiders concealed an even sharper rivalry between local Clubs and local supporters. But with such enthusiasm some success was inevitable in the competition and Wednesday was the first to achieve it. In 1882 they reached the semi-final with a team that included J. C. Clegg, such a power as player, referee, and Committee man, W. E. Clegg, and Billy Mosforth, the best outside-left of his day. A replay was necessary before Blackburn Rovers' superior fitness overwhelmed

Wednesday in the second half. Such had been the interest that 10,000 came to the first game at Huddersfield paying £142 6s. 5d. For the second at Whalley Range, Manchester, receipts were £282 11s. 0d. The takings went to the F.A. who minuted: 'The Association do give the amount of £70 to be divided between the charities of Sheffield and Blackburn equally.'

Sheffield were determinedly amateur in outlook with a principled approach to the game expressed by J. C. Shaw, President of the Association. 'Football so far from having the deteriorating effect upon the minds of the multitude which so many of our so called "sports" undoubtedly had, was in very large degree useful as a moral agency – cultivating as it did gentlemanly habits, good temper, coolness, self-denial, courage, and abstemiousness'.

They took some time to adjust to the advent of professionalism, which they strongly opposed. But once they had accepted the inevitable Wednesday built up a side that reached the Final in 1890. An official of the Bolton Wanderers team whom they beat in the semi-final commented sourly 'Sheffield Wednesday is one of the weakest Clubs which ever found its way to the Final tie'.

Blackburn's 6–1 victory at the Oval endorsed the view, but Wednesday's time was to come six years later. Meanwhile J. C. Clegg on the F.A. Council gave notable help in preventing the competition falling into disrepute over transfer squabbles. Sheffield themselves had been adept at protesting over the eligibility of other Club's players, while disputes and replays were becoming so common that the situation was farcical.

In 1893 there were over 1,000 registered players, there was a £10 bonus for signing for a new Club and the maximum wage was £140 per annum with an optional close season payment of not more than £1 per week.

With other inducements no doubt offered, many players, including the great Steve Bloomer, were found to be registered with two Clubs. As the confusion grew many clubs researched the opposition to find irregularities, then waited for the results of games before recording protests if they lost. Clegg now had his proposal accepted that all objections to players should be made beforehand. The *Sunday Chronicle* applauded: 'something of the sort was badly wanted and Mr Clegg has at least found a temporary remedy for a growing evil'. Firm handling soon eliminated the problem.

In 1896 Wednesday reached the Final after a replay with Bolton and Spiksley's two goals gave them victory at Crystal Palace. *The Times* commented:

'It is curious that such a great centre of football as Sheffield has always been, should have to wait 25 years from the institution of the competition before carrying off the football prize of the season. That they deserved it if only for their hard work in Cup ties alone, everyone will admit, while on Saturday they played the better game in a very keen match.'

But now the balance in the town tilted to Sheffield United. In 1898 they won the League title and the next year the Cup. Ernest Needham was, of course, one good reason for their success, as Liverpool found in the semi-final. United were a goal down but 'there was the little man at half-back who was ever on the alert for an opening and it was he who obtained the United equalising goal'.

In the replay, losing 2–4 with eight minutes to go Needham switched eight players into attack for Priest and Almond to equalise. The teams met again at Fallowfield, but so great was the crush that the crowd kept breaking on to the pitch and it was ten minutes to six before half-time was reached. The referee losing patience then abandoned the match with Liverpool a goal ahead.

They moved to Derby to settle the struggle, Sheffield United finally winning through by a goal from Beers five minutes before time. And it was Derby whom they met in the Final. Despite Steve Bloomer's presence and an early goal from Boag 'there was only one team in it' as United scored three in the second half.

Their courage was well expressed by Thickett. He was said to have broken two ribs and ruptured his side in the Fallowfield game, but he still played in the Final swathed in more than 50 yards of starched bandages interspersed with pads and consuming a whole bottle of champagne at half-time to keep himself going.

Little wonder that United should be in the Final again in 1901 and win the following year. But to preserve the balance Wednesday won in 1907 beating Everton in the Final. This is how the game was described in *The Only Authentic Record of the Cup* edited by D. Mackenzie.

'The long procession of beaten favourites in the Final had one more victim added to the score when the whistle sounded at the end of this game. A crowd of over 84,000 had assembled at the Palace and witnessed ninety minutes of what may be fairly described as interesting, if not artistic football. It was generally understood that Everton were intrinsically the next best side to the leaders of the League, and, naturally, expected to win. The character of the football had much in common with that usually associated with Final ties; neither side played quite as well as they were supposed to be capable of doing. There was much pace, the kicking was hard, the ball was much in the air, and fouls were plentiful. The Everton team included ten of the men who were successful in the previous Final, so that the ordeal of playing before a vast audience could not be urged as an excuse for the inability of Everton to find their real game. From the very first, however, they seemed embarrassed by the rushing and bustling tactics of the Wednesday. The play of Sheffield, if it did not often promise a score, kept the ball at the Everton end.

Everton on the defensive in the 1907 Cup-Final at Crystal Palace
which they lost 1–2 to Sheffield Wednesday.

In the Final replay at Old Trafford in 1911, Bradford City beat Newcastle United to
become the first holders of the present Cup made, appropriately, in Bradford.

This cartoon was based on a popular song of 1910 –
'Saturday-attur-day Afternoon'.

'In the first half of the game, a mix-up on the part of the Everton backs enabled the first goal to be scored at the end of 20 minutes' play, Chapman swinging the ball into the mouth of the Everton goal for Stewart to give it the final touch. During the closing minutes of the first half there was a glimpse of real football from the Everton side when the best goal of the match was scored by Sharp.

'There was a general feeling that Everton would easily turn the game in the second half, but anticipations were not realised. From a throw-in about four minutes from the finish, the ball was hooked by Wilson across the mouth of the goal for Simpson, all unmarked, to quietly head it in the net.

'This was one of the softest goals imaginable, but proved the deciding factor towards the defeat of Everton.'

But for all Yorkshire's success in the competition, with Bradford City and Barnsley also lifting the Cup in 1911 and 1912, it was a team from the North East that dominated the decade.

No side has built a greater reputation than the Newcastle team of these years. League Champions three times and Cup-Finalists five times in seven years they were the most formidable of opponents. The fact that they won the Cup only once was an unkind jest by the fates or the working out of a mysterious hoodoo.

Crystal Palace was the one name to upset them. They simply could not win on that lush ground. It was said that the longer grass disrupted the smooth precision of their passing practised on the barer, swifter surface of St James's Park. But their League record with all the away matches, shows that their game was not as fragile and delicately balanced as that.

It was just one of those inexplicable footballing freaks and no doubt the more often they failed the more they worried.

To lose to Aston Villa and Everton was no more than a mild surprise. But why should the finest team of the generation be beaten by Wolves (ninth in the Second Division) and be held to draws by Barnsley and Bradford City (ninth and twelfth in the Second Division)?

It was not just the ground that mesmerised Newcastle. In 1907 they won the League Championship yet they lost at home to an indifferent Southern League side in the first round of the Cup. The side? why Crystal Palace, of course.

Only in 1910 could they carry off the Cup beating Barnsley in the replay at Everton. This was how the Final was described in Mackenzie's record:

'For the fourth time in five years Newcastle made their appearance in the Final at the Palace, but once again they were denied the satisfaction of winning in the Metropolis. It cannot be said that the football yielded by this game was either scientific or artistic. Except during the last quarter of an hour – when the Newcastle men, the majority of whom possessed International Caps, played up to their reputation and sustained their attack in a clever and resourceful style – many faults were glaringly obvious. Partly because of the haphazard kicking of the half-backs, but chiefly because of their inability either to pass accurately or try a little dribbling, both sets of forwards were singularly ineffectual during the greater part of the game. Barnsley's goal was the result of a fine inward pass and a clever shot by Tuffnell, which glanced in off the post. The Newcastle eleven did very well in the closing stages of the match, their backs and half-backs keeping the ball down and feeding the forwards accurately. The equalising goal for Newcastle was headed in by Rutherford, the fastest and cleverest wing on the field.

'In the re-play at Liverpool, the Newcastle men showed clearly that they were a splendid side, and in dribbling, passing and general tactics they out-played Barnsley completely. They displayed a remarkable control over the wet and slippery ball, while their pace never slackened. There was no score at half-time, but during the second period Rutherford and Howie were always prominent, although Shepherd, who was given more scope than on the previous Saturday, had the satisfaction of scoring both goals, the second one being from a penalty.

'Thus in this re-play Newcastle achieved what they had failed to do in four appearances at the Palace.'

There was welcome relief from earlier frustrations and Tyneside went wild with delight. But next year there was Bradford City beating them at Old Trafford in the replay.

Looking back in detachment we can see that the law of averages was at work. Later years were to even the score with Newcastle's record now nicely balanced – ten Finals and six wins. Fortune relented in the 'fifties, but if Colin Veitch and his team could have foreseen the future – it would have given no consolation. For all that matters to the players is today's game, not the record over the century.

Yet it is this record that brings Newcastle United immediately to mind as the best Cup team of them all, though it was in 1955 that they last won the trophy.

In quantity, Villa and Blackburn Rovers can boast of more Finals, but Newcastle's were all in the fiercer competition of the 20th century.

The distinctive feature of the Club was the cool intelligence and smooth precision of their game. There was a rhythmic beauty in their forward moves and neat triangular passing.

In defence they relied not on the long kick or physical dominance, but on clever interception or the off-side trap. McCracken was to tease and torment by his subtle anticipation and the perfection of the timing that disrupted so many attacks.

McCracken and Veitch typified the intellectual approach of the players. Before their great season in 1904 things had not gone too well and the Chairman told Veitch, Carr, and Aitken to lock themselves in a room and pick what they considered the best team. That was an unusual tribute to the player's judgement fully justified by the results.

It was at one of the post-mortem discussions within the team that Veitch, McWilliam, and McCracken first devised the off-side strategy. Appropriately the discussion was in a railway train. For their plan so played on opponents' nerves that when a visiting side heard the guard's whistle blow as they arrived at Newcastle station one forward exclaimed 'what – off-side already!'

McWilliam later managed Tottenham Hotspur and that great tactician, Arthur Rowe, was coached by him. He recalls that McWilliam started him thinking with the comment: 'It's a simple game in which positional play is everything.'

Those early Newcastle players had that instinctive understanding of the patterns of play that is called in today's jargon: 'ability to read the game'.

As Newcastle tailed off, the North-Eastern supremacy might so easily have been maintained by Sunderland's team of all the talents. Cuggy, Mordue and Buchan was a combination of such ability that the largest crowd in the history of Crystal Palace came flocking to the Final with Villa in 1913.

This was how the game was reported in *The Only Authentic Record of the Cup:*

'The Villa eleven, who were destined to win the Cup for the fifth time, were nearly as popular idols with the crowd of over 120,000 as if they were members of a Southern club. As things turned out, the game, though appreciably better than many of the Final Cup-ties of the last few years, was merely good in parts. It was fast and open at the beginning, but the promise of a brilliant start was not kept up – chiefly because the backs on either side soon took to high kicking, and were also anxious to dispose of the remotest possibility of danger by getting the ball away into touch. It was seldom, indeed, that either line of forwards justified their high reputation. There was little or none of the brilliant passing at top speed which had distinguished the Villa in previous victorious years. On both sides too much time was wasted in mere pattern-weaving, and when a concerted attack was delivered the obvious thing was always done at the critical moment. The head-to-head passing was at times uncannily clever; yet one felt that in some cases a piece of straight-forward dribbling would have been more effective. On the whole the best feature of the game was the superlative excellence of the defence on either side. However awkward the position the backs contrived to get the ball safely away. Hardy, the best goalkeeper England has had for a long time, gave a delightful exhibition.

'There can be no doubt that Aston Villa was slightly the better team at all points of the game – even at half-back, where Sunderland were supposed to have a distinct advantage. The more popular team ought certainly to have scored more than the single goal adroitly headed by Barber late in the second half, which Butler, the Sunderland goalkeeper, had no possible chance of saving. This winning goal was the outcome of a corner kick taken by Wallace and beautifully centred.'

Sunderland's side might well have developed into a team of Newcastle's stature had it not been broken and dispersed by the War.

Lancashire never fades quietly into the background, their challenge becoming more insistent and diverse as Merseyside and Manchester, Bury and Burnley added their weight.

The City of Liverpool's great impact on the Cup can best be seen in the results. Of all League teams Everton have the best and Liverpool the fourth best record if performance is judged on average progress each season, rather than the number of times the Cup has been won. Yet winning the Cup is the real goal of the competition and it is surprising that Everton have succeeded only three times and Liverpool but once.

It is surprising, too, how slow Merseyside was to take to its heart a game that was soon to become a fever in the blood of this great sea-port. When the competition was seven years old rugby was still the recognised sport in the City and there were few opportunities for the association football player. But before the end of 1879 St Domingo's Football Club had been formed and had won its first match against St Peter's. Once more the Church's interest in youth welfare had started a famous football club, for soon St Domingo's Football Club changed its name to Everton.

By 1882 *The Liverpool Daily Post* was to comment on a game between Bootle and Everton that 'those two Clubs were in advance of all others playing under the rules of Association in this neighbourhood.'

As Everton won the match 4–1 this seemed to stamp them as the district's leading team and this was certainly the case when they were elected as a founder member of the League six years later. But their Cup record by then was hardly impressive. True they had won the Liverpool Cup three times, including 1886 the year of Queen Victoria's visit to the Liverpool Exhibition. Yet in that very year the Lancashire Association resolved that Everton be not allowed to play for the Lancashire Senior Cup until they show proof of their ability. There was certainly no proof of their ability in that year's F.A. Challenge Cup for they withdrew from the competition when they found their best player ineligible after Glasgow Rangers had arrived to play the first tie. In this twilight period after the acceptance of professionalism credentials were, indeed, more important than ability. This was clear enough the following year as protests dogged the Cup games between Bolton Wanderers and Everton.

Bolton won the first match, but Everton successfully appealed against the eligibility of William Struthers, their best forward. A replay was ordered and ended in a draw. The next game also ended 'in darkness and a draw'. Finally Everton won 2–1, but now Bolton appealed and the F.A. ruled that some of Everton's players, registered as amateurs, were in fact professionals. By the time the decision was reached Everton had already lost to Preston in the next round and they were suspended for a month.

The Liverpool and District Association also removed the Liverpool Cup, but a replica was kept on the sideboard with a notice 'Gone but not forgotten'.

The famous Nick Ross was signed from Preston to captain the team in its first year in the League. He was paid the large sum of £10 per month, but was unable to command success. Under the heading 'Everton Football Fiascos' the *Liverpool Review* blamed the lack of attention paid to his views for the many away reverses the Club suffered.

By the start of the 1889 season Everton had a side good enough to beat Notts Rangers 11–0 in the first round and Derby County 11–2 in the second. Then they surprisingly crashed to Stoke.

It was 1893 before they reached the Final, for the unfancied Wolves to beat them by the only goal. With the kick-off at half-past three there were people waiting at the gates four hours earlier and the vast crowd nearly spilled on to the pitch. As the magazine *Out of Doors* recorded:

'At last the Wanderers appeared and then Everton and you will remember it was almost as difficult to reach the playing space as to kick a goal. But they did reach it, the toss was won and lost, and the game began. I suppose Evertonians thought it could have only one ending. They forgot what your good-natured British crowd can do. They back up the weaker side to begin with and encourage them and this weaker side, with all to gain and nothing to lose, play up valiantly. They play above form. Final-tie football is not like ordinary football; the stronger side (so-called) get just a bit flurried and then a little more and at last they lose'.

In its way it had been remarkable for Everton to recover so quickly from the stirring events of the year before which could well have left the Club 'a bit flurried'. Their Chairman at Anfield Road was the rumbustious self-made 'King John' Houlding, an assertive and domineering man whose brusque handling led to a split. The Club had difficulties over renting their ground from a Mr Orrell and Houlding tried to rush through a scheme for buying up both the land that Orrell leased and a further 15,000 square yards that Houlding himself owned. An opposition group led by Mahon and Clayton finally moved the Club to Goodison Park, purchasing the area for £8,090. Unabashed, Houlding started up the Liverpool Association Football Club.

The new Club was only recognised by the F.A. after some delay and a protest by the local Rugby Union organisation against the title. With W. E. Barclay as Secretary the new Liverpool Club was soon reinforced by a remarkable character, John McKenna. He was to be a Director of the Club for 30 years, President of the League in 1910, and later a Vice-President of the F.A.

Liverpool started in the Lancashire League, but next season when Accrington Stanley resigned from the Second Division and Bootle, in financial trouble, failed to secure re-election McKenna cheerfully applied by telegram for Liverpool to join. The Committee were, in fact, against leaving the Lancashire League and Barclay was quite unaware that the telegram had been sent in his name until he received the immediate reply 'Liverpool elected. Come to London meeting at three o'clock tomorrow to arrange fixtures.'

Andrew Hannah, late of Everton, was Liverpool's first captain. Though their football was described as 'kick-and-rush' this was not untypical of the Second Division and they won promotion by 1894.

Everton had treated the new Club with disdain and 44,000 spectators came to Goodison Park on October 13 to relish the first League match between the two teams. Everton won 2–0, but were held to a 2–2 draw in the return match at Anfield. Liverpool finished at the bottom of the First Division and, as was then the custom had to play a 'Test' Match to see if they stayed there or whether Bury were promoted in their place. Bury won 1–0 despite their goalkeeper being sent off for 'kicking an opponent in the abdomen'.

Liverpool bounced straight back the next season getting the best of the 'Test' Matches with Albion, Small Heath and Manchester City. Their hard relentless defence was beginning to make its mark, but they could not yet challenge Everton's performance. For in 1897 Everton reached the Final of the Cup for that magnificent game with Aston Villa in which 'the excitement knew no bounds and it was a positive relief to the spectators when the ball was put out'. Everton lost to the odd

Freeman, near the penalty-spot, scores the only goal of the 1914 Final
to give Burnley their win over Liverpool.

goal in five in what Lord Roseberry described as a 'splendid and Olympic' contest.

Liverpool ceased to be the poor relations in 1899, when they reached the semi-final of the Cup and were runners-up in the League. They were joined that season by Alexander Raisbeck, a centre-half rated by Gibson and Pickford as one of the giants of the game. In *Association Football* they describe him as 'like an intelligent automaton fully wound up and warranted to last through the longest game on record. To watch him play is to see a man pulsating to his finger-tips with the joy of life. Swift, rapid movement, fierce electric rushes are to him an everlasting delight.' He needed all his energy for the three replays with Sheffield United in the semi-final. At the last they lost by the odd goal and Sheffield United cruised home comfortably enough in the Final.

The nice balance of ability was further evidenced when Liverpool won the League and Everton the Cup in the 1905–06 season. It was third time lucky for Everton and, their good fortune was in catching Newcastle United on their hoodoo ground at

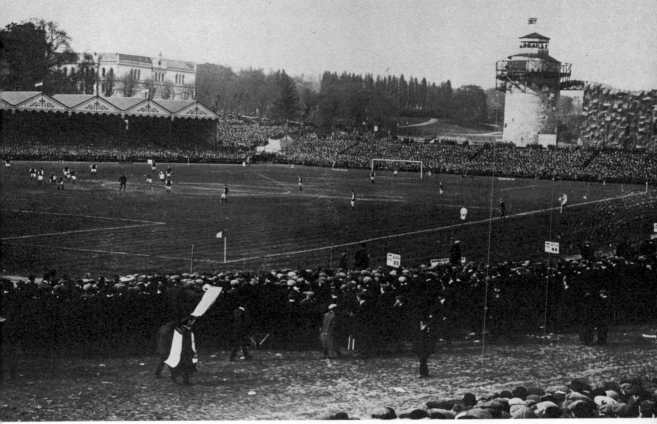

A view of the Crystal Palace ground with nearly 73,000
spectators watching the 1914 Cup-Final.

Crystal Palace. Young's goal was enough to give the game to an Everton side
whose success was ascribed by the *Athletic News* to 'English muscle, English skill,
and English pluck'.

Just as satisfying for Everton had been their win in the semi-final over Liverpool.
The game was decided in the second half when Dunlop put the ball into his own
goal and Hardman scored a second within a minute before Liverpool could regain
their poise.

Everton were back in the Final the next season, but despite their consistency in
the earlier rounds of the Cup, Liverpool were to have to wait another 59 years
before they could emulate their neighbours. They had their chance in 1914, but
Burnley gained the only goal of an undistinguished match. It was Freeman whose
fierce shot and fine play illumined a drab game. That all-Lancashire Final just
before the war was a reminder of the County's continuing power in the competition
and the City of Liverpool was to play a full part in maintaining that reputation to
the present day.

12

Pick of the Finals, 1872–1915

The 1915 Final was played at Old Trafford with khaki prominent among the 70,000 spectators and the day as gloomy as the mood. Gone was the gaiety, the spontaneous expression of feeling, the total commitment. The drum of war was so insistent it filled men's minds, even though the *Sheffield Telegraph* felt confident enough to comment on United's future prospects, 'Given the final triumph of the Allies and the resumption of football next season . . .'

Their equally optimistic assessment of the Sheffield team was better justified by events. The fine half-back line of Sturgess, Brelsford, and Utley took firm charge of the midfield. Chelsea were rarely in the game after Simmons had headed in Utley's lob, and two late goals by Fazackerley and Kitchen destroyed them. Vivian Woodward might have brought some life to Chelsea forwards. He had obtained leave from the 'Footballers Battalion' but watched from the stands. 'Bob Thomson has got you to the Final and he must play now' said Woodward.

Lord Derby presented the Cup and exhorted the crowd, 'You have seen the Cup played for and it is now the duty of everyone to join with each other and play a sterner game for England'.

Forty-three years had gone by since the competition's modest start. It was now a national institution and the pace of development had been hectic. In the changing kaleidoscope of clubs and rules, players, and tactics the picture can be a confused abstract. But with the footballers marching off to Flanders we can look back in detail at four of the more memorable Finals and by focusing on key games get a clearer view of the whole.

In the Final of 1875 the Royal Engineers survived an unfair handicap to go on and win the replay. Their experience, as set out in their Sports Club record, led to an updating of the rule about changing ends.

Royal Engineers 1   **Old Etonians 1**

'The final contest for the Cup between the above Clubs was arranged for Saturday the 13th. The attendance was large and the corps well represented as on former occasions. Although our fellows were hot favourites and an easy victory for them had been anticipated, it was evident with the strong wind blowing right down the ground from goal to goal that everything depended on the toss and the consequent choice of station. Unfortunately for us the Old Etonians won the toss, and gained the advantage of the wind at the outset. For 40 minutes they tried their utmost to score, but our fellows invariably got the ball away at

DOYLE (Burnley) and FERGUSON (Liverpool), the rival captains, had the honour of being presented to His Majesty. — KENNETH CAMPBELL (Liverpool) about to repel a shot coming in over the heads of several players.

Headline news in 1914 was the King's first Cup-Final when
Burnley beat Liverpool 1–0.

the critical moment. Our backs kicked in splendid form, but it was no use. The wind was too strong and the ball came careering back into the neighbourhood of our goal. Five minutes now remained to "half-time", and if the R.E.'s could only defend their goal for this short space of time, the game was certainly theirs. However, as luck would have it, Bonsor at the last moment by a magnificent "corner kick" sent the ball through the goal, the wind making the ball curl back in a most wonderful fashion and utterly dashing all calculations of the goal-keeper as to its probable line of descent. Ends were now changed and the Sappers, boiling over with rage at this terribly hard stroke of luck got hold of the ball and carrying it straight down to the opposite goal sent it spinning through the posts amidst great applause. The relative merits of the opposing team could thus be judged to a nicety. The Old Etonians with the wind had scored one goal after 40 minutes play. The R.E.'s with the wind scored their goal almost instantly. It was therefore pretty apparent that the Sappers were by far the superior team. Fate had decreed, however, that they should have to battle once more against the wind. Ends were changed and the fight again carried on with renewed energy. At last Ruck, who by his determined charging had frequently threatened to lay up some of the enemy came into collision with Ottaway with such effect that the latter was carried off the field. This reduction in the members of the Old Etonians produced no material result and when time was called the match remained undecided, each side having scored one goal. Before the commencement of the match arrangements had been made between the two captains to continue play for half-an-hour in the event of the match being undecided in the first period. As the Old Etonians, however, had lost one of their men a discussion arose as to the advisability of their continuing the game with reduced numbers. Although we were anxious to go on and fight the match out, confident in our superior lasting powers, still our captain would not press the question and left it entirely to the Etonians to decide whether the match should be continued or not. After a short consultation they agreed to play on. The ground was cleared and stations tossed for and again the Old Etonians won the toss and gained the advantage of the wind. In the next 15 minutes however they failed to score a goal and it having been agreed to change at half-time our fellows now changed over and for the second time commenced playing with the wind in their backs. Our prospects now looked brilliant. There was no chance of the enemy scoring against the wind and every chance of our fellows repeating their former performance, but it was not to be done. Our forwards did their very utmost, but the enemy abandoning the offensive, confined themselves to a strictly defensive game and thus baffled them completely so that the match still resulted in a draw after two hours hard fight.

Next choice is Preston's unique performance in 1889 described by a player of keen perception:

Preston North End 3   Wolverhampton Wanderers 0

'The Final of 1889 was of special interest not only because of the excellence of the play, but because of Preston's remarkable achievement in winning the Cup without conceding a goal and the League without losing a match. The coveted "double" was much easier in those far-off days, but this remains the most unusual feat in the history of the Cup.

'Although no Southern team was involved Preston's reputation was such that the record Oval crowd was no surprise.

'In Press comments before the match it was noted that the London and North-Western railway was running excursion trains from Birkenhead, Chester, Shrewsbury, Wolverhampton, and Preston at remarkably low rates. Wolverhampton, however, had been so apathetic in supporting their team that no great crowds were expected from there. The kick-off was set for 4.00 p.m. to allow those who wished to see the Boat Race first to get to the Oval on time. The match officials were to be Umpires: Lord Kinnaird and J. C. Clegg: Referee, Major Marindin R.E., C.M.G. As one paper put it "We compliment the Association on appointing three old and experienced players because in our opinion no matter how well versed in the laws they may be, officials who have not had some considerable experience as players can never be relied on as an efficient Umpire or Referee".'

106

An eye witness account of the game recorded its highlights giving us a vivid picture of the scene and of the more boisterous methods of play then in vogue. Modern goalkeepers are advised not to read on unless they have strong nerves.

'Few of the 23,000 spectators who were at the Oval grudged the winners their hard-earned victory. For three years the Preston men and their supporters have confidently expected to secure the "insignificant pot" and year after year their aspirations have been dashed. But neither the team nor their leader, W. Sudell, whose motto is "nil desperandum", shared any doubt. Mr Sudell's face was wreathed in confident smiles before the game and after it the pleasure depicted was sublime.

'We have reason to believe that the crowd exceeded the record gate for a football match. It was both orderly and impartial otherwise it would have been impossible for the game to have been played. One incident alone proved this. A few minutes before time and following a questionable custom of the Surrey crowd at a cricket match several spectators rushed across the enclosure in front of the pavilion to get a closer glimpse of the players. This stupid action caused the crowd to break in on all sides and for the last few minutes only those who were close to the touch lines could get a sight of the play.

'Early comers had a long wait for the 4.00 p.m. start and various methods of amusement were tried by the young blood present. An old International player, now a clergyman, sat on the reserved enclosure wearing a top hat which apparently formed a tempting target for the marksmen behind who kept up a continual fire of paper pellets until their stock was exhausted. Then they had the assurance to ask the policeman within the enclosure to collect and return their missiles to them.

'Some of the spectators thought both teams played viciously but as a player I must contradict this. Save for one or two exceptions for which the prevalent excitement was sufficient cause it was generally agreed that all concerned played a thoroughly fair game. There was plenty of charging and it was good heavy charging, but there is little or no danger in fair charging; it certainly was not accompanied by what some apparently prefer, unfair practices such as lifting the knee, pushing and deliberate tripping.

'In consequence of the enormous crowd already admitted the gates were closed some time before the start and when Umpire, Lord Kinnaird, arrived he could not get into the ground. After quite a severe struggle he managed to gain admission and reached the pavilion just as the teams were ready to take the field.

'London evening papers give little space to football and rarely publish reports of matches but on Saturday some of them issued special editions for the occasion while the *Pall Mall Gazette* actually gave portraits of the officials and the players with their positions on the field.

'Let us view the scene. The game was played in the centre of the Oval and the ring round it was almost as large as at a cricket match. The wooden tiers facing the pavilion were moved near to it and turned round. Two rows of seats surrounded the enclosure inside the ropes and provided an excellent view of the game as also did the covered stands adjoining. By three o'clock every point of advantage was secured and the doors were closed but as the disappointed crowd outside threatened to become riotous they were opened again and those who cared to take a chance of getting a peep at the play were admitted. Some two thousand, however, turned away being satisfied with the assurance that there was really no room for them.

'At five minutes to four Preston in white shirts and dark knickers came from the pavilion and received a hearty welcome and the cheers had hardly died away when they were renewed to pay a similar compliment to the Wolverhampton team in broad red and white striped shirts.

Preston North End
R. H. Mills-Roberts

R. H. Howarth				R. Holmes
G. Drummond		D. Russell		J. Graham
J. Gordon	J. Ross	J. Goodall	F. Dewhurst (Captain)	S. Thompson

T. Knight	H. Wood	J. Brodie (Captain)	D. Wykes	T. Hunter
	A. Lowder	H. Allen		E. Fletcher
	C. Mason			R. Baugh
		J. Baynton		

Wolverhampton Wanderers

'Dewhurst beat Brodie in the toss and chose to defend the Crown Baths goal. A few minutes of wild rushing and reckless kicking showed that the players were somewhat excited but soon they settled down and the Wanderers attacked. First Knight, then Wood had chances to score but failed. Had these opportunities been utilised properly the fortunes of the day might have been turned. The Midlanders got no other easy chances in the first half and Mills-Roberts dealt with the long shots in his best style.

'As the teams got into their strides it was easy to note the marked difference in their styles. The one aim and endeavour of the Preston forwards was to keep the ball on the ground as much as possible and the Wolverhampton forwards on the other hand were apparently trying to see how long they could keep it bobbing about in the air. This quickly confirmed my view that short passing on the ground is as superior to long passing in the air as the neat placing of the ball by a half-back to his forward is to the wild heave in which novices at half so freely indulge. The Wolves half backs headed more often than they kicked whilst the Preston men rarely headed when they could use their feet. If a Wanderer's outside half got the ball he generally kicked it hard across to the other wing, the

North Enders did nothing of the kind but simply passed it along the ground to a well placed forward.

'After less than fifteen minutes play the Preston right wing went forward and Ross shot. Baynton punched away and Dewhurst returned the ball and put it between the posts to the accompaniment of vociferous cheers.

'Ten minutes later Ross dodged Allen and Mason and sent a shot straight at the goalkeeper who "muffed it" and literally allowed the ball to slip through his fingers for goal number two.

'Then the Wanderers attacked and Hunter centred. Had Brodie been smarter Mills-Roberts would have lost his "clean sheet" for he just touched the ball with his finger tips from the long shot before he was sent flying through the goal and onto his back. Howarth kicked the ball away and Thomson got it. He was steadying himself for a shot when Fletcher promptly floored him with a vigorous but fair charge. So the half-time score was Preston 2 Wolverhampton 0.

'Wanderers re-started with great dash and Mills-Roberts was very busy, ably backed by Russell who dropped back to defend the Preston goal. Long shots poured in but one doubts if these spelled danger as much as would have been the case had the Wolverhampton men dribbled or passed until nearer to the Preston goal. Whilst the goalkeeper had much to do only two or three of the shots were difficult to stop.

'Then this attack gradually weakened and the North End's forwards got away. Twenty minutes from "time" pretty passing by Gordon and Ross left the latter in possession but challenged by two or three opponents. He dribbled beautifully and when close to the goal line middled splendidly. Mason tried to kick away, touched the ball and slightly diverted its course, the goalkeeper was rushed through the goal by Dewhurst and Thomson got possession to get the third and last goal.

'Wolverhampton still strove hard, but when the final whistle was blown they were still in the defensive.'

The 1897 Final was remarkable for the quality of the play and the tingling excitement of the game as well as for Aston Villa's double:

Aston Villa 3   Everton 2

These extracts from *The Times* of Monday, April 12th 1897 tell the story of the game.

'The Crystal Palace is the only place in England where such a crowd could get a view of some sort of the game. Quite half of Saturday's huge crowd were gathered on the turf slopes on the Eastern side of the field and the mass of people presented a wonderful sight from the pavilion. The afternoon was bright and the keen wind not much felt in the hollow in which the ground is situated. The arrangements for dealing with the company were efficiently carried out under the direction of Mr Henry Gillman, the Manager of the Crystal Palace.

'Aston Villa won the match beating Everton by three goals to two after a

109

contest in which the excitement continued to the end. The enthusiasm was raised to a high pitch by the variations of fortune and the high scoring. All the scoring occurred in a period of 25 minutes in the first half. That Aston Villa deserved their victory was unquestionable for they played the better football and were consistent to the end, whereas the Everton men were rather uneven.

'The game was remarkable for the superb defence at both ends and the high standard of the half-back play.

'It was the Villa half-back play which enabled the forwards to do so well and time after time broke up the Everton attack. Everton too were not lacking in this respect though demonstrating it to lesser degree.

'The halves placed the ball for the forwards with wonderful accuracy Reynolds and Holt, both approaching the veteran stage, were particularly clever. As for full-backs, Spencer and Storrier distinguished themselves amid the general excellence.

'Athersmith, Devey and Bell were the pick of the forwards and it was a wonder the forward work was so good in view of the fine defence by which it was opposed.

'The game began at 4 o'clock Everton kicking towards the north goal which meant they had to face a fresh breeze. Aston Villa seemed at once to settle down, their halves looking too clever for their opponents. It was only the stout defence of Everton which prevented any score. Athersmith, with his great pace and his cleverness in dribbling was dangerous. Twice he got up, but being pressed he had to shoot at difficult angles and the ball went behind.

'There was one sharp attack by Everton, caused by one of the Birmingham men "fouling" Hartley. The scrimmage in front of goal passed away without result, but it immediately preceded the scoring of the first goal for Villa. The ball went upfield from Spencer to Reynolds and then on to Athersmith who reached a position 20 yards from the posts. He passed to Campbell who made a long shot and the ball swerved owing to the wind and passed into the net.

'Aston were not long in possession of their advantage for after a spell of even play Bell broke away and went between the two full-backs. Whitehouse's only policy was to go out and meet Bell, but the Everton forward got in his kick before he was charged and the ball went into the net.

'The pace seemed to increase and inside the first half-hour Everton took the lead. They had a free kick not far from goal and Hartley scored out of a scrimmage. For a moment the Everton men again strongly attacked and seemed likely to get through. But in the course of five minutes Aston Villa got two more goals. The first was put through out of a scrimmage following a free kick by Wheldon, the second was cleverly headed by Devey.

'Whitehouse made two good saves for Villa in the three minutes remaining to the interval. The cut and thrust continued through the second half.

'When the last twenty minutes were reached the teams were still playing at a wonderful pace. Aston Villa attacked for a long time without gaining anything

CRYSTAL PALACE.
Saturday, April 10th, 1897.

FINAL TIE
FOR THE
CHALLENGE CUP of the FOOTBALL ASSOCIATION.

ASTON VILLA.

Colours—
Claret and Light Blue Shirts,
White Knickers.

Goal.
× WHITEHOUSE.

Backs.
× SPENCER. × EVANS.

Half-Backs.
× REYNOLDS. × JAMES COWAN. × CRABTREE.

Forwards.
× ATHERSMITH. × DEVEY. × CAMPBELL. × WHELDON. × JOHN COWAN.

○

Forwards.
× MILWARD. × CHADWICK. × HARTLEY. × BELL. × TAYLOR.

Half-Backs.
× STEWART. × HOLT. × BOYLE.

Backs.
× STORRIER. × MEECHAN.

Goal.
× MENHAM.

Colours—
Blue Shirts, White Knickers.

EVERTON.

RIGHT. LEFT. LEFT. RIGHT.

Referee—J. LEWIS (Lancashire). Linesmen—J. HOWCROFT (Redcar). A. SCRAGG (Crewe).

Official Programme. ONE PENNY.

One penny was the charge for the programme for Aston Villa's
great game against Everton in 1897.

and then the enthusiasm of the spectators was aroused by several brilliant efforts on the part of Everton to get level. Bell, Milward and Hartley each shot low, swift and straight, but Whitehouse, the goalkeeper, came off with flying colours and each was saved. These were anxious minutes for Villa, but time at last ran out and the victory remained with them. The crowd rushed to the enclosure and the players were heartily cheered.'

Tottenham's win in 1901 over Sheffield United was a unique performance by a non-league Club:

Tottenham Hotspur 2:3   Sheffield United 2:1

Tottenham's appearance in the 1901 Final put the Crystal Palace crowd up from 68,945 the previous year to 110,820. Several thousands may have entered London's great pleasure ground for other pastimes than watching the Final, but this was a crowd of record proportions and 'Grasshopper's' report in *The Athletic News* sets the scene for this memorable game.

'On Saturday with us in town it was a case of the Cup! the Cup!! and nothing but the Cup!!! I never remember such keen interest being taken in a match before and this was borne out by the record gate which assembled on the Palace enclosure.

'It was said that 75 special trains were run to London all of which were filled. This would make about 75,000 provincials present, which I do not believe, as to judge from the cheering and hat-waving after each point scored, I am confident the Hotspur supporters were in a majority of at least 2 to 1.

'It was a wonderful sight that Palace enclosure around which the crowd assembled. One vast mass of humanity was closely packed around a big saucer-shaped circus while trees, roofs of buildings – indeed every point from which a view of the game could be obtained – were availed of by eager enthusiasts.

'The glorious spring-like weather which has burst on us all at once was no doubt responsible for much, but at the same time there is no getting away from the fact that many of those present had travelled at least one hundred miles to see the match, and would have been present had it been raining cats or dogs, or even French nails.

'The players I daresay would have ordered a little cooler and less dusty atmosphere. The great lesson of the day is the immense amount of interest that is shown by all classes of society not only in football, but in the much derided, in some quarters, professional branch of the game.

'As to the game itself, it was one of the most interesting and keenly contested that I ever remember in a final tie, and what is more satisfactory, it was played by both sides in a fair, although naturally vigorous, and sportsmanlike spirit. The Northerners combined better, but lacked the dash and "devil" of the Hotspur forwards.'

The caterers at least were not surprised by the size of the crowd. *The Athletic News* records the preparation of: 2,500 sandwich loaves, each weighing 8 lbs; 1,000 bread and butter loaves each weighing 5 lbs; 1,000 household loaves, 12,000 batons, 21,000 rolls, 120,000 slices of bread and butter, 30,000 pats of butter, 45,120 portions of best cake, 16,000 portions of lunch cake, 1,000 sponge cakes, 1,000 pieces of short-bread, 20,000 French pastries, 10,000 bath buns, 10,000 plain buns, 24,000 scones, 6,000 sixpenny pork pies, 2,000 smoked sausages, 1,728 gallons of milk, 200 rumps of beef, 250 chines of mutton for chops, 150 best ends of mutton for cutlets, 60 fore-ribs of beef, each weighing 40 lbs., 40 whole lambs, 300 quarters of whitebait, 500 pounds of soles, 22,400 lbs. of potatoes, 2,000 cabbages and cauliflowers, 400 fowls, 200 ducks, and 120,000 bottles of mineral waters.

And though some of the crowd could only see the ball when it was kicked high in the air their behaviour was impeccable as was recorded in the inevitable verse:

'The Sydenham slopes are unsurpassed
In their essential fitness
For letting monstrous crowds and vast
The sports arena witness.

112

But, oh, the wobbling, whelming surge
That ever swayed those masses;
And on your minds this fact I urge –
John Bull's behaviour passes.
All praise, for that good humour blithe
which – in the crush terrific –
Made each crammed Sydenham slope, mid writhe
and roar, a Slope Pacific!'

Such was the background to a game which a Sheffielder described in the *Athletic News*:

'I went full of confidence in the ability of the United team to beat Tottenham Hotspur and returned with that confidence somewhat shaken. True the United were not beaten, but the great superiority which thousands of the excursionists who went up to town from Sheffield expecting to see Needham and his merry men display was entirely absent.

'When the manner in which their equalising goal was scored is taken into consideration the United may be somewhat fortunate to have another chance of tackling the "Spurs".

'The Bramall-lane Brigade found their opponents to be a team with more speed, agility, and dash than the Aston Villa combination whom they vanquished in the semi-final.

'The teams were very evenly matched and I think United were rather the better side in the first half and Tottenham in the second. United began in promising style and when Priest scored eleven minutes from the start Sheffielders settled themselves comfortable to enjoy the victory they had gone to London to see.

'But the Tottenham defence in the first half was superb, whilst several brilliant flashes suggested the possibility that later on their smart attack might cause trouble. And so it did.

'An equalising goal for Spurs left matters level at half-time. When a splendidly executed forward movement ended in the now famous Brown putting the "Spurs" ahead five minutes after resuming I was troubled with doubts. These were greatly lessened two minutes later when the score was level again. The great point of argument is whether Mr Kingscott was right in deciding the ball had been over the line.'

Free Critic had no doubts of Mr. Kingscott's correctness:

'He was in a capital position to judge, and there was no necessity to appeal to linesmen. He was convinced the ball was over the line when Clawley cleared, and consequently gave it a goal. There were afterwards many sarcastic shouts of "goal" when the ball passed yards wide of the posts, but I am standing by Mr Kingscott who refereed a difficult game very well.'

113

The replay was at Burnden Park, Bolton but the crowd now was a mere 22,000 with gate receipts of £1,173.

The ground could have held 45,000 but alarmist reports prevented many going for fear of being 'crushed to death'. Bolton had been chosen because of difficulty over the terms at Crystal Palace and a Liverpool objection to the match being played at Everton. The Bolton shopkeepers were the main sufferers having stocked up with thousands of their famous pies which had to be sold off cheap. Again the *Athletic News* account gives us a picture of the game:

'With only a handful of sympathisers from London behind them the Tottenham players were not in such great esteem among the crowd on stepping out, but they speedily ingratiated themselves into popular favour when the ball had been set rolling. A fair idea of how the game went in its early stages is that for nearly half-an-hour Clawley had no work to do.

'Certainly the Southerners by winning the toss gained whatever advantage accrued from a choppy wind which blew diagonally. Such tall kicking were their backs able to indulge in that it seemed imperative the forwards should score this half to do the team any good.

'Several hard drives from Brown, Copeland and Jones were warded off more through good luck than merit on the part of the defenders. Foulke had to come out to meet some others which escaped the ruck in the goalmouth, but reasonable chances were neglected.

'When United did at last get under way they were, even with fewer opportunities, the more dangerous.

'Thickett, from full-back, was actually firing away at Clawley on one occasion and this was a much better attempt to score than some by the crack marksman on the Sheffield side.

'However, a little bit of skirmishing by Needham led to Lipsham passing to the centre and Priest obliged with a shot just inside the post which gave Clawley no chance.

'The wind had dropped when the Hotspur came out to face the second half, a goal in arrears, and they suffered no such handicap as had United for the first half-hour.

'Recollecting two previous Cup-ties in Lancashire when the Tottenham team after the interval made the enemy look like so many inanimate barrels I looked for events at the Sheffield end. They were not long in coming. Six minutes after the change Cameron fastened on a ball twenty yards out and with a hard drive beat the giant in goal all ends up.

'It was now that the war was at its hottest and for a quarter-of-an-hour a rare up-and-a-downer it was. Ever so little luck might have meant a score at either end and the United came nearest to accomplishing their ends.

'Clawley had one or two awkward customers and a ball from Hedley, which glanced off Tait's back, all but caught him unawares. The attack, however, was

The old markings are clearly shown in this picture of the 1901 Cup-Final with Brown scoring for Tottenham Hotspur against Sheffield United.

gradually beaten back and the result of another invasion of the terrace end was that Cameron tried another shot much the same as that which had scored earlier on. This time the ball was deflected, but came out to Smith who made no mistake.

'Tottenham well deserved their lead, but it looked like being discounted the next minute as Priest arrived in front of Clawley in undisputed command. Up came Erentz however and down went the Sheffielder just as folks were counting on his equalising.

'The fate of the Yorkshiremen was by no means sealed yet although there were periods when their half-backs were simply run around. However, eight minutes from the close and from a series of corners taken almost in succession, Brown found his chance to keep level with his previous Cup tie exploits.

'Smith put the ball well across and with a stupendous effort the Tottenham centre got his head to it and it glanced into the rigging. I thought it the best goal of the day and it won the Cup right enough.'

115

13

The 'Little Tin Idol'

The competition is rich in reverse and misfortune and the Challenge Cup itself has not been immune from disaster. The original Cup was hardly the most impressive of trophies bought for a mere £20. Only two firms had been asked to submit designs and on February 13, 1872 the small sub-committee selected one of Martin, Hall & Co.'s.

The Cup was made of silver, though it was soon to be referred to as 'the little tin idol'. It was inscribed 'The Football Association Challenge Cup' and could hold little more than a quart, when it was filled for victory celebrations. On its lid was the figure of a footballer symbolising that the game's the thing. These were the days when ornate and enormous trophies were popular and the small Cup was soon to be dwarfed by the imposing prizes for lesser competitions. Indeed it was soon to be affectionately christened 'the insignificant pot' by the teams who battled for it. The Northern view was more direct and crushing. As Alf Warburton waved it aloft in triumph before Blackburn Olympic carried it away from London a supporter shouted 'Isn't that t'coup? Why it's like a tea kettle'.

The original entries were hardly enough to warrant a more imposing purchase. But anything more ostentatious would also have undermined the amateur principles of the founders of the competition who saw the game as much more important than the prize. It was for this reason that the winning team were to receive only badges or medals of 'trifling value'.

It might have proved necessary to replace the trophy when Wanderers won it three times in succession and became entitled to keep it. But as Alcock returned the Cup on condition that no other Club should ever be allowed to retain it, neither Wanderers', nor Blackburn Rovers' hat-trick of victories cost the F.A. dear.

The magic attraction of the Cup can be measured by the swelling attendances at the Final and the changed value of a ticket. For that first game at the Oval a mere 2,000 came to watch, put off, *Bell's Life* recorded, by the excessive gate charge of one shilling. Compare that with the £50 that the touts could get for a ticket a hundred years later and the desperate struggle for a seat in a stadium holding 100,000.

The explosion of interest followed the provincial success. In 1884 there were still only 4,000 to watch Blackburn Rovers get the best of Queen's Park. But by 1895 interest had grown ten-fold and 42,500 came pouring in to watch the first all Midlands Final and the first at Crystal Palace.

Aston Villa got the better of Albion in that game to become the only Club ever

Goal-area and penalty-area markings had changed by 1905.
Over 100,000 spectators again saw the Final
when Aston Villa beat Newcastle United.

to win, and lose the Cup in the same season. To reward their supporters' enthusiasm Villa put the Cup on display and that was the last that was ever seen of it.

On the night of September 11, 1895 the Cup was stolen from the shop window of William Shillcock football and football boot manufacturer of Newton Row, Birmingham. Extracts from an account in the local paper describe what happened after the Villa Committee handed the Cup to Messrs William Shillcock & Co. for exhibition at their football works. As reported in a Birmingham paper:

'It remained there in the day for the admiration of the crowd and it stayed there at night to invite the envy of the burglar. These premises were locked up at 9 o'clock last night and the Cup was then safely occupying a prominent position in the window. The shop is a one storeyed construction and abuts from the main building. This, of course, facilitated the thieves' plans. The place is a lock-up one

The original F.A. Cup.

£10 REWARD.

STOLEN!

From the Shop Window of W. Shillcock, Football Outfitter, Newtown Row, Birmingham, between the hour of 9-30 p.m. on Wednesday, the 11th September, and 7-30 a.m., on Thursday, the 12th inst., the

ENGLISH CUP,

the property of Aston Villa F.C. The premises were broken into between the hours named, and the Cup, together with cash in drawer, stolen.

The above Reward will be paid for the recovery of the Cup, or for information as may lead to the conviction of the thieves.

Information to be given to the Chief of Police, or to Mr. W. Shillcock, 73, Newtown Row.

The scene of the theft in 1895.

The old Cup winners' medal was
withdrawn after World War I.

The new medal brings the design of
the dress up to date.

and directly the premises were fastened there was little difficulty in gaining access
to the roof of the shop. The zinc covering was removed and a hole large enough
to admit a man was made through the ceiling. Everything then was plain sailing.
The sliding window was pushed back and the Cup abstracted. A few shillings in
the till did not pass unnoticed and then the thieves made good their escape.

'The theft has created a good deal of excitement in football circles. To the
enthusiast the loss has come with so much surprise he is scarcely able to credit
the actual theft of the cherished trophy. Evidence of the amount of feeling the
incident has aroused is marked by the crowd to be seen at the scene of the rob-
bery throughout the morning. The juvenile section of the assembly seemed very
troubled.

'Mr Shillcock is anxious for its historic associations the Cup should not be
lost. He states he is willing to give £10 for its recovery and should the thief take
steps to send back the Cup no enquiries will be made as to who was responsible.

'The real value from the refiners standpoint would not be more than £5 so that
with the offer of £10 there may yet be a chance of getting the trophy returned,
unless it is already either broken or melted.

'When the Aston Villa Committee received the Cup from the National Football Association they were called upon to give a guarantee of the value of £200. The Club insured the trophy for that amount and on lending it to Mr Shillcock made provision for a movable policy which would ensure payment in case of loss. Messrs Shillcock also insured the Cup against burglary. The prize is thus well insured for a good round sum, but no amount would replace the trophy which has played such a thrilling part in the history of football in England. The police, under the direction of Inspector Dobbs, are making active enquiries, but the hope remains that the offer of a reward will be effectual and that the Cup will be sent back. The average football enthusiast would look on the smashing of the English Cup as little short of a National disaster.

'Thus another chapter has been added to the vicissitudes through which the Cup has passed. It is a battered old relic that has done duty at many a banquet; rumour does say that it has been dropped and otherwise maltreated by those who in the hour of victory have consumed more champagne out of it than they could stand. It has been passed round among thousands of pairs of hands; it has been carted round to various towns on chara-bancs and wagonettes; it has been exhibited at bazaars, art galleries, and museums, hostelries, tradesmen's establishments, and public functions innumerable.

'It has been used as a loving cup by a dozen famous clubs and now it is . . . where? there's the question. It must not be forgotten, however, that even when stolen three times in succession it does not become the property of the stealer!'

Despite the enticement of the reward and the zealous efforts of Inspector Dobbs the Cup disappeared without trace and for more than 60 years the mystery remained unsolved.

Then in February 1958 the *Sunday Pictorial* carried as a front page scoop the confession of Harry Burge, an 83-year-old in a Birmingham Corporation Welfare Hostel, who admitted to having stolen the Cup all those years before. There can be no certainty that he was telling the truth for there were some clear discrepancies from the details of entry recorded at the time. Burge claimed that the theft had been on his conscience too long and in the twilight of his days he wished to relieve his mind by giving the details. Memory might now be suspect, but his story was simple and plausible and on the record he was just the person to have carried out the theft. He related that he and two others had broken into the shop about midnight, forcing the back door with a jemmy. Burge had snatched up the Cup while his companions took several pairs of boots and the money in the till. The three then sneaked off to Burge's house close by in Hospital Street. There they broke up the Cup and melted down the fragments in an iron pot. The silver was used to make counterfeit half-crowns. for which they had the moulds. Some of these were passed in a public house kept by Dennis Hodgetts, the Villa forward. With Villa players regularly visiting there several of them may well have handled pieces of the Cup they had won some months before. The plain truth or the fancy of an old man – who can tell? But the story is entirely in keeping with the irony and coincidence of the Cup.

Burge, twice married with a family of five, had been convicted of theft two years later and thereafter was in gaol off and on for a total of 46 years. So he had the right credentials for a raid that aroused as much excitement as the theft of the Crown Jewels. He set an unfortunate precedent for it was in England too that the World Cup was stolen. Neatly lifted from the Stampex Exhibition at Westminster Hall it was sniffed out by the dog 'Pickles' where it had been discarded under pressure of the search. Another strange and mystifying tale with the golden trophy fortunately escaping the melting pot and surviving to be presented to Bobby Moore on that July day of triumph.

Aston Villa were fined £25 by the F.A. – no hardship with all that insurance – and the sum was used to purchase a new Cup from Messrs Vaughton's of Birmingham. But Villa did more than put up the money, they took a personal pride in the replacement. Howard Vaughton was a director of the firm of silversmiths and helped to make this second challenge cup. He had been Villa's first ever international, a fine forward who was at inside left in that first notable Cup victory at the Oval in 1887. One suspects that more than £25 of effort went into the new 'insignificant pot'.

To maintain the past tradition the Cup remained a small and humble trophy. In style and in size there was little change. The honour of winning the Cup continued to dwarf the trophy itself.

To guide him in the work Vaughton was able to obtain exact replicas of the Cup from Wolverhampton Wanderers. Their Chairman, Sir Alfred Hickman, had received permission only two years before to award his players ten-inch-high copies of the Cup to celebrate their victory.

Newcastle were the last team to hold this new trophy. Success had been long delayed for them, the Cup always slipping from their nerveless fingers as the Crystal Palace ground cast its strange spell over their formidable side. But in 1910 they won at last and the excited Tynesiders were only just in time to savour the prize that had eluded them so long. For the Cup itself was presented to Lord Kinnaird by the Council of The Football Association to mark his completion of 21 years as President. They had already decided that the Cup must be replaced, having discovered that the design had been pirated in Manchester and that they were powerless to prevent copies being put in wider circulation. In July the Council passed a resolution 'That the present Football Association Challenge Cup, having been duplicated without the consent of the Association, be withdrawn from competition and a new Cup offered the design of which should be registered.' The third Cup was to cost only 50 guineas with the pattern and craftsmanship to be of more importance than size or weight. Hardly the most attractive or profitable commission in itself, but the trophy's reputation had always been of more importance than the trophy. So the designs and models flowed in from all the leading silversmiths and from the vast number submitted the one chosen was by Messrs Fattorini and Sons of Bradford. Third time lucky indeed for the City as Bradford celebrated by winning the Cup. Never before or after have they even reached the semi-finals.

121

14

The Bridge

'As we were saying when we were so rudely interrupted . . .' was the attitude after the war, with the Cup going on as if nothing had happened. There was a proposal that the Qualifying Competition be dropped and the First Round Proper confined to 40 Clubs, mainly from the First and Second Divisions and the Southern League's First Division (which was about to become the Third Division of the League).

The big Clubs never shared the general amusement if they were tripped up by some unknown team. None of them relished this sort of contest, so the suggestion was natural. But the right to take a tilt at the mighty, was part of the Cup's special appeal. Very properly the F.A. refused to accept an emasculated tournament and 445 teams entered.

But one thing had to change. Crystal Palace had been a War Service Depot and was no longer available, or likely to be fit for use. London by long association and the right of capital was the established centre for the Final, whatever the legitimate claims of Birmingham, Manchester, Liverpool or Sheffield. So for three years the Cup-Final crowds came down the Fulham Road to Stamford Bridge.

There was a comfortable feeling of continuity in 1920 when Aston Villa came through to win. As Andy Ducat, England cricketer and football International, came up to collect the Cup from Prince Henry there were four members of the winning 1913 side behind him. Sam Hardy that most reliable of goalkeepers, Weston, Wallace, and Clem Stephenson had bridged the war years. Their experience and Frank Barson's strength at centre-half took them to the title.

But they had been fortunate indeed to earn the chance at Stamford Bridge. In the quarter-final Tottenham Hotspur would have overwhelmed them, but for the hypnotic brilliance of Sam Hardy. His reputation as the 'Keeper of Keepers' was based on the quiet competence of his handling, the sure instinct of his positional play. As with Gordon Banks, the hallmark of his style was composure and confidence, rather than agile acrobatics.

Billy Walker, who was to make such an impact on the game as player and Manager, was the young Villa centre-forward. Later he wrote of this game that he hardly had a kick at the ball and for 60 minutes it was Hardy against Spurs.

The frustrated crowd kept shouting 'straight at him again' as the ball homed unerringly to Hardy's hands. Villa's winning goal was a sad error by Tommy Clay, that most precise of backs, who sliced the ball into his own net to make the final result a total distortion of the pattern of play.

In the semi-final it was Billy Walker who saw Villa through and saved the

Huddersfield's strong defensive play kept Aston Villa in check for
much of the 1920 Final, the first at Stamford Bridge.

authorities some embarrassment. He scored two of the three goals that defeated
Chelsea, whose powerful team came so close to appearing in the last Final before
the war and the first after it.

Under the rules of the competition the Final should be played on a neutral
ground, but arrangements were too far advanced to alter the venue from Stamford
Bridge even had Chelsea won. With 'home' advantage Chelsea, who finished third
in the League, would have been well placed to win had they survived the semi-final.
But they still had an influence on the Final. For Aston Villa's opponents were
Huddersfield Town whose remarkable revival had been helped by Chelsea.

At the start of the season Huddersfield were in such desperate financial difficulties that they were seriously considering transferring the Club to Leeds, where the
Leeds City team had just been closed down by the F.A. for making illegal

Aston Villa won for the sixth time in 1920.
Prince Henry presented the Cup and medals.

payments during the war. Huddersfield were rescued in part by an appeal to the townspeople to support their soccer and in part by the £2,500 paid by Chelsea to acquire their international centre-forward J. G. (Jack) Cock.

From the threat of dissolution Huddersfield built success, the determination that had saved the Club now fashioning one of the most powerful teams of the decade. They were still a Second Division side when they took on the redoubtable Villa in the Final. But they had one unusual advantage. Their semi-final with Bristol City had been played at Stamford Bridge giving them a preliminary practice on the pitch.

In the end it was the greater experience of the Claret and Blues that proved more important than this trial run. Villa's quick interpassing had Huddersfield at full stretch in those anxious early minutes when nerves affected their play. Only Tom Wilson's sterling play at centre-half gave Huddersfield time to settle. But soon their strong spoiling style jolted Villa out of their rhythm, their moves now too hasty and inaccurate to create the openings.

Huddersfield had suffered a sad blow during the final week of preparation. Their young outside-left W. H. Smith was suspended after an enquiry into an incident in a League match nearly two months earlier. The timing made this a harsh penalty for the individual and his team. Without Smith Huddersfield's attack had little penetration and there was no score at full-time. The players were indulging in handshakes for a hard-fought game when the referee reminded them that it was not yet over. For the first time there was to be extra time at the first meeting of the

124

finalists – a new rule introduced shortly before the war and forgotten by the players. The Referee, Mr Howcroft, was nick-named 'He Who Must Be Obeyed' and the match re-started without delay under his firm control.

In the seventh minute a corner was lobbed into the Huddersfield penalty-area, glancing into the net off the back of Kirton's head. In the press of players not even the scorer was at first quite sure what had happened but Howcroft had no doubts 'The ball went straight in off Kirton's head'.

The Huddersfield team had a good-luck charm – the Aladdin's lamp from a local pantomime which they all touched before taking the field – but no genie appeared to save them.

Despite their last despairing attacks Sam Hardy kept the Cup safe for Villa.

Villa's win briefly concealed the great shifts of power that had taken place. For Huddersfield was to dominate the early twenties along with Bolton Wanderers and neither of these had been the fashionable team of the past. In the wings were Cardiff and Arsenal, while the South generally was much more formidable than before.

The next season, for instance, was Tottenham's. They still had Tommy Clay, a back of the same calibre and outlook as Alf Ramsey, always using the ball to advantage and with a positional sense that concealed a lack of speed. At inside right, Jimmy Seed, later to manage Charlton so effectively, was the find of the season. Arthur Grimsdell, the captain, was the best attacking wing-half in the country and in front he had Bliss and Dimmock as a formidable left-wing. In their first match against Bristol Rovers, Tottenham were rated 'artistic, scientific, and cohesive' taking six goals off a side reduced to ten men. Seed was in great form in the next round against Bradford City the headlines reading:

'Great hat trick – two goals in 30 seconds.' Thereafter the going was harder, but two goals by Bliss from Grimsdell's passes were enough to defeat Preston in the semi-final.

In the Final the rugged Wolves side played above their Second Division form on a pitch muddied by a downpour. But Dimmock, winning a ball back from Woodward made the thrust that mattered. The *Sporting Life* recorded: 'Converging on goal he drove in a great low oblique shot and the ball entered the far corner of the net well out of reach of George.'

Once more, Tottenham fought through to the semi-final the following year and again they met Preston. Spurs had won 5–0 and 2–1 in the League, but as usual that proved meaningless on the day. A goal from Seed put them ahead, but Preston were revived by Joe McCall's defensive skill and by champagne at half-time. Soon they were level, but then Bliss drove home a fierce shot. As the ball was about to cross the line the referee blew his whistle to attend to an injured Preston player and the goal was disallowed. Instead Preston soon scored the winner, going on to meet Huddersfield.

Preston North End have a Jekyll-and-Hyde quality about them, their reputation for skilful play and good sportsmanship occasionally sullied by unaccountable

125

lapses. There had been these lamentable scenes with Queen's Park and now they were concerned in a valedictory game at Stamford Bridge that was rough and un-distinguished. It was fair comment on this match that Huddersfield should win by a penalty and clearly the referee's patience was greater than the Football Association's. Mr Fowler indeed seems to have lost control of this game for even a good referee, like a good player, can have an off day.

It is unusual for the F.A. Minutes to comment on any Cup-Final beyond the bare details of the score. Even the following year's sensational events at Wembley were chronicled with stark simplicity:

'5. Final Tie. The Secretary reported that Bolton Wanderers beat West Ham by two goals to nil at Wembley on 28 April, 1923.'

No mention then of the 200,000 swarming over the ground, of the start delayed 40 minutes, of the questions asked in the House of Commons.

But for this Preston–Huddersfield match the relevant Minute is a little more dis-cursive adding to the bare details of the score the stern rider:

'The Council expressed its great regret at the conduct of some of the players during the match. The Council further expressed the strong hope that there will not be any similar conduct in any future Final tie.'

Huddersfield Town were disposed to discuss the matter further, but received a crushing retort. At the August meeting the Minutes recorded:

'A letter was read from Huddersfield Town enquiring whether the Resolution expressing regret at the conduct of some of the players during the last Final Tie referred to any of their players and asking for names of players and nature of conduct. The Secretary was instructed to reply that the resolution was not con-fined to the players of one team and as the members of the Committee of the Club were present at the match the Council regret that by their enquiry they do not appreciate the discredit brought upon the game by such conduct.'

The F.A. were very wise to leave the culprits anonymous and so shall we.

The decisive goal came as Smith racing into the penalty-area at the end of a long dribble was sent sprawling by Preston's right-back, Hamilton. Despite J. F. Mitchell's efforts to distract him by jumping up and down on his line, Smith drove home the penalty. But should it have been awarded? Here too the unfortunate Mr Fowler gave cause for controversy. For it was strongly held that the crime was committed outside the area and the amateur detectives pointed to a long scar in the ground made, they said, by the tackle and proving their point. Fortunately there were no slow motion play-backs to add to the arguments and no disputing the result.

All three post-war games had ended 1–0 and only Dimmock's flashing goal had relieved the curious anonymity of this interlude at Stamford Bridge.

But the new stage was ready and there was to be no lack of drama from the opening curtain.

126

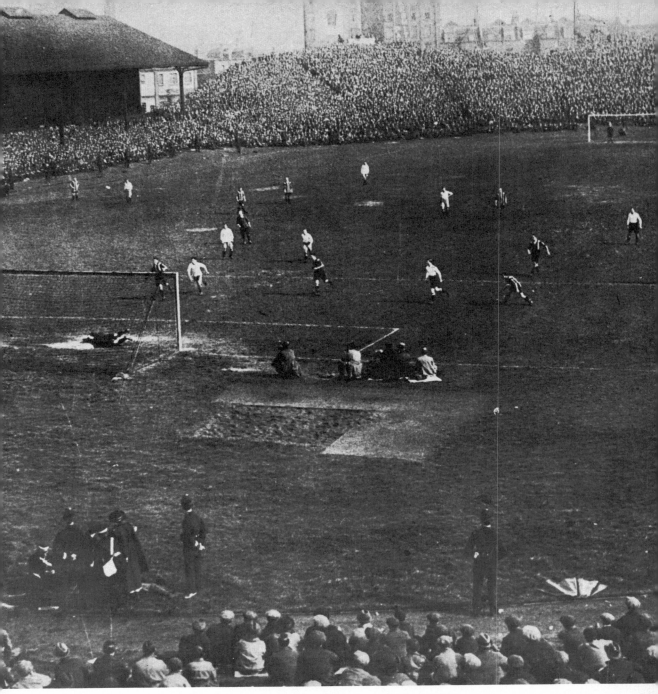

After an interval of twenty years the Cup came south in 1921.
Dimmock, Tottenham Hotspur's outside-left, scored
the goal against Wolverhampton.

15

Wembley – The Early Years

The move to Wembley proved beyond doubt how vast was soccer's appeal; everyone was taken by surprise as a tidal wave of people flooded in for that first Final in 1923.

The number who passed through the turnstiles was 126,047, but the press and the pictures indicate that close on a quarter of a million were at the ground.

The Stadium was ready for football a year before the British Empire Exhibition officially opened. It was completed only four days before the match at a cost of £750,000. Construction required 25,000 tons of concrete and it had taken only 300 working days to build. The site in Wembley Park had previously been a golf course. A pond there had been a haunt of herons, who left countless footprints in the concrete before finally accepting the loss of their home. Sir Thomas Watkin had planned earlier to build in the park a massive tower to rival the Eiffel in Paris. But the foundations shifted and the project was abandoned.

The F.A. Ground Committee visited Wembley in 1921 and Sir Charles Clegg, as President of the F.A., completed a 21-year agreement with the authorities.

As the work neared its end an infantry battalion was brought in to mark time on the terraces testing their strength. Amid the final trials and precautions the one point overlooked was the need to limit the crowd. This was understandable. Stamford Bridge had only attracted 53,000 the year before and Wembley was thought capable of holding 127,000. The arrangements for the seating and control were the responsibility of the British Empire Exhibition authorities and they did not foresee the need to make this an all-ticket occasion. There was no check at railway stations, no warning of the human torrent that swept into the stadium breaking barriers, taking over turnstiles, flooding the pitch. Only the mounted police and Constable G. A. Scorey on his white horse made play possible. The white horse symbolised for everyone the way in which order was miraculously re-established out of total chaos. Policeman Scorey is now dead, but his tale was told by Eric Todd in *The Guardian*:

'Anyway, you want to hear about the Final. Well, whatever credit there was went to Billie (his horse). It was the first time he really behaved himself too. Funnily enough, neither of us had expected to be at the match, and I wasn't bothered as I wasn't keen on football. In any case I was always on duty for Saturdays. A detachment of mounted police was in reserve about four miles away from the Stadium, standing by just in case anything out of the ordinary cropped up, although we weren't expecting to be called on. I know I was thinking about my wedding and not about football.

128

Sir Frederick Wall and Sir Charles Clegg look at Wembley Stadium
as it nears completion for the 1923 Cup-Final.

'It would be about 2.30 that we got the order to mount and proceed to
Wembley as soon as possible. We arrived there about the time kick-off was due
with orders to clear the pitch. Clear the pitch indeed! You couldn't see it. I felt
like giving it up as hopeless because there was nobody in charge I could see and
I just didn't know where to start. Anyway, Billie knew what to do. He pushed
forward quietly but firmly and the crowd made way for him. He answered all my
orders beautifully and although it was hard work, the crowd – and they were
good-natured – seemed to respect the horse. I told them to link hands and push
away from the touchline and I remember telling one chap with one leg to get in
the goal and stay there.

'Inside half-an-hour the job was done and the match started. I stopped there,
of course, although I can't remember much about the game. As I say, I wasn't
very keen on football and have never seen a match since, but I believe Jack
scored one of the goals . . .'

April 28, 1923 was the date of the first Wembley Final. An estimated
crowd of 200,000 people forced their way into the new stadium.

And he remembers putting the horse in its stable and then calling round to Kitty,
his girl friend. He remembers too, her asking him what sort of a day he had had –
and the answer he gave her. 'Oh, just ordinary, lass. Just ordinary!'

Scorey gave further details of what happened as his horse went up the touchline
easing people back. He had continued up the touchline until some of the crowd got
a bit stubborn and he had to call out 'Don't you want to see the match'. 'Yes' they
shouted back and Scorey said 'So do I. Now those in front join hands.' Then he
gave the word to heave and they went back step by step until the lines were clear.
When the teams tossed George Kay, captain of West Ham, said 'What about the
white horse on the penalty-spot, ref?' Without that horse many other people might
have been on the spot.

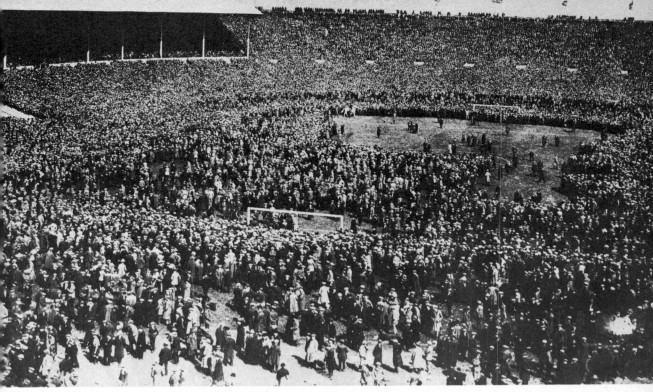

The famous picture of the policeman on the white horse helping
to control the over-eager spectators.

It was fortunate indeed that no one was killed and in the House of Commons
there were calls for an Inquiry. But complaints of hooliganism were quickly refuted.
The record of the debate includes: Mr J. Jones: 'May I say that as far as the crowd
were concerned they were good-humoured? (hear, hear). If it had not been for the
conduct of the police and the good humour of the crowd there would have been
murder. Therefore the hon. gentleman has no right to talk about hooliganism.'
(Ministerial cheers). Mr F. O. Roberts: 'Is the Home Secretary aware of the almost
universal praise of the conduct of the police especially of the officer who was
mounted on a white horse?' (laughter and cheers).

Altogether 12 Inspectors, 53 Sergeants, and 530 constables struggled to bring
order, but it was the presence of the King that was as effective as anything else.
'As the King appeared the whole vast gathering turned towards the royal enclosure
and stood to attention as the National Anthem was played. It was followed by
three mighty cheers which must have been heard far beyond Wembley and then,
after this display of enthusiastic loyalty the work of clearing the field was continued.'

Watching was an exhausting affair that day. 'I've paid a guinea for my ticket and
cannot get to my seat,' grumbled a man wedged in the crowd. 'I'd pay double that
to get out!' was his neighbour's response.

131

King George V acknowledges the cheers of the crowd
spilling over Wembley's pitch.

But it was even more difficult on the pitch. 'It isn't true that I said the best pass I received was from a spectator,' commented a West Ham winger. 'But it is a fact that, when taking corners, I had to lean on the spectators and say, "Now if you will give me a push I can take one stride and kick the ball".'

Ted Vizard, Bolton's outside-left, gave this account of the game:

'After finally shoving our way on to the pitch we had the unforgettable sight of a solid wall of spectators round the touchlines. It felt as though we were going to play football in a human box.

'The game started and within a few minutes we were one up. That early goal was just what we needed to put us on our game after that long anxious wait in the dressing room. I shall never forget David Jack's shot flashing past Ted Hufton – nor the pass that Joe Smith gave me later in the game, nor my long dribble to the corner flag. Cutting in down the goal line I saw J. R. Smith running into

David Jack of Bolton Wanderers scoring in the first-ever
F.A. Cup-Final at Wembley two minutes after the start.

position. As he fastened on to my centre I watched him screw the ball into the
net before the West Ham defenders knew what was happening.

Few other people on pitch or in the crowd realised at once what had happened
as the ball bounced straight back into play from the mass of spectators wedged
against the back of the net.

The conditions may have hampered West Ham most. Certainly their trainer,
Charlie Paynter, had a different view of the white horse, whose hooves had
helped to churn up the touchline.

'It was a pitch made for us until folks tramped all over the place and that white
horse thumped its big feet into the pitch. When the game started it was hopeless.
Our wingers, Ruffell and Richards were tumbling all over the place, tripping up
in great ruts and holes.'

In 1924 Newcastle took their revenge for Aston Villa's victory
of 1905 when Harris gave them the lead eight minutes from the end.

The West Ham plan had depended on flying wingers and the smooth forward
play that had brought them five goals in the semi-final. At centre-forward they had
Vic Watson, the most prolific scorer in the Club's history, and in better conditions
this attack was good enough to have taken the Cup. But on the day their captain
commented: 'The better team won. We did not touch our real form.'

West Ham still celebrated that night, driving through cheering crowds in a tram
decorated with crossed hammers and with a congratulatory message on the side
illuminated in electric lights.

Bolton Wanderers relished their first taste of Wembley coming back for more at
regular intervals. The Cup was theirs in 1923, 1926, and 1929 and over all that
period only seventeen players were needed to achieve those honours. No goal was
scored against them in the three matches so chief praise must go to the defence. In
goal Pym, the Devon fisherman, was competent and agile. But he was well protected by Seddon's command in the air and Nuttall's hard tackling. Forward there was
David Jack, tall and slim with the feel for an opening. It was he who decided the
game against Manchester City sending his shot arrowing into the net from Vizard's
centre.

But it was the nice balance of the forward line that made it so dangerous – Joe
Smith and Ted Vizard, a menacing left-wing, Butler fast and forceful on the right.
And it was Butler whose tremendous shot put Bolton ahead against Portsmouth
with only twelve minutes left. Blackmore moving as threateningly in the centre as
J. R. Smith had done before him, settled the game with another fine goal.

Lewis, the Arsenal goalkeeper, made a tragic mistake in the 1927
Final, allowing Cardiff to take the Cup out of England for the first time.

Ferguson, who scored the goal, raises his arms in triumph as
Davies jumps over the prostrate Lewis.

Johnson of Sheffield United in one of the three fierce semi-final
battles with Huddersfield Town in 1928.

In 1924 Newcastle United wiped out one bitter memory, the score against Aston
Villa a neat reversal of Crystal Palace in 1905. Both teams played stylishly and well
to contrive a match worthy of their varied talent. For long it looked as if the skills
of the great William Walker would drive Villa to yet another victory. But with only
eight minutes to go it was Newcastle's centre-half, Spencer, who worked the ball
up and Harris who slammed it home. Before Villa could recover their wits Seymour had sent another fierce shot flying into the net. Newcastle's luck had matched
their skill at last. But fortune kept a sting in the tail. Shortly before the Final Villa
had beaten them 6–1 in a League game and Newcastle were fined £750 for playing
weak teams in this and six other matches.

Thirty-six years later Leeds were to be fined £5,000 when their exhausting chase
for three titles forced them to a similar expedient.

The year 1925 saw a meeting of old masters and new hopefuls. Sheffield United
had won crushingly in that last Final before the war and now they played with a
confidence that Cardiff never matched. Gillespie, the Sheffield captain, was the
outstanding player, but for all his authority and his team's dominance the game
was settled by one momentary hesitation. Cardiff's left-half, Wake, waited to
intercept Pantling's long swinging pass, but Tunstall gathered the ball first to go
through and score.

Arsenal reached the Final for the first time in 1927, transformed by Herbert
Chapman's shrewd leadership. When he joined Arsenal the year before he had
taken them from 20th to second in the League, the first step in building them to be
the outstanding team of their time.

It was surprising that Arsenal had taken so long to make a decisive impact in

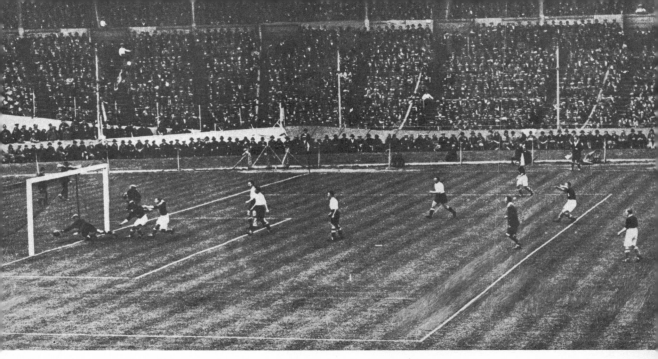

A sensational opening to the Final of 1928, Roscamp scoring
for Blackburn Rovers with sixty seconds gone.

Cup or League. The Club had been started by a group of men from Nottingham who had come down for employment at Woolwich Arsenal. These ammunition workers of the Dial Square section formed their own club, the Royal Arsenal F.C., at a meeting at Royal Oak in 1886.

By 1890 they were good enough to win the Kent Senior Cup beating Thanet Wanderers 3–0 and to run the Old Westminsters close in the Final of the London Senior Cup. Their success led to election to the Second Division of the Football League in 1893 together with Newcastle United, Middlesbrough Ironopolis and Rotherham Town.

Not until 1904 could Arsenal win promotion to the First Division, where they were to remain, except for 1913–14 and the following season.

When they were relegated they established a record for the lowest number of points and goals of a First Division Club. And in the Cup the only record Arsenal had established was to lose the longest tie ever played, five meetings with New Brompton. Not until 1924 was this to be exceeded in time, when Barrow and Leyton each took nine hours to beat Gillingham and Ilford respectively. True Arsenal twice reached the semi-final, but there they had lost to Newcastle and Sheffield Wednesday.

In 1920 they were talked back into the First Division when its numbers increased by two. In the last full season before the war Chelsea and Tottenham had been due for relegation, but were now expected to get the two extra places.

Sir Henry Norris's eloquence on behalf of Arsenal had his Club substituted for

Arsenal, 1929–30: *back row:* Baker, Lambert, Preedy, Seddon, Hapgood, John; *middle row:* Mr Herbert Chapman (*Manager*), Jack, Parker, James, Mr T. Whittaker (*Trainer*); *front row:* Hulme, Bastin.

Spurs, in preference also to two teams who had finished higher in the Second Division.

For five seasons Arsenal did little to justify the decision. Then came Chapman with new tactics, new players and an infectious confidence. Buchan was brought in from Sunderland to captain the side, Hulme from Blackburn to give speed to the attack, Parker from Southampton to give poise to the defence. To counteract the change in the off-side law, the centre-half was converted to a 'third-back' and an inside-forward brought deep to link defence and attack.

With 'Policeman' Roberts taking over as centre-half Arsenal reached the Final at last the following year, despite an unusually poor performance in the League. They were lucky to survive the game at Port Vale when Parker put through his own goal and also conceded a penalty. Brain finally earned the replay with two minutes left.

The Cardiff side they met were then at the height of their powers, with eight

A shot by Alex James surprises the Huddersfield
defence and Arsenal are on the way to winning the
Cup for the first time in 1930.

internationals in the team. City's strength was at half-back with Keenor peerless in
his play and leadership.

The quality of the football was not in keeping with the great potential of the
footballers on the field, but it was a unique occasion for all that. For the only time
in its history the Cup was to go outside England, won through a sad error by the
Welsh International in Arsenal's goal.

From a Cardiff throw-in Ferguson the centre-forward took a pass to shoot hard
and low. Down went goalkeeper Dan Lewis on his right knee getting the ball in the
crook of his left arm, to be challenged by Davies. Instead of throwing it clear his
desperate fumblings sent the ball trickling back over the goal line. According
to Lewis the ball 'twisted on his chest'. For him it was a moment of heartbreak,

The Graf Zeppelin crossed Wembley Stadium during the
Arsenal and Huddersfield Final in 1930.

but for Cardiff and Wales the heady triumph of success. The ball was in the net.
What matter how it got there?

With their great half-back line of Keenor, Sloan, and Hardy and competent backs
in Nelson and Watson, the remaining seventeen minutes gave Cardiff few worries.

Buchan with his deceptive swerve and sharp intuition had made three clear
chances that had been cast aside. He could do no more, And in truth, Cardiff,
second in the First Division, had taken the Cup by right, teaching Arsenal one
lesson on the way. Ever afterwards it has been an Arsenal tradition that a new
jersey is always washed before use so that no grease remains in the wool.

Dejection at Highbury, jubilation in the valleys, was followed by one of those
strange reversals of fortune. For the losers it was the curtain-raiser to great achieve-

Lambert heads one of Arsenal's eleven goals against Darwen
in the third round in 1931.

ments, for the victors prelude to a disastrous slide that saw them applying for re-
election only seven years later.

Much of Arsenal's success was in the League, but they were back to win the Cup
in 1930, and again in 1936, losing out in between to Newcastle in the 'ball over the
line' Final of 1932. Their first success came against Chapman's old team Huddersfield, the other dominating Club of the day. It was started when James slipped a
quick free-kick to Bastin and took a perfect return in his stride. The ball was in the
net before Huddersfield could cover – a goal by James as surprising as the move
itself. For the mid-field genius with the baggy pants and sly footwork was not
given to scoring. And it was a telling pass from James that sent Lambert through
to score the second, decisive goal.

Small wonder that Huddersfield's defence was stretched to destruction despite
men of the calibre of Goodall at back and Wilson at centre-half. For the Arsenal

141

In 1931 after an equaliser by Birmingham, Richardson
tapped the ball into the net for West Bromwich Albion
immediately following the re-start.

line had Hulme's burning speed on the right, Bastin's dash and power of shot on the left, Lambert to link the line in the middle, and the elegant David Jack to hover as a second striker. With Alex James pacing and directing the game, David Jack's third winning medal came easily enough. But Huddersfield's relentless endeavour made for a struggle so absorbing that few were distracted when the Graf Zeppelin floated overhead.

In 1932 Newcastle were their opponents, about to enjoy the good fortune that so cruelly eluded them at Crystal Palace. Within quarter-of-an-hour Arsenal had moved smoothly into the lead by a goal from John now teamed with Bastin on the left. The challenge fired Newcastle who came driving back with fierce insistence.

Davidson, Newcastle's centre-half, intercepted a clearance of Hapgood's and sent a long pass arching down his right flank. Richardson, who had switched places with Boyd, raced after the ball while Arsenal covered carefully. The final bounce seemed to have taken the ball over the line and the defence pulled up with Hapgood ambling out of play. But Richardson hooked the ball back and Allen headed home.

Mr W. Harper, the referee, pointed to the centre and a disbelieving Arsenal team made a momentary show of protest. But Parker, the captain, lived up to his nickname of 'Gentleman Tom'. At once he waved his players to their places.

This was the first of the inquisitions by camera and film shots appeared to confirm that the ball had been over the line. But in a fast-moving game such errors – if

142

error it were – are to be expected once in a while and the disciplined restraint with which Arsenal accepted misfortune recognised this fact. Yet such an incident nags at the mind and Newcastle steadily took charge of the game until Allen, not too popular a choice on Tyneside, became their hero with a second goal.

Sheffield is never far from the centre of football's stage and both its Clubs were quick to add to Wembley's pageant. After United's success in 1925 came Wednesday's in 1935.

Manager William Walker's instructions were to shoot low and often, playing on a suspected weakness on the ground of goalkeeper Pearson. But the decisive goal of that swaying contest with Albion was a desperate chase for a bouncing ball, which Rimmer flicked past Pearson to put Wednesday 3–2 ahead with five minutes to go. The other ace in Walker's pack was the captain, Starling. He was one of those footballers like Len Shackleton of Sunderland in a later day, whose sleight of foot baffles friend as well as foe. Such individualists are difficult to fit into a team, but so good was Starling that Walker fitted the team to him. And in the Final Starling was told to save himself for the second half when his shadowers would tire and might be less vividly aware of his menace. Starling's influence was decisive in the closing phase with Rimmer adding another goal seconds from time.

United were carrying Sheffield's colours the next year, the red and white replacing the blue and white. But Arsenal were their opponents, still in full pride of their powers, still not fully rewarded in the Cup for their mastery of the period. There were no new faces in their team, no change in the lethal power of their forward line or the cold certainty of their defence. At back, Hapgood and Male were a combination as powerful for England as Crompton and Pennington had been.

Joe Mercer, that outstanding Everton and Arsenal player, who was later to take Manchester City to such success in English and European Cups, rates Hapgood as the best captain he has ever seen, a powerful leader of men, and an inspiration in his play. 'Policeman' Roberts was still there flanked by Copping, the iron man of football, and Sheffield could find no weakness in that formidable defence.

Up front there was now Ted Drake, who ranks with Dean, Lawton, and Lofthouse as one of the great exponents of the typical English centre-forward game. Robust, courageous, and goal-hungry he was a menace to centre-halves and goalkeepers. Not for him the delicate mid-field skills of a Bobby Charlton, or the clever laying off of the ball with which Lambert had made openings for others. Direct and challenging his method was best expressed in a game against Aston Villa where he had eight openings and scored seven goals.

Smith, leaping, diving, throwing himself at the forwards' feet, kept the score to a single goal, scored inevitably by Drake despite a strapped knee.

For all the reputation that Arsenal established there were other great teams challenging them throughout the seasons. In the Cup Manchester City were almost as dangerous with the formidable Sam Cowan at centre-half, the cool and cultured skills of Matt Busby midfield and the dash of Eric Brook on the left-wing. City had

143

Everton F.C. 1933; *back row:* H. E. Cooke (Trainer), C. R. Britton, W. Cresswell, E. Sagar, W. Cook, T. White, J. Thomson; *front row:* A. Geldard, J. Dunn, W. R. Dean, T. C. F. Johnson, J. Stein, E. Critchley.

lost narrowly in 1926. That had been the first Final played under the new off-side rule which so defeated the legislators' aims. Introduced to aid scoring its effect was circumvented by the new emphasis on defensive play and the rugged 'stopper' centre-halves. City's clever forwards were usually good enough to break out of this strait-jacket, with their quick passing and swift interchange of positions. For the 1933 Final, however, they left out Tilson, a vital link at centre-forward, and they came too early to Wembley dressing-rooms, letting the tension build. Their nervous intensity gave them early control of the game, but the goal did not come and they faded sadly to leave the field to Everton. The new numbering was 1 to 22 and City were the high-numbered also rans. Langford with double figures on his jersey was also doubly in error. Goalkeepers then kept close to their line, not yet developed into the mobile, handling third back who can dominate the whole area. Centres that would now be cut out, too often reached the centre-forward. And to let the ball reach the head of William Ralph Dean – the immortal 'Dixie' – was to make disaster certain. In the age of the defensive centre-half he scored 379 League goals, beating Bloomer's record of 352 and bringing Everton's football back to the peaks.

In 1931 Everton won the Second Division Championship; the First Division Championship in 1932; and here was the hat-trick of success, the greatest triumph of them all, the Cup in 1933. No wonder Merseyside came flocking to see Dean and that poised elegant player Warney Cresswell, once of South Shields and Sunderland, capped twelve years before for England and now with a mellow maturity. These two destroyed Manchester as they had destroyed so many other sides. The goals came in orderly confirmation of Everton's command. Stein first, then Dean, then Dunn so that there was no twist, no surprise on that sunny afternoon. How different next year. In one of the outstanding Wembley Finals City came back to win the Cup with a young goalkeeper only 19-years old.

The 1934 Final had a full measure of excitement, coincidence, and personality, with fast attacking football as a pleasant bonus. There was the 19-year-old Frank Swift in goal for Manchester City and so lacking his later confidence that he fainted at the final whistle. There was Jack Tinn, Portsmouth's colourful Manager, whose side had no luck despite his ritual donning of the white spats that had become part of soccer's pageant and his team's success. There was Matt Busby, City's resourceful midfield player who was later to be United's organising genius, the doyen of modern football. There was Fred Tilson, a forceful Yorkshireman to lead a Lancashire attack. The referee was Stanley Rous who was to become such a power in football administration the world over.

The portents and the traditions of the Cup pointed to a Manchester victory and the day was to bring no surprises. City had been beaten at Wembley the previous year and any losing team that had bounced straight back to the Final had always won the following season. In the semi-final they had annihilated Aston Villa overwhelming them 6–1 on Huddersfield's ground with some masterfully aggressive play. In April they had beaten Portsmouth 2–1 in the League. That was a prophetic preliminary; but City were to need all their tenacity and the favours of fortune to repeat the score when it really mattered.

The goalkeeper's eye view of the game is an unusual one as if peering through alternate ends of a telescope. The figures are now remote miniatures in the far distance, now larger than life and in sharp relief. As for the soldier, there are long periods of boring inactivity alternating with brief spells of frenzied action. It was this that played on Swift's nerves and left every move, every word, every thought seared in his memory. He was to die later in that grim emotive crash on Munich's snow-swept airport. But he had recorded his impressions of the game and we can live it again through his eyes. In *Football from the Goalmouth*, edited by Roy Peskett, Swift described his feelings.

The night before his captain, Sam Cowan, had kept him awake into the small hours telling endless stories as much to take his own mind from the memory of the previous year's defeat as to still the apprehensions of the eager youngster. As he talked, Cowan had bathed a septic toe, unreported for fear of missing the match.

145

A late lie-in, a brisk walk, the youngest member's standard chore of purchasing chewing gum for the team, those were the time-honoured preliminaries to the drive to the Stadium. But while Bud Flanagan kept the Portsmouth players' minds off the game by cracking jokes in their dressing room there was no such relief across the corridor. One City player was so nervous the reserve had to lace up his boots and the sight suddenly made Swift sick with apprehension. When he fumbled his way to the washroom Alec Ball the trainer give him short shrift and no sympathy. A slap in the face, a tot of whisky and a 'Get back in there you big lug, no one's going to eat you', was the successful treatment.

Now Sam Cowan calls: 'This is it, lads, lets get going,' and beyond the long cavernous tunnel looms the bright sunlight and the massed faces. The shock wave of cheering hammers at the players. Sam Cowan introduces his team to the King commenting on Fred Tilson, reputedly the most kicked player in football: 'This is our centre-forward, Tilson, Your Majesty. He is the man who plays with two broken legs.' Gravely Tilson puts the record straight 'He's nobbut kidding thee, thy Majesty'. The ripple of amusement relieves the anxious wait.

The pitch was a vivid green with the lines standing out like white silk ribbons. But the surface lacked the usual smoothness and Sam Cowan grumbled that it was so rough he would not play a wood off it.

Hardly has play started than the ever-thoughtful Matt Busby pushes a pass back to Swift so that he can get a feel of the ball. On the quarter-hour a sudden shower makes Swift peer upfield to see if Gilfillan in the Portsmouth goal is putting on his gloves. He would have done better to trust his own instincts, rather than follow the Portsmouth goalkeeper's example, and leave his gloves in the corner of the net. For soon the ball is nestling there as well. Rutherford comes coasting in from the wing and his cross shot slithers off Swift's outstretched fingers.

'Just another Wembley goalkeeper!' he thinks bitterly. At half-time City are still a goal down and he sits disconsolate and miserable. Fred Tilson walks up. 'What's up with thee?' 'I thought I should have saved their goal.' 'Thee doesn't need to worry. I'll plonk in two next half.'

An easy promise to soothe a dejected youngster, but incredibly he is as good as his word. The game, hard fought in midfield, begins to flow away from Swift's view as City drive forward ever more determinedly. But the tall blond Allen at the heart of Portsmouth's defence coldly snuffs out the surging assaults. Only 17 minutes to go and Sam Cowan moves up for a corner. As he races in with his eyes on the ball he cannons into Allen. Allen is carried off the field in pain to be treated beside the goal.

Gone now is the hinge of Portsmouth's defence and the door to goal swings open. Matt Busby's quick, long throw finds Eric Brook moving to the right. Cutting inside he flicks a pass to Tilson on his left and the centre-forward moves through unchallenged to slide the ball home. Allen comes stumbling back, white and shaken, and Portsmouth rage upfield to keep Swift at full stretch. But ten minutes later Toseland pushes the ball up to Alec Herd and again Tilson picks up the pre-

146

cise pass. Again he hits the ball smoothly home, a careful, confident left-foot shot. A moment later Swift is diving full length to save Worrall's header at the foot of the post. And now his ordeal intensifies. His own words recall the tension:

'I'll tell you why I fainted at the end of this terrific battle. On either side of the goal, near the posts, two or three photographers were still perched, presumably in the hope of snapping Portsmouth's equaliser – should it come. One of them, probably seeing how tense I was, waiting for the final whistle, began to tick off the minutes for me. His colleagues at the other post helped.

'"Three minutes to go." The photographer's excited voice heightened the terrific tension. My heart was pounding away, and I had difficulty in focusing my full attention on the field of play. The City lads were still keeping the play in the Portsmouth half. I was glad, for I'm sure had somebody shot the ball at me at this moment, I would have fumbled.

'"Only two minutes left, Frank." Jackie Bray had the ball now, juggling with it before sending a long, looping pass up the field, the ball running out of play near the Portsmouth corner flag. The play seemed a long way off, or was it because things were becoming a little hazy. Sam Cowan, still tucked handy near the burly Weddle, has a quick glance over his shoulder to see where his full-backs are positioned.

'"One minute to go." Mr Rous is looking at his watch. Then he glances across to his linesmen to check their times, I wish he'd blow the whistle. Laurie Barnett glances back reassuringly at me. How I envy Laurie his coolness. Above the hubbub of the vast crowd, I hear an agonized voice shout, "Come on Portsmouth". I wondered idly if he were a sailor, and where . . .

'"Only fifty seconds, you're nearly there lad." I thought how pleased Mother would be, and brother Fred, and all of my dear family, at the glory which had come to their youngest member . . . Alec Herd tackles Nichol. There's no letting up with the Cup so close. Odd thoughts are beginning to run through my mind . . . I wonder if the Cup takes much cleaning . . .

'"Forty seconds, you've done 'em now" . . . Up in the Royal Box the King and Queen are still intently watching as the 1934 Cup-Final slowly runs out into history. I try to remember the drill we've been given. Winning team goes up first after the National Anthem, the captain takes the Cup and his medal. Then the rest of the team receive their medals. Then the losing team. I expect I'll drop my gloves, or my cap, or both . . . I hope the King says something to me. And I'll bet I'm so nervous if he does, I won't know what to say . . .

'"Thirty seconds, it's your Cup, son." Matt Busby smashes the ball into touch. A Portsmouth player despairingly tries to hurry it from the hands of a ball boy. I notice there's a flurry of movement near the entrance to the tunnel leading to the Royal Box. The Guards have come out, ready to line up on the grass. Eric Brook stands out on the left wing, beaming. I'm glad for all the lads who lost the Final last year. This time its O.K. Racing through my brain is the thought, I

147

Mutch scores for Preston in the last minute of extra time in 1938.

must shake Sam Cowan by the hand. Good old Sam. It's his Cup, if it's anybody's, and Fred Tilson, and Tosey, and Alec Herd, and Jackie Bray . . .

'"There's the whistle, it's all over." I stoop into the net for my cap and gloves,
take a couple of steps out to meet Sam . . . Then everything went black.

'I had fainted. I still think it was because of the tremendous nerve strain,
through the mounting tension and excitement, as those photographers, helpful
as they were, ticked away the dying moments of the game.

'Sam helped me to my feet, and I limped across to where the other players and
officials were waiting for our skipper to lead the parade up to the Royal dais.

'"How are you feeling now, my boy?" says a deep voice. It is the King
speaking.

'"Fine, Sir," says the lad.

'"That's good. You played well. Here is your medal, and good luck." '

16

Prelude to War

The three seasons before Hitler put a six-year stop on the Challenge Cup were notable for two great matches and one memorable incident.

The incident was Mutch's penalty in the last minutes of 1938. In the Cup history is apt to reverse not repeat itself. And here were Preston and Huddersfield once again locked in dour, inconclusive struggle. Extra time was nearly spent when Mutch was tripped and this time it was Preston with the chance to avenge the defeat of 1922.

For so many of these Wembley years the radio had brought the Cup-Final into the homes of those not fortunate enough to be at Wembley. The pace at first was leisurely with one commentator keeping us informed of the position of the ball by reference to a plan of the field divided into squares. But as in the game itself the pace of the presentation soon quickened and it was realised that possession not position was the key to football. The voice of the broadcaster quickened also, though still calm and controlled compared with the excited intensity that reflects today's more uninhibited approach. Here was how the millions at their sets heard Tommy Woodruffe describe that most dramatic moment in the long history of the Cup, everything depending on a single kick at the end of two hours desperate struggle:

> 'It goes into the centre of the field again. Everyone's having a bit of a kick at it. Preston's inside left gets it and passes back to O'Donnell who passes to Mutch, who's got it on the edge of the area. He tries to shoot – and he's tripped and that IS a penalty.
>
> 'Mutch is taking it himself with Hesford standing on his goal line. Hesford is licking his fingers – he's got to stand still. Mutch is taking it. Here it comes. And it's a goal. It's a goal! But it very nearly wasn't a goal. The shot hit the bar and I must say Hesford had no chance at all.'

Preston had their reward at last. An overdue win for a Club whose periods of pre-eminence are too little reflected in the competition's results. One driving force in the team had been Bill Shankly, later to lift Liverpool to the heights that are demanded as of right in that football-wise, football-crazy city. The determination was always there, the conviction that one never accepted second best from any man or any team.

In the first game the great Tom Finney played for Preston. Shankly kept him going with lusty shouts of 'Come on, we can still do it'. They were a mere four goals behind with two minutes to go!

Shankly's dedication was evident in the way he played with the palms of his hands turned outwards creating the illusion of a sailing ship striving for that little extra help from the wind. 'I played on ma toes all the time. Like a ballet dancer. That gave me strength in me calves and ah've still got it' was his recent description of his play. Had Mutch been injured in that tackle by Young it was Shankly who would have taken the penalty.

The story goes that Mutch was told: 'Shut thee eyes and hit the ruddy thing,' and the shot ricochetting down from the underside of the bar looked as if that was indeed his method.

Until that penalty, Huddersfield had been splendidly served by Young, a square-shouldered, destructive centre-half who dominated the middle. On their right was Joe Hulme, a little slower than in his Arsenal days, but still a dangerous winger. Sadly he was on the losing side for this his fifth final and the last game of his career. In 1924 he had cost Blackburn Rovers only £250 and a year later Arsenal paid £3,500 for him. What a small price by today's standards for a man who scored 108 goals in his Arsenal career.

Preston North End had been in the Final the previous year taking the lead before they were bewitched by Horatio Carter. There was another man to stand out amid the masters of the game – 'Raich' still a name that rings down the years. He played at a time when the key to success was the power of wing-halves and insides. They were expected to be both the labourers and the brains of the side, doing the hard work in midfield and being creative enough to make the openings.

All this Carter achieved. His swift intelligence and instinctive understanding of the game allowed him to cover the ground without appearing to hurry, to split the defence without appearing to have considered the pass. Sunderland born he led a Sunderland side that had been League champions the year before.

Yet for all Carter's urging Sunderland were curiously restrained in the first half. Preston went ahead as Dougal darted from the right into the centre. O'Donnell veered outside him, anticipated his pass, and beat Mapson with his shot.

But this was a tale of two halves and Sunderland wrote the second. Thomson and McNab drove upfield to release the latent power of their forwards. Within six minutes Gurney had put them level and with twenty minutes still to go Carter's genius expressed itself in a goal of brilliant design. Before the end Burbanks made sure with a powerful shot from the acutest of angles. Sunderland with their great record in the League and their many fine teams had waited long in the wings of the competition. This was their moment of triumph.

Having captained one side to its only Cup victory, Carter was to achieve the same for Derby County. His hair silvering, but his brain as shrewd as ever, he helped them to success in the first of the post-war Finals.

The bright spring of 1939 was shadowed by the remorseless march of Nazism. But still there was hope of 'peace in our time' and absorption with soccer. The Challenge Cup went on unheeding with supporters' minds on Wembley rather than the Rhine.

Smith, in Sheffield United's goal, kept the score to 1–0 when
Arsenal won the Cup for the second time in 1936.

Wolverhampton Wanderers were the most exciting team in the country, their
eager young forwards with a string of fine performances behind them. In a League
match, the leaders, Everton, had been beaten 7–0 and in the semi-final Grimsby had
been crushed 5–0.

Portsmouth were a more prosaic team just out of danger at the bottom of the
table, while Wolves were lying second. But on the day the favourites faltered while
Portsmouth were full of ideas and running. Barlow, who had earlier that season
been in the Wolves side, made them regret his transfer. He started the scoring and
never stopped causing them trouble. Anderson added a second before half-time
and afterwards Parker scored twice, the fourth goal headed in from Worrall's
centre. With a lucky sixpence in his boot and a miniature horseshoe in his pocket
Worrall had a splendid match on Portsmouth's right-wing.

Wolves ravenous forwards had turned tame and listless on the day that mattered.
Dorsett's one goal was no more than a passing gesture as Portsmouth took their
fortune at its tide. Portsmouth had done it at the third time of asking and they were
to keep the Cup for the six dark years of war.

151

17

Post-War Selection

Running through the hundred years of the Cup are two constant strands of criticism. The players aren't as good as they were and the football is always poor in the Finals. Let us consider these complaints in relation to Wembley's post-war record.

Though styles may become less attractive, standards have, in fact, risen. With the money, effort, and thought that has been poured into the game no other outcome was possible. Technical and tactical skills have improved even if the play is often more sterile. Were the old attacking half-backs more ebullient than Bremner, more subtle than Blanchflower? Were the goalkeepers more agile than Bonetti? The inside-forwards as strong in the tackle and graceful in dribbling as Best, or as tireless as Ball? Were the defenders harder to pass than Tommy Smith or more versatile than McLintock? Were the backs as poised as Lawler, as clever in attack as Cooper? I suspect the present are better players than the past, but then they have better training and better opportunity. There are brilliant players in every age and their talents are conditioned by their time. Comparison is fun but futile.

The other myth is easier to expose.

Let us look at a selection of memorable post-war Finals – Blackpool and Manchester in 1948, the Matthews' Final, Tottenham's 'double' and their game against Burnley, West Ham's struggle with Preston, Leeds and Chelsea's breathless fight, and finally Arsenal's 'double'. Even that list leaves out some splendid matches.

Sir Stanley Rous rated Arsenal's other game with Liverpool as the purest in football skill, Derby's win in 1946 and Everton's in 1966 were as thrilling as could be; and what of Newcastle and Milburn? Or of that strange game in 1959 with critical comment divided as to whether Nottingham Forest's win was the most exciting or the most boring of Finals.

All who saw the 1948 Final regard it as a classic for the quality of the play and the entertainment. Geoffrey Green recorded this account for *The Times*:

'In the presence of the King and Queen and some 100,000 people, Manchester United won the F.A. Cup for the second time in their history when they beat Blackpool by four goals to two in the Final at Wembley Stadium on Saturday in a match that will long be remembered.

'Here, indeed, was a Final worthy of the name and worthy of the occasion, a match of overflowing talent, glorious and dramatic. First let us begin by saying that both Manchester United and Blackpool, by their insistence upon attack and by their very enjoyment of it, have not only set a new standard of quality for Wembley, but have pointed a lesson to the game of football as a whole that

152

In 1937 Horatio Carter (*in striped shirt behind the goalkeeper*) put Sunderland ahead after Preston North End had led at the interval.

Tommy Lawton turns away after scoring Chelsea's second goal in a drawn fourth round Cup-tie with Derby County in 1947.

Duffy scores Charlton's winning goal six minutes
from the end of extra time in 1947.

should be marked. Defence is negation; attack, as we saw it, perfectly executed,
is life, and on Saturday we were taken by the hand and led into a world where
the colours were a bit brighter and the outlines sharper.

'So much for quality, but what of the pattern of the afternoon, the excitement
that kept one's scalp tingling, and the twist at the last that brought a very right
and proper end to the story? With only 20 minutes left Blackpool were in the
lead by two goals to one, and once again it seemed that there was to be an addition to the long list of favourites who have failed in the supreme test. Blackpool,
after surrendering an early lead through a defensive misunderstanding, had
regained it before half-time, and now with the game having run three parts of its
course they still held a position of command. It was a position they had gained
not because of any superior quality in their football, pure though it had been,
but by snatching their chances. Manchester, in fact, had perhaps enjoyed the
greater share of the attack. Certainly they held a long lead in the matter of goal-
kicks and corners forced on both wings, but the mechanism had just not clicked
near goal. Their putts on the green, so to speak, had failed to drop.

'Here we were, then, at the last phase, with Blackpool looking all the world
like winners and the curve of Manchester's hopes at its lowest point of the
afternoon. For a period after half-time the fire and precision had gone out of the
Manchester game; they lost touch, and inspiration clearly now eluded them.
With 20 minutes to go, however, Morris prepared to take a free-kick gained to
the right of the Blackpool penalty-area. As he advanced to the kick a gentle
breeze, had we but sensed it, had already begun to stir. A moment later the ball
lay snug at the bottom of the Blackpool net, headed there like a flash by Rowley,
who had timed his advance perfectly between Hayward and Shimwell. Manchester United were level.

154

The turning point of the great Final of 1948. Rowley, Manchester United centre-forward, headed home a quickly-taken free-kick by Morris, making the score 2–2 twenty minutes from the end.

'Even then Blackpool had one more chance to recover the prize that only a short time ago seemed to be theirs. Chilton, who spent a thoroughly anxious and uncomfortable afternoon, took one more unnecessary liberty with Mortensen, lost the ball, and there was Mortensen streaking through an open Manchester defence. It looked any odds on a goal and Mortensen's shot was hard and true for the far corner. But Crompton saved brilliantly at full length. That, if anything, was surely the turning point, for within seconds Manchester had their noses in front for the first time with a piercing thrust at the other end by Pearson. There was no stopping them. The gentle breeze had now become a strong and friendly wind, and Manchester sailed home with an astonishing outburst of brilliance.

'Whether Mortensen would have been a great danger at inside-right must always remain a matter of opinion, but the fact remains that his tactical switch to centre-forward nearly won Blackpool the match. It was clear they were going to hammer Chilton, and this they did with a fair measure of success from the beginning. Actually the Blackpool forwards, with Munro doing the work of two men as a mid-field link, moved the ball about beautifully on the ground amongst themselves far more than one had expected, but the opening approach, especially before half-time, was usually left to Matthews and the final thrust to Mortensen. Certainly Mortensen, with his great speed and opportunism, was a danger from first to last – he snatched his usual goal, to score in every round of the competition – but the game flowed away from Matthews in the later stages after he had left Aston facing the wrong way many times in the first half. But Aston stood the test coolly enough and came out of his duel with credit.

'The Manchester forwards, apart from that phase soon after half-time when they lost their rhythm, were usually moving together as a single unit, and if things could not go right for them for a long time near goal they certainly came with a glorious burst at the end. Within the superior frame of the Manchester teamwork came the power, intelligence and thrust of Rowley, Pearson and Morris, and this was the deciding factor. They saw to it that Delaney, against the experienced Crosland, was used as much as possible. Crosland was not disgraced, but Blackpool were never quite sure where to find Delaney next. Both pairs of wing half-backs, especially Cockburn and Johnston, played their parts splendidly, but the most polished and studied defender on the field was Carey, who finally subdued a lively winger in Rickett.

'The presentation to the King and the opening ceremonies over, it was Blackpool who set the standard at the beginning. After only quarter of an hour Manchester had their first real shock when Mortensen, gathering a long pass down the middle, swept past Chilton. Mortensen was just clear when a despairing tackle by the centre-half from behind brought him down. The referee, who controlled the game excellently, decided it was inside the penalty-area, and Shimwell duly shot past Crompton. Manchester, unmoved, began to settle down to a beautiful smooth approach, and at the end of half an hour, after a constant stream of corners, they were level. Carey found Delaney on the right and as Hayward and Robinson left the winger's forward lob to each other Rowley slipped between them to flick the ball sideways and roll it into an empty net. It was sheer tragedy for Blackpool, but within five minutes they were ahead again. This time a free-kick by Matthews, square and cleverly placed, reached Kelly, and there was Mortensen once again to pounce on the forward pass and beat Crompton with a cross-shot.

'So they went in at the interval. For the first quarter of an hour of the second half Blackpool slowly but surely began to take a grip of affairs. Hope at last seemed to be draining away from Manchester. They had little to show for all their studied attack earlier. With but 20 minutes left Blackpool, it seemed, were

156

Smyth scores Wolverhampton Wanderers' third goal
in the 1949 Final.

now nearly home. But at that moment came Morris's vital free-kick and the
beginning of the Manchester whirlwind.

'Rowley's superb header, as one has said, snatched the equaliser. Ten minutes
from the end Pearson, in a quick, closely-linked approach with Morris, aimed
for the bull, hit the target, and Manchester were ahead. A few moments later
Anderson shot home past a bewildered Robinson from some 30 yards and Blackpool were left gaping. It was a stirring climax, indeed, to a clean and glorious
game in which both sides had brought the best out of each other.'

Emotionally 1953 was the Matthews Final with old 'Matthewselah' only passed
fit just in time and the whole crowd rising to his magic. But in football terms this
was the other Stanley's match as well; Mortensen's three goals were the decisive
factor and little Ernie Taylor's subtle passing 'produced' the stage drama of the
finish. H. E. Bates's account of the game exactly catches the mood of that wonderful afternoon:

'This was a match that might have come straight out of the pages of the *Boys
Own Paper* – every schoolboy's miraculous dream of glory come true.
'From the day in September when scores of small local clubs begin to oppose
each other in the preliminary rounds to the moment when a hundred thousand

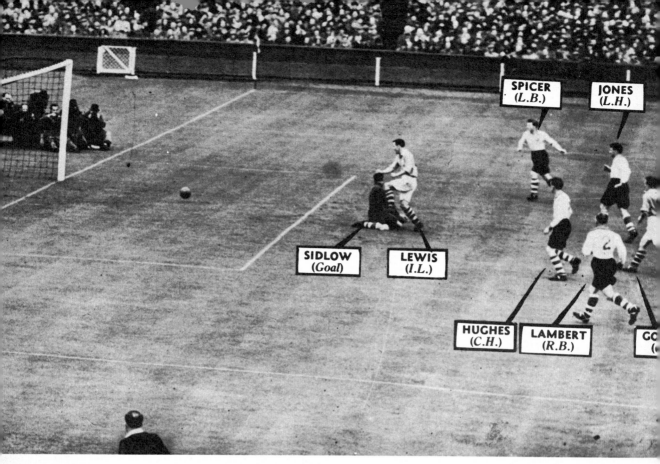

A superbly-planned goal: Lewis glides in Logie's through-pass
to score the first of his two goals by which Arsenal overcame
Liverpool in 1950.

people begin to yell themselves hoarse at the Final Tie, the competition for the
Challenge Cup is something unique in our sporting calendar. We have nothing
else quite like it in any other sport. In cricket the only comparison would be a
series in which hundreds of sporting little local clubs began to knock each other
out in the chilly days of April for the completely remote and impossible honour
of appearing in the final match at Lord's; I do not suppose that anyone has ever
thought such a competition to be possible. Yet *the* Cup has been going on in this
fashion since the days of Queen Victoria, offering its glamorous chances for any
little David to be drawn in battle with Goliath. And in that, I think, lies much of
the excitement and fascination it has for any lover of football.

'To most of us the idea of playing at Wembley even once is quite absurd and
impossible. But supposing you were a player who had been to Wembley several
times, not only to play in the Final Tie (these are the modest official words that
always appear on the tickets) but to represent England too? Not only is it not
easy to get to Wembley. It is not easy to play there. Many players find its power-

This overhead kick by Doug Lishman nearly gave Arsenal the lead
in the closing minutes of the 1952 Final against Newcastle.

ful atmosphere too much for them: there are others who find its rich thick turf
tiring and unsuitable to their game. But supposing you were a player who had
played there again and again, in Final Ties and Internationals, and had played
brilliantly and yet had never been able to step up to receive the highest and most
coveted honour the game in England has to offer – the winner's medal? And
supposing, when you were thirty-eight, surely near the end of your playing career,
the chance to gain the medal came once again, and probably for the last time –
the third chance in five years? You would say that that, I think, was the most
difficult and impossible thing of all.

'Yet this was the situation when Stanley Matthews walked out with the Blackpool team to confront their neighbouring Lancastrians, Bolton Wanderers, on
May 2nd, 1953. The day was beautifully bright; the turf was a vivid juicy emerald
after nearly fifty hours of rain. Perhaps it was an augury that the tangerine shirts

Ball hits post

Robledo headed from here

SWINDIN

L. SMITH

G. ROBLEDO

Robledo's header goes home in 1952, ten Arsenal men are beaten, and
Newcastle United take the Cup to the north-east for the second successive year.

of Blackpool were even brighter than the sun. The scene was made more re-splendent too because the Queen was there and because a hundred thousand people waved her welcome with thousands of Union Jacks printed on the backs of their song sheets. All of us indeed had high hopes of a great match and all of us who were not raving supporters of Bolton hoped that for one man's sake it would be won by Blackpool – yet not one of us had the slightest notion of what a great match it was going to be or in what a great moment it was going to be won.

'The game, for Blackpool, started most disastrously. Within two minutes that fine player Nat Lofthouse, England's centre-forward, hit a long, low and curiously curling ball from outside the penalty area towards the far Blackpool goal post. It seemed utterly to deceive Farm, a goalkeeper of splendid reputation, and it swung away from his hands and into the net. Farm looked horribly disconsolate and more than half the spectators must have felt in their hearts that it was going to be neither Blackpool's nor Matthews' day. A little later Lofthouse

160

hit the post; then another shot skimmed the Blackpool bar and then still another and to both of them the poor unhappy nervous Farm had really no answer. At the other end of the field the Bolton goalkeeper was not much better. He too made a mistake as Blackpool equalised and then, to our utter astonishment, Farm blundered again and allowed Bolton once more to take the lead.

'This was the score at half-time. Farm looked utterly dejected as he came from the field; his backs had little confidence in him and there was a possible weakness at left-half; some of the football had been scrappy and we had seen something, but not a very great deal, of Matthews. I ought perhaps to explain to those who have not seen him that Matthews is thin, stooping and, like many great footballers, a little pin-toed. I have seen him play many times for England and I remember particularly one extraordinary day when he put an entire Swiss defence into a state of abject mesmerism. But until Saturday, 2nd May, I have never thought him a more brilliant player than Tom Finney, whose superb display against Wales last November I shall never forget. Both are two-footed players of the greatest class who do their work with perfect economy, impeccable accuracy and a smooth coolness that is wonderful to see. But up to 2nd May I had not seen – and nor had anyone else of this generation – all that Matthews could do.

'For Blackpool the second half soon looked as disastrous as the first. The score was soon 3–1 against them and Bolton, even with a man injured, looked most deadly and dangerous whenever they raided, especially down the Blackpool left. Farm stood staring disconsolately at the penalty spot and I think all of us felt that it was not, after all, Matthews' day. Yet I noticed that Blackpool had never given up trying to play football. Mortensen, and Taylor their tiny inside-right, were playing beautifully, and it seemed to me that Taylor had still not touched the peak of his form. And sure enough, about twenty minutes from time he seemed to grasp that he had the measure of every one in front of him. He began to feed Matthews with a series of inspired passes. And presently one of these gave Matthews the chance to show us that genius has always something extra to give that is beyond the capacity of ordinary people. He put the entire Bolton defence into the same mesmerised tangle as he once put the Swiss and over went the typical low perfect centre. A one-legged tramp could have pushed it in with the side of his foot – yet every tangerine shirt missed it hopelessly.

'Even so, the touch of inspiration in the movement was so great that it seemed to set the entire Blackpool team on fire, and it was no surprise when, a few minutes later, the performance was repeated. And this time there was no mistake – and the score was 3–2. I had then no idea – and nor had anyone else, I think, except the referee and his linesmen – how much longer there was to play. The entire ground was in a state of growing pandemonium, and then a still more amazing thing happened. Blackpool were awarded a free-kick just outside the Bolton penalty area, at about the inside-left position. I had some impression that it was going to be taken either by Shimwell or Johnson, the Blackpool captain,

The injured Bell heads Bolton's third goal watched by Lofthouse.

who had all along played a fine cool game, but in fact it was Mortensen who
calmly aimed at the top corner of the net and slapped in such a fierce rocket of a
shot that the Bolton goalkeeper had not time to move a finger.

'After that there could not have been more than two or three minutes of added
time left for play and my impression was that everyone on the ground stopped
thinking. All of us became stupefied with excitement as the stooping pin-toed
figure of Matthews went time and time again through a series of swerves, dum-
mies, switches and above all that remarkable short swift burst of speed that is so
astonishing in a man of nearly forty. I think Taylor was hardly less inspired. He
fed Matthews at last with a perfect spoon of a pass and with it Matthews seemed
to beat the entire Bolton left-flank – almost exactly as Finney had done to make
Froggatt's great goal against Wales – and then the perfect low cross was over to
the middle and Perry whipped it in the net.

'A few mad seconds later the whistle went, and in front of me several otherwise
respectable gentlemen threw their overcoats high in the air. I cannot ever remember spectators at a football match throwing their overcoats away – hats,
often, but overcoats never – but then I cannot ever remember such an inspired

162

Stanley Mortensen beats the defensive wall to make the score 3–3
direct from a free-kick.

piece of football as was given us by Matthews and his colleagues that day. I do not think Wembley has ever seen anything like that miracle of Blackpool's recovery and the sheer beauty and skill of Matthews' part in it, and I shall be surprised if it ever does again. It was a masterpiece of a match, and a triumph for a masterpiece of a man.'

Tottenham's 'double' in 1961 and their second successive Cup win the following year were remarkable achievements against such fierce competition. Danny Blanchflower tells the story as the captain saw it:

'I heard a door slam somewhere. The window curtain was a glow of orange, the room inhabited by soft shadows. Tony Marchi, in the other bed, was still asleep. I looked at my watch. It was 8.15 a.m. The big day had arrived – and I had slept well.

'I gathered the newspapers squeezed under our door at The Hendon Hall Hotel. The *Daily Express* said that I had spent the night before in a gay mood – telling stories to the other players to keep their minds off the big game. The *Daily Mail* reported that I had looked tense and strained. In fact we had gone to the last performance at a West End Cinema – the idea being that if we got back to our hotel late enough we would be ready for sleep.

'Tony and I had breakfast in an almost deserted dining-room. Most of the other players had breakfast in their rooms. We got together in the television room about 11.30 a.m. when the BBC started setting the Cup Final scene. Their experts were cautious. They thought we might be the better team but doubted that any team could win the Cup as well as the League in one season. What interested us more was the big match news – Leicester City had dropped centre-forward Ken Leek. We watched in amazement as the B.B.C. showed film clips of how Leicester had got to the Final. Theirs had been a strangely hesitant path to glory, its one notable feature being the goals headed by Ken Leek. His being left out made us feel more confident.

163

Stanley Matthews before making the winning pass
against Bolton Wanderers in 1953.

'We lunched at noon. At 1.40 p.m. we boarded the coach for Wembley. At five minutes past two we hung our coats in the Wembley dressing room. I went out onto the pitch with some of the others. Not to examine the turf because we had done this the previous afternoon in time to get our boots ready. This time I wanted to get the feeling and atmosphere of the stadium and to note the wind and position of the sun so that I could anticipate their movement better when I came out later to toss up with the Leicester captain.

'Getting ready in the dressing-room was not as noisy as it usually was with us at Tottenham. The Wembley dressing-rooms are clean and airy but they seem bare and lacking in warmth – nobody lives there for most of the year. Time passed quickly and I was soon walking up that dark tunnel behind Bill Nicholson towards that square of light to the arena. I felt calm and confident as I walked

164

Stanley Matthews' moment of triumph as he shakes hands with the Queen.

across the green turf, not as revved-up as I had been before some of the previous cup rounds.

'Leicester were introduced first to the Duchess of Kent. She seemed lost in thought when she came over to meet us. Half way down the team-line she stopped and spoke to me. "The other team have their names on their track-suits," she said. I could not resist a quip. "Yes ma'am," I said, "but we know each other."

'We looked like strangers to one another for most of the game. We could not move that ball between one another as accurately as we usually did. Our timing was off and the team rhythm was hesitant and jerky. I think we misjudged our timing on the slower tempo of the Wembley turf. By the time we might have adjusted to this it started to rain and we were faced with a different condition on a strange surface. In some way I was more preoccupied with the conditions and atmosphere of Wembley Stadium than with the opposition. I can hardly re-member anything about Leicester except that Len Chalmers was injured early on and that must have been a great handicap for them, wrestling with the strange conditions too.

'The game seemed unreal. The crowd felt far away on the other side of that grey-hound track, as if they were part of another game somewhere. The sacred green turf was rich alright but it was a lush trap. An ideal pitch should have a little give in it – enough to take a stud. But Wembley was too soft. It pulled at the lower muscles of the leg, braking ones' efforts and natural timing. More players get cramp at Wembley than anywhere else.

'At times it felt like a purposeless dream . . . a distant crowd . . . an unflattering pitch. It was not immediate, emotional, nerve-wracking like the semi-final had been. There seemed no doubt, no uncertainty, no excitement in my feeling. Although we hardly looked like scoring I never felt we could lose. "It might last forever . . . but let's hope a goal comes quickly and get the damn thing over with."

165

Tottenham Hotspur appeal in the 1962 Final after Burnley's
centre-half, Cummings, has handled on the line.

'When Bobby Smith scored late in the second half I knew it was over. When
Terry Dyson scored a second I remember looking above their goal and seeing the
huge scoreboard for the first time during the game: Tottenham Hotspur 2,
Leicester City 0.

'It was no great thrill climbing the stairs to the Royal Box and collecting the
Cup. The thrill had been the achievement through the season, the excitement at
Crewe in the fourth round, at Villa Park in the fifth round, at Sunderland in the
sixth round, and the most tense game of all against Burnley in the semi-final.
Wembley was the end of the road and it felt a disappointment, an anti-climax.
Some of the others seemed to enjoy the victory lap but it was nothing more than
a tolerable duty for me.

'I enjoyed it all a bit more when we met Burnley the following season at
Wembley. They were our arch rivals of the time. It was a better match and we
played much better than against Leicester. The whole experience did not feel so
unreal possibly because I did not expect too much after the experience of the
year before. Perhaps there was that bit of extra feeling in it too because we
opposed Burnley.

'I remember taking a penalty-kick in the second half. We were leading 2–1. It
was a vital moment in the game. 'I bet you miss it,' Jimmy McIlroy, the Burnley
inside-forward teased me. McIlroy was a Northern Ireland team-mate of mine
and he had been taking the penalties for us and missing a few. 'I am damn glad

Danny Blanchflower strokes home the penalty to make sure
of Tottenham Hotspur's second successive win.

you are not taking it,' I gibed back. Had I been younger in the game he might
have distracted me. But I was 36 years old, an old pro with a lot of experience
behind me.

'I am glad the Wembley Cup-Finals came later in my career. Otherwise they
might have confused me in the years that followed. I was old enough to know my
own feelings and to register them in such a way that I could understand it all a
good deal better with the passing years.

'In truth we are all brain-washed about the Cup-Final. A player hears and
reads a great deal about it before he ever gets there. He hears about the 'Majestic'
twin towers . . . the 'Hallowed' green turf . . . the 'Royal' greeting . . . the crowd
singing 'Abide with Me' . . . It all sounds like some distant religious ceremony
that takes place every year in the promised land at the end of the football season.
The reality of it can never live up to the dream. The dream is not for the player.
It is for the fan, the worshipper without whom there would be no professional
game at all. It is for the lover of the game who doesn't really know what it's like
out there on the field and never *will* know. It is as *he* imagines it, a football
heaven. It is the fans' day, not the players', and that is why some 400 million fans
all over the world tune in on Cup Final Day. Long may it prosper.'

167

Bitter battle in the mud as Swansea duel with Preston
North End in the 1964 semi-final.

West Ham's only Cup win was a clash with Second Division Preston, its quality
and excitement sustained until the end. This was my account in *The Observer*:

'No matter what anyone paid for a Wembley ticket, it was cheap at the price.
This was one of the great Finals, a stirring mixture of graceful movement,
colourful enthusiasm, and sustained excitement.

'It seemed harsh that either of these sides playing such determined and delightful football should be without the Cup as just reward. Yet the decisive goal was a
fitting climax to a splendid game.

Dawson, Preston North End's centre-forward, heads the
second goal against West Ham in 1964.

Boyce's last-minute goal wins the 1964
Final for West Ham.

To err is human. McCreadie lets Charlton's header bounce through
his legs for Leeds United's first goal in 1970.

'In the second minute of injury time Hurst came driving down the field to
sweep a pass out to Brabrook. The winger's centre floated beyond Ross's despairing leap, beyond Sissons and there was Boyce to head home. Boyce who had
spent most of the game deep in defence had chosen his moment with perfect
timing. The quiet unobtrusive player with the flair for the dramatic had done it
again. Goals are a rarity with him yet it was his two that crushed Manchester
United in the semi-final and now he was the destroyer of Preston's hopes.

'It was a bitter moment for North End who had been twice in the lead and
whose precise clever play had made this a game of flowing movement and fluctuating fortune. Yet on balance West Ham deserved to come from behind to win in
a photo-finish. They were never flurried, although they had more than their
share of the easy chances that somehow got away as the ball evaded the net like
some lucky and lively fish.

'Who were the memorable performers in a memorable match? In defence

170

there was Moore, cool and masterful, with a magnetic attraction for the probing pass that should have laid bare the goal.

'Cruder, but no less effective was the solid power of Singleton's tackling. Kendall too was ready to take on Hurst or Byrne with the precocious confidence that marks the modern teenager. Yet this was a day that belonged to forwards of contrasting styles and skills.

'Sissons with his sinuous dribbling and quick perception of an opening, Hurst with his thrusting energy, were both prompted by Byrne roaming elusively in mid-field.

'In Preston's attack the delicate dribbling of the wingers was linked to the battering power of Dawson and Ashworth. Both have surprising speed for men of their bulk and they tested to the full the courage of West Ham's close-knit defence. Strength has its place in soccer as well as finesse, and from the start the two elements were finely and fairly balanced.

'It was Preston in the opening minutes who set the pattern of the match and made nonsense of the estimate that they were merely a tough, competent Second Division side. Poised and penetrating, they moved smoothly into the lead in the tenth minute. Dawson's drive from the edge of the area slid gently for the corner – the very slowness of the shot deceiving Standen into diving too early. As the ball slipped from his groping fingers Holden was there to stroke it into the net.

'Preston had no time even to consider closing the game up. Almost before the embraces were ended Moore had sent Sissons racing down the wing. Byrne played the ball back with a perfect wall pass and Sissons, his stride unchecked, shot at the last second to avoid his tacklers. The ball squeezed neatly between Kelly and the post to make him the youngest scorer in Wembley Finals.

'Neither team had given any hint of dark defensive thoughts, but in any case this instant riposte ensured that the game remained free and open.

'The close interpassing of Preston's forwards was swift and subtle enough to infiltrate the tight defence, but it was the high ball to Dawson and Ashworth that tortured Brown and his backs. The mid-field was controlled by Lawton, their attacking wing-half who kept moving into open spaces with Spavin in close and intelligent support. Together they pressed in relentlessly and it was West Ham who were forced to rugged and despairing tackles.

'Yet the Hammers should have gone ahead with the move that had brought them so many goals. Byrne's pass sliced through the defence to leave Hurst running free and Kelly's wrist was nearly sprained by the power of this shot. Before the interval Preston were ahead as Dawson rose high to head home Wilson's corner, leaving Brown flattened behind him.

'In the second half West Ham's marking was closer with the busy Bovington moving into midfield to lessen the menace of Lawton. Soon they were level and again it was from a corner. Brown headed it on to Hurst whose shot bounced down from the bar to hit Kelly and trickle over the line.

'Encouraged West Ham surged ceaselessly in on goal, looking for a time as if they would take charge of the game. Hurst fell as he was racing through, then missed Byrne's low cross as he stood two yards from an open goal. Byrne too could have scored a moment later had he realised that behind his back the goal was at his mercy.

'But Preston could also fight back and they had their chances as Dawson shot straight at Standen and Holden forced his way past Bond's tackle only to shoot into the side netting.

'As the game went into injury time, the cut and thrust looked to have ended in stalemate, until Boyce's header at last decisively tilted the delicate balance.'

Of all the Finals my own pick is Chelsea and Leeds' great struggle, not just for the swaying fortunes, but for the extraordinary skills and stamina on a desert of a pitch. Hugh McIlvanney wrote this in *The Observer*:

'After two hours of exhausting effort and almost unbearable excitement Leeds United and Chelsea still could not decide which of them should break their shared record of frustration in the F.A. Cup.

'It was the first time since the occasion moved to Wembley in 1923 that a Final had ended in a draw after extra time. But if that fact made the match historic there was much more to make it memorable. No two teams have ever shown themselves more worthy of the climactic moment of the English football season or vindicated more fully the bold predictions of their admirers.

'There will be no empty spaces at Old Trafford when they meet again on April 29th. If Eddie Gray went there on his own he would draw a crowd. Yesterday this young Scot played with an irresistible brilliance no winger has approached since Matthews hypnotised Bolton Wanderers into submission in 1953. Someone said cruelly after the game that Gray should send Webb an autographed picture – of the No. 11 on the back of his shirt. It was poor Webb's most consistent view of his tormenter throughout the match.

'Cooper's fluent running from behind added so excitingly to Gray's skills that United's left wing was by far the most offensive weapon on view. Had it been balanced by a similar strength on the right Chelsea would undoubtedly have been destroyed. Fortunately for them Lorimer is no Gray and while Madeley showed some assertiveness McCreadie never had Webb's worries.

'It was additional luck for Chelsea that the central attackers of Leeds took much longer than usual to make an impression. Jones and Clarke played forcefully after half-time and Bonetti three times heard the most relieving sound a goalkeeper knows – the slap of ball against wood – but Chelsea were never pushed out of reach of survival and their wonderful spirit saved them.

'No one exemplified this spirit more than Cooke, who can never have covered more ground in two hours of his life, or finished with more running left in him. Whether dribbling thrillingly at the front, building intelligently in the middle, or battling and harassing at the back he was a revelation to those who have seen him as a frail and peripheral figure. Switching him to a deep position late in the day was an inspiration.

172

Sprake dives over a simple shot from Houseman and Chelsea are level.

'From the beginning Chelsea gave clear warning that the absence of Hudson was as damaging as they feared it might be. On a surface of sand packed into the frail rearguard of Wembley's vanishing turf, Hollins and Houseman simply could not equal the mobility of the Leeds midfield players.

'With Hunter finding occasional opportunities to leave the side of Charlton, who was largely reassured by the return of this strong man to the side, United's authority in the middle of the field grew steadily.

'However, if that was a confirmation of the obvious so too was the more widespread aggression of the Chelsea attack and by half-time it was still impossible to tell which advantage would be decisive. After the interval Leeds found the sharpness that persuaded their trainer, Les Cocker, to say subsequently – with pardonable exaggeration – that they might have scored five goals. Yet Chelsea might have taken two more than they did.

'Osgood took some time to show that the uncertainty which afflicted Jack Charlton against Celtic in the European Cup had not disappeared altogether. Once the centre-forward had discovered the residue of uneasiness he played with a confident freedom for a while, but eventually sank to a level far more moderate than his talent.

'The harsh restriction Hunter imposed on Hutchinson led before long to a brief ill-tempered scuffle between them. For all the strain of one of the most tense of Cup Finals, the bitterness did not spread through the match. Most of the players were totally concerned with the legitimate pursuit of victory.

'The crowd were soon provided with convincing evidence that if such a victory

173

Hutchinson's header beats Sprake for Chelsea's second equalising
goal in the first-ever draw in a Wembley Cup-Final.

went to Leeds, no player would have had more to do with it than Gray whose
balance and precise control frequently reduced Webb to desperate headlong
dives at his feet. Gray's penetrative excellence did much to make up for the subduing effects of the splendidly functional Dempsey and the robust if erratic
Harris on Jones and Clarke. Chelsea and Leeds both made early openings, but
the first genuine escape was a tribute to Gray's deadly importance. The winger
skipped past Webb twice with the unhurried ease of a father showing off to his
small son on the beach and slid the ball back to Giles. Even a miskick from Giles
was dangerous enough to make Bonetti punch hurriedly into touch.

'Then a centre from Cooke gave Hutchinson a low header that was un-
comfortably close to Sprake's left-hand post. But when the ultimate discomfort
came it was to Bonetti. Of course Gray was concerned in it. His corner from the
left found Bonetti vainly trying to barge his way upwards through a bunch of
players and finding his hands able to make less telling contact than Charlton's
head. The header sent the ball in at a trickle, but Harris and McCreadie on the
goal line appeared preoccupied with protests about a foul on Bonetti. McCreadie
completely missed his kick and the ball ran wearily into the net. McCreadie said
later that the ball which would have bounced on a normal pitch went into a
deadened slither as it struck the ground. This like the almost grotesque slowness
that eventually affected the shattered players of both sides was one of the penalties of the worst field Wembley has provided for a Final.

'Leeds might have scored again when Gray once more passed Webb without
effort and shot over the bar. When the goal did come it was reward for the in-

creasing purposefulness of Chelsea, though in execution it was no more satisfactory than its predecessor.

'Houseman appeared to be in the most innocuous of positions. He was all of 20 yards out far on the left edge of the penalty area with an army of players separating him from goal. His shot was simple and without exceptional force, but as it dipped in on Sprake's left-hand side the goalkeeper dived feebly over it and was left squirming in an agony of remorse.

'At the start of the second half Gray took Madeley's pass, slipped past Webb and shot hard at Bonetti. Chelsea retaliated strongly. Hutchinson came boring fiercely through in a packed penalty area to force Sprake to dive twice at his feet to smother shots. The second time the ball spun loose for Osgood to stab it on and Hunter to clear off the line.

'Leeds, stronger and more persistent, soon took up the running convincingly. Their pressure was constant as Gray and Cooper bewildered Webb and the assaults came rippling in on the left. Gray drove a fierce right-footer against the bar. Bremner driving his team on ruthlessly sent Giles down the right. Clarke dived in to head his cross against the base of the post and as the ball ran loose Jones steered his left foot shot into the far corner. Leeds had only a few minutes to hold on to this lead. For at once Chelsea thrust back. Charlton was penalised for holding Osgood on the left. Harris pushed the kick back for Hollins to curl a cross close to the near post and Hutchinson burst through to glance the ball past Sprake's right shoulder.

'Harris, whose appearance had been a minor triumph for medical science could not be asked to face extra time and Hinton came on in his place.

'A free-kick was inadequately headed out to Dempsey and he struck a marvellously powerful shot. Somehow the goalkeeper standing three yards off his line hurled himself far enough to push the ball over the junction of crossbar and upright. Immediately Gray evaded two tackles and chipped the ball across goal to be met by a well judged volley from Giles. Almost everyone was sure that Giles had scored, but Webb careering in like an agitated locomotive struck out a foot and the ball was deflected in a blur over the bar.

'Leeds stayed better into the second half of extra time and as Chelsea's lungs burned Clarke and Lorimer were able to make a careful opening for the outside-right on the left wing. He went clear of all challenges except that of Bonetti who used his feet to save, then his hands to do so again inches under his crossbar. His resistance did a great deal to avert a defeat that would not have been unjust.'

Leeds had missed their moment and Chelsea drove on to their first Cup win in a replay that again went to extra time. So nice was the balance between the teams. And the man who settled it? It was Webb who forced the ball in to win the match. The leprechaun in the Cup was laughing again. The man who had been so outplayed for so long had first saved his team from inevitable defeat then snatched a remarkable win.

18

Managers', Referees', and Writers' Eye View

It is part of the Wembley tradition to see the Managers file out at the head of their team, their sober clothes contrasting with the players' bright track suits. What are their feelings and what will they contribute to the match?

Ron Greenwood remembers standing in the crowd for the 1962 Final and being near to tears with shared pride and pleasure as he watched Bill Nicholson and Harry Potts lead out Tottenham Hotspur and Burnley. It was his first season as West Ham's Manager and this he felt must be the greatest moment in a Manager's career. Two years later he was himself bringing West Ham out into that clamorous and colourful scene, yet there was no elation, no sense of fulfilment. His mind was absorbed in the coming game and the majestic preliminaries were just an irksome necessity. It was as well that he remained alert and committed for Preston were so dominant in the first half that a change of tactics was imperative. The pattern of the game was much clearer from the sidelines than for the players involved in its hectic action.

Bobby Moore was the sweeper waiting to cut out every infiltration. But Preston had made him superfluous crushing the other defenders back on to him as they attacked with the high ball to Dawson and Ashworth, their two tall and powerful strikers. With an extra man committed uselessly to defence, West Ham were losing the midfield to the dashing energy of young Kendall and Lawton.

At the interval Greenwood switched Moore to act as the second centre-half releasing Bovington for the midfield battle against Lawton and allowing Boyce to thrust further upfield. The change of tactics effectively swung the balance of the game as a tiring Preston team failed to counter the new challenge.

The following season West Ham became the second English side to win the European Cup Winners' Cup beating T.S.V. Munich in a Wembley match of marvellous quality. This time it was pre-planning that helped. English forwards, when they break through, tend to shoot on the run close to the goalkeeper's legs on the assumption that they react instinctively with their hands, but slower with their feet. Continental forwards by contrast like to flaunt their skills in dribbling round the goalkeeper as if he were just another defender. Jim Standen was given special practice in how to spread himself to have the best chance of interception. Twice his saving dives smothered a break-through by the German centre-forward and his carefully rehearsed skill kept the game safe for West Ham.

These instances are typical of the way English Managers tend to start from firm tactical plans, but accept that their players are intelligent enough to adjust if practice proves them imperfect. This is in contrast to most Continental Managers who keep rigidly to systems that have been rehearsed, for fear of any change confusing their players.

Many a Final has been lost in the dressing room before the game has started. The mind goes back to Sheffield Wednesday waiting miserably for Blackburn Rovers to slaughter them at the Oval in 1890, or to Wolverhampton Wanderers in 1939 too shaky, the story goes, to sign their names properly in the autograph book. That is where the Manager can be a vital influence.

Jack Tinn's white spats were a gimmick, helping by well-established ritual to give the players confidence that everything was normal.

Sir Matt Busby was always meticulous about another aspect. He had played and lost in 1933, played and won in 1934. In the earlier match Manchester City had arrived at Wembley an hour and a half before the game and the long wait had unsettled the team. So he always ensured that his side got to their dressing rooms with enough time for preparation, but none to spare for worrying.

Joe Mercer could also appreciate the pressures of the Final from his games at Wembley with Arsenal. When he took Manchester City there in 1969 he knew that his players would be keyed up, but would have to accept the tension as normal. 'Are any of you nervous?' he asked on the morning of the match. When any admitted it, he said 'Well I've got news for you, son. It will get worse!'

But as the team waited to go out Malcolm Allison the Assistant Manager told them: 'Out there people are worried sick, but here there's nothing but cool confidence,' and Mercer added the punch line: 'I *dare* you to go out and play football. I *dare* you to control the ball, juggle it, flick it around.'

And in those early minutes of the game Summerbee and Bell were to do just that establishing a mastery that gave City the match.

What a pity that was not said in 1922 when Huddersfield and Preston's two talented teams went out and made mock of the skills of the game!

Some Managers have brought in well-known comedians whose cheerful presence has kept the players entertained. But most have concentrated on keeping the atmosphere as normal as possible with the Manager acting as it if was just another match. This relaxed atmosphere was particularly noticeable as Managers Don Revie and Dave Sexton prepared Leeds and Chelsea for one of the most gruelling of Wembley Finals. Some of the players watched the scene outside on a television screen passing comment on the commentators. This was a more sophisticated distraction than the gramophones occasionally brought in in the past years.

While calming their players before the game, Managers know that they themselves will have to endure even greater nervous tension without the relief of action.

My personal appreciation of Cullis's great qualities as a centre-half is confined to sitting in front of him while Wolves beat Luton 4–1 in a Cup tie. That made me realise painfully that he played the whole 90 minutes himself on behalf of his team.

177

Before so important a game as a Cup-Final, no Manager is likely to try a major tactical innovation and the pre-planning is usually a minor adjustment to take advantage of known weaknesses or guard against known strengths in the opposition. But these alterations can be vital.

For Tottenham's Final in 1967 Nicholson's planning was helped by Chelsea's abandonment of their usual defensive 'sweeper'. Spurs forwards had never relished playing against this formation and now they were given greater freedom. Earlier in the season Tottenham had been playing without orthodox wingers and their backs had found themselves harassed as their opposite numbers came driving up unchallenged. This Nicholson had countered by reverting to normal wingers who chased back if necessary. From Spurs' own discomfiture earlier in the season he had learnt enough to take advantage of Chelsea playing without a regular left-winger.

Right-back Joe Kinnear was briefed to go driving up the wing and with Mackay covering in behind him he had a decisive influence on the game.

Pre-match planning or a change of emphasis at half-time gives no problem in implementation, but during a game it can be difficult to get a message to the team. Two examples illustrate its possible importance.

Arsenal's coach, Don Howe, always sat close enough to the touchline to attract the attention of his players. In the second half of extra time against Liverpool he passed the message for Graham to drop back and George, who was tiring in midfield, to be pushed up as a striker. No sooner was the switch effected than George scored the goal that gave Arsenal the double.

For Don Revie there was a quite different experience the year before. Everyone sees the player's moment of triumph or humiliation. The Manager's joy or grief is rather more private. But Revie experienced both extremes in a few seconds of the 1970 Final. Six minutes from time Jones put Leeds ahead for the second time and Revie sprang, feet in the air, arms thrown high in elation. Leeds had done it! After all their near misses and disappointments of the past, the Cup was theirs. Revie knew and everyone in the stands knew, that that formidable defence should have now no difficulty in holding on. Six hours might be a problem, but surely not six minutes. Yet as his feet touched the ground Revie went ice cold. For on the field Jones and Bremner were turning somersaults and the team was lost in a heady euphoria. All it needed was for the players to concentrate their minds and reinforce their defence. Yet joy unconfined left no room for thoughts on formation or for cold, careful assessment. They were celebrating too soon and Revie could get no message to them. As a player he had once known with perfect certainty that against all odds he would be brought back into Manchester City's Cup-Final team and that they would win. Now he sensed disaster just as clearly. To confirm his fears there was right-back Madeley gaily overlapping with Lorimer, an unnecessary gamble that left Leeds exposed.

Retribution was as swift and inevitable as in a Greek tragedy. The thrust back, the free-kick, the dreamy defence letting Hutchinson in to score – his mind had

178

Bertie Mee and Bill Shankly lead out the Arsenal and Liverpool teams.

Kennedy slices wide when well placed to score shortly
before the end of full time in the 1971 Final.

traced it all before it happened. And at the end of the road he could already sense not the Cup, but the dust and ashes of defeat, the bitterness of 'IF ONLY . . .'

To the victor the spoils, to the vanquished a lifetime of regret – that is the exquisite agony and ecstasy of the Cup – and for no one is it more acute than the Manager.

Most Managers complete their planning well in advance and, except for some unexpected development, the rest is up to the players and the captain. But this relationship between Manager and captain, captain and players can be vital.

When Tottenham were losing 0–1 to Manchester City in the 1956 semi-final their captain, Blanchflower, switched centre-half Norman to lead the attack. The Spurs' forward line had been rearranged for the game and had achieved little. In the final assaults, Norman's height and power put City's defenders under pressure. The bar was hit. Just before the end goalkeeper Trautmann clawed down Robb as he dribbled past him and was fortunate to escape a penalty. But Spurs lost and Blanchflower later lost the captaincy because his Manager disagreed with the change.

Blanchflower was a captain of unusual insight and independence and Tottenham's double in later years was to stem from the fine working relationship achieved with his new Manager, Billy Nicholson. But in general the influence of the captain on his Cup team is more in the leadership by example and the encouragement than the tactics.

This has followed from the development of the status of Manager and coach. We have seen Colin Veitch and his Newcastle players working out their own tactical gambits and in the early days it was the Management who concentrated on the finances and the selection of players, the captain and his team who worked things out on the field – with or without the authority to do so.

Billy Bassett, in his role as Chairman of Albion, was perhaps the first to influence his team in the way a modern Manager would. But it was not until Herbert Chapman that the new image was built.

His success in creating champion teams at Huddersfield and Arsenal gave a new status and public respect to the Manager. Chubby, cheerful and shrewd he built two great sides by his identification with, and confident handling of, players. It was at his suggestion that the teams first walked out side by side into the expectant stadium. That was in 1930, and appropriately, the teams that filed out were Huddersfield and Arsenal, the two that his magic touch had built to greatness. But it was Arsenal's destiny that he was now guiding and it was Arsenal who won the match with ease. In the heat of the game there is little place for sentiment.

The confidence he gave to his players was well illustrated by Cliff Bastin. He was worried when Chapman first asked him to play out of position on the wing. But he left Chapman's office convinced that he could be a great winger – and here he was at Wembley with a reputation as the best outside-left in the game. More than that he also built the reputation of the Clubs by an equal flair for publicity. Typical was his purchase of Charles Buchan for £5,000 plus £100 for every goal he scored in his first year. He got a great player and the daring deal was endlessly discussed. It was

180

said of Chapman that if he found there was one player a Club would never transfer that was the man he would get.

Major Buckley had this same flair for making the players realise their interests were put first and for attracting publicity to his side. His glandular treatments and his special equipment were typical of this approach.

With such Managers came a closer study of tactics and theory which was not then so readily accepted. The first time a blackboard was produced by Jimmy Dimmock's Manager he commented, 'I came here to play football, not listen to long words and be confused by diagrams. Any more of this and I'll have to ask for my cards.' He was not risking much financially by his stand as he was on a top wage for that period of the twenties of £8 per week with £6 in the close season and was making more by 'totting' with his horse and cart. A slight difference from the £12,000 Arsenal's players collected for 1971!

Perhaps it was from an understanding of this attitude that Arthur Rowe developed the 'make it simple' approach to the game that Spurs spread through soccer as Ramsey and Buckingham refined and developed this system for other teams.

Another in sympathy with this style was Billy Walker, player for Villa in the Finals of 1920 and 1924, Manager of Sheffield Wednesday when they won in 1935, and of Nottingham Forest when they took the Cup in 1959 – a remarkable record indeed.

But though the game remains basically simple it is the Managers who have had to develop training and coaching techniques that meet the needs of today's sharper pace and greater pressures.

Sir Matt Busby with his ability to gather players of talent and help them express themselves; Don Revie with his technical knowledge and the competent professionalism throughout his staff; Bill Shankly with his driving enthusiasm typify both the contribution of today's Manager and their understanding of the game.

The referee has long been a central figure never safe from criticism. Major Marindin's interpretation of the off-side law was thought by Queen's Park, Glasgow, to have cost them the Cup in 1884 and 50 years later the incident still rankled in Scotland.

There was endless argument also over the decision to let play go on in the Newcastle–Arsenal Final of 1932 when spectators, Arsenal players, and the camera photographs all maintained that the ball had crossed the line before Richardson centred.

Such is the referee's power to make or mar a game and as the Cup fever has steadily grown it is a tribute to the referees' quality that there have been so few disputed incidents in the Finals.

Of special interest is the fact that no one has yet been sent off or even booked in a Cup-Final. This indicates good control and the fact that for all the tension of the match the occasion tends to put players on their best behaviour. From many years of watching a number of occasions spring to mind where referees have seemed

181

lenient, but the Finals have in general been fair and sporting clashes played with restraint although the stakes are so high.

That great expert, Sir Stanley Rous, had to speak sternly to Mackie, Portsmouth's Irish full-back, in the 1934 Cup-Final. He warned him he might be sent off if he continued to use threatening language to Eric Brook. 'Ah, you'll no be sending me off at Wembley,' said Mackie. 'Do it again and you'll soon find out,' was the rejoinder that kept him quiet.

It was in this game that Stanley Rous introduced the diagonal system for the first time in a Final, with linesmen each patrolling one half of the field. He had developed this partly through thinking over the disputed decision of two years before in Arsenal's match. His new idea had not had general approval and one of his linesmen on the day was loath to use it, claiming that the system was strongly opposed by Mr Sutcliffe a Vice-President of the F.A. Sir Stanley is now amused to recall that a few days later he was being interviewed for the post of Secretary to The Football Association. On the selection panel was Mr Sutcliffe who complimented him on the success of the system.

The referee's job was initially something of a sinecure. His only function was to resolve any disagreement between the two umpires, while many matters, such as whether extra time should be played, were left to the two captains. As in the Queen's Park dispute, players were expected to claim for offences and goals. The referee who for important matches was usually a member of the F.A. Council, answered appeals like a cricket umpire. Not until 1895 did he have any power to award a penalty without appeal.

Once the professional teams took over, the stakes in money and prestige brought sharper pressures on the referee. He could no longer rely on the 'scout's honour' codes of conduct and Clubs were no longer prepared to accept any haphazard arrangement. Sharp practice was not unknown – the best example being the Cup tie between the Swifts and Crewe Alexandra. After Swifts won 3–2, Crewe lodged a protest on the ground that the bar was two inches below the regulation height. A replay had to be ordered, but it was then found that a Crewe official had measured the post with a two-foot rule before the match and kept his knowledge as 'insurance'. Crewe were censured for this conduct which was generally condemned and an addition was made to Rule 28 'any protest relating to the ground, goalposts, etc must be reported to the referee before the match begins'.

In 1891 the 'umpires' who had sometimes been highly partisan, were converted into linesmen and the referee was put in full control of the game.

Inevitably that put him at the storm centre of any disputed decisions. In Finals there are few that stand out. There was the goal given against Tottenham as Clawley fumbled the ball. Was Smith tripped inside the area as the Preston back tackled him in 1922? Was the ball over the line when Richardson centred? Was it a fair charge on Gregg as Lofthouse hustled him into the net? In the main controversy has been kept in a low key; the game has flowed smoothly without his becoming a central figure.

182

From the time the film cameras analysed that Newcastle centre, he has been open to slow motion play-backs of his every decision. That makes it the more remarkable that there have been so few arguments, so few identifiable mistakes.

The referee's role can be vital, so how does he see the Final? Ken Aston refereed when Manchester United won in 1963 and this is how he describes the procedure and the problems:

'Some referees take great care on Cup Final morning to pack their favourite tossing-up coin or whistle, or some lucky charm, but I'm not superstitious. I used to change whistles half a dozen times a season. You travel to the F.A., where you collect your expenses. There was no fee in my day. Today it is ten guineas but any referee would willingly pay for the privilege.

'Another job at Lancaster Gate is to choose the match ball from a heap of 30 or so – white balls, yellow and orange. The manufacturers' names are kept secret.

'One chap had written to me saying he was 82 and would be watching on TV. He asked if we could use a white ball so he could follow play more easily. But white was not really on in May, so I chose yellow. The three match balls were then weighed, measured and tested.

'It is about then that you start feeling really important. A large F.A. limousine wafts you to Wembley about midday, and there you are given lunch.

'Now you start wondering – will Lady Luck smile on me? Will press or TV pictures prove me wrong?

'At the age of 47, will I be able to pace myself so that the Wembley pitch, which saps the strength of players in peak fitness, does not handicap my performance?

'Wembley's cruel crop of injuries stems from over-tension, which warps judgement and results in players going into tackles that are not "on". The thick, clinging turf is usually blamed but I believe it's merely a contributory factor.

'Refereeing is an exercise in communication, and I decided that if I could appear calm and relaxed to the point of casualness in the early stages it must help. I think I succeeded. The first time we had a trainer on was five minutes from the end when a player went down with cramp.

'In fact refereeing a Wembley Final can be easier than controlling a normal First Division game. Certainly the 100,000 crowd makes a terrific din, but rival fans are grouped largely at either end and separated by 'neutrals' in the middle areas. Because of the greyhound track, you are comparatively remote from the crowd, and this helps towards relaxation. And the players, though excited and tense, tend to be better disciplined when taking part in this soccer showpiece.

'There is a fable about Cup Final referees being instructed not to send anyone off. It simply isn't true. The F.A. gives referees only one instruction:

'You will not signal the kick-off at the start of the game or after half-time until you receive the signal from the Royal Box that the Royal party are sitting comfortably. Then you may begin.'

'The only incidents in my Final, if you can call them that, were infringements by the two goalkeepers. Gordon Banks cleared the ball out of his hands from beyond the penalty-area, and David Gaskell broke the old four-step rule.

'After the game the winners usually invite you to their celebration banquet – Manchester United's was at the Savoy.

'I'm often asked about the referee's dressing-room at Wembley. It's a small room reached via a spiral staircase.

'When I was senior linesman at the 1957 Final we got a bit behind time. The referee was being hurried by the F.A. official and, halfway down the spiral staircase, he realised he had forgotten the ball. But I had picked it up along with my reserve ball so off we went behind the two teams – Manchester United and Aston Villa – up the tunnel.

'Suddenly I realised I had left my flag behind. I raced back up all those stairs, grabbed it, skipped back down again and, puffing heavily, caught the procession up just as it was going into the arena. Our double memory lapse probably had its root in nervousness. Yet I can truthfully say that I was not the least bit nervous before my Final.

'I did a little test by putting my hands on the dressing-room table. They were not shaking. It was just another game to me. I say that with a little reservation for I believe that "butterflies" before a big test are an indication that your arousal level is at its peak. I told my linesmen that day: "Perhaps it's a good thing I'm retiring." '

The Manager and the referee have a special view of Wembley. But what impression does it make on a writer? This is how Brian Glanville described the 1960 Final in his book *People in Sport*:

'Wembley on Final day doesn't change, except in the colour of the favours. The banners are up along the Olympic Way – JESUS SAVES, FLEE THE WRATH TO COME – and the ex-servicemen's band is thumping and strumming with awful, rending jollity. Above the banjos, the trumpets and the concertinas, the faces of these poor, elderly men are set in desperate concentration. A man is holding up a black and white placard inscribed THREE BLOKES NO TICKETS: CAN YOU HELP? and inside the stadium the usual big man in the rumpled white suit is leading the usual community singing. On the steep terraces, programmes wave to him like a sudden flight of seagulls.

'"You're good this afternoon", he says, like Everybody's Uncle, "You're wonderful. Thank you for the way you're singing". The climax, as always, is "Abide With Me" – "Everybody join in this wonderful great hymn". Everybody does. As usual, no one's quite sure whether to stand or not, as though "God Save the Queen" were being played on the radio. Some do, some don't; there's a sheepish hiatus in the grandstand, until everyone *is* standing – or almost everyone.

'The teams file out on to the field side by side, led by their Managers. For once, Mr Stanley Cullis, Wolverhampton's volatile Manager, is without his familiar hat with the drooping brim: his bald head gleams in the sunshine.

'The teams line up to be presented. Blackburn, oblivious of the sunshine, are wearing track suits. The Duke of Gloucester comes on to the field to inspect them, ushered by The Football Association Secretary, Sir Stanley Rous, as tall and stately as the Duke himself. It is a triumph of . . . what? Osmosis? Twenty-six years ago, Rous was a Hertfordshire schoolmaster and a soccer referee. To-day, the gesture with which he waves the band into the National Anthem might have come from a palace balcony. The players stand to attention. McLeod, Blackburn's outside-left, ceases to wave at friends in the crowd.

The game begins. Wolverhampton win easily enough, Whelan's broken leg preventing a fair trial of strength.

'There remains the ritual of the winning team's joyous rush to the terraces, where their supporters stand. Slater waves the Cup – with which he's at length hoisted on to his team's shoulders, as captains always are.

'In the dressing-rooms, Wolves are jubilant, Blackburn are taking it well. Journalists besiege each player in turn. "Can we say you were delighted, Stan?" Clayton, Blackburn's captain, a young and earnest Lancastrian, radiating sincerity, says, "I'm proud of the lads, they played wonderful. But the goals Wolves got were right bloody scrappy."

'In the high, gloomy stone corridor between the dressing-rooms, the dialogue continues. Both teams' motor-coaches loom there, a motor-cycle policeman stands by, huge and helmeted, the inevitable mute, seedy hanger-on has some-how joined the group; a small, sallow man whose tie hangs far below his collar. Schoolboys proffer autograph books, and Clayton signs them automatically, continuing to talk, as though he were merely buttoning his jacket.

'In the Wolves dressing-room, Slater, a slim, curiously ascetic figure for a Cup-Final captain, wearing a white shirt buttoned at the sleeves, is carefully combing his hair at the mirror. A journalist comes in and says: "Well done, Bill: no hard feelings," and Slater replies, "The only thing that got me was when you said Wolves' success was *depressing*. I said, well, there may be one more melancholic admitted to hospital, after Saturday."

'Stanley Cullis, for once relaxed, has just changed his suit; he's in his braces, packing the original jacket into a suitcase. Another journalist asks, "Can we say it was a shock, the way Stobart played, Stan?"

'Cullis says, "It's a shock to them, it isn't to me. Whenever we make a gamble and it comes off, I always say, thank goodness." He's actually smiling. "When they call me a genius, they little realise how near it is to calling me a fool. They'd have hung, drawn, and quartered me if it hadn't come off." He drinks off a glass of water; he is a teetotaller.

'Someone asks: "When Blackburn were pressing in that first quarter of an hour, did you think of 1939?"

'"I did," says Cullis. "Bill Slater said he was thinking of me, then I said, 'That makes two of us.'"

'A man comes in. "They're waiting, Stan."

'"I would hate to make them wait for me," says Cullis. He turns to one of the journalists. "Is my hair straight, Alan? Will I do?" The accent is Black Country, with an underlay of Ellesmere Port. He crosses to the mirror, saying, "I ate my bag of sweets during the match," smooths a hand over his bald head and asks "Have you got my vaseline to keep my hair down? Where's my chapeau?"

'He retrieves it from a peg, and blows dust off it. "Been on the floor a few times."

'"So was I," says Joe Gardiner, the club trainer, who played at Wembley with him in 1939, and sat next to him today.

'"Joe was," says Cullis. "I had him on the floor in the first five minutes."

'"When the ball nearly hit the bar?" asks a journalist.

'"*No!* When one of their players was going through, and I was tackling him!"

'He pushes a pound note into the hand of a dressing-room attendant, and makes for the door. "Have we got everything?"

'"You've got the Cup, anyway," says a journalist.'

19

Giant-Killers

Some years ago Les McDowall, then Manager of Manchester City, remarked:

'If I were given the choice of being drawn at home in the Cup against a First Division side or somebody non-League, I would take the first every time. At least you know what you are up against; with these other little beggars, you don't. You just can't trust 'em.'

'Since the beginning of football, the so called aristocrats of the game have had bad dreams about "these other little beggars" who are also known in the trade as "small fry", "minnows", "Davids", "upstarts" and "giant-killers". They show little respect for reputation; even less for class distinction. They are instinctive iconoclasts, and I never think of any of them without being reminded of those wartime tip and run raiders who wrought damage and chaos before getting the Hell out of it. Not all of them came back for a second time, but for them and their victims, once was more than enough.'

So wrote Eric Todd in the *F.A. News* about the joyous agony the little teams cause. The Managers hate them, the footballing public love them, and their success gives the competition its special flavour. Yet before there is any chance of a non-League side tripping up one of the League Goliaths it has to fight many a stirring battle that never makes the headlines. 20 Clubs are exempt to the First Round along with the Finalists from the Amateur Cup and Challenge Trophy. For the rest it is a long rough road. Consider the progress of Rhyl in 1970:

	Rhyl versus	*Score*	*Venue*
	Pwllheli	6–0	a
	Portmadoc	2–1	h
	Oswestry Town	1–1	a
		2–1	h
	South Liverpool	3–3	h
		2–2	a (extra time)
		1–0	Chester
1st round	Hartlepool	1–0	h
2nd round	Barnsley	0–0	h
		1–1	a (extra time)
		2–0	Old Trafford
3rd round	Swansea City	1–6	a

Twelve hard matches and no major sensation at the end – but for a small Club like Rhyl there is mounting excitement in a Cup run like this. Rhyl had started in one of the 36 Divisions in which the Qualifying Rounds begin. Let us look at the draw in one of them:

Lostock Gralam *v.* Stalybridge Celtic

Northwich Victoria *v.* Buxton

Byes: Prestwich Heys, Burscough, Horwich Railway

Mechanics Institute, Rossendale United,

St. Helen's Town and South Liverpool.

There's a catholic collection of the sides who travel hopefully, but only rarely arrive at the First Round.

Non-league Hereford United, helped for some years by the gentle giant, John Charles, set a record by reaching the Competition Proper for 21 successive years. To achieve it once is beyond the dreams of many.

In the past more than 600 teams have entered the competition but now the numbers are kept to around 450. In case of doubt acceptance of entry depends on the condition of the ground and the size of the gates, as well as the playing record of the Club and the view of its County Association. These are the yardsticks for the Challenge Cup Committee, chaired from 1958 to 1970 by Mr David Wiseman.

What impact have the non-League Clubs had on the competition? Consider the chart on pages 190 and 191 which shows the furthest progress of such teams in every year since 1888.

As the League has enlarged the outsiders have found it more difficult to reach the final rounds. But they still make their mark on the competition, still give Managers sleepless nights.

In the early days of the Midland Alliance or the Southern League the difference of standards was not so great that it was a surprise for these teams to reach the semi-final. To put it in perspective, Tottenham's unique win in 1901 must be viewed in the light of Southern League Southampton reaching the Final in the seasons before and after.

More surprising was Swindon Town's success in reaching the last four in 1910 and 1912. In recent years it was Yeovil Town who made the nation's pulse beat faster as they humbled Romford, Weymouth, Bury, and First Division Sunderland. A crowd 81,561 came to see them challenge the might of Manchester at Old Trafford and there the fun ended. Eight goals slapped them down for their presumption. That was in 1949 and the season before Colchester United had also reached the fifth round, aided by their narrow pitch and Manager Fenton's secret plans, code-named F. & M.

Blackpool finally put them in their place with a crushing 5–0 defeat to avenge Huddersfield Town and Bradford, their earlier League victims.

Bradford now have slipped from League Football to the Northern Premier League while Colchester continue their giant-killing act from the respectability of the Fourth Division.

188

For it is not only the non-League Clubs who stand form on its head. Defeat from a Third or Fourth Division side can be just as cruel. There have been countless upsets in the Challenge Cup, but the two matches that really sent the shockwaves reverberating round Britain (and the many countries abroad that so keenly follow our competition) were Walsall's defeat of Arsenal in the third round of 1932 and Colchester United's defeat of Leeds in the fourth round of 1971.

I can still recall my schoolboy disbelief at hearing that Arsenal at the height of their powers had lost to a Third Division Club. The news was as stunning as England's defeat by the U.S.A. in the World Cup. The result had no basis in logic and one sensed the hilarious excitement at Walsall, the utter dejection at Highbury.

In the book, *Cliff Bastin Remembers*, written with Brian Glanville, Bastin frankly recorded his feelings. The bias is natural, but so too is the genuineness of the feeling. This is what it is like for the great team that is humiliated.

'We never liked to play against Third Division teams. Such teams, when pitted against the glamorous Arsenal, found they had everything to gain and nothing to lose. Consequently, they would fling themselves into the game with reckless abandon and, win, lose, or draw, the gashed, bruised legs of the Arsenal players, after the game was over, would bear grim testimony to their misguided enthusiasm. The Third Division footballer may not be a soccer artist, but when it comes to a heavy tackle, he ranks with the best.

'As was now the Arsenal custom, we went down to Brighton to tune up for the Cup-tie. Whether the opposition was to be Walsall or Aston Villa made no difference to this routine.

'At this period, a severe influenza epidemic was sweeping the country, and three of our regular team – Eddie Hapgood, Bob John and Jack Lambert – fell victims to it, shortly before our match was due to be played. Further, Joey Hulme was in the middle of one of those bad periods which come to even the greatest of footballers at one time or another, and, in consequence, Mr Chapman had some team selection problems on his hands.

'In an endeavour to solve them, he chose Tommy Black, who had recently joined Arsenal from a junior Scottish team, to replace Eddie Hapgood. Norman Sidey, our reserve centre-half, took over at left-half, from Bob John; while to take over from Lambert and Joey Hulme, Mr Chapman chose, respectively, Charlie Walsh and Billy Warnes. In doing so, he made two of his very rare mistakes.

'Warnes, an amateur international who had come to us from the Isthmian League Club, Woking, was entirely the wrong kind of player for such a match as we were going to play. Essentially an artistic footballer, robust methods were liable to shake him off his game, and he was very chary of involving himself in a full-blooded tackle.

'Charlie Walsh had long been trying to bring Chapman round to his own way of thinking – that he was the best centre-forward on Arsenal's books – so far,

PROGRESS OF NON-LEAGUE CLUBS

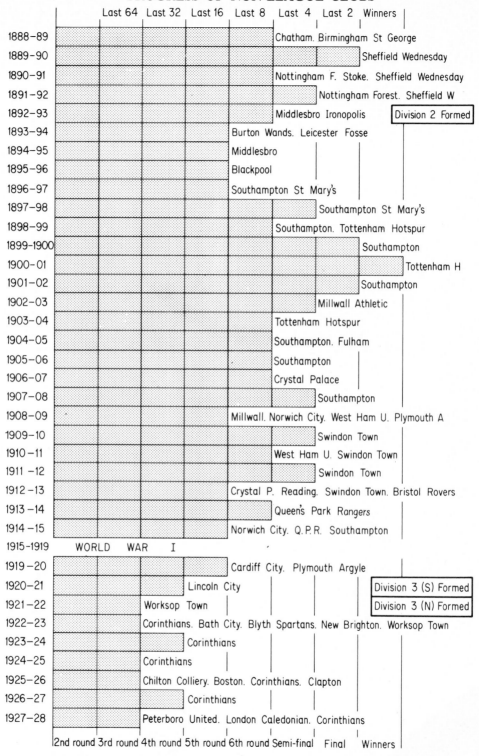

	Last 64	Last 32	Last 16	Last 8	Last 4	Last 2	Winners
1888–89					Chatham. Birmingham St George		
1889–90						Sheffield Wednesday	
1890–91					Nottingham F. Stoke. Sheffield Wednesday		
1891–92						Nottingham Forest. Sheffield W	
1892–93					Middlesbro Ironopolis	Division 2 Formed	
1893–94				Burton Wands. Leicester Fosse			
1894–95				Middlesbro			
1895–96				Blackpool			
1896–97				Southampton St Mary's			
1897–98					Southampton St Mary's		
1898–99					Southampton. Tottenham Hotspur		
1899–1900						Southampton	
1900–01							Tottenham H
1901–02							Southampton
1902–03						Millwall Athletic	
1903–04				Tottenham Hotspur			
1904–05				Southampton. Fulham			
1905–06				Southampton			
1906–07				Crystal Palace			
1907–08					Southampton		
1908–09				Millwall. Norwich City. West Ham U. Plymouth A			
1909–10					Swindon Town		
1910–11				West Ham U. Swindon Town			
1911–12					Swindon Town		
1912–13				Crystal P. Reading. Swindon Town. Bristol Rovers			
1913–14					Queen's Park Rangers		
1914–15				Norwich City. Q.P.R. Southampton			
1915–1919	WORLD WAR I						
1919–20				Cardiff City. Plymouth Argyle			
1920–21			Lincoln City			Division 3 (S) Formed	
1921–22		Worksop Town				Division 3 (N) Formed	
1922–23		Corinthians. Bath City. Blyth Spartans. New Brighton. Worksop Town					
1923–24			Corinthians				
1924–25		Corinthians					
1925–26		Chilton Colliery. Boston. Corinthians. Clapton					
1926–27			Corinthians				
1927–28		Peterboro United. London Caledonian. Corinthians					
	2nd round	3rd round	4th round	5th round	6th round	Semi-final	Final	Winners

Note: The names indicate the non-league clubs that reached the furthest round marked.

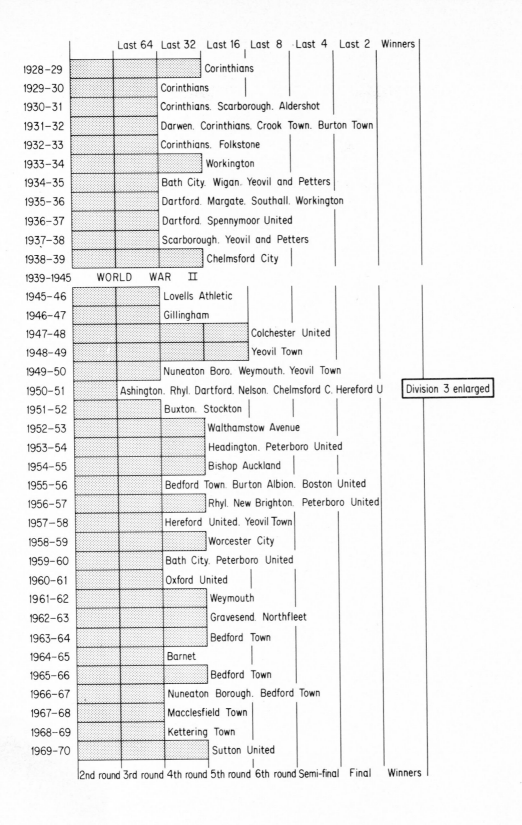

	Last 64	Last 32	Last 16	Last 8	Last 4	Last 2	Winners
1928–29			Corinthians				
1929–30		Corinthians					
1930–31		Corinthians. Scarborough. Aldershot					
1931–32		Darwen. Corinthians. Crook Town. Burton Town					
1932–33		Corinthians. Folkstone					
1933–34			Workington				
1934–35		Bath City. Wigan. Yeovil and Petters					
1935–36		Dartford. Margate. Southall. Workington					
1936–37		Dartford. Spennymoor United					
1937–38		Scarborough. Yeovil and Petters					
1938–39			Chelmsford City				
1939–1945	WORLD WAR II						
1945–46		Lovells Athletic					
1946–47		Gillingham					
1947–48				Colchester United			
1948–49				Yeovil Town			
1949–50		Nuneaton Boro. Weymouth. Yeovil Town					
1950–51	Ashington. Rhyl. Dartford. Nelson. Chelmsford C. Hereford U						
1951–52		Buxton. Stockton					
1952–53		Walthamstow Avenue					
1953–54			Headington. Peterboro United				
1954–55		Bishop Auckland					
1955–56		Bedford Town. Burton Albion. Boston United					
1956–57			Rhyl. New Brighton. Peterboro United				
1957–58		Hereford United. Yeovil Town					
1958–59			Worcester City				
1959–60		Bath City. Peterboro United					
1960–61		Oxford United					
1961–62			Weymouth				
1962–63			Gravesend. Northfleet				
1963–64			Bedford Town				
1964–65		Barnet					
1965–66			Bedford Town				
1966–67		Nuneaton Borough. Bedford Town					
1967–68		Macclesfield Town					
1968–69		Kettering Town					
1969–70			Sutton United				
	2nd round	3rd round	4th round	5th round	6th round	Semi-final	Final	Winners

Division 3 enlarged

without success. In this match, however, Chapman gave him his chance. He missed it, all too emphatically.

'Almost as soon as play had started, on the microscopic Walsall ground, it became quite clear to me that all our fears about the tactics our opponents might employ were fully justified. As soon as the ball came out to me on the left wing I was blatantly fouled by the Walsall right-back, who bowled me over without ceremony. No foul was given, however. Throughout the game, the referee was curiously lenient.

'Walsall could not have complained had five of their men, at least, been sent off the field in the first quarter of an hour. Arsenal were awarded ten free-kicks in as many minutes after the first whistle. Compared with this apology for a football match, the replayed semi-final against Hull City, three seasons back, had been child's play.

'Soon after the kick-off, big Herbie Roberts sustained a cut eye, in a violent aerial collision, and was handicapped accordingly for the rest of the game. Do not misinterpret me. I don't want to level an indictment at the Walsall players. They played, a little too vigorously, perhaps, the game which was right in the circumstances. If David had worn heavy armour against Goliath, the Philistine might have lived to a ripe old age! But it was rather disconcerting for Arsenal.

'Yet for all Walsall's crude tactics, and for all the difficulties imposed by the tiny pitch, and the proximity of the spectators who sat around it, I still say we should have won. We had quite enough chances to have banged in half a dozen goals. Not one was accepted.

'Charlie Walsh was the chief offender. His nervousness was pitiful to behold. On one occasion, during the first half, I crossed the ball right on to his head, with not one Walsall defender standing within yards of him. He misjudged the centre hopelessly and missed the ball completely. It bounced off his shoulder, to be pounced on by a thankful Walsall defence.

'Half-time came without any score. The Walsall supporters cheered their team to the echo, as it came off the field. It had held the mighty Arsenal for fully three-quarters of an hour! How this had been done was a matter that did not need to be discussed.

'For the second half, Charlie Walsh was switched to inside-right. David Jack took over from him as centre-forward. Perhaps, we thought, this switch will do the trick. We were wrong.

'Walsall took the lead after fifteen minutes. Gilbert Allsop their centre-forward, headed in a corner taken by the outside-right, Lee. The resultant clamour was heard fully two miles away.

'Far from converting the Walsall players to less vigorous ways, this goal only served to encourage them to further excesses of zeal. Alex James, who was literally knocked off his game, was a particularly bad sufferer. The gravest casualty of the second half was, however, left-half Norman Sidey. Norman – a sound player, but always inclined to be a little slow – was moving in leisurely

In 1953 amateurs Walthamstow Avenue held Manchester United to a draw at
Old Trafford before losing the replay 2–5 at Highbury. Centre-forward Lewis
scores Walthamstow's second goal watched by Trevor Bailey (7).

fashion for a ball which he seemed to have plenty of time to bring under control,
when a Walsall player appeared on the scene, and kicked him very scientifically
on the knee. Sorry as I was for Norman, I must confess that I had to laugh at his
resultant antics. He doubled up with pain, then sank slowly, very slowly, to the
ground. If he had collapsed at once, it would not have been in the least amusing.
But the sight of Norman sinking to the earth in slow motion brought a ray of
humour even into this evil-tasting game. Still, isn't it said that humour is always
just a step away from tragedy?

Bournemouth upset Wolverhampton Wanderers in the fourth
round match in 1957 bringing down their goalpost and
beating them 1–0 at Molineux.

'If Arsenal had had plenty of chances in the first half, we could not complain of lack of opportunities in the second. On one particular occasion, we would almost certainly have equalised, had it not been for the presence of one Charles Walsh.

'I gave David Jack a head-high centre. It was a golden chance, and I could sense that David was picking his spot in the Walsall net. But just as the ball was about to reach him, who should come thundering up from behind like a runaway tank but . . . Charlie Walsh!

In 1971 Fourth Division Colchester United went
one better as giant-killers, beating Leeds United 3–2,
aided by this goal from Crawford.

The giant-killers rejoice. Colchester United celebrate
after beating Leeds United in the fifth round in 1971.

'The astonishing leap through the air with which he ended his run deserved a better fate than it actually received. Alas, all Charlie did was to divert the ball away from David Jack, far, far from the Walsall goal. I can remember vividly to this day the look which David Jack gave Charlie.

'Walsall ultimately made things sure by converting a penalty. It was, I felt, rather curious that we, and not they, should give away a spot-kick, after the manner in which some of their players had behaved. However, there was no doubt at all that the penalty award against us was thoroughly deserved.

'It came as the climax of a long series of duels between one of our defenders and a Walsall forward. Relations between these two had gradually been becoming more and more strained, until it ultimately came to a point at which the question was which of them would be the first to vent his feelings on the other. Unfortunately for us, it was our man.

196

Radford scores Arsenal's first goal to prevent
any upset at Yeovil in 1971.

'Sheppard, the Walsall inside-right, took the penalty. His hard, low shot gave our goalkeeper, Frank Moss, no possible chance of saving.

'Never have I seen Herbert Chapman look so miserably unhappy. He made a brave, desperate, but unavailing effort to cheer us all up. "Never mind, boys," he said, "these things do happen." But we were all inconsolable, and so, for that matter, was he. I think he felt the blow more than any of us. Here was the team which he had come to when it was struggling pathetically at the bottom of the

In 1948 Colchester United took the country by storm,
their run ending in the fifth round at Blackpool.

First Division; the team which he had made one of the greatest in the history of
football, beaten by a fifth-rate side. Napoleon must have felt like that in Russia,
120 years before.'

A sequel to this ever-remembered game was the transfer to another club of the
man who gave Walsall their penalty. His foul was undoubtedly the result of great
provocation, but Mr Chapman would not suffer behaviour like that from any
player at Highbury.

The same sense of desolation engulfed Leeds when they lost to Colchester and
there was the same disbelief throughout the country. The experts had been saying
that the leading Clubs' standards were now too high, the gap in class too great for
them to be upset by the small fry. Leeds was taken as the exemplar of consistency
and competent professionalism, iron-nerved and unassailable. And suddenly they
fell apart before the enthusiasm of a Fourth Division side and Ray Crawford's
remembered skills. His power at centre-forward had once won Ipswich Town the

League Championship and now aided by Sprake's misjudgments he made good his confident forecast that Leeds would be his rabbit.

Miracles don't strike twice in the same place and Colchester, for all the brave efforts of their goalkeeper, were over-run by Everton at Goodison Park.

Frank McGhee recorded Colchester's wonderful win in the *Sunday Mirror* under the headline 'Mighty Leeds Crash Out to Crawford'.

'The shock waves of probably the greatest F.A. Cup upset of all time are still rippling through the bewildered minds of everyone who saw it, and who played in it.

'None of them will ever forget the day a numb, glum Leeds team, favourites for the trophy, went under to a Fourth Division side, happy to concede that they are made up of other club's rejects.

'It was essentially the story of those who will remember it most vividly, the men involved in the moves, the goals, the misses, the mistakes of a match that had everything.

'The immediately obvious man to mention is that hero whose performance could have been stolen from schoolboy fiction, the 34-year-old ex-England centre forward Ray Crawford, whom Colchester rescued from non-League football this season.

'He promised he would have a good game – and had a great one. He threatened he would score a goal – and got two.

'He boasted that Jack Charlton was his favourite centre half – and proved it by harassing the great old warrior into a nightmare of errors.

'But there was much more to it than just one man's memorable contribution.

'There was the tremendous fight-back by Leeds from 3–0 down and out of it to 3–2 and on the edge of survival that was denied them by one fabulous save from Colchester's Graham Smith.

'There was the disastrous error in attitude that spread through the whole Leeds team at the start – and eventually proved to be fatal.

'Perhaps that's the obvious place to start – the folly of the Leeds response to the early and successful disruption of their rhythm by Colchester.

'Instead of attempting to ride out the storm. Leeds fed it with illegalities of their own, careering into tackles that descended to levels which disgraced the standards they have been setting for the past three years.

'I have never seen the Leeds defence, Jack Charlton and right back Paul Reaney in particular, so miserably inept.

'They should have gone a goal down when Colchester's striker Mick Mahon roared through an inviting gap in the eleventh minute to have a shot strike keeper Gary Sprake's legs.

'But that miserable moment was delayed only seven minutes. In the eighteenth Brian Lewis, the Colchester winger who throughout the match lobbed passes

199

that were mortar bombs, sent a free kick dropping towards the far post for Crawford to race at, rise to and direct into the top of the net.

'In the twenty-fourth he added a second – a goal with admittedly an element of the freakish about it.

'After a cross from the right by winger Brian Gibbs, Crawford squeezed past Reaney, fell in a heap with Sprake and as the ball broke free, squirmed on his backside to hook it and send it rolling gently in.

'It became even worse for Leeds in the fifty-fifth minute when Colchester went further in front, with Sprake again taking much of the blame.

'He was caught flat-footed, off his line, moving neither forward nor back as inside-right Simmons burst between him and Reaney to head another Lewis long lob into an empty net.

'And then Leeds, at last started to play. They pulled one back in the sixty-first minute when Giles took a short corner and left half Norman Hunter rose high above them all in the goalmouth to nod Lorimer's cross into the net.

'They made it 3–2 in the seventy-fifth when Colchester centre-half Brian Garvey misplaced a clearance that was snapped up by Bates and worked through to Giles whose snap shot flashed in from the edge of the area.

'And suddenly all Colchester's confidence drained away.

'Colchester's three tight markers in defence, Garvey on Mick Jones, left half Joe Kurila on inside right Allan Clarke and full back Brian Hall on Lorimer, became distinctly shaky sentries.

'Colchester still had their moments – notably a couple of breakaways by Crawford, once miskicking through sheer weariness with only Sprake to beat.

'But it was Leeds who really gave the game its climax, settling at last to a spell of football that was summed up afterwards by Colchester manager Dick Graham.

'Unashamedly wet-eyed at the warmth of the way his players had mobbed and hugged him he still found time to say:

' "Leeds finished up playing the best and most controlled football I've ever seen." '

Four Third Division sides have reached the semi-final, Millwall the first to battle through in 1937 had previously reached the last four when in the Southern League. In 1954 Port Vale's iron defence conceded no goal to Queens Park Rangers and none to Cardiff or Blackpool or Leyton Orient. Wembley beckoned when they led West Bromwich at half-time, but at last Dudley and Allen found the way through.

The next year York City hunted Newcastle hard at Hillsborough. They had narrowly failed to reach the semi-final in 1938 holding Huddersfield to a goalless draw before submitting. Now they had their heads down for Wembley with hope surging high as Bolton gave them the lead. And, even though Keeble equalised York were twice only agonising inches from a decisive goal in the last minutes.

Scoular's harsh tackling kept them out and in the replay Mitchell's delicate dribbling deluded them to defeat.

But it was Norwich City who had the best chance of taking the Cup. Coached by that shrewd footballer, Archie Macaulay, they reached the semi-final and clearly had the ability to match Luton. This account by James Wilson in *The Sunday Times* tells how they held them:

'A DRAW at White Hart Lane yesterday was probably a fair result in a match exciting enough for even the most hardboiled spectator, and there will be many neutral observers, as well as Norwich supporters, glad to see the East Anglian club still carrying the Third Division flag proudly towards Wembley.

'Norwich's formidable earlier bag of Cup victims prevents one regarding their latest half-triumph as in any way a surprise.

'Their draw with Luton keeps them still in the game with a wonderful chance of becoming not only the first Third Division side to appear at Wembley but also the first Cup finalists from outside the First and Second Division since Southampton (then in the Southern League) in 1902.

'It is tempting but erroneous to ascribe Norwich's success merely to an astonishing run of sustained good fortune. To do so is less than fair not only to the players, but also to their astute manager, Archie Macaulay. By planning each match individually and by careful study of each set of opponents, he has shown how a well-organised team of moderate ability can hold a succession of sides of much greater potential.

'The Macaulay technique is well fitted to the Cup competition, where tension often reduces a better footballing side to the level of less skilful opponents; the credit for Norwich's magnificent achievement deserves, in fact, to be shared equally between their manager's analytical ability and his players' loyal interpretation of the resulting tactical ideas.

'Yesterday the hard ground seemed likely to suit Luton's polished style rather than Norwich's brand of sustained endeavour.

'Throughout the first half, indeed, Luton were much the superior side. In Cummins and Bingham they had the two best forwards on the field. But for a magnificent display of goalkeeping by Kennon these two might have sent Luton in for their mid-match cup of tea with such a clear lead that nothing Norwich could achieve later would make any difference.

'Great credit, however, is due to the whole Norwich defence for their fine rearguard action throughout the first half. They never panicked; despite intense Luton pressure, involving seven corners in the first 25 minutes, Butler and his fellow defenders continued methodically to push the ball away, and deliberately avoided wild aimless clearances.

'It was upon this fine defensive basis that was to be built the framework for Norwich's later counter-attack.

'The inevitable Luton goal came after 35 minutes. Bingham received a short free-kick on the right wing, beat Ashman yet again, and crossed a perfect centre for Brown to head easily home.

'For the only time in the game the covering of the Norwich defenders seemed at fault. They were, perhaps, unsettled by the speed with which Groves took the free-kick out on the right.

'To Norwich's great credit they continued to play good football even when behind. Even before the interval McCrohan raced up the right wing and centred perfectly but Crossan's header just skimmed the bar.

'Norwich's attacks at this stage were infrequent, and the tall Bly never seemed likely to get the better of the unhurrying Owen at the heart of the Luton defence. Nevertheless, they nearly scored in their first proper attack after 20 minutes.

'Brennan crossed a fine ball for Crossan, standing on the penalty spot, to see his header pushed round the post by Baynham.

'In the second half Luton, instead of going on where they had left off before the interval unwisely fell back on defence. Gradually Norwich came more into the game, and they thoroughly deserved their equaliser when it came 25 minutes from the end.

'It was not a great, or even a planned goal. McCrohan squared the ball hopefully across the Luton goal to Brennan, who, finding himself unmarked, pulled the ball down and coolly slammed a right-foot drive past Baynham.

'Both sides had their moments after this but Luton never managed to recapture their earlier rhythm. Too often Morton and Bingham were left unsupported in attack, and Cummins was by now too busy helping in defence to play his full part in attack.

'Nevertheless, only the finest of Kennon's many saves prevented Bingham from winning the game three minutes from time. By now, however, anything but a draw would have been grossly unfair to Norwich, and one was glad to see them live to fight another day.'

Luton edged home by a single goal in the replay, the ball obstinately declining to bounce Norwich's way when it mattered most. At least Norwich, like York City, had shown that a Third Division team could still hope to reach the Final. But that was twelve years ago and still they can only dream.

The non-league clubs have now the better chance of playing at Wembley for they have their own Challenge Trophy started by the F.A. in the 1969 season. But they will still be setting problems for the big clubs in the 'Cup'.

20

Tickets and Administration

No sport has such a massive following as association football and a Cup-Final ticket is both a status symbol and wish fulfilment. Sadly there is a limit to the supporters who can be accommodated and they try every dodge to get into Wembley. Someone tunnelled under the East entrance, but an alert official detected him as the tunnel caved in. To see Arsenal complete their first 'double' four young men climbed the walls in suction boots and were later rounded up by patrols. Tickets hopefully purchased from unofficial sources too often turn out to be photocopies or forgeries.

After that first Wembley Final the *Sunday Pictorial* commented: 'Cup Final chaos that was nearly a disaster.'

Good fortune had saved a forerunner of that terrible day when 33 died in the crush at a Cup-tie between Bolton Wanderers and Stoke City. But thereafter Wembley has always been an all-ticket match, the allocation decided by the F.A., the administrative arrangements controlled by the Wembley authorities.

The allocation has varied with the years, but progressively more tickets have been given to the Finalists, fewer to Clubs less directly involved. Originally tickets were still on sale at Wembley until a few days before the Final, but it soon became a matter of allocation. For 1971 the tickets, apart from the complimentary ones or those needed for officials on the day, were divided as follows:

	Tickets
The Football Association	2,560
The Finalists	39,210
County F.A.'s	33,396
Other Associations	97
First Division Clubs	8,690
Second ,, ,,	4,378
Third ,, ,,	2,136
Fourth ,, ,,	2,136
Other Full Members	1,980
Council Representatives	1,400
Wembley Stadium	500

These tickets have a scarcity value five to ten times greater than their price. No wonder special security paper is used for the printing so that forgeries can be easily detected. No wonder lists are kept so that it is known to whom every ticket was issued originally. No wonder that the touts still make a killing as disappointed supporters pay exorbitant prices.

From 1924 the difficulties were in the administration, not the crowd control on the day. Fred Jackson, Box Office Manager until he retired in 1967, dealt with them all with patience and precision. At every Final there are particular problems with those whose hard luck story of lost tickets has to be carefully checked. It is then that it is essential for the staff to know to whom each ticket was allocated. If the story is accepted, the person is guided to the seat and the nearest steward warned in case there is still any dispute over right to the seat. In a programme on Wembley Fred Jackson recorded this comment:

'Round about Cup-Final time I've been called the best hated man in England.

'But after all there's a limit to the Stadium capacity and we've always had a good many more applications than seats. And the trouble hasn't always ended with the issuing of tickets to the lucky ones – I remember particularly well the man who sent me the charred remains of two 2s. 6d. tickets in a matchbox. I was able to make out just enough to know that they were genuine ones which allowed me to issue him duplicates.

'Then there was the case of the man who produced two half-guinea tickets well chewed up by his dog after the postman had dropped them into his letter-box. Those too were proved genuine and replacements issued. No one has ever tried bribery and corruption on a large scale to get Cup-Final tickets, but I have to smile when I think of the fellow who each year used to enclose some rather squashed cigarettes with his application stating that he hoped that I would smoke these while I was allocating his seats.'

At least the applicant knew Fred Jackson was a heavy smoker! On another occasion he was shown the pulped up remains of some tickets that had gone with a suit to the cleaners and he was just able to identify the fragments. The F.A. too has problems from the piles of hopeful letters. One schoolboy sent in a thousand lines of 'Please can I have a ticket. Please . . .' The F.A. had to refuse the request as the allocations must keep to the standard pattern – but eventually a Liverpool Club supporter took pity on him and he saw the game with Arsenal.

For every Final a special booklet is prepared, the *Programme of Arrangements*, with its 14 sections from competing teams and officials, to bands, community singing and entertainment to transport. Every minute is covered, every official briefed.

In 1971 Mr Denis Follows, Secretary of The Football Association, described in the *F.A. News* the work behind the scenes that ensures such smooth presentation.

'The excellence of the arrangements made for the presentation of a Cup-Final at Wembley has now become accepted as part of the Wembley tradition. Everyone who sees a Final for the first time is thrilled by the spectacle, and the split second timing of the various activities which culminate in the kick-off. Anyone with the remotest association with the organisation of any event, however

Cup-Final preparation. The referee and linesmen select the balls
for the 1971 Cup-Final watched by F.A. Secretary, Denis Follows.
There is no maker's name on any of the balls.

humble, knows that the success of the enterprise does not just happen. It is the result of careful planning and painstaking administration. The Cup-Final is no exception. Years of experience lie behind the presentation of every Cup-Final and, whilst a general pattern is usually followed, rarely a year passes without the introduction of some small change as a result of new techniques or new social habits.

'Preparations for a Cup-Final in May begin in the previous autumn when a decision is taken concerning the pricing and allocation of tickets. The various interested parties are informed and printing is undertaken by Wembley Stadium. The tickets are not distributed until some three weeks before the match. Invitations are extended to the chief guest, usually a member of the Royal Family, at about the turn of the year.

'When the semi-finalists are known they receive a memorandum which is designed to help them make their preparations in the event of their winning their way into the Final. This is particularly helpful to those clubs who have not had any recent experience of appearing at Wembley.

'For the match itself, a very detailed programme of arrangements is printed, copies of which are sent to every individual who has any direct connection with the arrangements for the day. The booklet which consists of some eight pages covers the following items:

Section	I	**Competing Teams and Officials**
	II	**Referee and Linesmen**
	III	**Substitution**
	IV	**Footballs and Linesmen's Flags, Cup and Medals**
	V	**Ball-Boys**
	VI	**Programmes**
	VII	**Interval Entertainment**
	VIII	**Bands and Community Singing**
	IX	**Reception and Presentation of Officials and Teams**
	X	**Royal Box Guests**
	XI	**Dispersal**
	XII	**Catering**
	XIII	**Stewards**

The following extracts from the programme indicate the meticulous preparation and accurate timing which governs the detailed arrangements:

SECTION 1

Competing Teams and Officials.

X will occupy the North Dressing Room, and Y the South Dressing Room.

2.48 p.m. The players must be ready to leave the dressing rooms. A member of the F.A. Staff – Mr H. N. Bird – will inform the players, referee and linesmen, when to leave, and will conduct them to the entrance to the playing arena. They will enter the arena side by side on receipt of a signal from Mr Stanton at the arena end of the

Royal Tunnel, and will proceed across the field of play and take up their positions at the flags opposite the Royal Tunnel in two lines facing each other for presentation to the Royal Guest, the X team at the blue flag, and the Y team at the white flag. The referee and linesmen will take up their positions as indicated . . . Mr H. N. Bird will supervise these arrangements.

Photographers must wait until after the teams are in position before they can enter the playing field.

Plans are reproduced showing the location of the teams and photographers when the presentations are to be made.

Immediately the match is over the players and the three match Officials will assemble in front of the Royal Tunnel. The winning team, including the substitute, headed by the captain, will then walk up the steps on the right facing the Royal Box to receive the Cup and medals, followed by the captain and members of the losing team, including the substitute, and the referee and linesmen. The Royal Guest will present the Cup and a medal to the captain. The next player will then take the plinth and receive his medal. Immediately the second linesman has joined the players, the National Anthem will be played – Mr D. Follows, who will be standing beside The Royal Guest, will give the signal to the Bandmaster. As the players and officials return to the field they must form a line facing the Royal Box. A member of The F.A. Staff, Mr Bird, with the Wembley Officials detailed to be responsible for the ground arrangements, will direct these movements.

SECTION IV

Footballs and Linesmen's Flags.

A Member of the F.A. Staff, Mr N. Williams, will be responsible for taking the footballs and flags to Wembley and for taking them to the Officials' dressing room for the Referee to make his selection unless the choice has been made at the Offices of The Football Association on the morning of the match. The practice balls will be taken to the respective dressing rooms before the match. During the game these will be in the charge of the substitute linesmen and after the match they will be collected for return to Lancaster Gate.

Cup and Medals.

A member of The F.A. Staff, Mr J. Baylis, will deliver the Cup and medals to Mr K. Sutton on arrival at Wembley. At 4.30 p.m. Wembley officials will bring them to The Royal Box.

Reference is made in the first extract to a 'signal from Mr Stanton'. Signalling and communications form an integral part of the arrangements for a Cup-Final. Individuals are placed at strategic positions for the purpose of passing on messages by pre-arranged signals. In this way movement prior to the match is accurately controlled, so that the appearance of the Royal Guest coincides with the final line up of the players and officials for presentation and the playing of the National Anthem.

Crowd control is in the hands of Wembley Stadium and their co-operation with the police is again based on years of experience.

As one of the few privileged regular attenders at a Cup-Final with a job of work to do I am always moved by the atmosphere of the occasion and the ceremony attached to it. There is little wonder therefore that the Cup-Final is universally recognised as *the* event in the football year.

The draw for the Cup games is now an established ritual watched by millions on television. The Chairman of the Challenge Cup Committee is responsible for this and the smooth presentation to the viewers occasionally conceals a backstage problem.

Mr David Wiseman was once trapped in his hotel lift arriving for the draw with only a minute to spare. The bag with the numbered balls has also proved somewhat slippery on occasions until Sir Stanley Rous finally arranged for a special thong that attaches it to the Chairman's wrist. This has eliminated the possibility of the balls being spilled over the floor and there is a gloss to the whole operation that is very different from the early days at the Holborn Viaduct offices of the F.A.

Then folded pieces of paper with the names of the Clubs written on were dropped into a top-hat which was veiled with a handkerchief. An official holding the top-hat then lifted the corner of the handkerchief so that two Council officials could each draw out a slip, pairing off the teams.

The draw is the most obvious link for the public between the Cup and soccer's administration. But since the competition has been the mainspring for the whole of football's development the background administration has been vital to its success. The striking feature of this has been the continuity. Over the 100 years since the Cup began there have been only four Secretaries, Charles Alcock (1870–1895), Sir Frederick Wall (1895–1934), Sir Stanley Rous (1934–1962), and now Denis Follows.

Their experience, their strong guidance has played a vital part in the orderly organisation that this great competition demands.

21

Verse, Song, and Supporters

'Then strip, lads and to it though sharp be the weather
And if by mischance you should happen to fall,
There are worse things in life than a tumble in heather
And life itself is a game of football.'

'In riot revelry and rout
Pursue the football play.'

Sir Walter Scott

Cricket was the first game to unite all classes through a common love of sport. This fascination found expression in a wealth of fine writing. The quiet tempo of the game building up to unbearable climax, its easy grace of movement, its emphasis on sportsmanship and character values, its contemplative crowds, all stirred the imagination of writers. The spirit of the game was best expressed in print with raucous comment and total commitment left to the uninhibited spectators on the 'Hill' in Sydney.

Football with its faster pace, its fiercer challenge and its massive spectator involvement bred a different response. The supporters' commitment is passionate, voluble, and at times violent. There is none of the cathedral calm of the pavilion at Lords and the pent-up emotion finds immediate expression. There is a true 'folk' quality in the songs and verse this inspired, ranging from the rough and rude to the polished and penetrating. 'Poetry is the spontaneous overflow of powerful feeling,' said Wordsworth. It is all too evident that football – and in particular the Cup – excites an overflow of powerful feelings. Often this is channelled into poetry or ballad or song.

There is a classical simplicity in the poem by the Queen's Park player, H. N. Smith, after a match with Hamilton Gymnasium in 1869. Two stanzas sum up the spirit of association football in its formative years expressing in a few lines the essence of the game:

'Kick at the ball or not at all
No pushing with the hand,
Tripping, holding, quar'ling, scolding
(Two umpires council holding
The play close watching stand)

No nails or spikes or plated boots
The game is won by sleight of foot.
Strike if you list with hand or fist,
The ball but not the man!
No player hold, however bold
But with your shoulder, you are told
Avert him if you can;
Lift or carry, lead they to ill –
Football's the game and won by skill.'

Another poem printed in the *Football Post* of 1903 outlines the eternal dilemma of officialdom and the ethics of fair play. In the style of Gilbert's 'Bab Ballads' it comments with a player's crude commonsense on some observations by The Football Association:

'We mustn't kick the winger when he's passed us on the scent
We mustn't push him headlong over heels
We mustn't jump upon him to our very heart's content
Nor hack his ankle till the beggar reels?'

'Well I do say as its ridiculous to alter all the show
Because of splintered bone or twisted knee
Why bless your life the forwards like it – they expect it so
Why cannot the F.A. nibnobs let us be?'

The more it changes the more it stays the same! That controversy is just as lively 69 years on – and these verses may be some comfort to those who think soccer has suddenly got rougher. 'Don't worry about the ball, let's get on with the game,' has always been a popular cry with some players.

The 'winner take all,' death-or-glory aspect of Cup Games plays on the emotions. Supporters are more excitable and vulnerable than the players for they are denied the release of action. Their relief is in song or slogan and their team's victories may be celebrated in ballad or verse. The 'spontaneous overflow of feeling' has been rich and varied. There is humourous comment as in the poem of a Mr Kay of Tonge Moor, published in the *Bolton Evening News* when Nat Lofthouse announced his retirement.

The 1958 Final was won for Bolton Wanderers when Nat Lofthouse barged Harry Gregg over his line as he clutched the ball. That controversial incident drew the neat comment in one stanza:

'Harry Gregg just after t'Final
Went into Nat's for a beer
Who returned his money and told him
We don't charge goalkeepers here!'

But the heroic approach has been more favoured. Sandy Turnbull, hardly recovered from injury, won the Cup for Manchester United in 1909. His feat was lauded in the *Athletic News*:

> 'Why, we thought that you were crock'd –
> Dashing Sandy –
> That to Fame your road was block'd –
> Hard lines, Sandy!
> But you came up to the scratch,
> Made an effort for THE match,
> A great victory to snatch –
> Bravo Sandy!'

When Everton beat Newcastle United in 1906 there was fulsome praise for Young. In honour of his part in the 'Toffee Men's' victory an excited fan wrote:

> 'O Evertonians, such a day
> So fought, so sweetly won,
> Hath ne'er inspired a roundelay
> Since ever time begun;
> As sweet as toffee to the tongue
> Was that one splendid goal by Young.'

Football verse runs close to the folk tradition and was often unwritten at the time. An exhortatory piece thought to have originated in a pantomime at the Alexandra Theatre, Sheffield, was afterwards recorded though the words were varied every night in the pantomime tradition of topicality. The written version runs:

> 'There's a good old Wednesday Captain
> Fred Thompson is his name,
> And on each side of him are heroes of great fame
> There's Morley, Smith and Dogworth,
> There's Betts of great renown,
> There's Ingram, Woolhouse and Mumford
> They will never let him down
> For they're good 'uns one and all
> No names I need to call.'
> Chorus:
> 'So play up, my Wednesday boys,
> They try to win where'er they can
> By a little bit of luck,
> They will bring us home the Cup
> So play up, my Wednesday Boys.'

There speaks the eternal, resilient supporter. His team can do no wrong and even total defeat can be seen as triumph. Or that at least is how 12-year-old

211

Magdalen Hewitt saw Crewe Alexandra's performance in the 1961 Competition. First Division Chelsea had been defeated and Tottenham Hotspur held to a draw before Fourth Division Crewe crashed 13–2 at White Hart Lane in the replay. Undaunted Magdalen wrote:

'Some talk of Tottenham Hotspurs
And some of other teams
Yet the boldest are the Alex,
At least that's how it seems.

In all the Fourth Division
By far the best is Crewe,
Who went down to mighty Tottenham
But not before they drew!

They all are our town heroes,
Especially Jim McGill
Who was told "You'll never play again",
But he had a strong will.

Jones, Campbell, and Williamson,
All the team, too,
These lads who are playing for
The Alex and for Crewe.

Let us cheer on Alex
In the white and red socks
See them brave the enemy
And give the crowd great shocks.

I'll wear a gay red ribbon
And a white one, too,
And shout out, "Up the Alex",
When its Tottenham versus CREWE.'

But soccer also has its vast epic poem, a piece of enormous length on Sheffield United's Cup win in 1899.

'Then went there forth a chosen band
Eleven good men and true,
"United" called; for Sheffield's Fame
Their best resolved to do.

Burnley fell first, then proud Preston
In long and stubborn fight;
York once more countered Lancaster
The Red Rose 'gainst the White

212

But then came valiant Liverpool
And fortune, fickle Jade,
Turns from the Victors, who are thrice
Baffled, though undismayed.'

(It took four games to defeat Liverpool, and so to the Final, described in detail before its climax.)

'Brave they defence, thou sturdy Fryer!
E'en failure brings increased
Respect for thy skill 'gainst the attacks
Of Bennett, Beers and Priest.
Still louder, longer shouts declare
At length the battle done,
While heralds call, "Sheffield doth win
Handsomely – four to one!"'

Two verses from Dannie Abse's poem on Ninian Park so well describes the feeling before and after the game:

'Waiting, we recall records, legendary scores:
Fred Keenor, Hardy in a royal blue shirt.
The very names, sad as old songs, open doors
Before our time when someone else was hurt.
Now, like an injured beast, the great crowd roars.

'Silent the Stadium. The crowds have all filed out.
Only the pigeons beneath the roofs remain.
The clean programmes are trampled underfoot,
And natural the dark, appropriate the rain,
Whilst, under lamp posts, threatening newsboys shout.'

A verse from 'Men on the Terraces' by Gordon Jeffery evokes the same shared feeling of nostalgia:

'But sometimes during the dullest play
Something comes back from an earlier day.
A fleeting moment, a hint of grace
Brings back a feeling, a time, a place' . . . .

The feeling, the time, the place that so often recurs in Cup memories is the Matthews final of 1953. And of Matthews Alan Ross wrote with poetic insight:

'Only emptiness following him, pursuing some scent
Of his own, he weaves in towards,
Not away from, fresh tacklers,
Who, turning about to gain time, are by him
Harried, pursued not pursuers.
Now gathers speed, nursing the ball as he cruises,

213

Eyes judging distance, noting the gaps, the spaces
Vital for colleagues to move to, slowing a trace,
As from Vivaldi to Dibdin, pausing
And leisurely, leisurely swings
To the left upright his centre, on hips
His hands, observing the goalkeeper spring,
Heads rising vainly to the ball's curve
Just as it's plucked from them; and dispassionately
Back to his mark he trots, whistling through closed lips.
Trim as a yacht, with similar lightness
– Of keel, of reaction to surface – with salt air
Tanned, this incomparable player, in decline fair
To look at, nor in decline either,
Improving like wine with age, has come far –
Born to one, a barber, who boxed
Not with such filial magnificence, but well.
"The greatest of all time", *Meraviglioso* Matthews –
Stoke City, Blackpool and England.
Expressionless enchanter, weaving as on strings
Conceptual patterns to a private music, heard
Only by him, to whose slowly emerging theme
He rehearses steps, soloist in compulsions of a dream.'

Herbert Chapman's name stands out among Managers as does Matthews' among players. In 'The Lost Captain' Thomas Moult captured the feeling:

'Who shall challenge his name, who shall challenge the laurel
We hold out to him through the twilight? His love
Was of beauty of action, and clear limbs that move
With the pride of high combat above the mean quarrel.
He led others to share it. And that is enough.'

Writing verse and sending In Memoriam cards to the losers, was once the popular fashion. But much of the celebration and support has always been in song.

In 1893 as Wolves set off for their Final with Everton ballad sheets were on sale with the chorus:

'Then hurrah! for the Wolves of the Forest –
The lads from the Black Country town,
For they'll win the old Cup at the finish,
And gain for themselves great renown.'

But there is one song particularly associated with the Final at Wembley – 'Abide with Me' first sung there in 1927. Perhaps it is appropriate to have pride of place given to a hymn since for many of the more enthusiastic supporters football is almost a religion.

Radcliffe was the first official master of ceremonies at Wembley leading the 100,000 spectators in their community singing. The choice was his when 'Abide with Me' was first included, but it was known to be a favourite hymn of Queen Mary's.

Tradition has staled its impact, but for years it was a central part of the day – a moment of deep emotion that moved the great crowds. So popular did it become that there was a storm of controversy when public opinion was tested one year by the announcement that it was to be left out. In 1959 it was reported in *The Times* 'A Wembley Stadium spokesman said on Wednesday that a display by girls of the Coventry Keep Fit Association would take the place of the hymn (Abide with Me).'

A letter to *The Times* from the Reverend H. W. R. Elsley read:

'Sir – I am the vicar of the parish in which the Empire Stadium is situated and have been an appreciative guest at Cup Finals for many years. I can testify that the hymn, "Abide with Me," has been sung with perfect reverence; but with what amount of understanding is another matter. The words "fast falls the eventide, the darkness deepens" seem out of place in broad daylight and sometimes in strong sunshine. The reverend father, of course, was thinking of his approaching death at all too young an age. But this sentiment is also out of place on the lips of people almost all of whom are young and few beyond middle age.'

But popular opinion did not find the hymn out of place, preferring it to the Coventry Girls. On April 20, *The Times* was able to announce '"Abide with Me" ... will be included in the programme of community singing at this year's Final on May 2, Sir Stanley Rous, the F.A. Secretary, said last night.'

Popular tunes of the day have usually been taken over by supporters. Before the 1893 Final between Everton and Wolves, thousands gave a spirited rendering of 'The Man Who Broke the Bank at Monte Carlo'. After their win in 1921 the Spurs' coach was sung home from Stamford Bridge with the current hit tune,

'Omaha I'll be coming back to you.'

And at Wembley's first Final 'I'm forever blowing bubbles' had already become West Ham's theme song. When they won at last in 1964 this was slightly amended to:

'We have blown a lot of bubbles
Pretty bubbles in the air,
They've flown so high
Now they've reached the sky
Let's hope they never fade and die.'

Charlton Athletic were welcomed to Wembley with their song 'When the red red robins go bob, bob, bobbin'.

But when in 1947 they scored the winning goal against Burnley with only a few minutes left to play this was quickly changed for another song of the day:

215

'Only five minutes more
Only five minutes more of your charms'.

Quick adaptation of the tune of the moment helped smooth over one of the Cup's disputed incidents. In 1932 Arsenal suffered defeat, in the famous 'was-the-ball-over-the line?' Final. After their celebration dinner, Newcastle's players felt it would be a friendly gesture to call round on their defeated opponents over at the Savoy Hotel. As Jimmy Boyd led the Newcastle players into the banqueting hall they were seen by the leader of the orchestra. At once he stopped the band and switched them to 'After the *ball* was over'. The Arsenal players forgot their depression and joined in the song.

'Land of Hope and Glory' was sung at the opening of Wembley and became a popular tune for Cup-Finals. Wolverhampton were exhorted to adopt a version in 1939:

'Team of hope and glory
Up to win the Cup:
See them kick for victory
Beating opponents up . . .'

The last line one hopes was intended in a football sense, but it was not heeded by the team who lost despite the vocal support.

Thirty-two years later Associated Television was to run a competition to find Arsenal a supporters' song and again the tune proposed was 'Land of Hope and Glory'. In 1925 and again in 1927 Wembley echoed to Welsh voices singing 'Land of my Fathers' with deep fervour. The old favourite, 'Blaydon Races', urged on Newcastle to their quartet of victories. Even when the pop age brought with it the song leader and the supporting choir, there was still a preference for traditional tunes.

But there was a new intensity in the singing of 'Glory, Glory, Hallelujah' as Spurs swept on to the 'double' in a crescendo of excitement. Saints Marching in, the Happy Wanderers, the Blowing Bubbles and the Bobbing Robins all had their day in Wembley's cheerful preliminaries.

It was a new experience when Liverpool came to town for the 1965 Final. The supporters from the Kop came with them and that ensured a lively afternoon. The Anfield chorus built up an atmosphere of its own which Eric Todd described in *The Guardian*:

'Whenever Anfield's Kop is alive with the sound of music, strangers to the ground marvel at the topicality and the spontaneity of the songs and above all at the comfortable level of the key in which they are pitched. Unlike Bill Shankly on the subject of Liverpool, however, the Kop is reluctant to discuss the musical side of its character. Nobody seems to know much about the choir's antecedents, but I was told that a Ben Hendry of Crosby had a lot to do with it some 13 years ago. And Ben has not been seen around a lot these days. Not at Anfield anyway.

216

'Among the recently contactable choristers is Jimmy Lloyd who informed me that a few of the lads practised regularly in a Crosby public house to the accompaniment of a guitar.

'We've got some idea of what we are going to sing before we meet at the ground and it isn't all that difficult to fit new words to the music when something suitable turns up. Somebody will start a jingle and the rest join in so quickly that it sounds like they all started together. Or somebody else will turn up with a suggestion during a game and we fit the words to the old "ee-aye-Addeo".

'It's easy enough when you know how. Not that we're musically-minded like, but we enjoy a good tune and that's why we chose "You'll never walk alone" for our theme song. Real pretty.'

'"You'll never walk alone" rolled over the Stadium regardless of the tune on the official song sheet. And at the end the Kop could let itself go with the song that best expresses the joy of victory:

> "We won the Cup
> We won the Cup
> Ee aye addeo
> WE won the CUP."'

22

Training, Laws, and Tactics

In 1899 John Goodall of Preston North End and Derby County wrote:

'A common question invites comparison between ancient and modern football. I have had the benefit of the experience of both and yet I find the subject difficult to treat satisfactorily.

'In earlier days very little was known of training. Certainly it was not conducted on the scientific lines adopted now in the preparation of players for a match. Training carefully managed should prove beneficial to footballers, but I think there is a tendency to over-do training.

'The Derby County team never touched a football during the time they were preparing at Matlock Bridge. Weekend football is the best training for a player. If you put him to hard work on weekdays you make him stale and listless. The best training for important Cup-ties is rest and care; a good sharp walk before breakfast, a little billiards or fishing, vapour baths, early bed and above all temperance, though not necessarily total abstinence – these are the prime factors in good condition.'

More than 70 years later this still sums up the way in which soccer standards develop and the general approach to important Cup-ties.

Intensified training, new standards of fitness, new techniques for developing muscles or ball skills, these continue to raise the standards of efficiency over the years – no question now of hard work making players stale! But before the important Cup games most teams concentrate on rest and relaxation. They are already trained to peak condition, they have already perfected their tactical systems and this is no time for experiment. Golf is more likely than billiards, warm water than vapour baths, but the principles are unchanged from Goodall's day.

The first sign of a more professional approach to the Final was the week's special preparation in 1882 with the Blackburn Olympic team taken away to the seaside at Blackpool.

Again there is not much fundamental change since then. It is still the popular practice for teams to go away for special training. But the object now is to escape from the publicity pressures, to live in a relaxed atmosphere, and to tone up sufficiently to maintain fitness at the end of a hard season.

Yet Tottenham, the most successful Cup team in recent years, preferred to follow a normal stay-at-home routine. That indeed is the most logical approach, for the whole emphasis of Managers is to keep the routines as normal as possible and to avoid any heightening of the tension. The significant difference over the years has been in the training before and through the season, not in the special arrangements for important matches.

Each age has its own training techniques but, as the pace and the pressures of the game increase, these have become more sophisticated. In the early days, apart from the spontaneous kickabouts, a long walk in the best suit with watchchains in waist-coats and bowlers on heads was the favoured way of keeping fit. Walking still has its place in the schedule, but the emphasis on physical fitness led to other developments.

Everton in the early 1890s took systematic training to the point that thousands came to watch their pre-season practice and the team was noted for its 'machine-like precision'.

This was a considerable advance for a club once known as the 'moon-lighters', when their amateurs only had time to practise after the day's work was done and the moon was up. Such enthusiasm was now better channelled but by modern standards training and tactical theory were still in the elementary stage.

After the all-Lancashire Final of 1914 between Burnley and Liverpool that great authority Mr John Lewis commented: 'It is certainly true that our professionals evince no great anxiety to learn anything of the theory of the sport and that in most teams there is no evidence of pre-conceived tactics or thought-out-manoeuvres.'

Thirty years ago training techniques centred on running, skipping, abdominal exercises, and the medicine ball. These catered for the main requirements of the game – lapping for stamina and 'broken' running for short bursts of speed. The skipping kept players light and strong on their feet; the abdominal exercises and the medicine ball built up strength where it mattered.

But, once the Hungarians in 1953 exposed the limitations of the English game, much more emphasis was put on ball practice and ball skills. Weight-lifting and other techniques were adopted to add the strength of body-building exercises and give wider interest to the training.

The next phase was the development of tactical theory and the wider training of coaches, which received such impetus from Walter Winterbottom when England's Team Manager and the F.A.'s Chief Coach.

In recent seasons the greater prizes for Clubs, the greater incentives for players, have intensified the will to improve and the facilities to do so. It is this that has kept standards of performance rising.

Other experiments have been tried in plenty, from psychologists to improve the team's will to win to the Coverdale Management Training used by Bournemouth to give their players greater awareness and to make them think more about the game. These are usually the Manager's way of building interest and confidence and most of them rank as gimmicks comparable to Jack Tinn's spats – but like the spats they serve a purpose.

Inevitably there are fads about feeding – in which myth and common sense are mingled. Before the turn of the century, John Goodall's view was:

'Whole potatoes and vegetables are not the best food for a player, but they should not be strictly avoided if he likes them. The player can fall into the error of under-feeding himself which is almost as disastrous as gluttony; for faintness is an unpleasant feeling. Footballers should have a good square meal about three hours before the start of a match. I have sometimes indulged about an hour later and have felt the effects about half-way in the game with a "stitch in my side".'

The good square meal is by no means outmoded and steak for lunch is still the favourite with some players and teams. But in general fashions changed to boiled mutton and then to boiled chicken or steamed fish. Only in two aspects is there general agreement – a hearty breakfast in accordance with the player's particular likes and a lunch early enough for adequate digestion – usually eaten by noon, three hours before the kick-off.

Sherry and eggs was the special diet on which Revie trained to keep fit for his recall to the Manchester City Cup-Final side and eggs have always been popular. Before the 1921 Final, Spurs' centre-half, Charlie Walters, had eight eggs for breakfast and he was the fastest man on the field. In the closing minutes he sprinted across to charge down a shot by Brooks, which could have brought Wolves level.

Arsenal's preparation for the 1971 Final brought the headline in the *Evening Standard* 'Gunners go to it on an Egg'. It was typical of their thorough preparation that this should have been studied in detail and Manager Bertie Mee explained: 'Steak is protein and takes 48 hours to be absorbed and turned into energy on the field. Our diet of cornflakes, fruit containing plenty of glucose and poached eggs has a high sugar and carbohydrate content for instant energy.' This was the sensible adaptation of science to improved performance, preferable to Major Buckley's flamboyant gland treatment. But the principle is the same. In the words of the old quotation, 'Victory prefers the "man who takes trouble".'

Football's growth and development stemmed from the Cup and the competition has mirrored or promoted the changes in rules and tactics. The law-makers have been intelligent enough not to indulge in too much change for change's sake and the rules of the game remain relatively simple.

It had been one of The Football Association's main tasks on its formation to produce a common set of rules from the varying codes and practices of the Public Schools and the Universities. In 1863 J. C. Thring had set out 'the Simplest Rules' of the game – ten in number – and this had been a useful guide.

The problems of unifying practices that were so diverse as to represent fundamentally different types of game created the strains that led to the split with rugby. By the time the Cup competition started, however, the basic rules were clear cut and the F.A.'s laws were widely accepted though some other Associations, such as Sheffield, still had their own divergent rules for some years.

All the Cup games were, however, played under the F.A. rules. But in those first games of the competition there were many distinctive differences from present-day football.

The throw-in was an important feature of the game with the first player to get the ball having the right to throw it. The throw was one-handed and at first could be taken on the run. Experts like N. C. Bailey or J. F. M. Prinsep could usually throw the ball into the goalmouth from anywhere in the opponent's half. It was to restrict this advantage that the two-handed throw was introduced in 1882, and in 1895 it was ruled that the thrower must stand still. Only in recent seasons has technique improved to the point where a score of players can once more throw vast distances to use this as an attacking gambit. It was Hutchinson's long throw that finally broke the deadlock between Leeds and Chelsea showing how technique and performance improve over the years.

Changing ends after a goal was scored could cause much unfairness when there was a strong wind and it was the Royal Engineers' problem in the Final of 1875 that led to the present rule being introduced.

In the 1880's heavy charging was allowed even when the ball was not being played. The goalkeeper was particularly vulnerable and was often hustled through his goal by a couple of forwards while another scored.

Control of the game was exercised in the early Cup matches by two umpires with the referee appointed to decide all cases of difference between them. Not until 1891 were the umpires converted into linesmen and the referee made the autocrat of the game. Even then he had to wait four years before he was given power to penalise 'without an appeal being made to him'. The exception to this had been in allowing referees to award a goal if one was prevented by handling. E. C. Bambridge had been the first to do this in 1881 and the following season the referees were given the right to award goals. This they did with such largesse that the law was repealed after one year. But still it was not until 1891 that the penalty-kick was introduced, Heath of Wolverhampton Wanderers scoring the first penalty goal. So the game took modern shape with one vital exception. Other changes of detail were of limited importance, but the offside rule was central to the game.

The Football Association had insisted on an off-side rule that required three opponents to be between the attackers and the goal when the pass was made. At first other Associations like Sheffield, or some leading Clubs like Oxford University had been playing an off-side rule involving only one or two, rather than three players.

But The Football Association's rule gained general acceptance over the first 50 years of the Cup. Then it began to be exploited in a way that disrupted the whole flow of the game until there was a general call for revision. The man who emphasised the problem was Billy McCracken of whom Don Davies wrote in *The Guardian*:

'William McCracken was an Irish International right-back and a storm centre of his generation. He was a specialist in off-side tactics and, as such, was the cause of more demonstrations of hostility and resentment than any other player before or since. He had the same demoniac qualities as Spofforth, the same ability to get on players' nerves; his sardonic smile as he went about his disruptive task could rouse passions to fever-heat. Being an Irishman, he naturally took a deep delight in that most of his playing time was spent in twisting the tails of British players. Being an artist he played 16 times for Ireland and nigh on 20 seasons in one of the most illustrious club sides of all time, Newcastle United of the early 1900s. As a zealous student of association football as well as one of its foremost practitioners he applied all the resources of a keen mind to the problems of defensive strategy with such success in the off-side moves that in his day he could reduce the cleverest forward line to a rabble of hesitant and bewildered units.

'That McCracken, though widely respected as an individual and always feared as a player, was not exactly a universal favourite is understandable. Who but a snake-charmer would fall in love with a serpent? It was his province as a setter of off-side traps of unwonted slickness and cunning to jolt his contemporaries out of their conventional ruts and make them substitute adaptability and resource for rule of thumb; to force them to realise that the only antidote to subtlety and deceit was even greater subtlety and deceit. In short, he made them think and that has never been a popular mission. Crowds flocked to watch him, composed mainly of angry and prejudiced men, and few there were who had the patience to acknowledge the beauty of McCracken's technique in the abstract. All they saw was a player whose phenomenal mastery over a defensive mood could repeatedly disrupt and arrest a game, the smooth and rhythmic ebb and flow of which was its greatest charm; matches in which McCracken appeared usually degenerated into dull repetitions of tiresome infringements and stoppages. Tempers frayed and angry scenes developed. On one occasion at Hyde Road McCracken teased and tormented the Manchester City forward line to such purpose that the crowd felt obliged to intervene.

'Where McCracken outstripped all his rivals was in his ability to judge his opponents' intentions correctly and to time his counter-strokes effectively. Until he retired no one arose who could match his superiority in that. It followed that in all the furious disputes in the 1920s (and there were many), concerning the desirability or otherwise of changing the off-side law, a step which seemed inevitable as the only means of freeing forwards from the shackles which defences were increasingly putting upon them, McCracken's name was cited and remains so to this day as that of the arch-criminal. But even McCracken could not play for ever and by the early 1920s his appearances were growing rarer; Caspar's work was done or very nearly. Before the door closed finally on his career and he hung up his boots for the last time there could be heard, like the roll of revolutionary drums, the unceasing clamour for revision growing stronger and stronger, until in 1925 even the great W. I. Bassett lent his name to the popular cry for reform.

'At a meeting in London on 15th June, 1925, the F.A. adopted by the necessary two-thirds majority the "Two-for-Three Scheme" as it was called. Thus the old law which had stood untouched since 1866 (except for its limitations to one half of the field in 1907) was scrapped, mainly, as men thought, through the perverse genius of an Irishman who loved to meddle in British affairs. Not for the first time in our island story was a decision made which seemed to penalise those who used their brains in order to make things easier for those who either could not or would not use theirs. Off-side traps, even as perfected by McCracken, could still be sprung by forwards who had the wit to hold the ball and dribble well ahead of their colleagues before making their passes. But that was a new idea and it has been well said: "There is nothing so painful to human nature as the pain of a new idea", particularly when, as in this instance, it involved the abandonment of conventional rule-of-thumb methods and the substitution of creative thought.

'By the middle of the 1925–26 season, the first under the new rule, it appeared as though the earthly paradise had indeed arrived, for all, that is, except the poor goalkeepers. Forwards everywhere kicked over the traces, and scoring became fantastic. Seven league matches alone produced a crop of sixty-four goals in one afternoon! But amid general rejoicing, when Sunderland, for example, were averaging five goals per match, and centre-forwards like David Halliday were running amok, a certain Yorkshire Club, Hull City, was seen to be oddly stubborn in its refusal to conform to the prevailing fashion of giving away goals like largesse; on the contrary, it was making scoring so difficult that in the first five months of the season not a single goal had been scored against it. Chilly doubts again assailed observers. Not McCracken again, surely! But facts were facts and soon the alarming rumour spread, later confirmed by eye-witnesses, that the enterprising coach, critic, and tactical adviser to the Hull City Football Club was none other than our old friend Irish Mephistopheles, William Mc-Cracken, as ever a peerless defender in his own day, still adding cubits to his stature as the game's arch-obstructionist. Thoughtful men peered into the future with alarm and misgiving. The ghost was still walking.'

And the ghost is still walking today for the change in law led to the defensive centre-half and the refinement of defensive tactics. McCracken must have relished Liverpool's play in the 1965 and 1971 Finals.

Two other rules have had a vital effect on play in the Cup.

In 1965 substitutes were allowed, ending at last the series of one-sided Finals in which injury lessened interest and decided the course of the game.

Then there was the ending of the maximum wage in 1963. This has given further incentives to improve skills and by putting an ever-higher premium on results has further strengthened defensive convictions.

Yet whatever tactics are employed the goals still come. Jimmy Dimmock could outwit McCracken easily enough by holding the ball and breaking on his own. Packed defences hampered the goalkeeper and brought opportunity back to the tall striker good in the air. Teams like Manchester City or Manchester United that believe in attack and the encouragement of individual skill can find a way through the maze of modern defensive covering.

The tactical battle of wits adds spice to the game. But at first this amounted to little more than the concerted charging which made the Royal Engineers so formidable or the development of a simple gambit like the long pass from wing to wing that won Blackburn Olympic the Cup.

Major Suddell battling to buy players was of more importance to Preston than any plan. Dr Morley's famous exhortation to Blackburn in the 'eighties: 'For heaven's sake play FOOTBALL, Rovers', was not untypical of the vague generalities. What was to be understood by 'FOOTBALL'? In this case not much more than keep playing the ball instead of the man, keep cool, keep using your skill and strength and keep your temper.

Tactical developments there were, but these were mostly in the formation that teams adopted. Lieutenant Ruck well described the pattern in 1872 at the start of it all with one back, two half-backs, and seven forwards, two paired on either wing. But it was too early in the game for any standard system to be established. Two backs were an obvious development as goalkeepers needed more protection. Then in 1893 Accrington Stanley introduced three half-backs perhaps copied from Scotland where the game was more fluid and there was more experiment. Nottingham Forest and others also developed this new system at about the same time and it remains the standard pattern on the programme.

But defensive tendencies have continued with players steadily withdrawn from attack. The 'W' formation followed with the two insides dropping back to link with wing-halves in mid-field.

Newcastle's searching study of tactics led to the off-side trap and the new off-side law. That in turn led to Herbert Chapman's reappraisal and the conversion to the 'stopper' centre-half no longer allowed the attacking role that had made him for so long the hub of the game.

Everywhere the pace of development speeded up after Hitler's war. It was the same with football tactics. Arsenal soon revived old glories by new methods. With their traditions there was bound to be a heavy defensive emphasis in the plan. Herbert Chapman had preferred safety-first tactics and 'Policeman' Roberts had a place of honour in the Club's history. So too did that great amateur centre-half, Bernard Joy, for whose invaluable service in the late 'thirties, the Club wished to make a presentation only to be prevented by a ruling that it would jeopardise his amateur status.

Their new 'retreating defence' was based on not challenging opponents in possession in mid-field, but shuttling back to form an impenetrable screen 20 yards from goal. That way the defence could never be outmanoeuvred and the pressure could be contained if there was a tall centre-half to cut out the crosses and a goalkeeper who could not be beaten from long range or acute angles. To dominate the centre Arsenal had Leslie Compton, who was to win his first International Cap at age 38, the safest of goalkeepers in George Swindin. This gave them the edge over any imitators.

Inevitably the system gave the impression of siege at times, but once the opponents had been drawn forward they were liable to leave gaps for Arsenal's strikers. So the 'lucky' Arsenal legend was born, for they always seemed to have the worst of the game, but take the spoils. There was no 'luck' involved only shrewd planning.

This style tended to obscure another major tactical change. Goalkeepers were becoming more adventurous. Bartram in Charlton's Cup runs of 1946 and 1947 was often far from his goal, a third back whose anticipation cut out many a through pass. Look at the two goalkeepers in the pictures as Dean heads home in the 1933 Final, or as Allen nods in that controversial cross in 1932. Both stand rooted on their line while the centre-forward heads the ball in from a few yards out. By the 'fifties there would be strong words from the Manager for any goalkeeper who allowed that without challenge and their greater mobility gave fewer opportunities for forwards in the penalty-area.

The Spurs team that won the Second and First Division championships in successive seasons specialised in planned moves from set-piece plays, their well practised free-kicks bringing them many goals. This allied to the 'push and run' method was to be a basis of success. But their great Cup days in the 'sixties needed the addition of a dash of subtlety to the original mixture of 'keep it simple, keep it quick'.

The trickle of new ideas had been turned into a flood by two significant happenings. In 1953 Hungary not only became the first foreign team to beat England at home, but the millions who watched at Wembley on their screen saw a dazzling display of new skills and original method. Then came the ending of the maximum wage and the vast incentive to Managers and players. Top-class football became big business with big stakes.

Money and effort was lavished on improvement and there was a leap forward in tactics, fitness, and ball control. Before few players had maintained the interest to train with the dedication of a Matthews or a Meredith. Now Manager and footballer worked together with greater intensity.

Manchester City were the first to learn a lesson from the Hungarians, adopting their own version of Hidgekuti's deep-lying centre-forward play. This was to be known as the 'Revie' plan and the credit given to him and Manager Les McDowall. But like all good inventions it sprang in fact from a chance happening acutely observed. It was Fred Tilson, who had 'plonked in two' in that memorable Final of 1934, who had the idea. In charge of City's reserves he told the centre-forward to drop deep to get away from a close-marking centre-half. Johnny Williamson then linked so well with Ken Barnes that they tried it again – and again. For the last 20 matches of the season the reserves had a wonderful run and McDowall decided to try it for real the next season. In this numerate age we would more correctly call the system the start of 4–2–4 with the midfield the responsi-

The disputed Newcastle goal of 1932 was headed by
Allen while Hapgood was out of play.

bility of two players with a roaming role. But Revie, nominally centre-forward, was to be the key man in this development and inevitably the scheme was called the 'Revie plan'. City practised assiduously for a month, the secret tactics unveiled in the season's opening game. To the delight of critics and opponents they crashed 0–5. The players clamoured to get back to normal. But McDowall insisted they give it a fair run in mid-week matches. As Revie developed the feel and the timing the system demands – and as Barnes took over from McTavish – suddenly the mocking ceased and City shot to the top of the table. Revie as we shall see was to win a Final with his astute use of the method against Birmingham.

The essence of tactical change now was that nothing was fixed and static – not formations, not systems, not ideas, not individuals. Detailed and careful analysis of the other side – the strengths and weaknesses of their method, the instinctive habits of their players, all were studied in depth. The same scientific approach was

226

The 1933 Cup-Final: Dean scores in Everton's 3–0 win over Manchester City. This was the first Final in which players were numbered; Everton wore 1–11 and City 12–22.

brought to football as Jardine had brought to defeating the Australians at cricket – with all their strokes plotted and Larwood's fielders precisely placed. Those cold calculations, and the hard line approach, won the Tests, but raised a storm of protest.

The method teams like Leeds and Liverpool were no less successful and no more popular with opposing supporters. But one most attractive part of the new method was its emphasis on all-round ability and the versatile player. It was no good spotting weaknesses in other team's methods, or in individual's, if one's own players could not adapt to take advantage. So we moved to the era of backs overlapping as wingers, and of teams changing smoothly from 4–2–4 to 4–3–3 and understanding what the mystical numbers meant. The old numbering system of two backs, three half-backs, and five forwards, was now meaningless and served only to identify the players' names in the programme. The game was more fluid, more versatile, more demanding in fitness and intelligence – but not always more attractive to watch.

Typical of the varying way clubs adapted tactics to suit their players can be seen in the methods of Wolverhampton Wanderers and Manchester United. These two teams had been the most consistently successful in the 'fifties and remained powerful performers in the 'sixties.

Wolverhampton had a simple well-disciplined approach, exploiting with long passes the skill and speed of their wingers. Strength and stamina were fundamental to their game and they used this for one unusual tactic. This was the 'repossession' play still used when they won the Cup in 1960. The ball was sometimes played deliberately to a defender who was immediately put under challenge by a Wolves' forward. The sharp-shooters in the line hovered close behind ready to try a snap shot if the ball ran loose.

In contrast Manchester United has always put less emphasis on system, more on individual talent. Sir Matt Busby set out to acquire the players with the flair and self-confidence to win matches, then allowed them to express their talents within a sound and simple tactical framework.

By all calculations Manchester United have been the pre-eminent post-war team and this is pleasant confirmation that the great players can rise superior to any shackles others may design to fetter them.

With some teams it would appear that Lieutenant Ruck's formation has been reversed with the seven now in defence rather than attack. This has had one noticeable effect on individual skills.

As the defenders began to outnumber the front runners there has been a dearth of great midfield players, their genius stifled by the lack of opportunity to create openings. The refinement of defensive tactics emphasised teamwork and efficiency at the expense of the spectacular and the individual.

The Final of 1971 was the epitome of this tactical and technical battle. But even this scientific struggle showed that flair still has its place, that a touch of individualism can still win matches.

23

The Agony and the Ecstasy

Triumph or disaster, exhilaration or utter dejection these are the moods the Cup inspires even in a straight-forward match. But feelings are unbearably intensified by the fatal mistake or the vital goal on which a whole game turns. Inevitably the joy or despair is magnified in the Final with the vast crowds watching and the great prize so close. Yet it can be just as acute in the previous rounds. For some the suspense of the semi-final is more nerve-stretching than the Final. Then at least one has been part of the great day and the great occasion. In the semi-final there is even greater frustration in the plunge to obscurity on the brink of renown.

Two incidents emphasise the point. When Geoff Hurst is asked which goal is the most memorable of his career one wonders which he will choose from those three that destroyed West Germany and gave England her only World Cup. But the un-forgettable goal he describes is in the semi-final of 1964, when he took Moore's pass and ran through to score the third goal that finally crushed Manchester United.

And that day of triumph at Wembley cannot altogether erase from Sir Alf Ramsey's mind the bitter moment in the semi-final of 1953. This game was to be the prelude to the Matthews Final – perhaps the most memorable occasion in the Cup's long history. But how nearly were Spurs at Wembley, rather than Blackpool. For most of the game they had dominated the play. A breakaway goal by Perry had been cancelled out by Duquemin's equaliser. And as Blackpool struggled for survival against Tottenham's mounting pressure the ball was booted downfield. Ramsey, the most poised and precise of backs, brought it under instant control. Then, as Stanley Matthews saw it:

'he decided to pass back to his goalkeeper. But he did not connect with the ball properly and as it slowly rolled towards Ditchburn, Jackie Mudie nipped round Ramsey and kicked the ball into the back of the net. Ramsey held his head in horror and Ditchburn beat the earth with his clenched fists. A few minutes later the whistle went with the score Blackpool 2 Spurs 1.'

For Matthews it was the prelude to a life's ambition fulfilled, for Ramsey a night-mare of self-reproach.

Many Blackburn people go back to the quarter-final for their most exciting Cup Match – ignoring their three successive wins in the Final. On March 14, 1912, the Rovers were replaying on their own ground after a draw with Manchester United. In a game of fine football and fluctuating fortune they were 2–1 down with seconds to go. Then Chapman their centre-forward burst through the middle in a last desperate dash. Out came the goalkeeper, Edmunds, over raced left-back, Stacey, all three collided near the penalty-spot. But it was Chapman who got the final touch and the ball rolled slow, so slow towards the goal. The policemen behind the net took off their helmets and waved the ball on while the Blackburn crowd willed it to cross the line. When it trickled over the shout was heard for miles around as hats, sticks and caps were hurled into the air many to be lost forever. Two goals in extra time gave Rovers the match and they seemed all set for the double. But in the semi-final it was West Bromwich Albion who scored the late goal in extra time in the replay. No team can count for long on the favours of fortune and all taste of frustration as well as success.

One of the most thrilling finishes in Cup history came in a match between Everton and Spurs in 1937, which Joe Mercer and Arthur Rowe rate as their most remarkable game. It was a replay at White Hart Lane after a 1–1 draw at Goodison.

With four minutes to go Everton were leading 3–1 and the referee appeared to award them a penalty as Rowe tripped Dixie Dean. But after protest and consultation with a linesman the referee, Dr Barton, awarded Spurs a throw-in instead for the ball had been over the line when Mercer centred.

The throw-in was quickly taken, the ball pushed up to centre-forward Morrison and hit cleanly into Everton's net. Before Everton could regain their composure right-half Tommy Meads lashed in an equaliser from thirty yards. To Everton's dismay and the home crowd's exultation Morrison headed the winner seconds before the final whistle. Three goals in the last four minutes had the spectators dancing with joy.

But there can be more than mental agony and the Cup-Finals have their full share of physical injury or exhaustion. That first game at the Oval saw Lieutenant Cresswell with a broken collar-bone ten minutes from the start of it all. That pattern has been fitfully repeated throughout the years for football is still a game of physical challenge. Even Wembley has its formidable casualty list. Indeed, it is unique among stadia for heightening the tension of the big match. The players come out of the tunnel into a wall of sound shattering in its intensity. As they walk those last few yards to the pitch they are engulfed by the crowd and the noise. This can unsettle the anxious and unnerve the weak. But most of the other hazards are myths born of imagination and coincidence. The lush grass and moist surface have given it a reputation as a tiring pitch. This it is, with cramp afflicting many a player. Yet Wembley is easy going compared with a League ground on a muddy afternoon in winter. It is the excitement of the game that exhausts the average player. Everyone is keyed up by the occasion. They race into position when a brisk walk would be safe enough. They try twice as hard, run half as far again, and are that much sharper in reaction. It is this and the nervous tension that drains them, more than the Wembley turf.

In the 'fifties, Cup-Finals at Wembley acquired a sinister reputation for injury and it was the turf that was unfairly blamed. Barnes in 1952, Meadows three years

230

The despair of an own goal. *Above:* Turner, Charlton's right-half (*on the ground*) puts the ball into his own net to help Derby County to their first success in 1946. *Below:* McGrath of Blackburn Rovers turns the ball past his goalkeeper in 1960. Deeley of Wolverhampton Wanderers leaps with joy heedless of his agony.

later were two early casualties whose absence helped Newcastle United to victory. The list grew steadily as Dwight broke a leg in Nottingham Forest's win, Trautmann broke his neck keeping the Cup secure for Manchester City, Wood's injury cost Manchester United the double in 1957, the accident to Chalmers helped Spurs to the double, while Whelan's broken leg destroyed Blackburn Rovers chance in 1960. The stretcher bearers were kept busy and the Finals were crippled as well, the spectacle tarnished, and victory tinged with regret. So the Cup added to the sensible pressure for substitutes, first permitted in 1966. But there was nothing unusual about these accidents. Walley Barnes was the first of the Wembley casualties and he is quite clear that the cause was a muffed pass by Milburn and his own speed of reaction. Milburn was dribbling in on goal and Barnes had deliberately left a gap close to the line hoping Milburn would go that way. As Milburn went for the opening Barnes moved to cut him off, the distance nicely judged for an easy tackle. At that second the quick-witted Mitchell, hovering behind, called for the ball. Milburn checked and tried a back-heel with his weak right foot. Only the toe of the boot touched the ball which rolled a yard or two and stopped. Barnes, brain working quicker than his body, twisted round to go for the loose ball before Mitchell could pounce. Already committed the other way, inevitably he wrenched his knee. A few minutes later an awkward tackle with Robledo finally split a cartilage that was already torn. Robledo was later to head the one goal that crushed Arsenal's gallant fight against the odds. For Barnes it meant a season out of soccer for the injury was so unusual that the specialist took his time to diagnose it. But it was no fault of the pitch and perhaps the only culprit was the heightened tension of the Final.

For Barnes, like most other players, responded to the challenge of this unique occasion by an extra effort of mind and body. No one can live with the thought of being the player who lets his team slip when the Cup is at their fingertips. Alert and on edge, their responses are fractionally faster than usual, their tackles even more determined. So Barnes willed his body to do more than was physically possible and paid for his dedication.

It was the same with Meadows. Again, it was the elusive and intelligent Mitchell who was the unconscious destroyer. As Meadows went for the tackle Mitchell suddenly checked and pulled the ball back to leave him stranded. Again, the mind willed the impossible and his leg paid the price for the contorted effort to change direction against the whole momentum of his body. This time it was the skilful sleight of foot, the baffling dribble that twisted the over-eager Meadows to destruction.

Dwight's injury was the only one that could be charged against the turf, his studs catching as he slid at speed. But this is an injury that can happen at any time on any ground and one in nearly 50 years is no criticism of Wembley, no special coincidence.

Saddest of all the Wembley woundings was Wood's broken collarbone that undoubtedly cost Manchester United the 'double'. And that was a simple collision

232

with winger McParland. Or was it so simple? Again the heightened tension of the occasion may have been responsible. For McParland went in hard and fast, an unnecessary and intimidatory charge when Wood had already cleared the ball. This at least, was how I saw it. McParland himself was hurt and clearly the clash was judged unintentional for no free-kick was given. But it had been a reckless rush that won undeserved reward. For that special irony in which the competition delights decreed that McParland score both the goals which sneaked Aston Villa home. While Wood hobbled on the wing the elder Blanchflower gave a spirited but amateurish performance in his unwelcome role of goalkeeper.

The most serious injury was also the least noticed. Trautmann, that commanding and spectacular goalkeeper, plunged to make a daring save in the final minutes of Manchester City's winning game against Birmingham. Once more the clash ended with the bodies prone on the vivid grass and the anxious huddle round them. Trautmann soon waved away assistance and saw the game out unaware, like the crowd, that his neck was broken.

Unusual goals, tragic mistakes, crippling accidents, all have added to the agony and ecstasy of the Cup. But even in the tumultuous excitement and fierce pressures of the Final the last word is sometimes with icy intelligence and cold precision. That expert judge, Sir Stanley Rous, rated Arsenal's win over Liverpool in 1950 as the best football he had seen in a Final. A downpour before the kick-off drenched the pitch and damped the spirits of the crowd, destroying some of the frenetic atmosphere of the modern Final. Perhaps it was this that helped Arsenal's calm and reasoned play. Their decisive first thrust was as coolly executed as any that Wembley has seen – indeed a goal fit to set before a King.

Swindin threw the ball out for Compton to nudge it on to Barnes. Cox was free on the right but, as Barnes shaped to pass, Logie burst suddenly down the centre calling for the ball. Barnes's instant response sent a low, raking pass into his stride. At once Goring, the Arsenal centre-forward, ran across the face of the defence drawing centre-half Hughes with him to leave the vital space into which Logie stroked the ball. Lewis came gliding in to collect the pass, run smoothly on, and slip the ball past Sidlow with sure touch. The still, small voice of perfection can make itself heard amid the clamour of a Cup-Final crowd and the bustle on the pitch.

24

Wembley, the Modern Game

Twenty-six seasons of Cup football since the last war has involved more than 13,000 games. For players and supporters, each has been full of excitement and meaning, a game to be remembered with delight or regret.

But the competition is cruelly selective, acknowledging only the victor. That is the pattern we now follow concentrating on the Finals with the briefest of backward glances down the long, rough road to Wembley.

Other chapters have given something of the flavour and the highlights of the giantkillers, the hopeful travellers and the also-rans who every year are the making of this competition. But at the end all eyes are on Wembley and the losers, by the way, have to shed their own tears. There is always a certain lack of justice in that ultimate selection and only once in the Cup's history have the two leading League teams met in the Final.

On the hard or muddy grounds of January, February, or March many a team disappears that might have graced Wembley's smooth turf. As early as the 1890s newspapers were often complaining that there were better teams around than the Finalists. But all who win through must have some outstanding quality of courage or skill. And if the standards of play sometimes disappoint unrealistic expectations, the Cup-Finals never fail as a spectacle and as an emotional experience for the supporters. This is the climax of the sudden death competition and the result is more important and compelling for the team than the play.

After the war the country had turned to football with avid enthusiasm. For the only year in the Cup's history the preliminary games were on a home-and-away basis with extra time obligatory if teams were level after 90 minutes.

On the way to Wembley Charlton Athletic were beaten 2–1 at Fulham, but won 4–3 on aggregate. They remain the only team to have lost a Cup match and reached the Final. Their opponents, Derby, attracted a mid-week crowd of 80,407 for their replayed semi-final with Birmingham – decided in extra time when Birmingham's centre-half Ted Duckhouse broke a leg in a vain attempt to stop Doherty scoring. Most remarkable of the other matches were Bradford's two games with Manchester City. Beaten 1–3 at home, Bradford won 8–2 at Maine Road!

Both Cup-Final teams had great strength at inside-forward, the silver-haired 'Raich' Carter and the vivacious red-head Doherty providing Derby with a wonderful blend of experience and energy. Charlton's 'Sailor' Brown and Don Welsh were not such household names, but were nearly as formidable.

The game was fast and open – a splendid spectacle of sweeping movement and

234

shifting fortune with Derby making the early running. With 80 minutes gone Charlton's Welsh international, centre-half, Bert Turner, scored twice in a minute. This amazing double had a shattering start as he turned Duncan's shot into his own net. But there was a happy ending immediately afterwards when he drove a free-kick at the defensive wall and his shot deflected off Doherty to wobble over the line with Woodley clawing desperately after it. Not so happy was the ending for Charlton, for in extra time the powerful but ungainly Jack Stamps ran riot making a goal for Doherty with a perfect centre then scoring two himself.

Charlton's regular right-back, Peter Croker, missed the Final through injury as did Derby's left-back, Parr, one breaking a leg, the other an arm.

Luck and the game were even enough, but Derby deserved to win with Leuty the outstanding defender on the field. John Oakes, at 42 the oldest man to play in a Final, fought courageously against a Derby attack of whom it was said 'with forwards like these who needs a defence?' One shot of Duncan's had been safely caught by Bartram when he felt the ball deflating. At once he threw it towards the touchline to prevent the bounce-up with the new ball being taken on his goal-line. That was typical of Bartram's quick thinking throughout the match, but not all his ready wit or agile interceptions could stop Derby taking the Cup, their only win in their four Finals.

Charlton Athletic had been in two of the League South Cup Finals during the war and in 1947 there they were at Wembley for the fourth time in five years. The previous year's losers in the Final, they were to maintain the Cup tradition of returning to win.

Their Cup record was not matched this year by their League performance in a season savaged by the weather. An appalling winter that stretched into spring kept the grounds frost-bound and the fixture list so congested that games were still being played off in June.

Charlton were near the bottom of the First Division while Burnley were riding high in the Second on the back of a defence as hard and bleak as the weather.

In the 50 games before Wembley Burnley had conceded only 31 goals. Their play was not untypical of the dour and rugged approach developing in the game. It promised a dull, drab Final and there were to be no surprises. Only the weather relented and the match was played in gruelling heat. Defensive attitudes were reinforced as the sun and Wembley turf drained the spirit of the teams. There was no score in full-time and only a handful of incidents to stir the unusually somnolent and passive spectators.

Extra time promised little change in the stalemate. Then with six minutes to go a cross from the right was nudged on to Charlton's leading goal grabber, Duffy. The left-wing at last had a fleeting sight of goal. His instant volley was billowing the back of the net before Strong could move. Duffy's blistering shot and his ecstatic dance of joy, ending in the arms of Shreeve, gave the game its memorable moment and Charlton Athletic their one victory. The game was also marked by one of those extraordinary coincidences in which the Cup abounds. For the second

235

year in succession the ball burst during play as if to spite the radio commentator who had quoted it as a million-to-one chance. In an interview before the 1946 Final, Raymond Glendenning had said this before asking the Cup-Final referee, Mr E. D. Smith, what his ruling would be if it happened. Mr Smith was asked for an instant answer on the air, but at least he was well-prepared when it happened!

Mr Smith has a different memory of the incident, saying Bartram held up the ball in surprise as it deflated. Mr Smith had already decided that the point was not exactly covered by the rules and he could use his common sense in holding the bounce-up where there was no great advantage.

Contrast is the essence of the competition and one of the dullest of Finals was succeeded by one of the most exhilarating. Manchester United's win over Blackpool still rates as the most complete in entertainment value for its skills, its spirit, its goals, and its sharp shifts of fortune.

The year 1949 was more prosaic and predictable, though a clash between Second and First Division always adds spice to the occasion.

Leicester were a surprising side to survive to the last two out of the 617 entrants in 1949. When they went to Wembley on April 30 relegation from the Second Division was more likely than winning the Cup. For they were second from bottom with three matches to play. In the event both parts of the amazing 'double' eluded them, the Cup going to Wolverhampton Wanderers and a single point keeping them afloat in the Second Division.

The Final might have appeared a walk-over in prospect, but for Leicester's remarkable performance in the semi-final when they beat League leaders Portsmouth more easily than the 3–1 score suggests.

So Fleet Street hoped for sensation and was nearly rewarded. Without their key man, Don Revie, Leicester still played attractive and sporting football. Two goals down at half-time, their spirited recovery was crushed by a marginal decision. Griffiths, their Welsh international outside-right, had hooked a shot home off the post after Williams had parried Chisholm's shot. And in the 67th minute Griffiths lobbed the ball over his head to the far side of the goal where Chisholm drove it in. As Chisholm turned, arms aloft, for the congratulations he met only the referee's finger pointing for off-side. At once Smyth went weaving through on a 30-yard run to hammer a left foot shot past Bradley. This was one of Wembley's finest individual goals and it crushed Leicester.

There was no dishonour in that, for Wolves were riding high in the League and had outstanding individual players with Williams in goal and Wright at left-half. Hancocks, one of the smallest men to appear in League football, and Mullen, one of the youngest, were devastating wingers with lethal shots. Jesse Pye in the centre was an astute player who was at his best in this game, heading in a cross from Hancocks then stabbing home a close shot just before the interval. For 20 minutes in the second half, Leicester had Wolves at full stretch, but after Smyth's goal they were able to cruise home comfortably enough.

Hannah (*second from the right*) scores Newcastle's third goal in 1955 making sure of their third Cup victory in five years.

Wolverhampton's third Cup victory was a happy prelude to the decade in which they and Manchester United were the country's leading teams, and it was typical of the uncertainties of Cup football that neither should win again until the 'sixties.

Arsenal had steadily built another fine team with the emphasis, as in the 'thirties, on an impregnable defence. Retreating when possession was lost, their cover was so good that they were unruffled by constant pressure. Indeed they invited it, striking back with sudden and deadly effect. To spectators it often looked as if they had the luck, but Managers knew they had the players and the plan. And in 1950 they were to win the Cup for the third time.

Sometimes the run of the ball decides a Final, sometimes the tactical plan. But Liverpool were beaten by both. In a game of great technical competence nothing went right for them. Swindin turned the ball against his own bar, Stubbins's dive was an instant too late to meet Liddell's searching centre, and in the final spirited assaults the bar was shaken again by Jones's header.

Arsenal's plan to contain the dangerous Liddell by the double-marking of Forbes and Scott was effective and successful, but Manager Kay's decision to leave Paisley

A fearless dive by Trautmann stops Keeble scoring.

out of the Liverpool side was almost certainly an error. Paisley, who had won an Amateur Cup Medal in 1939 and was later to train many successful Liverpool teams, was a hard, quick-tackling half-back who had played a decisive part in earlier matches. He was left out for Jones, a more sophisticated player, who lacked the speed and relentless challenge to contain Logie. It was Logie who made Arsenal so dangerous with his perceptive passes to the strikers Goring and Lewis. In the

18th minute of the first half, a sweeping Arsenal move saw Logie send Lewis clear to slide the ball coolly past Sidlow. In the same minute of the second half Denis Compton's long centre was nudged on by Cox and again Lewis was clear to take his chance with a cold accuracy that gave the goalkeeper no hope. Not even the double shackles of the marking, or one cruelly harsh tackle that slowed him down, could totally subdue Liddell. His raking centres showed the havoc he might have wrought given more space and why his team was sometimes called 'Liddellpool'.

But Arsenal were deserved winners, the composure of Walley Barnes and Laurie Scott and the experience of Joe Mercer keeping their defence impregnable. Their's was the oldest side to play at Wembley and no doubt it was this, as much as the drenching rain, that kept their heads so cool.

Some experienced judges still rate this the best Wembley Final for pure football skill. And it was played throughout at an exhausting pace. Denis Compton had only come into the side at the fifth round and had not worked up to peak fitness. At half-time he sat in the dressing-room utterly drained until Alex James fetched him a large brandy. He recalls that this had much greater effect in reviving him than the Manager's exhortations to make a special effort for what was effectively the last 45 minutes of his footballing career.

Twenty-one years later Arsenal were again to defeat Liverpool in the Final that concludes this book. To Compton the main difference in the teams was the extraordinary fitness of the later side. The muscle-building techniques, culminating in exercises and warm baths shortly before their games, gave the team the toughness that was to take them to their 'double'.

That is fair comment on the way the game keeps changing over the years. A greater emphasis on work-rate, and physical challenge, more instinctive ball-control learnt from intensive training, this was to be the pattern of development. As techniques and facilities improve it is impossible to compare teams and individuals. Styles are different and training opportunities continually improve. Standards of performance rise over the years, and no fair comparison is ever possible, but the great player or the great team of one era would be great in another though differently shaped by the techniques of the time. The Arsenal of 1950, like the side of 1971, was an outstanding team that gave of its best at Wembley.

The following season saw Newcastle United snatch the first of the three victories that were to make them the leading Cup team of the 'fifties, just as Tottenham was to dominate the 'sixties. The Final was won by two superb goals from Milburn, the spectacular striker who typified Newcastle's dash and verve. 'Wor Jackie' was the idol of Tyneside, able to turn a match with his thrilling burst of speed and lightning shot. His opportunism and courage were typical of the traditional English centre-forward, but Milburn was in fact a converted winger. So perhaps it was not surprising that he lacked the other traditional virtues of power in the air and robust physical challenge. Yet his speed and shooting power were to play a decisive part in Newcastle's success and gain him 13 caps for England.

Blackpool were opponents of similar stamp and style. Mortensen was a centre-forward with the same lethal qualities as Milburn, an opportunist who needed only the half-chance to turn a match. And if he had Matthews' baffling sleight of foot to make the openings for him, Milburn was as well supported by Mitchell, whose elusive dribbling also qualified for the magic circle.

With two such forward lines it was surprising that for the first time since 1912 there should be no goals scored in either of the semi-final matches. Blackpool indeed were lucky to survive against Birmingham and both the replays were closely contested.

Newcastle had also failed to score at home against Bristol Rovers in the sixth round and in the replay they were trailing before a brilliant burst of three goals in ten minutes saw them through.

With the tall and powerful Brennan at centre-half and the busy Joe Harvey, captaining the side from right-half, Newcastle had an impressive defence. Impressive, but not impregnable for Tottenham Hotspur, whose push and run football took the League Championship, had just scored seven against them without reply.

Blackpool had the 'Player of the Year', Johnston, as an attacking right-half covered by the rugged Shimwell at back. But on the day the difference in the teams was in the centre of the field. Brennan's decisive tackling subdued Mortensen, while Hayward could not compete with Milburn's burning pace.

Blackpool relied on an off-side trap with backs standing wide, but once Milburn timed his run right there was no cover for Hayward. Just before the interval Milburn left him trailing for Farm to make a diving save. Five minutes into the second half he cantered clear again collecting Robledo's long through pass and sliding the ball inside Farm's right-hand post. Now he strode on to Ernie Taylor's clever back heel to hit an angled left-foot shot from outside the area that left Farm groping. Within four minutes Milburn had won the match with one breathtaking run and one shot of explosive violence.

The 1952 Final was the game that ended the myth of 'lucky Arsenal'. Newcastle won the Cup, but it was Arsenal who gained universal admiration and sympathy.

In the 22nd minute Walley Barnes injured his knee. For a few minutes he played on with his leg strapped, then split a cartilage in a tackle with Robledo. That was the end of Barnes' soccer for a year and the end of Arsenal's hopes of winning the Cup. In a season when they might have done the double injury deprived them of every trophy. Yet they did not easily accept their fate with Joe Mercer leading a magnificent fight against the odds. He was 38 years old and Wembley might well have drained his energy in a normal game. Now with Barnes gone and Daniel, Lishman and Logie far from fit, he drove himself and his team beyond the point of exhaustion.

Newcastle had scored a total of 98 goals in the League and this was the free scoring forward line that Arsenal came so close to containing. Only six minutes remained when Robledo at last headed the solitary winner and it was typical of Arsenal's ill-luck that the ball bounced in off a post.

Roper, deputising as full-back, Forbes and Smith helped Mercer beat off the

240

Tommy Taylor sits on the ground after heading Manchester United's consolation
goal in the 1957 Final against Aston Villa.

The 1954 Final: Charlie Wayman runs through to score Preston North End's second goal while West Bromwich Albion appeal for offside.

Newcastle attacks while Daniel was in dominating form at centre-half. Though Smith saved on the line and Milburn twice went near, Arsenal were on the brink of survival until Mitchell's centre caught them off balance. Yet five minutes before it was Arsenal who might have taken the lead when Lishman's header flicked up off the bar. No wonder Stan Seymour, Newcastle's director-manager paid generous tribute. 'We won the Cup, but the glory is yours.'

The glory next season was to be Matthews' and the whole country rejoiced in his and Blackpool's success. His popularity overshadowed the real architects of their victory, the ebullient Mortensen and the subtle Taylor.

Stanley Mortensen was the happiest of footballers as gay and irrepressible off the field as on it. He was also one of the most deadly strikers the game has seen. His sudden acceleration, his whiplash shot, his instant perception of an opening and his unquenchable courage, made him capable of winning a match on his own. And in the 1953 Final it was his three goals and the clever promptings of little Ernie Taylor that helped Matthews to his twenty minutes of inspiration and his only winner's medal.

After Stanley Matthews' triumph many hoped the next year would be the turn of that other great winger, Tom Finney of Preston North End. But it was Albion's

243

right winger, Griffin, who stole the Cup with a goal three minutes from time.

Albion had once looked a good bet for the elusive double. But after their semi-final win they were hit by injury, losing five matches out of seven and surrendering the League Championship to Wolves. Yet they recovered their form at Wembley in a game of fluctuating fortune that showed off the attacking skills of two attractive teams. Nicholls and Allen were a powerful spearhead for Albion and in the twenty-first minute Allen gathered Lee's low pass to score his team's 100th goal of the season. At once Preston thrust back with Morrison springing high to head in Docherty's lofted lob.

Early in the second half Docherty's pass sent Wayman clear and he scored with ease while the defenders appealed for off-side. Barlow, Albion's powerful attacking wing-half came driving back and his urgency soon levelled the score. Brushing aside two tackles he was finally felled by Docherty. Allen calmly slid home the penalty though Thomson's groping fingers nearly diverted the ball against the post.

It was cut and thrust for the final half-hour with Saunders brilliantly saving a shot from Preston's Foster, that flew out of a ruck of players. Then Ryan swept a pass up to Griffin, who for once raced past Walton. Near the corner of the area he stabbed the ball for goal and the shot squeezed slowly past Thomson for Albion's decisive thrust.

For the third time in five years Newcastle United were to take the Cup in 1955. Deservedly so, though once more injury was to play a decisive part in their success. Again, it was their opponents' left-back who was crippled and again there were nearly seventy minutes left for play. Jimmy Meadows twisted his knee when he was contorted by Mitchell's elusive dribbling. Only 24 years old Meadows had just won his first England Cap, but he was never to play again.

Once more the match was forfeit to Newcastle, but they already looked like winning it. Right at the start Milburn had been left unmarked and welcomed this curious lapse by heading home White's corner. Scoular's relentless challenge in midfield and Mitchell's dazzling dribbles kept Newcastle in command, stepping up the pressure once Meadows had gone. Yet shortly before the interval City's striker, Johnstone, found the inspiration to alter the character of the game. The little Scot went weaving past four defenders only to hit the goalkeeper's legs. Then he launched himself at Hayes' low cross to head the equaliser.

Trautmann had brought off some miraculous saves, but now Mitchell deceived him, arrowing the ball between his body and the post when he expected a centre. Again Scoular put Mitchell clear and Trautmann could only push out the shot. Hannah swept home the rebound to leave the last half-hour devoid of interest or challenge.

In Newcastle's great run of success two forwards of diverse talent stand out for their distinctive contribution. Jackie Milburn, a modest man always worrying about his ability, was decisive and confident in his play. His raking stride and explosive shooting played a vital part in his team's success. Ball control was not his

Goalkeeper Sanders cannot watch as Allen scores from a penalty for
West Bromwich Albion in the 1954 Final.

strong point, but that hardly mattered for a centre-forward who could conjure a goal out of nothing. His heading too was conspicuously ineffective – yet here he was scoring the vital goal against Manchester City. 'I just twisted my neck and found the ball in the net' was his surprised comment.

Mitchell on the left wing was an altogether different character, relying on cool cunning rather than dashing attack. His dribbling was a bewilderment to opponents and a delight to spectators. For he had the supreme confidence to take on and beat the defender, the timing and swerve to baffle the best. And the big occasion was for him a stimulant rather than an anxiety. With a strong defence based on Brennan's power at centre-half and with such talent in attack, Newcastle finally wiped out the memory of those sad failures at Crystal Palace.

Manchester City had little time to grieve reversing the previous year's score when they fought their way back to Wembley. On record Birmingham were favourites having won every tie away from home with an aggregate of 18–2. By contrast City had struggled through by the odd goal in all their matches. Yet on the day Birmingham were never in the hunt and not even an injury to Trautmann could help them. Fifteen minutes from the end he made a typically daring dive at Murphy's feet and played on in great pain. After the match it was found he had broken his neck, a sad climax to being elected Footballer of the Year and gaining a Cup winners' medal.

Yet it could be that an attack of boils decided this game. They forced Spurdle to drop out of the City team on the very eve of the Final and Revie was reinstated in his old role of deep-lying centre-forward with Johnstone moving to the wing. For Revie it had been a lean season in which he had lost his place in England's team and in his Club's. Now he came back to play with tireless efficiency. He and Barnes dominated the midfield and within three minutes he had made the opening goal. After a smooth interchange of passes with Clarke, Revie backheeled the ball for Hayes to score. Soon Brown gave Kinsey the chance to equalise and the teams were still level at half-time. But Birmingham, noted for their rugged tackling, were curiously hesitant and indecisive against Manchester's clever passing. The only surprise was that City's second goal was so long delayed. In the 65th minute Revie and Barnes split the defence for Dyson to run through and score. Three minutes later Trautmann's long clearance was headed on by Dyson and Johnstone went gliding down the centre to beat Merrick. Johnstone not only settled the issue, but became the first man to score in successive Wembley Finals. With Trautmann dazed and in pain Birmingham made a final effort to get back in the game. Dave Ewing, never the most delicate of centre-halves covered his injured goalkeeper with rugged efficiency. One clearance struck on the half-volley soared high into the stand opposite the Royal Box. Roy Paul put his hand on Ewing's shoulder and congratulated him on 'the longest kick ever seen at Wembley'. No accident was going to be allowed to deprive Manchester City of a game that was well won!

The following year injury shattered Manchester United's hopes of the double, but nothing could rob them of the title of the team of 1957. For the second season

Merrick dives to save at the feet of Hayes, Manchester
City's inside-right, in the 1956 Final.

they won the League and in addition they reached the Final of the F.A. Cup and the semi-final of the European Cup. Under Matt Busby's leadership United had been the most consistent of post-war sides in Cup as well as League. But Aston Villa's Cup record is second to none and once again they snatched the victory.

The decisive moment came after only six minutes. Goalkeeper Wood caught the ball and hesitated long enough for McParland to charge in, coming straight on even when the ball was cleared. The reckless rush ended with both players stretched in the turf. Wood was helped off with a fractured cheek-bone, coming back later to wander aimlessly on the wing. McParland was unharmed and by strange irony was to score the two goals that left United's hopes in ruins. With Blanchflower borrowing a photographer's cap and going into goal, Edwards fell back to centre-half and Whelan to left-half.

Before the match Matt Busby had only one worry – that illness or injury might cripple a team which appeared invincible. In the competition they had risen superior to every challenge. Hartlepools gave them a fright in the first round coming back from 0–3 down to equalise before United nosed ahead in a match that Busby regards as the most nerve-wracking he ever watched. Away again to Bournemouth they were a goal down and a man injured at half-time against a giant-killing team that had already disposed of Wolverhampton Wanderers and Tottenham Hotspur. Yet their nerve held and they won through. Now it seemed that they must outclass Aston Villa and Busby was happily confident once his team reported fit. So soon after the start the nightmare became reality and his hopes dissolved as Wood was helped off.

Inevitably United were driven back in defence holding out until only twenty-two minutes were left. Then Smith sent a cross into the area and McParland raced in to head home. There had been many near misses before this, but soon McParland scored again hitting in the rebound as Dixon shot against a post. Now United staked all in attack sending the dazed and concussed Wood back into goal. Soon their surging assaults showed how different the game might have been, but for the crippling re-organisation. Taylor headed in from a corner the ball floating over Sims to drop inside the angle of bar and post. With Edwards driving powerfully through the midfield Aston Villa barely survived the last five minutes, conceding five corners. As in 1952, the universal respect and sympathy was for the losers with Villa's victory ringing hollow.

The year 1958 is also linked forever with Manchester United, though again the Cup eluded them. There was to be no story book ending, no sop to popular emotion, no triumph of the 'goodies'. Once more Bolton Wanderers found themselves caught up in a Final steeped in emotion. In 1953 the crowd's will and Stanley Matthews had destroyed them. This time they were too competent, too decisive to give in to the United team resurgent after the fatal air crash.

Getting to Wembley was for Manchester a miracle of will and spirit, the players borne along on the surge of popular support. Eight of their team of all the talents had died in the snow of Munich Airport. Out of the ruins a new side was fashioned in a few days. The fifth round tie with Sheffield Wednesday was put back four days. The rules were bent for them and Stan Crowther of Villa, signed on the eve of the game, became only the second man to play for two League Clubs in the competition in the same season. Taylor, another player with Cup-Final experience, was signed from Blackpool. Incredibly their patchwork side won 3–0 in the glare of floodlights, and with a 65,000 crowd keeping up an incessant roar.

The enthusiasm and emotion destroyed Sheffield. Bobby Charlton defeated West Bromwich Albion in the sixth round replay, running fifty yards in the last minute of extra time to make a goal for Webster. In the semi-final Second Division Fulham were also beaten in a replay, two wonderful goals by Charlton saving United in the first match and Macedo's uncertain handling giving them an easy win the second. Dawson at 18 scored the first semi-final hat-trick since 1948 while Roy Bentley played in his seventh semi-final game without ever reaching Wembley.

The sustained intensity of feeling veered between the unforgettable and the unhealthy. But in the Final Bolton were proof against nerves or sentiment and the cold logic of their play brought the game back to earth. Within three minutes Lofthouse had slipped the ball into the net as Edwards' thirty-yard pass found him unmarked. Only Gregg's saves kept United in the game in that first half. Then, shortly after the interval, Charlton took Taylor's pass and sent a fierce drive smashing against the post. The ball slammed back into Hopkinson's hands and the cheers died stillborn. At once Bolton thrust back and Gregg could only knock up Stevens' rising shot. As he caught the ball Lofthouse charged him into the net. It was an unusual goal with goalkeepers now so carefully protected by the rules. But no argument about its fairness could obscure the fact that the best team had won by the right margin.

The season of upsets was 1959. Nottingham Forest were nearly defeated by amateurs Tooting and Mitcham. And in the semi-final Luton only just got the better of Third Division Norwich City in a replay. Finalists Luton and Forest were far from outstanding and indeed had both been playing so badly in the weeks before the Final that a dreary game was forecast. One writer did, in fact, call this the most forgettable final of all time.

But to me this was a prejudiced view for Nottingham Forest played above themselves and the match was full of challenge and good football. The best of the play was in the first twenty minutes as Forest's forwards swept through at will. In the tenth minute Dwight scored with a ferocious drive. Four minutes later Wilson headed in Gray's lob. And still Luton were stretched and tormented by those darting forwards as Baynham's fine goalkeeping saved them from being overwhelmed. Then, on the half-hour Dwight broke a leg as he collided with McNally. Inevitably the whole course of the game was changed and it was now the watchful defence of Burkitt, Whitefoot and McKinlay that preserved the lead. With less than half-an-hour left Pacey drove in Hawkes' low cross after a corner. But still Forest kept their poise and had few further worries.

The skill of the Final was a reversal of all expectation and a pleasant climax to a

249

curious season in the competition. To add to the oddities both teams had kept the same eleven for every Cup match while Luton had reached their first Final without having a Manager, since Duncan left them in October.

In 1960 double disaster hit Blackburn Rovers just before the interval and left them without hope. In the forty-first minute McGrath deflected Stobart's low cross into his own net. Then Whelan broke his leg in a tackle on Deeley.

Wolverhampton were too powerful a side to permit any recovery. They had failed by one point to win the League for the third successive year and nothing could now stop them taking the Cup. The rugged power of Flowers and Clamp had given them midfield command before the accident. Now they came driving forward relentlessly, backed by Slater's intelligent control from centre-half. Their forwards responded with wit and vigour as Broadbent, cool and inventive, gave scope to the speed of Stobart and Deeley. Deeley, his right leg bruised in the clash with Whelan, used it effectively enough to score the two telling goals. The first was laid on for him by Horne and his shot from near the penalty spot gave Leyland no chance. The second was generously presented by Woods, making his one mistake at centre-half. Failing to control a centre he left the ball ideally placed for Deeley to sweep in. Kevin Howley, at 35 the youngest man to referee a Wembley Cup Final, had disallowed two other goals for offside and that was clear indication of the run of play.

The crowd were on Blackburn's side and Wolves' professional power was little to their liking. Yet at the end one's respect was all for Wolverhampton. For Blackburn's cavalier approach to the Final had merited some retribution and their cruel luck was not altogether undeserved.

Clayton, Douglas and Woods gave unstinting effort, but Blackburn's was a brittle performance without noticeable team spirit and far from their great tradition in the Cup.

25

Decade of the 'Double' 1961–71

The last ten years start and end with the 'double' that had seemed so elusive of achievement throughout this century. Tottenham and Arsenal's successes exploded the myth that modern pressures make it impossible to win both Cup and League. As the rich and powerful clubs become ever stronger the magic circle of likely winners contracts improving their chances of the double.

Teamwork and team spirit were there in abundance as Tottenham showed the way in 1961. So too was individual skill. Blanchflower and Mackay were the ideal blend of subtlety and strength in midfield. Forward, Greaves, White, Smith and Jones had the talent to defeat any defensive plan. Perhaps this was the finest team of the century, and certainly it was the most attractive. In the Final they beat Leicester without revealing their true ability, then won again the following season in a clash with Burnley that was a joy to watch.

The Centenary Year of The Football Association was 1963 and there could be no more appropriate Cup winner than Manchester United. United was still the country's leading team and it was typical of their resilience that they should carry off this trophy while struggling for once to avoid relegation. The weather had been unco-operative for the Centenary, the freeze-up in January so congesting fixtures that the Final was put back until May 25. Manchester's team had been rebuilt, regardless of expense, with more than £300,000 paid for Cantwell, Crerand, Setters, Quixall, Law, and Herd. On this great occasion they looked a team without price, worth every pound that Busby had spent. Inevitably their side was laced with home-grown talent, the other five all products of minor football.

Leicester, however, were the favourites, well placed in the League and with only two goals conceded in the Cup. Their disciplined defence was expected to subdue the wayward genius of United's forwards while McLintock, Cross and Stringfellow had the attacking power to snatch goals. And for a time it seemed that this might be the pattern with Gaskell kept anxiously active by Leicester's swift raids. Then Banks, after a fine save from Charlton made a haphazard clearance straight to Crerand. There was no recovery from error. Crerand slipped past three men then stroked the ball through for Law to hook home.

With growing assurance Manchester pressed in on Banks and twelve minutes after the interval Charlton flashed in a shot he could only parry. Herd joyfully swept home the rebound. With ten minutes left Leicester hit back at last as Manchester still came driving forward.

Keyworth threw himself at a low centre, his courageous header slipping inside

Henry is the strong man at the bottom of this pyramid
in the 1962 Final.

The Manager's torture – Harry Catterick of Everton cannot
watch the closing minutes of the 1966 Final.

the post. Unconcerned, Manchester swept back with Law heading against the post
after a spectacular run. And now Banks, of all people, erred again, dropping Giles'
centre under pressure from Law. Herd, whose father had played in the Finals of
1933 and 1934 went two better than Dad by hammering home his second goal.

West Ham's only win in 1964 was compensation for that disturbed game at
Wembley's opening, when the pressures of the day threw them out of their stride.
This time Moore's cool direction and Boyce's finishing thrust saw them home
against Second Division Preston.

With two such competent defences it was almost inevitable that the 1965 Final
between Liverpool and Leeds should go into extra time. And indeed all the excitement was reserved for those last thirty minutes. Until then the forwards had had

1966: an over-enthusiastic supporter is collared by the police and lectured
by Brian Labone. Brian Harris tries on a police officer's hat.

Trebilcock, a surprise choice, scores one of his two goals which
helped Everton defeat Sheffield Wednesday in 1966.

short shrift against the relentless tackling and close marking. Yet Liverpool had
always looked the stronger and more inventive. Midfield, Smith and Stevenson
dictated the flow of the ball. Forward, St. John and Hunt quested eagerly for an
opening. Leeds were less impressive with Collins and Bremner unusually subdued
and Peacock ineffective against Yeats.

   Storrie was slowed by injury, but it should have been Liverpool who suffered
most from misfortune. For in the tenth minute Byrne broke a collar bone, playing
on with a courage reminiscent of Lieutenant Cresswell in that first Cup Final at the
Oval. But Byrne had more than courage, successfully concealing his injury and
containing Giles with calm assurance. And in the third minute of extra time – the
first since 1947 – it was Byrne who overlapped down the wing to meet Stevenson's

Alex Young beats Brennan and Gregg but his shot hits the post in this
1966 semi-final game which Everton won 1–0.

Graceful movement in the spring sunshine as Law slides home
the first goal for Manchester United in 1963.

precise pass. As he centred to the near post Hunt stooped forward to head in. The
singing of the Liverpool supporters had brought a new atmosphere to Wembley
and now the Stadium was alive with noise and colour. But the jubilation was pre-
mature. With Bremner switched into attack Leeds at last successfully finished off
one of their standard moves. Jack Charlton stole up unnoticed to head down
Hunter's high pass. Bremner turned to meet the ball and smashed his shot high
into the net.

But still Leeds hesitated to commit themselves to attack and Liverpool soon

Gaskell's leap cannot stop Ron Boyce scoring for West Ham in the 1964
semi-final against Manchester United at Hillsborough.

The 1965 Final: Bremner jumps for joy as his shot enters the net
for Leeds' equalising goal.

regained their poise, powering forward once more. With nine minutes to go Callaghan went racing on and on down the right crossing the ball just as he seemed to be squeezed out. The centre drifted beyond Sprake and St John flung himself forward to head home.

Over the years Liverpool have been in the top four for consistency in the competition yet surprisingly this was only their third Final and their first win. Leeds United were developing a side of formidable consistency, yet so often fated to be runners up. This was a characteristic achievement with the Cup remaining so near and yet so far.

The year 1966 was in cheerful contrast to the defensive tempo of 1965.

A colourful Final full of incident and goals saw the dramatic recovery of an Everton team that had looked well beaten. They were revived by two fine goals from Trebilcock an energetic little Cornishman who was a surprise replacement for the expensive and experienced Pickering. It was typical of the romance of the

St John's agile header scores the decisive goal for
Liverpool against Leeds United in 1965.

Cup that this one game should bring fame to a young player whose name was not
even in the programme and who could never afterwards establish himself at the top
level.

Sheffield Wednesday were in calm control of the first hour's play. They went
ahead after only four minutes. Ford squared the ball across goal and McCalliog met
it in full stride. His half-hit shot was deflected by left-back Wilson to leave West

Jeff Astle beats Gordon West to score the extra-time goal that gave
West Bromwich Albion the Cup against Everton in 1968.

stranded. With Quinn and Pugh busy in midfield Ford and Fantham kept Everton's defence at full stretch. The occasional counter-attacks centred on the elegant
Alex Young who was unfortunate to be denied a penalty as Springett's dive
brought him down when poised to score. Early in the second half Young was
again unlucky as his low volley was saved one handed by Springett. Then the
tenacious Fantham, tearing through the middle, hit a searing left-foot shot that
West could only parry. Ford ran the ball into the goal.

Within two minutes Everton struck back from two goals down and within a quarter of an hour they had won the Cup. Temple headed the ball into the centre for Trebilcock to drive it home. Then Scott's free kick was jostled out to Trebilcock and again his confident shot went true and straight. Police chased off two joyful supporters, but there was no holding Everton's elation. Under their surging pressure the competent Gerry Young made his one fatal error. Free from challenge he failed to trap a ball in midfield and before he could recover Temple sped smoothly past him to shoot low into the net.

The 1967 Final was the first all-London Final at Wembley and Tottenham's third Cup victory in the 60s. Chelsea, rivalling them for consistency of Cup performance in this decade, still found the main prize eluding them. On the day Tottenham were always the more confident and cohesive team. All the energy, enthusiasm, and skill of Hollins and Cooke merely went to prove that individual effort is no substitute for good teamwork. Throughout Spurs contained Chelsea's assaults with ease. MacKay reining back his attacking inclinations stayed deep at the heart of a composed and powerful defence, leaving the dashing midfield work to Mullery and allowing Kinnear to do some venturesome running down the wing.

Forward Gilzean's dominance in the air, the persistence of Saul, and Robertson's quick eye for an opening were a constant threat. Robertson came near to scoring with two blinding volleys, one saved at full stretch by Bonetti, the other grazing the bar.

Just before half-time it was third time lucky for Robertson's snap shooting.

Mullery came driving through the middle and his shot was blocked by Ron Harris. As the ball ran loose Robertson, loitering with intent, hit it first time into the net with Bonetti groping in vain. Another goal in the 68th minute was in keeping with Tottenham's calm control. Mackay's long throw-in was helped on by Robertson for Saul to hook the ball home on the turn.

At last Chelsea were stung to fierce retaliation. The game had begun in sunshine after a sharp thunderstorm, but now the rain came drifting back. The slippery ball contributed to Jennings one error five minutes from the end. Under challenge he missed Boyle's centre and Tambling headed the ball home. For all the vigour of Chelsea's final assaults Spurs allowed them no further hope, taking the trophy for the third time in seven seasons – Chelsea were left to reflect on five semi-finals and one Final in the same period with nothing to show for their efforts.

Chelsea's good fortune had been exhausted in reaching Wembley. In their semi-final at Villa Park Leeds a goal down with a few minutes left for play jubilantly saluted a shot from Lorimer that flashed into the net. A free-kick had been rolled across to him and it looked as if he had scored the equaliser. But Chelsea's players had not been far enough away and the referee had given no signal to take the kick. So for Leeds it was frustration again, the goal disallowed and their hopes of Wembley crushed.

Next year's Cup-Final was a sad anti-climax to a season of soaring interest and success for English football. The game between West Bromwich Albion and Everton was reminiscent of Verdun with 'They shall not pass' as the main tactical concept. There was a harsh reliance on physical strength to the exclusion of the arts and graces of the game. Close marking and ruthless tackling made this a match of disjointed movements and few openings.

For all the drive and determination there was no breaking of those massed and ruthless defences in the full ninety minutes. Then a contest that began in rain and graceless football ended in sunshine and overdue excitement.

Jeff Astle scored the decisive goal in the third minute of extra time. He had scored in every round getting eight of the sixteen goals that took Albion to Wembley.

With that wearing extra half-hour barely begun Astle moved casually through the middle brushing aside Kendall's tired tackle. His weak drive spun back off Harvey and now Astle lunged forward to hit a searing left-foot shot. The ball swept into the far corner of the net with satisfying certainty. Astle, leading scorer in English football that season, was just the man to strike the decisive blow though he was often more dangerous with head than foot. His skill at last rose superior to the destructive bustle of the play.

But others had already pointed the way. For Everton Morrissey, poised and purposeful, was an effective winger at his own deliberate pace, while Ball was endlessly inventive. Albion's Hope matched his craft with penetrating passes that kept the Everton defenders at full stretch. Only Wright and Wilson's cool control of the Albion wingers prevented Astle having earlier chance to prove his finishing power.

Until extra time the game belonged mainly to the destructive powers of Talbut and Kaye, Hurst and Labone. Yet Everton could so easily have stolen the match had Husband been more precise near goal. Of three clear chances he squandered, the easiest was just before full time.

Once more it was Morrissey who made the opening and Husband, unchallenged, headed over from a few yards out. That would have settled the game. But in extra time it was Albion who were the stronger though Kaye had to be replaced.

In 1969 Manchester City, League Champions the previous year, ended an otherwise disappointing season by carrying off the Cup. And that is consolation enough for any side whatever the other results may be.

How different for Leicester City. For them it was dust and ashes all the way as they slid into the Second Division and lost a gripping final by a solitary goal.

This Wembley match was always a game of character and challenge settled by one thunderous shot from inside-left Young. That chance was taken with a decisive authority which contrasted with the sad squandering by both sides of many another clear-cut openings.

Two bleak unmemorable semi-finals, with Everton and West Bromwich Albion nudged into oblivion, had given little hint of this fluent, swaying struggle.

Manchester City could be counted on for stylish football with Mercer and Allison preaching to their team the creed of class and fluency.

Leicester City's standards were much less certain. Their team had a tradition of

263

Robertson's joy at scoring Tottenham Hotspur's first goal
against Chelsea in 1967.

cup fighting resource and success, but there had been little flair or grace in their play that season.

Yet at the end they could take pride in their contribution to a Final of fluid movement and breathless excitement. Without defensive thoughts they played open attacking football challenging Manchester at their own level of excellence.

Manchester City were quickest into their stride and it was in the first 25 minutes that the match was won. Summerbee ran riot on the right, baffling Nish with his intricate dribbling and smooth acceleration. The Manchester attacks built up from Book's cool control at the back, through the inventiveness of Doyle, Bell and Young in midfield to the penetrating drive of Summerbee. Yet the restless, surging

Wilson saves at full stretch from Lindsay's free-kick.

assaults were countered by the steadfast determination of Cross and the agile interception of Shilton. Young shooting with his weak right-foot and Lee side-footing a close shot high and wide failed to finish with the neat precision that marked the approach play.

When Leicester thrust back Clarke and Lochhead were menacingly effective. Clarke with his languid looking runs went gliding past the tackles, or found the

Wilson leaves the near post unguarded and Heighway
scores from an acute angle.

gaps with precise and penetrating passes. An insolent dribble across the face of the
defence and an explosive shot stretched Dowd to save high to his right. As the
Leicester pressure mounted Booth intercepted a shot by Glover as he slid the ball
past goalkeeper, Dowd. Then full-back Rodrigues, up in attack, swung wildly as
the ball cannoned to his feet close to the near post.

Appropriately it was Summerbee who made the goal after 23 minutes. Losing
Nish and evading some crude lunging tackles he slid the ball back into Young's
stride. His deadly left foot sent the ball soaring high past Shilton's right shoulder.

For all the skill of Clarke, Man of the Match in the journalists' view, Leicester

City could never get back on terms. Lochhead sliced weakly wide as Clarke nodded the ball to him with delicate touch. That was the easiest of the openings, but both teams spurned chances in the cut and thrust of attack and counter-attack. Before the end Glover, injured in a harsh tackle, was replaced by Manley. Yet this was a match more notable for skill than strength, for style and speed than harshness.

After Chelsea's long drawn victory over Leeds, Arsenal and Liverpool contrived another marathon. A battle of attrition was the accurate forecast and not until extra time sapped their strength were two relentless defences to give space or opportunity to the forwards. Then it was that Arsenal's resilience and determination took them to the double.

Before the match, Manager Bill Shankly had declared that one goal would be decisive and if Liverpool nosed ahead they would never be caught. Yet Arsenal recovered from the dagger thrust of Heighway's opportunist goal, their nerves steady enough, their muscles hard enough to drive them to victory in this most exhausting close to an exhausting season. With 63 games already played, it was a remarkable tribute to their will, their courage, and their fitness that they could make a successful challenge late in extra time.

So often had teams destroyed themselves in the chase for the double that it had been regarded as impossible of achievement under modern pressures until Tottenham's triumph of 1961. Where so many other Clubs had faltered in the past Arsenal won through in a climactic finish of sustained and relentless intensity. In the League they trailed Leeds throughout the season coming through on the post with an extraordinary run of 27 points from the last fifteen matches.

On the Monday of Cup-Final week they beat Spurs in the decisive game, a goal from Kennedy two minutes from time inching them a point clear. Their one disappointment had been to lose to Leeds in a crucial match by a hotly-disputed goal at the very end of the game. What could have been a disaster proved only the spur to success. So it was in the Cup. In the semi-final they were two goals down to Stoke at half-time, yet Storey saved them with a fierce shot and a coolly stroked penalty. The penalty came in the last minute as McLintock's header was handled on the line. In the replay they raised their game to shatter Stoke. And now they faced a Liverpool side as hard and determined as themselves which had come to its peak late in the season.

This was a battle of the scientific soccer of the seventies. Both teams had steely defences, the ultimate refinements from the change in the off-side law and the ending of the maximum wage. The first had started the trend for stopper centre-halves and packed defences. The second had put so high a premium on success that teams could no longer afford to gamble. And, as any military man will tell, defence is so much easier to organise than attack.

Yet despite the destructive excellence and the disciplined teamwork the Final was decided at the last by players of flair and individuality.

Heighway wandering in lonely isolation on the wings nearly settled the match with one darting run, jinking dribble and unexpected shot. Thompson, the Liver-

Charlie George celebrates Arsenal's 'double' by standing on his head.

pool substitute transformed their play and the even tenor of the match with his subtle swerve, close control, and artfully precise centres.

For Liverpool's two Arsenal had three and that was a fair summary of the balance of the game.

Graham pacing and controlling the play in the centre of the field was masterful and assured throughout the long afternoon, his skill shining out amid the bustle. Radford, swift and strong, was clever enough to beat his man in confined space. He set up enough simple chances for Arsenal to have won without the aid of extra time and he had a foot in that last crushing goal.

Appropriately it was George who made that final killing thrust as he had threatened to throughout the game. His feel for the unexpected pass that un-balances opponents, and the raking power of his shot, made him the explosive force that no patterned defence could wholly smother.

Even among defenders the honours went to two confined in no rigid mould. McLintock, player of the year, inspirational captain, was a poised and constructive centre-half, immaculate in his ball control, thoughtful in his distribution. Twice before a loser in the Cup-Final it was skill not luck that brought him the winner's medal at the third attempt.

For Liverpool, Lawler's cool command and sudden attack steadied the defence and gave strength to the forwards.

Strength indeed was the first impression of the match as two hard sides fought for physical dominance. Liverpool came driving into attack with Hughes running powerfully in support of his forwards. The challenge was met head on and head down by Storey whose reckless tackling got the match off to a niggling start and a series of free kicks.

Fortunately there were few hard feelings between sides used to giving and taking hard knocks and if disruption was the keynote of the play there was no ill-humour. Technical excellence there was in the defensive covering, in the tackling, in the interception. But of smooth sweeping movement or spectacular attack there was little sign in the first hour. Chances were as rare as Coelacănths.

George ended Liverpool's brief dominance with a perceptive pass that sent Kennedy clear to drag his shot wide of the far post.

Armstrong, close in, headed Radford's centre hard and true but near enough to Clemence for an instinctive save and scrambling recovery. From a free kick just outside the area Callaghan pushed the ball sideways for Lindsay to arrow a low shot just inside the post – Wilson plunged across to turn it aside at full stretch of his elastic fingers.

So much for the first half; and until Kelly came on for the injured Storey and Thompson for Evans the stalemate persisted. Yet Arsenal kept working the occa-sional chance, only for Kennedy whose sure finishing had won them the League Championship, to squander the openings.

Radford's delicate overhead flick to beat Lloyd was followed by a precise pass that Kennedy stabbed wide from three yards out. Then Graham's backheader

270

flicked up off the bar and from the corner he once more rose high above the defenders for Lindsay to clear off the line. Smith was tackling with implacable resolve, but still Arsenal came sweeping through for Kennedy to shoot wide. But Liverpool too were now more lively in attack with Thompson's centres stretching Wilson. The ball at last was reaching Toshack's head, but with Evans off there was no one to pick up his glancing passes.

So to extra time and on the tiring surface the gaps at last began to appear in those impenetrable defences. In the second minute of the first period Heighway picked up Thompson's pass and strode clear until a huddle of defenders shepherded him wide on the edge of the area. A sudden shot from the acutest of angles caught Wilson out from goal to cut off the expected centre and the ball slid into the net, grazing the near post.

As Arsenal wilted Hall so nearly added the second, his close volley palmed away by Wilson's instinctive lunge. But now Kelly hustled in to challenge Smith and Hughes for a gently bouncing ball. Surprisingly he won it from these two strong men and Graham sped behind their backs to touch the shot home. Or so it looked and so Graham confirmed – but TV camera re-runs indicated that the ball rolled in direct from Kelly.

By the final period of extra time the blistering pace had taken its toll. George, tiring in midfield, was pushed up as striker swapping with Graham. At once Radford gave him a return pass and George's fierce shot from outside the area flew into the corner of the net. George salutes his own goals arms aloft in triumph, but this time he lay full length for his victory sign. That was fair comment on the tiredness of the teams, though exultation or desperation drove both to a rousing finish with Lawler's close volley soaring over the Arsenal bar.

It had been a Final rich in courage and skill with a climax of mounting excitement to end the two hours' struggle. The game was made more colourful by the swaying battle between South and North, and the double for Arsenal to better their great days of the thirties. What finer end could there be to this story or more perfect prelude to the Cup's centenary season?

271

Appendix A

F.A. Challenge Cup Winners 1872–1971

1872 and 1874–92	Kennington Oval	1895–1914	Crystal Palace
1873	Lillie Bridge	1915	Old Trafford Manchester
1893	Fallowfield, Manchester	1920–22	Stamford Bridge
1894	Everton	1923 to date	Wembley

Year	Winners	Runners-up	Score
1872	Wanderers	Royal Engineers	1–0
1873	Wanderers	Oxford University	2–0
1874	Oxford University	Royal Engineers	2–0
1875	Royal Engineers	Old Etonians	2–0 after 1–1 draw
1876	Wanderers	Old Etonians	3–0 after 0–0 draw
1877	Wanderers	Oxford University	2–0 after extra time
1878	*Wanderers	Royal Engineers	3–1
1879	Old Etonians	Clapham Rovers	1–0
1880	Clapham Rovers	Oxford University	1–0
1881	Old Carthusians	Old Etonians	3–0
1882	Old Etonians	Blackburn Rovers	1–0
1883	Blackburn Olympic	Old Etonians	2–1 after extra time
1884	Blackburn Rovers	Queen's Park, Glasgow	2–1
1885	Blackburn Rovers	Queen's Park, Glasgow	2–0
1886	†Blackburn Rovers	West Bromwich Albion	2–0 after 0–0 draw
1887	Aston Villa	West Bromwich Albion	2–0
1888	West Bromwich Albion	Preston North End	2–1
1889	Preston North End	Wolverhampton Wanderers	3–0
1890	Blackburn Rovers	Sheffield Wednesday	6–1
1891	Blackburn Rovers	Notts County	3–1
1892	West Bromwich Albion	Aston Villa	3–0
1893	Wolverhampton Wanderers	Everton	1–0
1894	Notts County	Bolton Wanderers	4–1
1895	Aston Villa	West Bromwich Albion	1–0
1896	Sheffield Wednesday	Wolverhampton Wanderers	2–1
1897	Aston Villa	Everton	3–2
1898	Nottingham Forest	Derby County	3–1
1899	Sheffield United	Derby County	4–1
1900	Bury	Southampton	4–0
1901	Tottenham Hotspur	Sheffield United	3–1 after 2–2 draw
1902	Sheffield United	Southampton	2–1 after 1–1 draw
1903	Bury	Derby County	6–0
1904	Manchester City	Bolton Wanderers	1–0
1905	Aston Villa	Newcastle United	2–0
1906	Everton	Newcastle United	1–0
1907	Sheffield Wednesday	Everton	2–1
1908	Wolverhampton Wanderers	Newcastle United	3–1
1909	Manchester United	Bristol City	1–0
1910	Newcastle United	Barnsley	2–0 after 1–1 draw
1911	Bradford City	Newcastle United	1–0 after 0–0 draw
1912	Barnsley	West Bromwich Albion	1–0 after 0–0 draw
1913	Aston Villa	Sunderland	1–0
1914	Burnley	Liverpool	1–0
1915	Sheffield United	Chelsea	3–0

Year	Winners	Runners-up	Score
1920	Aston Villa	Huddersfield Town	1–0 after extra time
1921	Tottenham Hotspur	Wolverhampton Wanderers	1–0
1922	Huddersfield Town	Preston North End	1–0
1923	Bolton Wanderers	West Ham United	2–0
1924	Newcastle United	Aston Villa	2–0
1925	Sheffield United	Cardiff City	1–0
1926	Bolton Wanderers	Manchester City	1–0
1927	Cardiff City	Arsenal	1–0
1928	Blackburn Rovers	Huddersfield Town	3–1
1929	Bolton Wanderers	Portsmouth	2–0
1930	Arsenal	Huddersfield Town	2–0
1931	West Bromwich Albion	Birmingham	2–1
1932	Newcastle United	Arsenal	2–1
1933	Everton	Manchester City	3–0
1934	Manchester City	Portsmouth	2–1
1935	Sheffield Wednesday	West Bromwich Albion	4–2
1936	Arsenal	Sheffield United	1–0
1937	Sunderland	Preston North End	3–1
1938	Preston North End	Huddersfield Town	1–0 after extra time
1939	Portsmouth	Wolverhampton Wanderers	4–1
1946	Derby County	Charlton Athletic	4–1 after extra time
1947	Charlton Athletic	Burnley	1–0 after extra time
1948	Manchester United	Blackpool	4–2
1949	Wolverhampton Wanderers	Leicester City	3–1
1950	Arsenal	Liverpool	2–0
1951	Newcastle United	Blackpool	2–0
1952	Newcastle United	Arsenal	1–0
1953	Blackpool	Bolton Wanderers	4–3
1954	West Bromwich Albion	Preston North End	3–2
1955	Newcastle United	Manchester City	3–1
1956	Manchester City	Birmingham City	3–1
1957	Aston Villa	Manchester United	2–1
1958	Bolton Wanderers	Manchester United	2–0
1959	Nottingham Forest	Luton Town	2–1
1960	Wolverhampton Wanderers	Blackburn Rovers	3–0
1961	Tottenham Hotspur	Leicester City	2–0
1962	Tottenham Hotspur	Burnley	3–1
1963	Manchester United	Leicester City	3–1
1964	West Ham United	Preston North End	3–2
1965	Liverpool	Leeds United	2–1 after extra time
1966	Everton	Sheffield Wednesday	3–2
1967	Tottenham Hotspur	Chelsea	2–1
1968	West Bromwich Albion	Everton	1–0 after extra time
1969	Manchester City	Leicester City	1–0
1970	Chelsea	Leeds United	2–1 after 2–2 draw both games extra time
1971	Arsenal	Liverpool	2–1 after extra time

* Won outright, but restored to Association.
† A special trophy was awarded for third consecutive win.

273

Clubs Which Have Won The F.A. Cup

Since 1871–72 there have been 90 F.A. Cup-Finals. The F.A. Cup competition was suspended during seasons 1915–16 to 1918–19 and 1939–40 to 1944–45. The Cup has been won by 37 clubs:

Aston Villa (*see facing page*)	7	Manchester United	3
Blackburn Rovers	6	Sheffield Wednesday	3
Newcastle United	6	Bury	2
Tottenham Hotspur	5	Nottingham Forest	2
Wanderers	5	Old Etonians	2
West Bromwich Albion	5	Preston North End	2
Arsenal	4	Barnsley, Blackburn Olympic, Blackpool, Bradford City, Burnley, Cardiff City, Charlton Athletic, Chelsea, Clapham Rovers, Derby County, Huddersfield Town, Liverpool, Notts County, Old Carthusians, Oxford University, Portsmouth, Royal Engineers, Sunderland, West Ham United	
Bolton Wanderers	4		
Manchester City	4		
Sheffield United	4		
Wolverhampton Wanderers	4		
Everton	3		1

Johnny Dixon, captain of Aston Villa, holds aloft the F.A. Cup after the
Club had won the Cup-Final for a record seventh time in 1957.

Appendix B

League Clubs' Comparative Performance 1888–1971

The table below evaluates the Cup performance of leading teams by the average round to which they progressed from 1888 onwards

		Round Average	Cup Wins	Placing in 1888–1915	Placing in 1919–39	Placing in 1945–71
1	Everton	5·08	3	1	15	5
2	Aston Villa	5·00	6	2	3	17
3	Tottenham Hotspur	4·96	4	22	5	2
4	Liverpool	4·90	1	9	12	4
5	West Bromwich Albion	4·88	4	7	8	6
6	Newcastle United	4·81	6	3	11	13
7	Wolverhampton Wanderers	4·75	4	5	15	11
8	Arsenal	4·72	4	23	1	6
9	Chelsea	4·71	1	21	12	3
10	Blackburn Rovers	4·68	3	4	12	20
11	Sheffield United	4·68	4	11	9	11
12	Sheffield Wednesday	4·67	3	5	15	16
12	Manchester United	4·67	3	20	29	1
14	Bolton Wanderers	4·63	4	14	7	17
15	Preston North End	4·62	2	16	6	15
16	Sunderland	4·56	1	10	9	23
17	Derby County	4·47	1	8	20	27
18	Burnley	4·42	1	19	23	9
19	Manchester City	4·39	4	27	4	13
20	Nottingham Forest	4·32	2	12	27	24
21	Huddersfield Town	4·29	1	–	2	30
22	Stoke City	4·26	0	15	34	19
23	Birmingham City	4·25	0	28	18	10
24	Leicester City	4·15	0	31	22	6
25	West Ham United	4·13	1	–	20	26
26	Portsmouth	4·04	1	–	19	28
27	Leeds United	4·02	0	–	31	22

Four other Clubs have ranked in the top 20 at various periods:

1888–1915	13th Bury	17th Notts County	18th Bradford City
1945–1971	20th Blackpool		

Restricted to one of the 3 periods under review the best performances have been as follows:

1888–1915		1919–1939		1945–1971	
Everton	5·69	Arsenal	5·45	Manchester United	5·46
Aston Villa	5·63	Huddersfield Town	5·35	Tottenham Hotspur	5·23
Newcastle United	5·50				

Note: It is stressed that the above and following figures and tables are *not* a record of a Clubs' complete results in the F.A. Cup, but only while as members of the Football League.

Several Clubs have changed their names during their membership of the League. While the tables use only the names as used by Clubs at the present day, they might well have been different at earlier periods. The number of rounds has also changed and in order to have a fair comparison these have been allocated as follows:

Round Allocation	1		2		3	4	5	6	7	8	9
									S-F	Final	Won
1888–89 to 1895–96	2nd	Q	3rd	Q	4th Q	1st	2nd	3rd	S-F	Final	Won
1896–97 to 1899–00	3rd	Q	4th	Q	5th Q	1st	2nd	3rd	S-F	Final	Won
1900–01 to 1904–05	*4th	Q	5th	Q	Intermediate	1st	2nd	3rd	S-F	Final	Won
1905–06 to 1924–25	4/5th Q		5/6th Q		1st		2nd	3rd	4th S-F	Final	Won
1925–26 to 1970–71	1st		2nd		3rd		4th	5th	6th S-F	Final	Won

*In 1900–01, the Intermediate Round was termed the Supplementary Round
Q Qualifying

The Also Rans

There are 8 current Members of the Football League who fail to average a 2nd Round appearance over their total League membership:

Rochdale	1·48	Crewe Alexandra	1·83
Barrow	1·61	Colchester United	1·90
Halifax Town	1·77	Gillingham	1·92
Hartlepool	1·83	Torquay United	1·92

Over a restricted period the worst records have been:

1919–1939	Rochdale	1·11	Barrow	1·28
1945–1971	Halifax Town	1·65		

Comparison of Divisional Performances

1888–1915 (27 Seasons)

Round	Pre 4th	4th	5th	6th	S-F	Final	Winners	Round Average
1st Division	72	137	111	64	42	22	23	5·04
2nd Division	235	111	40	20	5	2	3	3·28
Non League	–	184	65	24	7	3	1	–

277

The figures are influenced by the fact that the League consisted only of a single Division for the four seasons 1888–89 to 1892–93. Non-League results were influenced by the performance of the Southern League, formed two years after the addition of a Second Division. Between 1899 and 1902 the Southern League had three Cup-Finalists, Tottenham Hotspur winning in 1901. As late as 1911–12 the Southern League was providing a semi-finalist, Swindon Town, and, as the tables show, was as strong as the Second Division.

1919–1939 (20 seasons)

	Pre-3rd	3rd	4th	5th	6th	S-F	Final	Winners	Round Average
1st Division	–	141	116	78	45	24	16	19	4·59
2nd Division	15	223	103	53	25	15	4	1	3·79
3rd Division (South)	197	128	60	24	8	1	–	–	2·57
3rd Division (North)	270	87	29	3	2	–	–	–	1·93
Non League	–	61	12	2	–	–	–	–	–

The Third Division (South) participated in 19 of the 20 seasons, its original membership composed almost entirely of ex-members of the Southern League. The Third Division (North) participated in 18 of the 20 seasons.

1945–1971 (26 seasons)

	Pre 3rd	3rd	4th	5th	6th	S-F	Final	Winners	Round Average
1st Division	–	190	145	94	59	35	23	26	4·99
2nd Division	–	290	156	77	32	14	3	–	3·83
3rd Division (South)	177	80	28	13	4	–	–	–	2·29
3rd Division (North)	193	75	23	5	2	2	–	–	2·15
3rd Division	182	82	31	11	5	1	–	–	2·34
4th Division	213	71	20	6	2	–	–	–	1·99
Non League	–	44	13	2	–	–	–	–	–

The Regional Sections of the Third Division competed for 13 post-War seasons and the Third and Fourth Divisions also for 13 seasons.

Southern League Comparative Performance 1894–95 to 1920

	P	W	L
v. First Division Clubs	196	65	131
v. Second Division Clubs	116	54	62
v. Other non-League Clubs	24	18	6
Total	336	137	199

Four Southern League Clubs reached the semi-finals or Final

Millwall – semi-final 1899–1900, 1902–3

Southampton – semi-final 1897–98, 1907–8; Final 1899–1900, 1901–2

Swindon Town – semi-final 1909–10, 1911–12

Tottenham Hotspur – won Final 1900–01.

Appendix C

LEAGUE CLUBS' RECORD IN THE F.A. CUP
(Clubs' pre-League Cup performance not included)

Club	Best	In Season	Round Aver	Round Eliminated										1888–1915			1919–1939			1945–1971		
				0	1	2	3	4	5	6	Semi	Fin	Won	T	Best	Aver	T	Best	Aver	T	Best	Aver
Aberdare Athletic	3rd	3 Times	1·67	2	1	–	3	–	–	–	–	–	–	–	–	–	6	3rd	1·67	–	–	–
Accrington Stanley	5th	4 Times	2·40	1	12	9	10	4	4	–	–	–	–	5	5th	4·80	18	4th	2·11	17	4th	2·00
Aldershot	5th	1932–33	2·33	–	9	10	9	4	1	–	–	–	–	–	–	–	7	5th	2·57	26	4th	2·27
Arsenal	WON	4 Times	4·72	1	1	–	17	21	10	9	3	3	4	22	Semi	4·05	20	Won	5·45	26	Won	4·73
Ashington	3rd	3 Times	1·62	1	4	–	3	–	–	–	–	–	–	–	–	–	8	3rd	1·62	–	–	–
Aston Villa	WON	6 Times	5·00	–	1	–	16	19	12	9	8	2	6	27	Won	5·63	20	Won	5·05	26	Won	4·31
Barnsley	WON	1911–12	3·52	–	4	9	27	12	6	3	–	1	1	17	Won	3·94	20	6th	3·40	26	6th	3·43
Barrow	3rd	9 Times	1·61	3	20	12	9	–	–	–	–	–	–	–	–	–	20	3rd	1·28	26	3rd	1·85
Birmingham City	Final	Twice	4·25	–	–	–	27	15	11	8	4	2	–	23	6th	3·74	19	Fin	4·37	26	Fin	4·62
Blackburn Rovers	WON	3 Times	4·68	–	4	–	23	15	16	7	8	1	3	27	Won	5·29	20	Won	4·45	26	Fin	4·23
Blackpool	WON	1952–53	3·61	1	–	–	32	17	4	3	–	2	1	18	5th	2·67	20	6th	3·65	26	Won	4·23
Bolton Wanderers	WON	4 Times	4·63	1	1	–	21	22	11	6	5	3	4	27	Fin	4·81	20	Won	4·80	26	Won	4·31
Bootle	1st	1892–93	1·00	–	1	–	–	–	–	–	–	–	–	1	1st	1·00	–	–	–	–	–	–
Bournemouth & Boscombe	6th	1956–57	2·29	2	12	9	13	4	1	1	–	–	–	–	–	–	16	5th	2·37	26	6th	2·23
Bradford City	WON	1910–11	3·05	12	10	17	8	7	3	–	–	–	1	12	Won	4·50	20	6th	3·55	25	5th	2·00
Bradford (P.A.)	6th	3 Times	3·15	–	9	10	11	11	8	3	–	–	–	7	6th	4·28	20	6th	3·80	26	6th	2·32
Brentford	6th	3 Times	2·96	–	8	9	13	10	2	3	–	–	–	–	–	–	19	6th	2·89	26	6th	3·00
Brighton & Hove Albion	5th	5 Times	2·71	–	12	8	11	9	5	–	–	–	–	–	–	–	19	5th	3·16	26	5th	2·38
Bristol City	Final	1908–09	3·30	–	6	7	25	11	9	–	1	1	–	14	Fin	3·86	19	Semi	3·10	26	5th	3·19
Bristol Rovers	6th	Twice	2·78	–	8	10	16	8	1	2	–	–	–	–	–	–	19	4th	2·37	26	6th	3·08
Burnley	WON	1913–14	4·42	–	1	–	23	19	14	9	4	2	1	27	Won	4·44	20	Semi	4·05	26	Final	4·69
Burton United	4th	3 Times	2·47	1	2	4	5	3	–	–	–	–	–	15	4th	2·47	–	–	–	–	–	–
Burton Wanderers	4th	3 Times	4·00	–	–	–	–	3	–	–	–	–	–	3	4th	4·00	–	–	–	–	–	–
Bury	WON	Twice	3·84	–	2	2	26	23	9	3	–	–	2	21	Won	4·90	20	6th	3·80	26	4th	3·00
Cambridge United	2nd	1970–71	2·00	–	–	1	–	–	–	–	–	–	–	–	–	–	–	–	–	1	2nd	2·00
Cardiff City	WON	1926–27	3·73	–	4	–	21	10	5	2	1	–	–	–	–	–	19	Won	4·05	26	5th	3·50
Carlisle United	5th	Twice	2·32	–	12	9	10	4	2	–	–	–	–	–	–	–	11	3rd	1·91	26	5th	2·50
Charlton Athletic	WON	1946–47	3·64	1	2	–	21	11	5	1	–	–	–	–	–	–	18	6th	3·06	26	Won	4·04
Chelsea	WON	1969–70	4·71	–	1	–	13	16	10	6	7	2	–	10	Fin	4·20	18	Semi	4·45	26	Won	5·11
Chester	4th	6 Times	2·29	–	9	12	7	6	–	–	–	–	–	–	–	–	8	4th	3·00	26	4th	2·08
Chesterfield	5th	3 Times	2·67	–	10	10	25	6	3	–	–	–	–	10	5th	3·10	18	5th	2·72	26	5th	2·46
Colchester United	6th	1970–71	1·90	–	11	5	3	1	1	–	–	–	–	–	–	–	–	–	–	21	6th	1·90
Coventry City	6th	1962–63	2·57	–	11	10	17	5	2	1	–	–	–	–	–	–	20	5th	2·10	26	6th	2·92
Crewe Alexandra	4th	6 Times	1·83	3	20	13	6	6	–	–	–	–	–	4	4th	2·00	18	4th	1·72	26	4th	1·88
Crystal Palace	6th	1964–65	2·69	–	11	8	16	5	4	1	–	–	–	–	–	–	19	5th	2·89	26	6th	2·54
Darlington	5th	1957–58	2·11	–	15	14	11	3	1	–	–	–	–	–	–	–	18	4th	2·50	26	5th	1·85
Darwen	6th	1892–93	3·62	–	–	1	1	3	1	1	–	–	–	8	6th	3·62	–	–	–	–	–	–
Derby County	WON	1945–46	4·47	–	–	2	23	21	10	5	8	3	1	27	Fin	5·15	20	Semi	4·30	26	Won	3·88

Club Records (con.)

Club	In Season Best	In Season Season	Round Aver	0	1	2	3	4	5	6	Semi	Fin	Won	1888–1915 T	1888–1915 Best	1888–1915 Aver	1919–1939 T	1919–1939 Best	1919–1939 Aver	1945–1971 T	1945–1971 Best	1945–1971 Aver
Doncaster Rovers	5th	4 Times	2·40	3	11	7	17	3	4	–	–	–	–	3	2nd	0·67	16	4th	2·19	26	5th	2·73
Durham City	2nd	1925–26	1·00	1	4	1	–	–	–	–	–	–	–	–	–	–	6	2nd	1·00	–	–	–
Everton	WON	3 Times	5·08	–	–	–	15	17	13	11	9	4	3	26	Won	5·69	20	Won	4·40	26	Won	5·00
Exeter City	6th	1930–31	2·04	–	22	8	9	4	1	1	–	–	–	–	–	–	19	6th	2·42	26	4th	1·77
Fulham	Semi	4 Times	3·79	–	2	1	24	18	4	4	4	–	–	8	Semi	4·25	20	Semi	3·70	26	Semi	3·73
Gainsborough Trinity	5th	1897–98	2·37	3	2	1	7	2	1	–	–	–	–	16	5th	2·37	1	–	–	–	–	–
Gateshead	6th	1952–53	2·51	–	13	3	12	3	3	1	–	–	–	–	–	–	20	5th	2·65	15	6th	2·33
Gillingham	5th	1969–70	1·92	–	13	18	7	–	1	–	–	–	–	–	–	–	18	3rd	1·89	21	6th	1·95
Glossop North End	6th	1908–09	3·00	–	3	1	8	4	–	1	–	–	–	17	6th	3·00	–	–	–	–	–	–
Grimsby Town	Semi	Twice	3·22	–	10	4	29	16	6	1	2	–	–	22	6th	3·64	20	Semi	3·65	26	4th	2·54
Halifax Town	5th	Twice	1·77	1	24	9	6	2	2	–	–	–	–	–	–	–	18	5th	1·94	26	5th	1·65
Hartlepool	4th	1954–55	1·82	–	18	17	8	1	–	–	–	–	–	–	–	–	18	3rd	1·67	26	4th	1·92
Huddersfield Town	WON	1921–22	4·29	–	1	–	20	14	7	2	2	4	1	5	4th	3·00	20	Won	5·35	26	6th	3·73
Hull City	Semi	1929–30	3·54	–	2	3	31	8	5	5	1	–	–	10	6th	3·70	20	Semi	3·50	25	6th	3·52
Ipswich Town	5th	4 Times	3·15	3	3	12	5	4	–	1	–	–	–	–	–	–	1	3rd	3·00	26	5th	3·15
Leeds City	4th	4 Times	3·20	–	1	–	5	4	–	–	–	–	–	10	4th	3·20	–	–	–	–	–	–
Leeds United	Final	Twice	4·02	–	–	–	22	10	7	1	2	2	–	–	–	–	18	5th	3·83	26	Fin	4·15
Leicester City	Final	4 Times	4·15	–	1	2	26	16	10	7	1	4	–	21	6th	3·38	20	Semi	4·20	26	Fin	4·73
Lincoln City	5th	1901–02	2·30	3	16	13	27	6	1	–	–	–	–	21	5th	2·38	19	3rd	2·00	26	4th	2·46
Liverpool	WON	1964–65	4·90	–	–	–	11	19	18	11	5	3	1	22	Fin	5·09	20	6th	4·45	26	Won	5·08
Loughborough Town	2nd	3 Times	1·40	–	3	2	–	–	–	–	–	–	–	5	2nd	1·40	–	–	–	–	–	–
Luton Town	Final	1958–59	3·56	–	1	6	23	6	9	2	1	1	–	3	4th	3·33	19	6th	3·37	26	Fin	3·73
Manchester City	WON	4 Times	4·39	4	–	–	20	17	13	6	2	3	4	23	Won	3·78	20	Won	5·00	26	Won	4·46
Manchester United	WON	3 Times	4·67	–	1	–	21	17	10	8	7	2	3	23	Won	4·48	20	Semi	3·85	26	Won	5·46
Mansfield Town	6th	1968–69	2·24	13	8	9	1	2	1	–	–	–	–	–	–	–	8	3rd	1·75	26	6th	2·38
Merthyr Town	3rd	1922–23	1·40	7	2	1	–	–	–	–	–	–	–	–	–	–	10	3rd	1·40	–	–	–
Middlesbrough	6th	5 Times	3·87	1	–	–	26	18	12	5	1	–	–	16	6th	3·88	20	6th	3·90	26	6th	3·85
Middlesbrough Iron.	5th	1893–94	5·00	–	–	–	–	–	1	–	1	–	–	1	5th	5·00	–	–	–	–	–	–
Millwall	Semi	1936–37	3·16	–	6	7	16	10	3	2	1	–	–	–	–	–	19	Semi	4·05	26	5th	2·50
Nelson	2nd	4 Times	1·44	1	5	4	1	–	–	–	–	–	–	–	–	–	9	2nd	1·44	–	–	–
New Brighton	4th	3 Times	1·71	1	11	5	1	3	–	–	–	–	–	–	–	–	16	4th	1·75	5	3rd	1·60
New Brighton Tower	4th	1900–01	1·67	1	1	–	1	–	–	–	–	–	–	3	4th	1·67	–	–	–	–	–	–
Newcastle United	WON	6 Times	4·81	–	–	–	21	17	12	6	2	4	6	22	Won	5·50	20	Won	4·50	26	Won	4·46
Newport County	5th	1948–49	2·07	2	16	9	12	4	1	–	–	–	–	–	–	–	18	3rd	1·61	26	5th	2·38
Northampton Town	5th	3 Times	2·49	–	13	7	18	4	3	–	–	–	–	–	–	–	19	5th	2·47	26	5th	2·50
Northwich Victoria	5th	1892–93	3·00	–	1	–	1	–	1	–	–	–	–	2	5th	3·00	–	–	–	–	–	–
Norwich City	Semi	1958–59	3·09	–	6	8	19	3	7	1	1	1	–	–	–	–	19	5th	2·63	26	Semi	3·42
Notts County	WON	1893–94	3·58	–	9	4	25	19	9	4	1	1	1	27	Won	4·52	20	Semi	3·65	26	6th	2·54
Nottingham Forest	WON	Twice	4·32	–	2	2	26	13	13	10	3	–	2	23	Won	4·96	20	6th	3·90	26	Won	4·08

Club Records (con.)

Club	Best	In Season	Round Aver	Round Eliminated										1888–1915			1919–1939			1945–1971		
				0	1	2	3	4	5	6	Semi	Fin	Won	T	Best	Aver	T	Best	Aver	T	Best	Aver
Oldham Athletic	Semi	1912–13	2·85	–	7	11	25	8	1	1	1	–	–	8	Semi	4·37	20	4th	3·00	26	4th	2·27
Orient	6th	Twice	2·84	1	10	8	21	10	3	2	–	–	–	9	4th	2·78	20	6th	2·86	26	6th	2·85
Oxford United	6th	1963–64	2·78	–	3	1	3	–	1	1	–	–	–	–	–	–	–	–	–	9	6th	2·78
Peterborough United	6th	1964–65	3·09	–	2	2	2	4	–	1	–	–	–	–	–	–	–	–	–	11	6th	3·09
Plymouth Argyle	5th	3 Times	3·11	–	4	2	27	9	3	–	–	–	–	–	–	–	19	5th	3·37	26	5th	2·92
Portsmouth	WON	1938–39	4·04	3	1	–	19	14	6	1	1	2	1	–	–	–	19	Won	4·32	26	Semi	3·85
Port Vale	Semi	1953–54	2·68	–	11	10	19	12	3	–	1	–	–	13	5th	2·00	20	5th	2·85	26	Semi	2·88
Preston North End	WON	Twice	4·62	–	1	–	21	19	11	13	2	4	2	27	Won	4·61	20	5th	4·85	26	Fin	4·42
Queen's Park Rangers	6th	3 Times	2·84	1	6	8	24	2	2	3	–	–	–	–	–	–	18	6th	2·70	26	6th	2·88
Reading	Semi	1926–27	2·58	–	12	5	23	2	2	–	1	–	–	–	–	–	19	Semi	2·89	26	4th	2·35
Rochdale	4th	1970–71	1·48	1	28	9	5	1	–	–	–	–	–	–	–	–	18	2nd	1·11	26	4th	1·73
Rotherham Town	3rd	1895–96	1·00	2	–	–	1	–	–	–	–	–	–	3	3rd	1·00	–	–	–	–	–	–
Rotherham United	5th	Twice	2·78	–	9	7	17	11	2	–	–	–	–	–	–	–	20	3rd	1·80	26	5th	3·54
Scunthorpe United	5th	Twice	2·76	1	3	4	7	4	2	–	–	–	–	–	–	–	–	–	–	21	5th	2·76
Sheffield United	WON	4 Times	4·68	–	–	–	19	22	10	8	4	2	4	23	Won	5·00	20	Won	4·55	26	Semi	4·50
Sheffield Wednesday	WON	3 Times	4·67	–	–	–	19	19	15	5	7	1	3	23	Won	5·26	20	Won	4·40	26	Fin	4·35
Shrewsbury Town	5th	Twice	2·19	1	8	4	4	2	2	–	–	–	–	–	–	–	–	–	–	21	5th	2·19
Southampton	Semi	3 Times	3·73	–	1	3	20	12	4	2	3	–	–	–	–	–	19	Semi	3·90	26	Semi	3·62
Southend United	5th	3 Times	2·33	–	16	10	10	6	3	–	–	–	–	–	–	–	19	5th	2·63	26	5th	2·12
Southport	6th	1930–31	2·07	–	19	11	9	3	1	1	–	–	–	–	–	–	18	6th	2·33	26	5th	1·88
Stalybridge Celtic	3rd	1922–23	2·50	–	–	–	1	–	–	–	–	–	–	–	–	–	2	3rd	2·50	–	–	–
Stockport County	5th	Twice	2·35	–	18	11	17	9	2	–	–	–	–	14	4th	2·29	20	5th	2·45	26	5th	2·31
Stoke City	Semi	Twice	4·26	–	1	–	16	20	16	9	2	–	–	19	Semi	4·79	20	6th	3·75	26	Semi	4·27
Sunderland	WON	1936–37	4·56	1	–	–	21	17	17	7	7	1	1	25	Fin	5·04	19	Won	4·55	26	Semi	4·12
Swansea City	Semi	Twice	3·69	–	2	2	19	12	7	1	2	–	–	–	–	–	19	Semi	3·84	26	Semi	3·58
Swindon Town	6th	Twice	3·00	–	9	9	9	11	5	2	–	–	–	–	–	–	19	6th	3·10	26	6th	2·92
Thames	1st	Twice	1·00	–	2	–	–	–	–	–	–	–	–	–	–	–	2	1st	1·00	–	–	–
Torquay United	4th	3 Times	1·92	1	13	15	6	3	–	–	–	–	–	–	–	–	12	3rd	1·67	26	4th	2·08
Tottenham Hotspur	WON	4 Times	4·96	1	–	–	12	11	13	9	4	–	4	7	5th	4·14	20	Won	4·90	26	Won	5·23
Tranmere Rovers	5th	1967–68	2·00	2	17	11	8	5	1	–	–	–	–	–	–	–	18	4th	2·00	26	5th	2·00
Walsall	5th	1938–39	2·34	1	17	8	16	9	3	–	–	–	–	8	4th	2·12	18	5th	2·61	26	4th	2·22
Watford	Semi	1969–70	2·82	–	9	12	10	9	3	1	1	–	–	–	–	–	19	6th	3·05	26	Semi	2·65
West Bromwich Albion	WON	4 Times	4·88	–	–	–	17	23	10	9	–	3	4	27	Won	5·19	20	Won	4·65	26	Won	4·77
West Ham United	WON	1963–64	4·13	–	–	–	20	13	6	4	1	1	1	–	–	–	20	Fin	4·30	26	Won	4·00
Wigan Borough	4th	1922–23	2·00	1	4	2	2	1	–	–	–	–	–	–	–	–	9	4th	2·00	–	–	–
Wolverhampton Wanderers	WON	4 Times	4·75	–	–	–	17	26	10	10	2	4	4	27	Won	5·26	20	Fin	4·40	26	Won	4·50
Workington	3rd	7 Times	2·15	–	4	9	7	–	–	–	–	–	–	–	–	–	–	–	–	20	3rd	2·15
Wrexham	4th	4 Times	2·07	–	14	17	9	4	–	–	–	–	–	–	–	–	18	4th	2·00	26	4th	2·12
York City	Semi	1954–55	2·42	–	15	9	9	6	1	1	1	–	–	–	–	–	10	6th	2·60	26	Semi	2·35

T = Total seasons entered

COMPLETE F.A. CUP RESULTS 1888–1915 FOR INDIVIDUAL LEAGUE CLUBS

	88/89	89/90	1	2	3	4	94/95	6	7	8	9	99/00	1	2	3	4	04/05	6	7	8	9	09/10	1	2	3	4	14/15
ACCRINGTON STANLEY	4	5	5	5	5	–	–	–	–	–	–	–	–	–	–	–	–	–	–	–	–	–	–	–	–	–	–
ARSENAL	–	5	–	–	–	4	–	4	3	4	4	1	5	4	4	5	4	5	4	3	4	4	4	3	4	3	–
ASTON VILLA	6	5	5	F	4	6	W	4	W	4	4	6	Sf	4	Sf	5	W	5	4	3	3	5	F	4	W	Sf	4
BARNSLEY	–	–	–	–	–	–	W	4	W	–	3	2	2	2	5	3	3	4	2	3	F	F	4	3	4	3	3
BIRMINGHAM	Sf	–	–	–	4	4	4	4	4	1	5	3	6	3	4	6	4	6	6	3	5	3	3	3	4	5	5
BLACKBURN ROVERS	Sf	W	W	5	Sf	Sf	5	4	6	4	4	5	4	1	5	6	4	3	4	3	5	5	Sf	4	6	5	3
BLACKPOOL	–	–	–	–	Sf	–	–	–	3	1	4	4	1	1	0	1	3	5	3	–	4	3	3	4	3	3	3
BOLTON WANDERERS	1	Sf	4	4	4	F	6	Sf	5	6	4	4	5	5	4	F	6	3	5	5	3	3	3	5	3	5	Sf
BOOTLE	–	–	–	–	5	1	–	–	–	–	–	–	–	–	–	–	–	–	–	–	–	–	–	–	–	–	–
BRADFORD CITY	–	–	–	–	–	–	–	–	–	–	–	–	–	–	–	1	3	5	5	3	2	4	W	6	3	4	6
BRADFORD (P.A.)	–	–	–	–	–	–	–	–	–	–	–	–	–	–	–	–	–	3	4	–	–	4	4	5	6	3	5
BRISTOL CITY	5	4	5	5	5	4	4	5	4	6	4	5	2	5	5	4	5	3	4	3	6	4	3	3	3	4	5
BURNLEY	–	–	–	4	4	1	2	5	4	6	3	4	2	4	3	1	0	3	3	–	3	4	6	3	Sf	W	5
BURTON UNITED	–	–	–	4	4	1	2	4	4	1	3	2	2	3	3	3	3	3	3	–	–	–	–	–	–	–	–
BURTON WANDERERS	–	–	–	–	–	–	4	4	4	4	4	–	–	–	–	–	–	–	–	–	–	–	–	–	–	–	–
BURY	–	–	–	–	–	–	5	6	5	4	5	W	6	5	W	5	5	3	5	4	4	4	4	4	4	4	4
CHELSEA	–	–	–	–	–	–	–	–	–	–	–	–	4	3	1	3	3	1	3	4	4	4	4	4	4	3	F
CHESTERFIELD	–	–	–	–	–	–	–	–	2	3	4	3	3	4	1	3	3	4	3	4	3	–	–	–	–	–	–
CREWE ALEXANDRA	–	–	–	–	0	3	1	4	4	1	4	–	–	–	–	–	–	–	–	–	–	–	–	–	–	–	–
DARWEN	–	–	–	5	6	4	4	4	2	3	1	4	–	–	–	–	–	–	–	–	–	–	–	–	–	–	–
DERBY COUNTY	5	4	–	4	4	6	4	Sf	Sf	F	F	4	4	Sf	F	Sf	4	4	5	3	Sf	4	4	4	3	4	3
DONCASTER ROVERS	–	–	–	–	–	–	–	–	–	–	–	–	–	2	0	–	0	–	–	–	–	–	–	–	–	–	–
EVERTON	/	5	4	4	F	4	6	Sf	F	4	5	4	5	4	6	4	Sf	W	F	6	4	Sf	5	6	6	3	Sf
FULHAM	–	–	–	–	–	–	–	–	–	–	–	–	–	–	6	–	–	W	–	Sf	4	4	3	6	3	3	4
GAINSBOROUGH TRINITY	–	–	–	–	–	–	–	–	1	5	4	0	0	0	2	3	3	4	3	4	3	3	3	3	3	–	–
GLOSSOP NORTH END	–	–	–	–	6	4	4	4	5	4	4	1	3	4	4	1	2	3	3	6	3	3	3	3	3	4	3
GRIMSBY TOWN	–	–	–	5	5	4	2	5	4	4	4	4	4	4	5	4	4	3	6	3	3	–	3	1	3	3	3
HUDDERSFIELD TOWN	–	–	–	–	–	–	–	–	–	–	–	–	–	–	–	–	–	–	–	–	–	–	1	3	4	4	3

282

1888–1915 (con.)

	88/89	89/90	1	2	3	4	94/95	6	7	8	9	99/00	1	2	3	4	04/05	6	7	8	9	09/10	1	2	3	4	14/15
HULL CITY	—	—	—	—	—	—	—	—	—	—	—	—	—	—	—	—	—	3	3	4	3	3	3	4	4	4	6
LEEDS CITY	—	—	—	—	—	—	—	—	—	—	—	—	—	—	—	—	—	1	3	3	4	3	5	4	4	3	4
LEICESTER CITY	—	—	—	—	—	—	4	3	3	4	3	4	4	3	1	2	4	3	4	4	4	6	3	4	3	4	4
LINCOLN CITY	—	—	—	—	3	1	0	2	3	2	2	1	5	5	4	0	4	4	4	3	1	3	1	2	3	3	2
LIVERPOOL	—	—	—	—	—	6	5	5	Sf	1	2	Sf	4	4	5	4	4	Sf	6	5	4	3	4	5	5	F	4
LOUGHBOROUGH TOWN	—	—	—	—	—	—	—	2	1	4	3	—	—	—	—	—	—	—	—	—	—	—	—	—	—	—	—
LUTON TOWN	—	—	—	—	Sc	—	Sc	4	5	4	3	4	5	4	3	—	—	—	—	—	—	—	—	—	—	—	—
MANCHESTER CITY	—	—	—	—	4	5	4	6	5	4	4	4	5	4	6	W	5	3	3	5	3	6	4	4	4	6	5
MANCHESTER UNITED	—	—	—	—	5	4	5	5	4	1	0	6	3	3	5	5	3	6	3	5	W	3	5	6	5	3	3
MIDDLESBROUGH	—	—	—	5	—	5	—	—	—	—	—	0	4	3	6	6	4	5	5	3	3	3	5	4	5	3	4
MIDDLESBROUGH IRONOPOLIS	—	—	—	—	—	—	—	—	—	—	—	—	—	—	—	—	—	—	—	—	—	—	—	—	—	—	—
NEW BRIGHTON TOWER	—	—	—	—	—	—	—	—	—	1	0	4	4	4	F	—	—	—	—	—	—	—	—	—	—	—	—
NEWCASTLE UNITED	—	—	—	5	5	5	5	5	4	5	5	5	6	4	4	F	F	F	3	F	3	W	F	6	3	3	6
NORTHWICH VICTORIA	—	—	5	1	—	—	—	—	—	—	—	—	—	—	—	—	—	—	—	—	—	—	—	—	—	—	—
NOTTS COUNTY	5	6	4	5	4	W	4	4	5	4	5	5	5	Sf	6	4	4	3	6	3	3	3	3	4	Sf	3	3
NOTTINGHAM FOREST	—	—	—	5	6	6	4	6	W	5	6	Sf	Sf	5	5	5	5	F	3	3	5	3	3	Sf	3	3	6
OLDHAM ATHLETIC	—	—	—	—	—	—	—	—	—	—	—	—	—	—	—	—	—	4	5	4	3	3	3	4	5	4	3
ORIENT	—	—	—	—	—	—	—	—	—	—	0	—	—	—	—	—	—	3	4	3 / 0	3	3	3	3	4	3	3
PORT VALE	—	—	0	Sf	0	0	1	4	—	3	3	3	2	1	4	2	2	3	4	—	—	—	—	—	—	—	—
PRESTON NORTH END	W	6	4	5	Sf	5	5	4	6	4	5	6	4	4	5	5	6	3	3	3	4	4	3	3	3	5	3
ROTHERHAM TOWN	—	—	—	—	0	3	—	—	—	—	—	—	—	—	—	—	—	—	—	—	—	—	—	—	—	—	—
SHEFFIELD UNITED	—	—	5	4	5	W	4	5	4	4	W	F	4	5	5	6	4	4	3	3	3	3	3	3	5	Sf	W
SHEFFIELD WEDNESDAY	—	—	6	Sf	6	6	5	W	4	5	5	5	4	4	4	Sf	6	W	3	3	5	5	6	5	6	5	5
STOCKPORT COUNTY	0	6	—	—	—	—	—	—	—	0	Sf	0	1	3	3	4	1	3	3	4	—	4	1	3	2	2	3
STOKE CITY	0	6	4	4	5	5	6	5	5	4	5	4	4	6	6	4	5	4	3	6	—	3	5	3	4	4	4
SUNDERLAND	—	—	Sf	6	6	5	Sf	5	5	4	5	5	4	5	4	4	4	5	5	5	6	5	3	5	F	4	4
TOTTENHAM HOTSPUR	—	—	—	—	—	—	—	—	—	—	—	—	—	—	3	3	5	5	3	5	4	5	4	3	4	4	4
WALSALL	—	—	—	2	2	0	—	1	1	4	4	3	3	4	—	4	3	4	—	3	—	3	4	F	3	5	4
WEST BROMWICH ALBION	Sf	4	Sf	4	4	F	F	6	Sf	6	6	Sf	4	4	4	4	3	3	Sf	3	4	4	3	5	3	4	3
WOLVERHAMPTON WNDRS.	F	Sf	6	6	W	4	6	W	5	5	5	4	4	4	4	5	5	4	3	W	3	4	4	4	4	3	4

/—No Entry   Sc—Scratched   Numbers indicate round reached   Sf—Semi-final   F—Final   W—Winners

283

	19/20				24/25					29/30					34/35				38/39	45/46				49/50					54/55					59/60					64/65					69/70	
	20	2	3	4	25	6	7	8	9	30	1	2	3	4	35	6	7	38 39	R 46	7	8	9	50	1	2	3	4	55	6	7	8	9	60	1	2	3	4	65	6	7	8	9	70	1	
ABERDARE ATHLETIC	–	–	0	3	3	0	3	1	–	–	–	–	–	–	–	–	–	–	–	–	–	–	–	–	–	–	–	–	–	–	–	–	–	–	–	–	–	–	–	–	–	–	–	–	–
ACCRINGTON STANLEY	–	–	0	1	3	3	4	1	3	2	2	–	5	3	3	3	1	4 2	2	2	3	3	1	1	3	2	1	1	1	3	4	3	3	3	3	3	3	3	–	–	–	–	–	–	–
ALDERSHOT	–	–	–	–	–	–	–	–	–	–	–	–	6	3	6	4	3	2 3	3	3	4	6	5	4	4	3	3	4	3	5	4	4	4	3	3	5	1	4	3	3	4	4	3	3	–
ARSENAL	4	3	6	3	4	3	6	Sf	6	W	4	F	3	6	6	W	6	5 3	1	1	1	2	2	3	4	W	5	F	6	4	4	3	4	5	5	4	Sf	Sf	3	5	5	3	W	–	–
ASHINGTON	–	–	3	1	3	0	1	3	1	1	–	–	–	–	–	–	–	–	–	–	–	–	–	–	–	–	–	–	–	–	–	–	–	–	–	–	–	–	–	–	–	–	–	–	–
ASTON VILLA	W	6	6	3	6	Sf	6	3	5	Sf	6	3	4	4	3	6	3	4 3	4	6	3	W	3	Sf	Sf	5	6	4	4	3	4	5	5	4	3	5	3	1	–	–	–	–	–	–	–
BARNSLEY	4	3	5	4	3	4	1	4	3	5	4	6	3	3	4	4	3	4 2	2	4	5	3	1	1	2	1	1	3	3	3	4	5	5	3	2	1	3	2	3	2	3	3	2	2	–
BARROW	–	–	0	2	0	3	4	1	3	2	2	1	1	2	2	2	1	2 1	1	1	2	3	1	1	2	3	3	1	1	2	3	1	3	3	3	2	1	1	3	2	2	2	2	2	–
BIRMINGHAM CITY	5	3	/	3	3	5	4	4	5	4	4	F	4	6	5	6	3	Sf 3	5	3	3	4	3	6	3	3	3	3	5	3	6	Sf	5	3	3	6	3	4	6	Sf	3	5	5	3	3
BLACKBURN ROVERS	3	3	5	4	3	Sf	4	3	W	6	5	5	4	4	5	3	5	4 3	4	6	5	6	3	3	4	5	3	3	5	3	4	5	3	4	F	5	3	3	3	5	3	5	3	3	3
BLACKPOOL	4	4	3	3	4	6	3	3	4	6	3	4	5	4	3	4	3	4 3	W	5	3	6	4	3	5	4	3	4	3	3	5	3	6	4	3	4	3	3	3	3	3	4	4	4	3
BOLTON WANDERERS	3	3	4	W	4	4	W	3	4	5	4	W	3	4	3	5	6	3 6	3	5	3	6	Sf	3	5	3	3	3	F	6	4	4	4	3	4	5	3	4	3	3	4	4	3	4	3
BOURNEMOUTH & B.	–	–	0	0	0	4	3	3	5	3	1	4	1	2	1	3	3	5 4	W	6	4	4	3	5	6	2	1	4	3	6	4	4	4	3	2	1	2	3	3	4	4	3	3	3	–
BRADFORD CITY	6	4	4	3	3	5	5	4	4	2	1	1	5	5	3	5	3	1 1	1	2	2	1	2	1	2	3	5	3	3	2	1	4	3	5	2	3	1	2	1	3	2	2	1	2	–
BRADFORD (P.A.)	6	4	4	4	4	4	2	1	2	5	5	5	5	5	4	3	3	1 1	2	1	4	1	1	1	2	1	2	2	3	1	1	4	3	2	3	3	3	2	1	1	2	1	1	1	–
BRENTFORD	–	3	3	2	2	1	2	5	3	2	1	4	4	1	3	3	4	6 3	6	4	4	4	6	4	4	6	3	6	4	4	4	6	4	6	4	6	3	2	3	2	3	1	2	1	5
BRIGHTON & H. A.	–	4	4	4	5	4	4	1	3	2	5	4	4	3	2	1	1	3 1	3	5	4	3	5	4	3	1	1	4	2	2	3	1	1	4	2	2	3	2	2	4	2	2	2	2	3
BRISTOL CITY	Sf	3	4	5	4	3	4	5	4	3	2	3	1	1	3	2	2	3 1	5	2	1	1	6	4	5	2	1	1	3	5	5	3	4	4	3	3	5	5	3	3	5	2	2	4	3
BRISTOL ROVERS	–	3	2	2	1	3	1	3	2	2	3	4	2	3	3	2	1	4 3	3	5	5	6	4	1	1	6	4	4	5	5	4	4	6	5	3	3	5	3	4	3	3	5	5	3	2
BURNLEY	4	5	3	3	Sf	3	3	4	4	3	5	5	3	3	5	6	3	6 4	6	4	5	4	1	6	4	3	6	3	5	4	6	5	4	4	6	Sf	4	6	5	4	3	4	4	4	3
BURY	4	3	3	5	3	4	3	4	3	4	4	W	3	3	3	3	4	4 3	4	6	4	4	6	5	4	3	4	3	6	Sf	F	4	6	6	2	3	4	4	3	3	4	3	1	3	2
CAMBRIDGE UNITED	–	–	–	–	–	–	–	–	–	–	–	–	–	–	–	–	–	–	–	–	–	–	–	–	–	–	–	–	–	–	–	–	–	–	–	–	–	–	–	–	–	–	–	3	2
CARDIFF CITY	–	Sf	6	5	6	F	4	W	5	3	4	3	1	1	1	3	3	3 5	3	3	4	5	4	2	1	1	3	4	3	4	4	4	4	5	4	2	1	2	2	2	5	4	4	3	4
CARLISLE UNITED	–	–	–	–	–	–	–	2	3	3	3	3	2	1	2	3	1	3 4	2	3	2	2	1	1	3	1	1	3	3	3	2	2	4	3	4	2	1	5	2	3	5	4	4	5	4
CHARLTON ATHLETIC	–	–	–	0	6	4	2	3	2	4	4	6	6	5	4	3	4	F W	5	4	3	4	4	4	3	3	5	4	4	3	2	4	1	4	3	3	5	4	3	4	3	3	4	4	3
CHELSEA	Sf	6	3	4	3	3	4	6	3	5	1	3	3	2	3	3	5	4 5	4	4	5	3	5	Sf	5	3	5	5	4	4	4	4	3	4	4	2	3	5	4	Sf	Sf	F	6	6	W
CHESTER	–	–	–	–	–	–	–	–	–	–	–	–	–	–	3	2	3	4 2	–	2	4	2	2	1	3	5	5	3	4	4	4	4	2	2	2	3	3	3	3	3	2	3	3	3	2
CHESTERFIELD	–	–	1	2	2	3	3	1	3	1	4	5	3	2	3	2	3	2 3	2	2	1	4	3	2	2	4	1	3	2	1	4	4	3	2	2	2	4	4	2	2	2	4	2	2	3
COLCHESTER UNITED	–	–	–	–	–	–	–	–	–	–	–	–	–	–	–	–	–	–	–	3	1	4	5	3	3	1	4	5	3	2	2	4	1	1	3	3	3	1	2	2	3	2	1	6	2
COVENTRY CITY	3	2	2	1	1	0	2	3	1	4	5	3	3	1	3	3	4	4 4	4	3	1	5	3	3	4	3	1	5	3	3	2	6	2	3	5	5	4	4	4	3	3	3	2	1	6
CREWE ALEXANDRA	–	1	0	1	0	2	3	4	1	2	2	1	1	2	1	1	2	2 1	2	1	2	1	1	3	3	1	1	5	3	1	1	4	4	2	1	1	4	3	2	3	1	4	3	4	3
CRYSTAL PALACE	4	4	3	5	4	5	1	2	5	3	4	2	1	4	1	3	1	3 4	4	3	3	2	2	3	2	1	1	4	3	2	1	4	3	2	6	2	3	1	4	1	3	2	1	2	2
DARLINGTON	3	3	2	3	3	3	2	3	3	1	5	1	3	4	1	2	3	3 1	3	3	1	2	3	4	1	2	3	2	3	1	4	2	3	2	3	4	6	3	3	2	6	3	2	1	2
DERBY COUNTY	3	4	3	Sf	4	3	6	4	3	5	3	3	4	3	3	4	2	W 5	Sf	6	6	3	6	4	3	3	4	3	2	4	3	3	4	3	3	4	4	3	3	3	3	5	3	5	5
DONCASTER ROVERS	–	–	0	3	2	3	1	1	4	2	2	1	1	4	5	3	3	4 2	1	1	4	5	3	3	1	3	1	1	3	4	3	3	3	1	2	3	3	1	3	5	3	5	3	2	1
DURHAM CITY	–	–	1	1	0	1	2	–	–	–	–	–	–	4	–	–	–	–	–	–	–	–	–	–	–	–	–	–	–	–	–	–	–	–	–	–	–	–	–	–	–	–	–	–	–

284

1919–71 (con.)

	19 20	1	2	3	4	24 25	6	7	8	9	29 30	1	2	3	4	34 35	6	7	8	38 39	W A R	45 46	7	8	9	49 50	1	2	3	4	54 55	6	7	8	9	59 60	1	2	3	4	64 65	6	7	8	9	69 70	1
EVERTON	3	6	3	3	4	5	3	4	3	4	3	4	3	6	3	5	4	6	3	4		5	4	Sf	3	3	3	5	6	4	5	4	3	3	5	5	4	5	4	W	6	F	F	Sf	3	Sf
EXETER CITY	–	3	1	1	4	3	4	4	4	6	3	3	3	3	3	2	1	2	1	3		3	4	2	4	4	4	4	3	1	1	3	1	1	2	1	3	3	2	2	1	2	3	2	1
FULHAM	3	5	4	3	4	4	6	4	3	5	4	3	2	2	2	3	3	3	3	3		Sf	3	3	4	2	1	2	2	2	1	1	2	2	1	1	2	1	1	2	2	2	1	2	3	3
GATESHEAD	3	4	3	5	3	5	5	5	3	1	4	4	6	3	1	3	1	1	3	4		3	3	1	3	3	3	3	3	3	3	3	3	4	4	4	4	4	4	–	–	–	–	–	–
GILLINGHAM	–	2	3	3	2	2	2	2	2	2	3	1	1	2	2	1	2	2	1	3		3	1	4	2	2	2	2	1	3	1	3	3	3	3	4	4	4	3	4	4	4	4	2	1
GRIMSBY TOWN	3	4	3	1	3	1	1	3	3	3	3	5	4	4	5	2	2	1	2	Sf		3	4	3	4	4	4	2	1	1	1	3	3	3	3	3	3	3	3	3	3	3	1	2	5	1
HALIFAX TOWN	–	0	3	4	1	1	1	3	3	5	3	3	3	3	3	2	1	2	1	1		1	2	1	1	3	4	2	1	1	3	3	4	5	3	4	4	3	4	1	1	1	3	4	1	1
HARTLEPOOL	–	–	1	2	2	3	3	3	3	2	1	1	1	1	1	2	2	2	2	2		2	5	1	2	3	2	2	2	2	1	1	2	2	2	3	3	2	3	3	3	4	1	1	2	1
HUDDERSFIELD TOWN	F	5	W	5	5	3	4	3	F	3	5	5	3	4	3	4	3	3	F	Sf		1	2	1	2	1	1	2	1	1	1	2	2	1	2	2	3	1	2	2	3	3	3	3	2	4
HULL CITY	3	6	4	3	3	4	3	3	5	3	Sf	3	3	4	3	3	1	2	3	2		/	3	3	4	4	5	4	4	3	4	4	3	4	4	3	2	3	3	3	3	3	3	3	3	6
IPSWICH TOWN	–	–	–	–	–	–	–	–	–	–	–	–	–	–	–	/	3	3	3	3		2	2	1	3	3	6	4	5	3	3	3	4	5	3	4	4	3	4	4	3	3	3	5	3	5
LEEDS UNITED	–	/	3	4	5	3	3	4	1	1	1	1	1	2	3	3	2	1	3	3		3	3	3	6	4	3	3	3	4	5	5	4	3	3	4	5	3	5	F	4	Sf	Sf	6	F	5
LEICESTER CITY	5	3	5	4	3	3	1	3	5	3	3	5	3	3	5	3	2	2	1	1		5	3	5	F	3	F	3	3	6	F	3	5	3	6	5	3	6	F	5	5	6	5	6	3	6
LINCOLN CITY	3	–	1	0	1	1	3	3	3	3	3	2	2	3	2	3	2	2	3	2		3	1	1	3	3	2	3	3	3	1	1	1	3	1	1	3	1	3	3	1	1	3	2	3
LIVERPOOL	6	4	4	5	6	6	4	5	4	4	5	6	6	4	5	4	5	Sf	3	3		4	4	Sf	6	W	3	5	6	5	6	F
LUTON TOWN	–	5	4	3	3	2	3	3	3	2	1	2	3	6	3	3	1	2	3	3		3	5	5	3	3	4	6	5	3	5	5	3	3	2	3	6	3	3	2	2	2	3	2	3
MANCHESTER CITY	4	3	5	Sf	3	F	3	5	5	4	3	3	1	2	3	6	F	W	3	5		4	5	5	3	4	6	5	3	4	F	3	3	4	5	3	6	6	4	W	4	5
MANCHESTER UNITED	4	3	4	4	3	Sf	3	6	4	4	1	1	1	1	3	4	4	5	3	2		4	4	W	Sf	6	6	3	3	F	3	F	F	3	5	4	Sf	4	Sf	Sf	4	3	6	Sf	3
MANSFIELD TOWN	–	–	–	–	–	–	–	–	–	–	–	1	1	1	3	3	1	2	3	3		3	1	2	5	1	3	1	1	3	2	5	1	3	2	1	2	4	1	4	1	6	5	2
MERTHYR TOWN	–	1	2	3	1	1	1	1	1	2	1	–	–	–	1	2	1	1	–	–
MIDDLESBROUGH	4	3	3	4	3	3	3	4	3	5	4	5	4	5	6	5	6	3	5	4		5	6	3	4	3	3	3	4	3	3	4	3	3	4	3	4	4	5	3	3	3	3	4	3	6
MILLWALL	–	3	6	4	3	3	5	6	4	3	5	3	4	4	3	4	4	3	Sf	3		4	3	2	3	2	1	4	2	3	1	1	2	1	4	2	2	1	4	2	3	3	4	3	3
NELSON	–	2	1	1	2	1	2	1	2	1	–	–	–	–	–	–	–	–	–	–		/	1	2	3	1	1	–	1	2	3	1	1	–	1	–	–	–	–	–	–	–	–	–	–
NEW BRIGHTON	–	–	–	0	1	4	1	4	1	1	2	1	2	1	2	2	1	2	1	4		/	1	2	3	1	1	–	1	2	3	1	1	–	1	–	–	–	–	–	–	–	–	–	–
NEWCASTLE UNITED	4	5	4	3	W	4	5	5	3	3	6	4	3	5	3	4	4	3	3	3		3	Sf	3	3	4	W	W	3	4	4	6	4	3	3	6	4	W	4	3	3	4	3	3	3	3
NEWPORT COUNTY	–	0	3	1	0	1	2	1	1	2	2	2	2	2	2	2	1	2	3	3		3	3	2	5	4	1	2	2	2	4	4	1	1	4	3	1	3	1	3	1	3	1	3	3
NORTHAMPTON TOWN	–	3	4	1	3	3	3	3	3	2	3	3	1	4	2	5	3	1	1	1		3	2	5	4	1	2	2	5	3	1	1	4	2	1	3	3	3	1	3	3	1	3	5	1
NORWICH CITY	–	3	3	3	3	3	3	3	3	3	3	3	4	1	3	2	1	2	2	1		3	2	2	2	5	4	1	2	2	2	1	3	Sf	3	1	5	6	3	3	5	4	3	3	3
NOTTS COUNTY	5	4	Sf	3	4	5	5	3	4	3	4	5	5	3	4	3	3	4	1	1		2	3	4	4	3	1	2	1	3	1	1	1	3	2	1	3	2	1	3	5	4	3	3	3
NOTTINGHAM FOREST	3	3	5	3	4	3	4	6	4	6	3	3	4	4	3	5	3	3	4	3		3	5	3	4	4	6	3	3	5	5	3	6	4	W	4	3	6	4	3	4	Sf	3	4	3	5
OLDHAM ATHLETIC	3	3	4	3	3	4	3	3	5	3	4	3	4	4	4	3	4	4	1	2		2	2	2	3	3	2	2	3	3	2	1	2	4	1	3	2	2	4	3	4	4	3	2	1
ORIENT	3	3	3	3	3	3	3	6	3	4	4	4	1	2	1	2	2	2	2	2		1	1	1	5	1	6	2	4	3	2	4	3	4	3	2	4	1	3	5	4	3	3	1	4
OXFORD UNITED	–	–	–	–	–	–	–	–	–	–	–	–	–	–	–	–	–	–	–	–		–	–	–	–	–	–	–	–	–	–	–	–	–	–	–	–	–	–	3	6	1	2	1	3
PETERBOROUGH UTD	–	–	–	–	–	–	–	–	–	–	–	–	–	–	–	–	–	–	–	–		–	–	–	–	–	5	3	3	3	3	3	3	4	4	3	1	6	2	4	3	1	3	5	3
PLYMOUTH ARGYLE	–	5	3	5	3	3	3	3	3	4	3	3	3	4	4	3	5	5	3	4		3	4	1	4	3	1	3	1	3	3	3	3	2	3	3	3	1	3	3	3	3	1	2	1
PORTSMOUTH	5	5	3	3	4	3	3	4	3	4	3	4	4	5	5	5	3	F	4	W		3	4	3	4	1	1	3	6	3	3	1	3	1	4	3	5	3	1	3	5	4	3	4	4
PORT VALE	3	2	3	1	1	3	3	4	4	5	3	2	4	4	3	3	3	4	3	2		3	4	1	1	4	3	1	2	Sf	4	4	4	3	2	1	5	3	5	3	3	3	2	3	1

285

1919–71 (con.)

Round reached in the F.A. Cup, by season (1919/20 – 1970/71). W = Winners, F = Finalists, Sf = Semi-final, Sc = ?, numerals = round reached, A/R = war/abandoned, – = not competing.

Club	20	1	2	3	4	25	6	7	8	9	30	1	2	3	4	35	6	7	8	39	46	7	8	9	50	1	2	3	4	55	6	7	8	9	60	1	2	3	4	65	6	7	8	9	70	1
PRESTON NORTH END	5	Sf	F	4	4	4	3	3	3	3	5	6	4	5	3	4	6	F	W	6	5	6	6	4	3	4	4	3	F	4	3	5	3	3	6	4	3	4	F	4	6	4	4	4	3	1
QUEEN'S PARK R'NG'S.	–	4	3	6	3	3	3	2	1	1	4	3	3	1	1	1	2	1	3	2	5	3	1	3	3	4	2	2	3	1	1	3	2	2	2	3	3	3	3	3	3	3	3	3	6	3
READING	–	3	3	1	1	2	3	5	3	3	1	1	1	3	2	4	3	3	1	1	1	3	1	3	3	5	4	5	3	1	3	4	4	3	3	3	2	1	2	4	3	2	3	3	1	4
ROCHDALE	–	–	1	0	1	2	2	1	3	1	3	1	1	3	1	2	1	1	1	1	3	3	2	1	3	4	1	2	3	3	1	1	2	3	1	3	1	1	2	1	1	1	1	1	1	4
ROTHERHAM UNITED	2	2	1	3	2	2	1	3	1	3	3	1	1	3	2	2	1	2	1	1	4	3	4	4	3	4	4	3	4	5	3	3	5	3	4	4	3	3	4	3	4	5	2	2	3	3
SCUNTHORPE UNITED	–	–	–	–	–	–	–	–	–	–	–	–	–	–	–	–	–	–	–	–	0	–	–	–	4	4	3	3	1	2	2	5	3	3	3	4	4	3	1	2	1	5	3	1	5	3
SHEFFIELD UNITED	4	3	Sf	4	4	W	4	3	Sf	3	4	5	4	4	4	3	4	F	4	5	4	6	4	4	4	6	5	4	3	3	5	3	5	6	Sf	6	5	4	4	4	5	6	5	6	4	3
SHEFFIELD WED.	3	4	3	5	4	4	4	4	5	4	5	3	5	3	5	W	4	4	3	5	5	5	4	4	3	3	3	3	3	Sf	3	3	3	3	6	5	3	4	4	3	F	5	4	4	3	3
SHREWSBURY TOWN	–	–	–	–	–	–	–	–	–	–	–	–	–	–	–	–	–	–	–	–	–	–	–	0	1	4	1	2	1	2	1	3	4	3	1	3	4	3	1	5	5	3	3	1	2	2
SOUTHAMPTON	–	5	4	6	5	Sf	3	Sf	3	3	3	3	3	2	1	2	4	3	3	3	4	6	3	3	4	3	5	4	1	1	2	1	2	3	4	4	3	Sf	3	3	4	4	4	4	4	5
SOUTHEND UNITED	–	5	4	1	2	1	5	2	2	1	3	3	2	1	2	1	3	2	3	4	1	3	1	1	3	1	2	2	3	4	3	4	3	1	3	2	2	1	3	3	4	1	1	2	2	2
SOUTHPORT	–	3	1	2	2	3	4	4	2	1	6	4	2	1	6	4	2	1	1	3	3	1	1	3	1	3	2	2	1	1	2	1	1	3	1	3	1	2	3	5	1	3	2	1	1	1
STALYBRIDGE CELTIC	–	2	3	–	–	–	–	–	–	–	–	–	–	–	–	–	–	–	–	–	–	–	–	–	–	–	–	–	–	–	–	–	–	–	–	–	–	–	–	–	–	–	–	–	–	–
STOCKPORT COUNTY	3	3	1	1	2	4	3	1	2	3	3	2	3	2	1	2	5	3	1	4	1	3	4	5	4	1	1	3	4	3	2	1	1	4	3	2	3	2	3	1	1	3	2	1	3	1
STOKE CITY	3	3	5	4	3	3	3	4	1	6	3	3	5	4	6	4	3	4	4	3	1	6	5	4	6	5	3	4	4	5	4	3	3	6	4	5	3	4	3	5	4	3	5	3	Sf	3
SUNDERLAND	5	3	4	3	4	3	4	5	4	3	Sf	4	4	5	4	3	4	W	Sf	5	5	3	3	4	6	4	5	3	4	Sf	Sf	4	3	4	6	4	5	2	4	3	3	3	3	3	5	3
SWANSEA CITY	–	4	5	1	4	4	Sf	6	3	4	3	3	3	5	4	3	5	4	3	3	3	4	2	4	3	5	3	5	3	3	4	Sf	5	1	2	4	3	4	Sf	3	5	1	2	4	2	2
SWINDON TOWN	–	4	4	3	6	3	4	1	4	5	4	1	1	3	4	3	4	1	2	4	1	2	5	3	2	2	5	3	2	1	4	2	1	2	1	4	5	3	3	5	4	3	6	4	3	4
THAMES	–	–	–	–	–	–	–	–	–	–	–	1	1	–	–	–	–	–	–	–	–	–	–	–	–	–	–	–	–	–	–	–	–	–	–	–	–	–	–	–	–	–	–	–	–	–
TORQUAY UNITED	–	–	–	–	–	–	–	–	–	Sc	2	1	3	1	2	2	2	1	1	2	1	3	4	2	1	1	4	3	3	2	3	2	3	2	1	1	2	1	4	2	1	1	3	1	2	4
TOTTENHAM HOTSPUR	6	W	Sf	6	3	5	4	3	6	3	3	2	1	1	3	5	6	6	6	4	3	3	Sf	3	5	3	4	5	5	Sf	5	4	5	5	W	W	W	3	3	5	W	5	6	4	6	6
TRANMERE ROVERS	–	0	0	2	1	1	1	3	2	1	1	3	4	4	2	4	1	3	3	4	3	3	5	3	3	4	5	5	3	3	3	5	2	1	2	5	1	4	1	1	2	5	1	4	1	1
WALSALL	–	3	2	2	1	2	2	1	1	3	2	1	3	4	3	1	4	2	4	1	2	3	1	4	1	1	3	3	1	1	2	3	1	2	4	3	3	1	3	1	4	3	4	3	3	2
WATFORD	–	4	4	3	5	3	2	2	1	4	2	5	6	3	1	2	4	1	3	3	4	2	1	1	4	1	4	2	1	3	3	2	1	2	5	3	3	3	4	2	1	2	3	4	Sf	4
WEST BROMWICH ALB.	3	3	5	5	6	6	4	3	3	6	3	W	3	4	3	F	4	Sf	5	4	4	4	6	3	3	5	5	3	W	4	5	Sf	6	5	3	3	4	3	4	4	3	3	W	Sf	3	4
WEST HAM UNITED	5	3	3	F	4	5	3	4	4	6	3	3	1	1	1	W	4	3	3	5	4	3	3	4	4	3	3	4	4	3	3	3	6	4	5	3	3	3	W	4	5	5	3	3	3	3
WIGAN BOROUGH	–	–	4	2	1	3	2	1	3	1	1	–	–	–	–	–	–	–	–	–	–	–	–	–	–	–	–	–	–	–	–	–	–	–	–	–	–	–	–	–	–	–	–	–	–	–
WOLVERHAMPTON W.	4	F	3	4	5	3	3	3	6	4	3	3	6	4	3	4	4	4	6	F	4	4	4	3	W	5	3	3	4	3	3	3	6	4	W	3	4	3	3	6	5	4	3	3	3	4
WORKINGTON	–	–	–	–	–	–	–	–	–	–	–	–	–	–	–	–	–	–	–	–	3	1	1	2	2	2	3	2	3	2	1	2	2	3	1	3	3	2	2	2	3	1	2	2	2	3
WREXHAM	–	2	3	2	1	1	2	1	1	4	3	2	1	1	3	3	2	2	1	1	3	2	2	1	3	1	3	1	3	1	4	1	3	2	1	3	2	2	3	1	2	2	1	2	4	4
YORK CITY	–	–	–	–	–	–	–	–	–	–	3	3	1	1	3	1	4	6	3	3	4	1	2	1	3	1	3	1	Sf	4	2	4	1	3	1	2	1	3	1	2	1	2	1	3	4	4

Appendix D

Non-League Clubs' Cup Achievements 1925-71

League Clubs undefeated by Non-League Clubs

In the period under review, from 1925–26, the number of League Clubs currently in Membership who have yet to be beaten by a Non-League Club is 29.

Arsenal	Everton	Plymouth Argyle
Aston Villa	Fulham	Portsmouth
Birmingham City	Grimsby Town	Preston North End
Blackburn Rovers	Hull City	Scunthorpe United
Blackpool	Leeds United	Sheffield United
Bolton Wanderers	Leicester City	Sheffield Wednesday
Burnley	Manchester City	Tottenham Hotspur
Cambridge United	Manchester United	West Bromwich Albion
Charlton Athletic	Middlesbrough	West Ham United
Chelsea	Nottingham Forest	

At the start of the season of 1971–72, the Divisional allocation of the 29 Clubs is as follows:

1st Division 12	3rd Division 4	
2nd Division 10	4th Division 3	

Non-League Sides in the F.A. Cup: Summary of Performances 1925–26 to 1970–71

Most Victories over League Sides

> Yeovil Town   10
> Peterborough United 8

Most Away Victories over League Sides

> Bedford Town & Peterborough United 3

Furthest Progress in F.A. Cup in a Season

> 5th Round – Colchester United 1947–48
> Yeovil Town   1948–49

Most Victories over a League Side in a Season

> 3 – Colchester United   1947–48
> Beat Wrexham (H) 1–0, Huddersfield Town (H) 1–0, Bradford (P.A.) (H) 1–0

Victories over League Sides in a Season

> a) *The Most* 11 1956–57   b) *The Least* 1 1949–50
>   10 1953–54   1950–51
>   1968–69

287

Rounds Reached by Non-League Clubs in a Season

	Most	*Least*
2nd Round	13 – 1965–66, 1967–68	5 – 1932–33
3rd Round	5 – 1931–32, 1965–66	0 – 1929–30, 1950–51
4th Round	3 – 1956–57	
5th Round	1 – 1947–48, 1949–50	

Biggest Victories over League Sides

Home

Walthamstow Avenue	6	Northampton Town	1	1936–37
Barnet	6	Newport County	1	1970–71
Hereford United	6	Queen's Park Rangers	1	1957–58

Away

Carlisle United	1	Wigan Athletic	6	1934–35
Derby County	1	Boston United	6	1955–56

Heaviest Defeats Against League Sides

Home

Scarborough	0	Mansfield Town	8	1952–53
Barnet	2	Southend United	9	1946–47

Away

Bristol City	11	Chichester	0	1960–61
Arsenal	11	Darwen	1	1931–32

Most Appearances by a Non-League Side in the Competition Proper

(Maximum 40)	Yeovil Town	28	Rhyl	20
	Hereford United	23	Walthamstow Avenue	20
	Scarborough	21		

Most Defeats by a League Club against a Non-League Side

Aldershot, Crystal Palace, and Newport County 7 each

Most Home Defeats by a League Club against a Non-League Side

Carlisle United, Walsall and York City   3 each

Worst Run of Defeats by a League Side against Non-League Side

Hartlepool were eliminated by a non-League Side in 4
consecutive seasons viz. 1926–27, 27–28, 28–29, 29–30

Victories by Non-League Sides over Football League Clubs from 1925–26

10 Times   Yeovil Town (2)

8 Times   Peterborough United (3)

288

6 Times	Bath City (1)		
	Bedford Town (3)		
	Rhyl (2)		

5 Times	Hereford United (1)	Walthamstow Avenue (1)
	Scunthorpe United (1)	Wigan Athletic (2)
	South Shields (1)	Workington (2)

4 Times	Gainsborough Town	
	Margate (1)	
	Scarborough (2)	

3 Times	Bishop Auckland (1)	Folkestone (1)
	Boston United (2)	Gillingham (1)
	Burton United (1)	Guildford City
	Chelmsford City	New Brighton (2)
	Colchester United	Weymouth (1)
	Dartford	

Twice	Aldershot (1)	King's Lynn (1)
	Carlisle United	Leytonstone
	Corinthians (2)	Mansfield Town (1)
	Crook Town	Nuneaton Borough
	Gateshead (2)	Runcorn
	Gravesend & Northfleet (1)	Tooting & Mitcham United
	Headington United	Worcester City
	Kettering Town (1)	Worksop Town

Once	Altrincham (1)	Darwen	Newark Town
	Ashington (1)	Finchley	Newport (I.O.W.)
	Bangor City	Goole Town (1)	Poole
	Barnet	Grantham	Shrewsbury Town
	Blyth Spartans (1)	Great Yarmouth	Southall
	Brentwood Town	Hastings United	South Liverpool
	Buxton	Hillingdon Borough	Spennymoor United
	Caernarvon Athletic	Ipswich Town	Stockton (1)
	Cambridge United (1)	Leyton	Sutton United
	Cheltenham Town (1)	Lovells Athletic	Tamworth
	Chilton Coll: Welf: (1)	Macclesfield Town	Tow Law Town
	Clapton	Merthyr Tydfil	Wimbledon
	Corby Town	Morecambe (1)	Wisbech Town

Note: The figures in brackets indicate the number of away victories. N.B. In 1945–46, Cup Ties were decided on a Home and Away basis. In this season, a few victories in single matches against League sides were recorded although the Tie was lost on aggregate scores. These are *not* included.

Victories by Non-League Clubs over First and Second Division Sides
First Division
  Home

  Colchester United beat Huddersfield Town   1–0............1947–48
  Yeovil Town beat Sunderland   2–1............1948–49

  Away

  None

Second Division
  Home

  Bishop Auckland beat Ipswich Town   3–1............1954–55
                                                (after 2-2 draw)
  Chelmsford beat Southampton   4–1............1938–39
  Colchester United beat Bradford (P.A.)   3–2............1947–48
  Rhyl beat Notts County   3–1............1956–57
  Worcester City beat Liverpool   2–1............1958–59
  Yeovil Town beat Bury   3–1............1948–49

  Away

  Bedford Town beat Newcastle United   2–1............1963–64
  Mansfield Town beat Wolverhampton Wanderers   1–0............1928–29
  Peterborough United beat Lincoln City   5–4............1956–57
                                                (after 2-2 draw)
  Peterborough United beat Ipswich Town   3–2............1959–60

Record of Football League Clubs' defeats by Non-League sides

7 Times	Aldershot (1)	
	Crystal Palace (1)	
	Newport County (1)	
6 Times	Exeter City (1)	
	Stockport County (1)	
5 Times	Halifax Town (1)	Queen's Park Rangers (1)
	Hartlepool (1)	Rochdale (2)
	Millwall (1)	Watford (1)
4 Times	Bournemouth & B (2)	Norwich City (2)
	Bradford (P.A.)	Torquay United
	Carlisle United (3)	Walsall (3)
	Darlington (2)	York City (3)
	Gillingham (1)	
3 Times	Coventry City (1)	Notts County (2)
	Crewe Alexandra	Shrewsbury Town
	Gateshead	Southend United
	Ipswich Town (1)	Southport (2)
	Lincoln City (2)	Wrexham
	Northampton Town (1)	

Twice	Bradford City	Mansfield Town (1)	
	Brighton & Hove Albion	Orient	
	Chester (1)	Oxford United	
	Colchester United	Reading	
	Derby County (2)	Swansea City	
	Doncaster Rovers	Swindon Town	
	Luton Town (1)	Tranmere Rovers (1)	
Once	Barrow	Merthyr Tydfil	Sunderland
	Brentford	New Brighton (1)	Wigan Borough
	Bristol City (1)	Newcastle United (1)	Wolverhampton W (1)
	Bristol Rovers	Oldham Athletic (1)	Workington (1)
	Bury	Peterborough United	
	Cardiff City	Port Vale	
	Chesterfield	Rotherham United	
	Huddersfield Town	Southampton	
	Liverpool	Stoke City (1)	

Figures in brackets indicate the number of home defeats.

Table of Victories over League Sides each Season

	Round				Total		Round				Total
	1	*2*	*3*	*4*			*1*	*2*	*3*	*4*	
1925–26	3	2	–	–	5	1951–52	2	1	–	–	3
1926–27	3	1	1	–	5	1952–53	2	2	1	–	5
1927–28	3	–	–	–	3	1953–54	6	3	1	–	10
1928–29	3	1	2	–	6	1954–55	1	1	1	–	3
1929–30	4	–	–	–	4	1955–56	1	4	–	–	5
1930–31	1	2	–	–	3	1956–57	5	3	3	–	11
1931–32	3	3	–	–	6	1957–58	3	1	–	–	4
1932–33	2	1	–	–	3	1958–59	3	2	1	–	6
1933–34	2	2	1	–	5	1959–60	4	2	1	–	7
1934–35	2	2	–	–	4	1960–61	2	–	–	–	2
1935–36	6	1	–	–	7	1961–62	4	3	–	–	7
1936–37	2	–	–	–	2	1962–63	2	–	1	–	3
1937–38	2	–	–	–	3	1963–64	3	1	1	–	5
1938–39	2	2	1	–	5	1964–65	3	–	–	–	3
1945–46	3	–	–	–	3	1965–66	5	4	–	–	9
1946–47	2	1	–	–	3	1966–67	–	2	–	–	2
1947–48	2	2	1	1	6	1967–68	5	–	–	–	5
1948–49	2	–	1	1	4	1968–69	1	–	–	–	1
1949–50	1	–	–	–	1	1969–70	3	2	–	–	5
1950–51	1	–	–	–	1	1970–71	5	2	–	–	7

A Non-League Merit Table

In an attempt to rank the performances of the non-League Clubs in the F.A. Cup from 1925–26, a merit table has been drawn up with points awarded on the following basis. One point is allocated for each round played in the Competition Proper, and for a victory gained against a non-League Club; 3 are awarded against a Third or Fourth Division side; 4 against a Second Division, and 5 against a First Division side. The headings A and B below, indicate the category of points gained, A for the number of rounds played and B for wins against a League side.

Club	A	B	Total	Club	A	B	Total
Yeovil Town	51	33	84	Margate Town	24	12	36
Peterborough United	31	26	57	Workington	20	15	35
Hereford United	37	15	52	Bishop Auckland	24	10	34
Bath City	32	18	50	Dartford	25	9	34
Rhyl Athletic	29	19	48	Scunthorpe United	19	15	34
Walthamstow Avenue	31	15	46	South Shields	19	15	34
Scarborough	30	12	42	Boston United	24	9	33
Bedford Town	23	19	42	Folkestone	23	9	32
Gainsborough Trinity	29	12	41	Guildford City	23	9	32
Weymouth	31	9	40	Kettering Town	26	6	32
Chelmsford City	27	10	37	Corinthians	25	6	31
Wigan Athletic	22	15	37				

N.B. In the period under review Corinthians received a Bye to the third round six times.

Club	A	B	Total	Club	A	B	Total
Blyth Spartans	23	4	27	Leytonstone	11	6	17
Barnet	23	3	26	Spennymoor United	14	3	17
Crook Town	19	6	25	Gravesend & Northfleet	10	6	16
Burton Town	14	9	23	Nuneaton Borough	10	6	16
King's Lynn	17	6	23	Mansfield Town	9	7	16
Grantham	18	3	21	Worcester City	9	7	16
Wimbledon	18	3	21	Gateshead	9	6	15
Colchester United	8	12	20	Hastings United	12	3	15
Headington (Oxford Utd.)	13	6	19	Leyton	12	3	15
Wellington Town	18	0	18	Runcorn	9	6	15
Cheltenham Town	17	3	20	Stockton	12	3	15
Gillingham	8	9	17	Sutton United	12	3	15

Index

294

296

297

HOT FAST

BBQ
ON YOUR WEBER SMOKEY MOUNTAIN COOKER

MASTER *the* QUICKEST METHOD TO SMOKING MOUTHWATERING MEATS

BILL GILLESPIE
BESTSELLING AUTHOR *and* AWARD-WINNING PITMASTER

WITH TIM O'KEEFE

PAGE STREET

Copyright © 2021 Bill Gillespie

First published in 2021 by
Page Street Publishing Co.
Congress Street, Suite 105
Salem, MA 01970
www.pagestreetpublishing.com

Distributed by Macmillan, sales in Canada by The Canadian Manda Group.

24   23   22   21   1   2   3   4   5

ISBN-13: 978-1-64567-282-1
ISBN-10: 1-64567-282-4

Library of Congress Control Number: 2020947804

Cover and book design by Laura Benton for Page Street Publishing Co.
Photography by Ken Goodman

Printed and bound in the United States

I DEDICATE THIS BOOK TO ALL MY FAMILY AND FRIENDS
WHO HAVE SUPPORTED ME FROM THE BEGINNING

CONTENTS

FOREWORD

Ever since the dawn of time when man first began cooking meat over an open fire, we've been constantly trying to improve on this concept.

Next to chili, barbecue is the most proprietary food on planet Earth. Everyone has at least one secret ingredient from generations gone by that supposedly gives that extra "edge."

You know the drill.

How can we all take essentially the same spice ingredients in preparing a rub, apply it to the protein of choice, labor over the fire and have some turn out so badly you're ashamed of it and some turn out so incredibly slap-your-mama-on-Christmas-Day-Sunday-melt-in-your-mouth delicious?

Ask Bill Gillespie.

Bill is the award-winning pitmaster of Smokin' Hoggz BBQ, and he's been doing it "low and slow" for well over 25 years.

When I say, "He's been doing it well," I mean he's been doing it *extremely* well.

As a Master of Ceremonies, I've personally handed Bill over $25,000 in first-place prize winnings at The Jack, plus thousands upon thousands of dollars in lower place winnings and ancillary prizes.

Seriously, his truck and wallet are always heavier when leaving Lynchburg, Tennessee, not to mention other locations where Bill and his team are firing up their grills.

Bill and his Smokin' Hoggz team have competed in more than 200 contests covering 20 states and Canada.

Since forming the Smokin' Hoggz team in 2008, he's cooked his way into a whopping 35 Grand Championships and 22 Reserve Grand Championships, not to mention more than 140 overall top-ten finishes. Plus, well over 400 individual category wins in chicken, ribs, pork and brisket.

Oh yeah, he's also won numerous dessert awards, including a first place, "perfect-perfect" score of 180!

I could go on to tell you Bill and Smokin' Hoggz have been named team of the year multiple times by the Northeast BBQ Society.

I could also tell you they've repeatedly been honored by the Kansas City Barbecue Society as a top-ten Team of the Year, or they've cooked a number of times at the American Royal Invitational World Series of Barbecue in Kansas City, Missouri. The list of accolades goes on, but you get the picture.

Bill and his team have an impressive barbecue résumé, no doubt. But to me, one of the truly striking things about Bill Gillespie is this: His love and knowledge of barbecue is so wide-ranging, he's forgotten more about this art form than most of us will ever know, and he is willing and able to share it with future and current generations. In fact, he knows sharing that knowledge is one of the fundamental keys to furthering this food form we all love.

And make no mistake, creating great barbecue is a combination of hard work, science, art and love.

Bill Gillespie works a crowd the same way he works a pit—with total ease and confidence—and he does it simultaneously.

He's always happy to dispense cooking tips to friends and competitors alike, and his words of advice are highly treasured among those less skilled and gifted. Bill knows—instinctively knows—that cooking with a live fire is a craft unto itself, built on tradition and truly mastered by few.

For many folks, barbecue is anything cooked over a flame of any sort, or even worse, the actual piece of equipment used to cook on.

Think back to the movie *Crocodile Dundee*, where actor Paul Hogan says, "I'll slip an extra shrimp on the barbie for you."

Please.

That obviously isn't barbecue. Not even close.

In the heart of barbecue country, and especially on the circuit itself, barbecue is not just food; it's a staple of life. It's a necessity. It's a social event and a reason to gather with family and friends—maybe even some friends we haven't yet met!

Barbecue is a love language all its own, and seeing a personal creation going from the grill to the palate is a pleasure for all. It lifts the spirits and brings a gleam to the eye and a smile to the heart. It is truly food for the soul.

Barbecue as a whole wouldn't be where it is today without the dreams, visions and accomplishments of Bill Gillespie.

CHIP CHAPMAN
Master of Ceremonies
Jack Daniel's World Invitational Barbecue

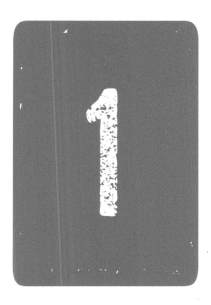

INTRO TO HOT, FAST and EASY COOKING ON The WSM

The Weber Smokey Mountain Cooker remains one of the best outdoor cookers on the market today. I'm not endorsed by Weber, but I've been active on the competition barbecue circuit for about fifteen years. When I first started competing, I used a WSM, and numerous competition cooks still use them today. The price point and quality of this product makes it accessible to most backyard cooking enthusiasts, and its ability to produce consistent results makes it a worthwhile expense.

The WSM is comprised of three primary sections: the base, the middle and the lid. Each section is porcelain enameled, which means the smoker is easy to clean, highly resistant to corrosion and retains heat fairly well.

The base of the WSM contains a metal ring that houses lit charcoal. The base of each model has three vents, the 14-inch (36-cm) and 18-inch (46-cm) model have three holes per vent, and the 22-inch (56-cm) model has four holes per vent that control airflow. The amount of oxygen that reaches the hot coals directly influences the overall cooking temperature of the smoker. For the hot-and-fast cooking method, you want to keep the bottom vents open about three-quarters of the way during the cooking process.

The middle section contains two cooking grates and a water pan. While the water pan can help create a moist cooking environment, its main purpose is to act as a heat sink that helps stabilize and maintain the smoker's internal cooking temperature. For the hot-and-fast cooking method, you cook with a dry and more direct heat. Do not fill the water pan with water. It's also a good idea to cook on the top cooking grate because the top grate runs about 15 to 20°F (8 to 12°C) hotter than the lower cooking grate, when using the empty water pan.

The lid contains one air vent. This vent usually remains fully open and is crucial for sustaining the hot charcoal and channeling smoke through the cooker. As smoke flows through the cooker, it imparts flavor to food.

PRODUCT OVERVIEW

The WSM is available in three different sizes. All of the recipes in this book were created using the mid-sized model. Slight adjustments to the amount of charcoal or cook time length may be necessary if you cook on a product of a different size. The mid-sized option is my recommendation as the best entry-level smoker for new backyard cooks—it's the perfect size when you're cooking for friends and family.

SIDE NOTE: Seasoning a new WSM is optional, but I recommend it. Before you cook food on your WSM, you should burn a batch of charcoal to help season the smoker. Seasoning helps remove residue left over from the manufacturing process, such as trace amounts of dust, powder or oil. Seasoning also helps cure the paint, remove chemical odors and promote rust prevention. To season properly, apply a light coat of cooking spray to all interior surfaces, including the cooking grates, the interior walls, the water pan and the interior of the lid. Then, burn two chimneys of charcoal at 350 to 400°F (177 to 204°C) for at least 2 to 3 hours, or until the charcoal burns out. You should also clean the smoker every three or four times you cook on it. Clean the interior of the lid after every cook—otherwise, particles of soot can build up, flake off and fall into your food.

DIAMETER	TOTAL COOKING AREA	DESCRIPTION
14.5 inch (37 cm)	286 square inches (20 cubic cm)	Most portable. Easy to pack in your car to bring camping, tailgating or to similar outdoor events. Least-expensive model, about $220, and a good choice if you have limited space, such as an apartment building or a cramped yard in the city. It's great for cooking smaller things, like tenderloins, kabobs, sausage, Cornish hens or a small pork butt.
18.5 inch (47 cm)	481 square inches (30 cubic cm)	Costs about $320 but is a more versatile model that is great at holding temperature. Can cook two racks of ribs but more will be a challenge, unless you use a rib rack. Can cook up to a 14-pound (6.4-kg) brisket and can handle two 8-pound (3.6-kg) pork butts per cooking grate.
22.5 inch (57 cm)	726 square inches (50 cubic cm)	Coming in at about $420, this is the most expensive model but allows you to cook a bountiful feast. This smoker can cook four pork butts, up to a 20-pound (9-kg) brisket or four whole chickens. For an alternate approach, you can hang ribs and cook them. They'll cook a little faster and have great flavor from fat dripping directly into the fire, which creates more smoke.

HOT 'N' FAST BASICS

The hot-and-fast cooking method uses a hotter cooking temperature and shorter cooking time than the low-and-slow cooking method associated with traditional barbecue. Essentially, the basic definition of barbecue is using wood or charcoal to cook meat over a low-heat source for a long period of time. The reason for this is related to the history of this unique cuisine. Many of the cuts of meat we associate with barbecue were less than ideal—tough and fatty—but these unwanted proteins were turned into desirable delicacies through creative innovation.

One of the creative innovations is that when you cook at a low temperature, the fat, collagen and connective tissue in the meats melt down, creating layers of flavor in a moist, finished product. However, with a little bit of knowledge and practice, you can achieve very similar results, in roughly half the time, using the hot-and-fast cooking method.

Typically, grilling meat over direct high heat, even at 500 to 600°F (260 to 316°C), can cook the outside of large cuts, but the inside remains undercooked. By using the hot-and-fast cooking method on the WSM, you're cooking around 350 to 400°F (177 to 204°C). While it's not the searing intensity of a high-heat grill, cooking on your smoker at this temperature does get the inside of the meat to cook properly.

The key to the hot-and-fast cooking method is to bring the protein you're cooking to a higher internal temperature than you would if you cook low and slow. This, along with the fact that your smoker is cooking at a higher temperature, is what causes fat to melt and collagens to break down into soft gelatin in less time. In cooking, generally speaking, temperature gets you close, but many times feel is the final determining factor in the perfect finished product. If you work your way through this book, I'm confident that you will be able to create the perfect finished product each and every time you step up to cook on your WSM.

ADVANTAGES OF THE HOT-AND-FAST COOKING METHOD:

- Shorter cooking durations that generally last 4 to 6 hours
- It's a time saver and allows you to spend more time with your guests
- More crust can form on the meat's surface than if you cook at lower temperatures
- Typically does not require additional charcoal during the cook time
- Favored when you prefer that charcoal be fully lit during cooking process

THINGS TO KEEP IN MIND:

- If the WSM runs too hot, bringing the temperature down can be problematic

- Ideal temperature range is 350 to 400°F (177 to 204°C)

CHARCOAL

On the WSM, charcoal is the fuel source that generates heat. The WSM cooks using convection, and the fire resides at the bottom of the cooker. Heat rises, filling the cooking chamber, and the unique design of the product's lid helps deflect heat back inward, toward the cooking grates. When cooking on the WSM, you have two primary types of charcoal to choose from as your fuel source: lump charcoal or charcoal briquettes.

When cooking hot and fast, lump charcoal is my choice. Lump charcoal is essentially chunks of burnt wood. It burns at a hotter temperature than briquettes, but it has a shorter burn duration. Several brands of lump charcoal are available, and it's easy to find at home improvement stores. Bags of lump charcoal often contain chunks of varying sizes, which can create temperature spikes while you're cooking. For the hot-and-fast cooking method, this usually isn't a problem.

SMOKE WOOD

Smoke is a key component in the traditional barbecue flavor profile. There are various smoke woods you can use, and each imparts its own unique flavor into the food you're cooking. I like to think of smoke as just another seasoning ingredient. When you're first learning to cook with smoke wood, just use a little bit, because like any other ingredient, it can overseason the food. Oversmoked food tastes bitter. Learning to pair the type and quantity of smoke wood to use with various proteins is part of the fun of backyard cooking. As you become experienced, your personal preferences should always be the primary factor in making these decisions.

- You can find bags of smoke wood at large home improvement stores. Sometimes, smaller hardware stores, fireplace stores or even specialty shops known for carrying a variety of ingredients will stock bags of smoke woods. Smoke wood is available in two sizes: chunks and chips. For the hot-and-fast cooking method, chunks are preferred. Chips burn up quickly and should be avoided.

For bigger cuts of meat, such as brisket, whole pork shoulder, pork butt or picnic shoulder, three chunks of wood are usually sufficient. For smaller items, such as a dozen wings or a few chicken breasts, one chunk is usually fine. Place the smoke wood on top of the lit charcoal, about the same time you put the food you're cooking on the cooking grate. Typically, you do not have to add additional smoke wood during the cooking process.

The table on page 15 provides details about common types of smoke woods.

BRINES

Brines are salty liquid solutions that are used to add moisture and flavor to meat. It's a technique that might come in handy when cooking with the hot-and-fast technique. When you brine a meat, keep the brine at or below 40°F (4°C) to stunt the growth of bacteria. You must fully submerge the meat into the brining solution, and the process works best if the meat soaks from as little as a few hours to as much as overnight. Essentially, you can brine most things you would marinade. While the process works well for chickens, turkeys and pork, I usually don't recommend it for beef, unless you are making corned beef or pastrami. When applying rubs, be mindful that the brining process adds salt to food and adjust your rub usage accordingly.

MARINADES

Marinades are acidic liquids used to add flavor and tenderize meat. While I don't recommend the use of marinades on larger cuts, like brisket or pork butt, the technique works very well on thin cuts, such as pork chops, steaks or chicken breasts. Typically, marinades don't penetrate much beyond the surface layer of meat. You can marinate anywhere from 30 minutes to overnight. I usually let chicken breasts or steaks marinate for a few hours, but fish I limit to an hour or two. Generally speaking, I don't recommend making a marinade more than a day in advance of when you'll use it, to help keep the acid strong and the flavors potent.

WOOD TYPE	DESCRIPTION
Alder	A mild wood from the Pacific Northwest that is good to use with seafood, poultry, pork and light game.
Hickory	A popular wood that lends a hint of bacon flavor. It goes well with pork and beef.
Mesquite	Typically associated with Texas barbecue and works well with beef. Use a little at first to get adjusted to its flavor, as mesquite can easily dominate food.
Oak	A milder form of hickory, oak produces a medium smoke flavor that goes well with all barbecue meats, especially beef and pork.
Pecan	An all-around good smoke wood, pecan has a sweet and mild flavor.
Sugar Maple	Frequently found in the Northeast, and a staple on the competition circuit, sugar maple provides a mellow smoke flavor. Works well with poultry, pork and cheese. For an interesting flavor combination, try mixing one or two pieces of this wood with apple or cherry wood.
Walnut	Produces a heavy flavor and often matched with beef. Walnut is best when used alone. If you want to mix flavors, try adding a little fruit wood.
Apple	Perhaps the most common of the fruit woods, apple works well with pork and chicken. Produces a subtle fruit flavor.
Cherry	Creates sweet-tasting smoke that goes wonderfully with pork and poultry. Also offers great color!
Peach	A milder wood that is great for a variety of white and pink meats.

INJECTIONS

An injection is a seasoned liquid you add to meat using a syringe. Injections penetrate deeply into large proteins, such as pork shoulder, beef brisket, whole chickens and whole turkeys, and can be applied moments before you begin to cook a protein. I think injecting is the easiest way to create a finished product that is juicy and flavorful. Keep in mind that many of the herbs and spices that injections contain can get stuck in a syringe. It's a good practice to strain injections before you use them.

RUBS

Rubs are a vibrant mixture of dry herbs and spices you apply to raw meat, seafood and vegetables prior to cooking. During the cooking process, rubs infuse food with aromas. As meat cooks, fat melts away, and the rub forms a savory bark at the meat's surface. When using with the hot-and-fast cooking method, bark can form more quickly. Spritzing the surface of the meat with liquid can help prevent burning.

You can apply a rub to large cuts of meat, wrap them in plastic and let them sit in the fridge overnight. Most rubs contain a fair amount of salt. If you apply a salty rub to ribs and let them sit overnight, the rub will almost create a curing effect, and the ribs will have a ham-like texture. For smaller selections, including ribs, steak or chicken breasts, apply the rub up to a few hours before cooking. With the hot-and-fast cooking method, sugars burn more easily. Use rubs with less sugar content, if you can find them. If you make your own rubs, I recommend using turbinado sugar because it has a higher burn point and can take more heat without burning.

SAUCES

A sauce is simply a liquid that adds flavor and visual appeal to food. While numerous sauces can be found throughout the culinary world, it should come as no surprise that one of my favorites is barbecue sauce. A variety of barbecue sauces can be found throughout the United States, and each has a distinct flavor. My favorite barbecue sauce is the tomato-and-brown-sugar variant strongly associated with Kansas City. This style of sauce contains a lot of sugar, so you should only apply it during the last few minutes of cooking. This becomes especially important when you use the hot-and-fast cooking method.

WORKFLOW FOR HOT 'N' FAST

1. Fully open the top and bottom vents. This configuration will help channel a significant amount of air throughout the entire cooking process, allowing the WSM to maintain a high cooking temperature.

2. Dump one chimney of unlit charcoal inside the charcoal ring.

3. Light one full chimney of charcoal. Wait for the charcoal at the top of the chimney to begin to turn gray or until you see flames rising out of the top of the chimney.

4. Using heat-resistant gloves, dump the hot charcoal into the center of the charcoal ring.

5. Cover the top of the water pan with aluminum foil to catch grease and prevent it from burning. DO NOT fill the water pan with water.

6. Assemble the WSM, and place the lid on top.

7. Let the WSM come up to temperature (350 to 400°F [177 to 204°C]). This typically takes 15 to 30 minutes. With no water in the water pan, the temperature stabilizes quickly. If you are having trouble bringing up the temperature, open the side access door to let more oxygen reach the hot charcoal. More oxygen reaching the hot coals will help raise the temperature.

8. After the temperature stabilizes, add your smoke wood and place the meat on the cooking grate. For hot-and-fast cooking, the top grate is preferred.

ADJUSTING THE VENTS FOR TEMPERATURE CONTROL

During the cooking process, you'll have to adjust the bottom vents from time to time in order to control the cooking temperature.

If the temperature falls below the range specified in the recipe, open the bottom vents more to allow more oxygen to reach the hot charcoal. Once the temperature begins to rise, close the bottom vents slightly.

Typically, you should try adjusting the three bottom vents equally so the charcoal burns more evenly.

When managing the WSM temperature using the vents, you will want to adjust the vents accordingly. For cooking at or around 325°F (160°C), adjust the bottom vents so they are 25 to 30 percent open; for cooking around 350°F (177°C), adjust the bottom vents so they are 50 to 65 percent open; and for anything above 375°F (190°C), you want the bottom vents 75 to 100 percent open.

There's a lot to consider when adjusting for temperature: the outside air temperature, wind, rain and type of charcoal you're using. So don't be too fussy when it comes to small temperature variations. As long as you're close to the target temperatures in the recipes, your dishes should be fabulous!

Opening or closing the vents increases or decreases the amount of oxygen that reaches the hot charcoal. This is essentially what controls temperature. It can take a little while for the WSM's temperature to respond to vent adjustments. One skill of an experienced backyard cook is the ability to anticipate when temperature changes might occur and act before it is necessary. This way, only small adjustments to the vents are needed.

2 QUICK *and* JUICY SWINE

Pork is a wonderful meat that is rich in flavor and frequents dinner tables in a variety of ways: chops, tenderloin, baby back ribs, pulled pork and holiday ham. The good news is that you can prepare all of these selections using the hot-and-fast cooking method.

The hot-and-fast cooking method is great for leaner cuts, with less fat content, such as pork loin. This cooking method produces a juicy finished product and is particularly well suited for thin cuts, like chops.

Larger offerings, like pork butt, seem betrothed to the low-and-slow cooking style, where it takes hours and hours to melt down the meat's fat content, turning the meat into a moist, flavorful delight. But here is a little something that just might tug at someone's heart: By using the hot-and-fast cooking method, you can achieve the same end result in less time by bringing the meat to a higher internal temperature during the cooking process.

I know there is passion in the barbecue community. A lot of people love barbecue, and many of those people swear by the low-and-slow cooking method. But if the definition of love includes the ability to push beyond, while sharing mutual trust, and being able to forgive, then I ask, that just one time, you cook pork butt using the hot-and-fast cooking method. You just might find a whole new experience with food!

SIDE NOTE: **The FDA recommends that pork is cooked to an internal temperature of 145°F (63°C).**

BABY BACK RIBS IN 2½ HOURS

I love ribs! In fact, baby back ribs were my first BBQ love, and I have such fond memories of them. At restaurants, I would order them every chance I got. Then one day I thought, *Hmmm, I bet I could make these at home.* So, I ventured out and got a smoker. It was a small round charcoal smoker, and the temperature gauge read low, ideal and hot—I'm sure some of you know exactly which model I'm talking about. The first set of ribs I cooked came out awful. I think there were about two bones from each rack that were even edible. It was a complete disaster! That was over 25 years ago. I have honed my barbecue skills since then, and this recipe will not only speed up your learning curve, but the hot-and-fast process will allow you to serve ribs in time for dinner even if you start them at 5:00 p.m.

Set up your WSM for 325 to 350°F (160 to 177°C). Use an empty water pan lined with foil to allow for easy cleanup after the cook. You will need one chimney of lit charcoal and 1½ chimneys of unlit charcoal. Add the chimney of unlit coal to the charcoal ring, add the fully lit chimney on top of the unlit, then the half chimney of unlit to that, wait 10 minutes and then reassemble the WSM.

Apply the honey mustard to both sides of the ribs, just enough to lightly coat them.

For the dry rub, in a small bowl, mix the salt, sugar, chili powder, cumin, cayenne, black pepper, granulated garlic and onion powder. Store the rub in an airtight container. Sprinkle the bone side of the ribs lightly with the rub (reserving 2 tbsp [20 g] for later) and let them sit for about 15 minutes. Flip the ribs and dust the meat side of ribs with the rub. Let them sit for 15 minutes. Letting the ribs sit after applying the rub allows the salt in the rub to work its magic and penetrate into the meat, creating a perfect layer of flavor.

Place the ribs on the top rack of the WSM. Add the smoke wood right after putting the ribs on the smoker. Place the cover on the smoker and cook for 2 hours.

Just before the ribs are ready to come off, lay out two pieces of heavy-duty aluminum foil, one for each rack of ribs. Make sure the length of foil is longer than the rack of ribs by about 4 inches (10 cm) on either end. Onto each of the foil sheets, pour ¼ cup (60 ml) of the BBQ sauce, ¼ cup (55 g) of brown sugar and 2 tablespoons (28 g) of butter.

Now remove the ribs from the WSM and place each rack, meat side down, onto the sauced foil sheets. Apply ¼ cup (60 ml) of BBQ sauce over each of the racks and sprinkle each rack with 1 tablespoon (10 g) of the reserved rub. Wrap the racks tightly with the foil and place them back on the WSM for 30 minutes.

You will know they are done when you can see the meat shrink back from the bone about ½ inch (1.3 cm). Take the ribs out of the foil, and glaze them with the juices that collected in the foil. Allow the ribs to rest for about 20 minutes.

(continued)

COOK TIME:
approximately 2½ hours

YIELD:
about 8 servings

¼ cup (60 ml) honey mustard

2 racks of loin back/baby back ribs with the membrane removed

DRY RUB

¼ cup (72 g) kosher salt

¼ cup (51 g) turbinado sugar (see Notes)

2 tbsp (13 g) chili powder

1 tbsp (6 g) ground cumin

2 tsp (4 g) cayenne pepper

2 tsp (4 g) freshly ground black pepper

2 tsp (4 g) granulated garlic

2 tsp (4 g) onion powder

2 chunks apple wood

Heavy-duty foil

1 cup (240 ml) Sticky Sweet BBQ Sauce (page 121), divided

½ cup (110 g) brown sugar

4 tbsp (56 g) butter

BABY BACK RIBS IN 2¹/₂ HOURS (CONTINUED)

> **NOTES:** This recipe works well with St. Louis–style spareribs. Follow the recipe exactly except add 1 hour to the cook time before wrapping the ribs in foil. The reason for the extra time for St. Louis ribs is they have a lot more meat on them than baby backs, and the extra time allows for them to cook properly.
>
> Sugar in the raw has a higher burn point and is better for cooking hot and fast.

Wrapping ribs, layer of sauce

Wrapping ribs, layer of brown sugar

Adding butter

Laying ribs meat side down

Sprinkling dry rub on ribs

Adding more sauce to ribs

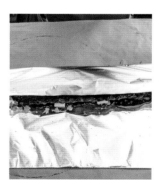

Wrapping tightly in foil

HOT AND FAST PULLED PORK

This is a great recipe if you don't have all day to cook, and the best part is that you don't have to get up before the birds to have pulled pork ready for dinner! Using the hot-and-fast cooking method, you'll have tender, flavorful pork in about half the cooking time as the low-and-slow method most cooks typically use.

COOK TIME:
approximately 5½ hours. Note: Cooking at low-and-slow temps around 250°F (130°C) would take this about 12 to 14 hours to cook.

YIELD:
about 12 servings

For the dry rub, in a small bowl, mix together the turbinado sugar, paprika, pepper, salt, chili powder, garlic powder and onion powder. Set it aside.

For the simple pork injection, in a medium bowl, mix together the apple juice, Dry Rub, apple cider vinegar, honey, Worcestershire sauce and salt.

Inject the pork butt with the pork injection. You probably won't use it all, but that's okay.

Apply the dry rub liberally all over the pork butt.

Let the pork butt sit in the fridge for at least 4 hours; overnight is fine.

Set up your WSM for 350°F (177°C) using an empty water pan lined with foil, and add about 2 cups (480 ml) of water to the water pan. You will need one chimney of lit charcoal and two chimneys of unlit charcoal. Add a chimney of unlit coal to the charcoal ring, add the fully lit chimney on top of the unlit coal, and then add the last chimney of unlit coal to that. Wait 10 minutes and then reassemble the WSM.

Place the pork butt on the top rack of the WSM, and place the lid on the smoker. Add the smoke wood when you place the pork butt on the smoker. Cook it for 3½ hours or until the pork butt reaches an internal temperature of 160 to 165°F (71 to 74°C).

When the pork butt reaches the desired internal temperature, remove it from the cooker and prepare it for wrapping. Lay out a piece of heavy-duty foil large enough to wrap the entire pork butt.

(continued)

DRY RUB

¼ cup (51 g) turbinado sugar

4 tbsp (28 g) paprika

1 tbsp (6 g) coarse black pepper

1 tbsp (18 g) kosher salt

1 tbsp (7 g) chili powder

1 tbsp (8 g) garlic powder

1 tbsp (7 g) onion powder

SIMPLE PORK INJECTION

2 cups (480 ml) apple juice

2 tbsp (20 g) Dry Rub (above)

2 tbsp (30 ml) apple cider vinegar

2 tbsp (30 ml) honey

1 tsp Worcestershire sauce

2 tsp (12 g) kosher salt

PORK BUTT

1 (8-lb [3.6-kg]) pork butt

1 chunk each apple wood and sugar maple

Heavy-duty foil

Sticky Sweet BBQ Sauce (page 121)

HOT AND FAST PULLED PORK (CONTINUED)

Place the pork butt on the foil, wrap completely and return it to the smoker. Cook for 1½ to 2 hours, or until it reaches an internal temperature of 200 to 205°F (93 to 96°C).

Remove the pork butt from the smoker. Open the foil and vent the pork butt for 10 minutes to help stop the cooking process. Wrap the pork butt back up in the same foil and set it aside in a dry, empty cooler to rest for about 1 hour, up to 4 hours. The empty cooler acts as an insulator, and the pork remains hot for a long time.

Remove the pork butt from the cooler. Unwrap the pork and shred it using your hands. Strain the juices from the foil and mix it back in with the pork. Serve the pulled pork on rolls with coleslaw and your favorite BBQ sauce.

> NOTES: When cooking hot and fast, I usually leave the water pan empty. However, pork butt contains a lot of fat, and having some water in the water pan helps prevent the fat drippings from burning up.
>
> Don't worry about cooking to this internal temperature. Using the high heat cooking process, you can cook meat to a higher internal temperature and the meat won't turn mushy.
>
> When shredding pork by hand, it's a good idea to wear a pair of cotton gloves, and then put your food-safe gloves over them. The cotton gloves provide a nice layer of insulation that allows you to more easily shred the pork without burning your hands.

SCOTCH EGG-STUFFED SAUSAGE FATTY WITH HOT SAUCE

COOK TIME:
45 minutes

YIELD:
4 servings

Have you ever had a Scotch egg? Well, I've had many, and they sure are succulent! A Scotch egg is a hard-boiled egg that is wrapped in breakfast sausage, rolled in breadcrumbs and then deep fried to a golden delight. A Scotch egg is typically served with either hot sauce or a spicy mayo. This recipe takes the traditional Scotch egg and turns it into a delicious sausage fatty.

For the Spicy Mayo, in a small bowl, mix the mayo, sour cream, mustard, hot sauce and chipotle powder. Store in an airtight container in the fridge until you're ready to use it.

Set up your WSM for 350°F (177°C) using an empty water pan lined with foil. You will need one fully lit chimney of charcoal, which should be plenty.

Form the ground breakfast sausage into a 6-inch (15-cm) square about ½ inch (1.3 cm) thick.

Season the inside of the sausage with 1 tablespoon (10 g) of Everyday/Everything Rub. Place all four eggs on top of the seasoned ground sausage. Roll the sausage around the eggs to form a log, making sure to seal up the ends.

In a large resealable plastic bag, add the cornstarch and the remaining tablespoon (10 g) of the dry rub. Place the rolled sausage log in the bag and coat its entire exterior with the cornstarch mixture.

Place the apple wood on top of the charcoal, and then put the sausage roll on the top cooking grate and cook for 45 minutes, or until it reaches an internal temperature of 160°F (71°C).

Remove the sausage roll from the smoker and let it sit for 5 minutes. Slice and serve with the Spicy Mayo.

SPICY MAYO

2 tbsp (30 ml) mayo

2 tbsp (30 ml) sour cream

1 tbsp (15 ml) Dijon mustard

2 tbsp (30 ml) Frank's hot sauce

½ tsp chipotle powder

SAUSAGE

1 lb (454 g) breakfast sausage, such as Jimmy Dean ground sausage

2 tbsp (20 g) Everyday/Everything Rub (page 120), divided

4 soft-boiled eggs, centers still slightly liquid

¼ cup (32 g) cornstarch

1 chunk apple wood

> **NOTE:** Coating the outside of the rolled sausage log in cornstarch helps form more surface crust when cooking on the smoker, almost like it was deep fried.

MAPLE-CHIPOTLE GLAZED PORK TENDERLOIN

Pork tenderloin is a very lean piece of meat that can easily dry out when it's overcooked. Similar to its beef counterpart, the beef tenderloin, this delicate piece of meat needs to be cooked over high heat, and it needs to be done quickly. This is a simple recipe with some great flavor, and it lends itself well to the hot-and-fast cooking method.

COOK TIME:
approximately 30 minutes

YIELD:
4 servings

MAPLE-CHIPOTLE GLAZE
½ cup (120 ml) pure maple syrup, not the fake stuff

¼ cup (55 g) light brown sugar

2 chipotle peppers in adobo sauce, finely chopped, plus 1 tsp sauce

1 tbsp (15 ml) Dijon mustard

2 tsp (5 g) chili powder

TENDERLOIN
Butcher's string

1 lb (454 g) pork tenderloin

2 tbsp (30 ml) olive oil

Salt and pepper

1 chunk sugar maple wood

Heavy-duty aluminum foil

Set up the WSM for 400°F (204°C) and remove the water pan. One fully lit chimney should do the trick for this recipe.

For the Maple-Chipotle Glaze, in a small bowl, mix together the maple syrup, brown sugar, chipotle peppers with sauce, mustard and chili powder. Cover and keep it in the fridge until you're ready to use it.

Using the butcher's string, tie the pork tenderloin so it looks uniform in thickness from one end to the other. Be sure the ends are tucked in and are the same thickness as the center of the tenderloin.

Coat the outside of the tenderloin with the olive oil and season with salt and pepper.

Place the maple wood on top of the charcoal, put the tenderloin on the bottom cooking grate and cook it for 13 minutes. Flip the tenderloin over, brush on some of the Maple-Chipotle Glaze, just to coat, and cook it for 13 minutes or until the internal temperature reaches 135°F (57°C). Flip the tenderloin over, brush on some of the glaze, just to coat, and cook for 5 minutes. The finished internal temperature should be 140 to 145°F (60 to 63°C).

Remove the tenderloin from the heat. Loosely tent it with foil and let it rest for 15 minutes.

While the tenderloin is resting, in a small saucepan over medium heat, simmer the remaining glaze for 10 minutes.

Slice the tenderloin into ½-inch (1.3-cm) pieces, and serve it with the Maple-Chipotle Glaze.

NOTE: Tying the pork tenderloin with string helps it cook evenly from end to end because it's all the same thickness.

CHORIZO-STUFFED PORK LOIN

One of my favorite things to do to a pork loin is to stuff it with something bold and flavorful. Let's be honest, pork loin can be very boring by itself. So why not add a little bit of flavor to it by stuffing it, right? The stuffing in this recipe is the perfect complement to the pork loin. It's absolutely full of flavor, and the spices from the chorizo mixed with the bitterness of the cooked spinach really helps bring this dish together.

COOK TIME:
45 to 60 minutes. This is less than half the time if cooking low and slow at 250°F (130°C).

YIELD:
about 8 servings

Set up the WSM for 350°F (177°C). Leave the water pan in it and line it with foil. This will greatly help with cleanup. You will need one fully lit chimney plus half of an unlit chimney of charcoal. Dump the fully lit chimney into the center of the charcoal ring, and then add the unlit charcoal to that. Wait 10 minutes and then reassemble the WSM.

For the stuffing, in a medium bowl, combine the spinach, cheese, chorizo and garlic. Season with salt and pepper.

Trim any of the white "silver skin" membrane and loose fat from the pork loin. Butterfly the pork loin. The easiest way to do this is to slice it across the middle like a hot dog bun, stopping about ½ inch (1.3 cm) from cutting all the way through. Next, pile on the stuffing and close up the loin using the butcher's string. Tie it up every 2 inches (5 cm). Lightly coat the entire tenderloin with olive oil. Season with salt and pepper.

Place the pork in the smoker and cook until the internal temperature of the pork reaches 145°F (63°C). Start checking the temperature after 30 minutes. When the desired internal temperature has been reached, remove the tenderloin and rest for 10 minutes.

Slice the pork into ½- to ¾-inch (1.3- to 2-cm) slices.

> NOTE: You can prepare this ahead of time, like the day before. Wrap the uncooked tenderloin tightly—stuffed, coated with oil and seasoned—in plastic wrap and keep it in the fridge overnight until you are ready to cook it.

STUFFING

1 (10-oz [283-g]) package frozen spinach, thawed and squeezed dry

½ cup (57 g) shredded extra-sharp cheddar cheese

½ lb (227 g) chorizo, crumbled

3 cloves garlic, minced

Salt and pepper

TENDERLOIN

1 (4-lb [1.8-kg]) pork tenderloin roast

Butcher's string

2 tbsp (30 ml) extra-virgin olive oil

Salt and pepper

HOLIDAY HAM

One of the things I love about the holiday season is that someone in my family will be cooking ham. Think of that aroma. The holidays are just not the holidays without that aroma! I love the saltiness of the ham mixed with the sweetness of the glaze. For the holidays, I like to use a ready-to-cook ham. That means the ham has already been cured, is partially cooked, and all you have to do is finish cooking it to 160°F (71°C). This makes preparation much simpler, and you can still add your favorite seasonings and a little bit of smoke flavor to help make for a memorable holiday gathering.

COOK TIME:
approximately
2¼ hours. Typical low-and-slow cooking time is about 4 to 5 hours at 250°F (130°C)

YIELD:
10 to 12 servings

3–4 chunks apple wood

1 (6-lb [2.7-kg]) ready-to-cook ham

½ cup (120 ml) pure maple syrup, not the fake stuff

Everyday/Everything Rub (page 120), enough to coat the ham

Simply Delicious Ham Glaze (page 35), enough to coat the ham a few times, plus extra for serving

Heavy-duty aluminum foil

Set up your WSM and let it heat up to 325 to 350°F (163 to 177°C). Use an empty water pan lined with foil for easy cleanup. You will need one fully lit chimney and one unlit chimney of charcoal. Add the fully lit chimney of coal, add the unlit on top of that, wait 10 minutes and then reassemble the WSM. Add your smoke wood at the same time you put the ham on the smoker.

When you remove the ham out of its packaging, it'll probably have a thin jelly-like layer on it. Run the ham under cold water to rinse off the jelly, and pat it dry with a paper towel.

Score the fat with the traditional diamond/checkerboard pattern you normally see with hams. Not only will this look great after it's cooked, but it also helps with rendering the fat during the cooking process. To form the pattern, use a paring knife to cut lines ¼ inch (6 mm) deep and about 1 inch (2.5 cm) apart across the surface of the ham. Rotate the ham 90 degrees and slice it again, creating perpendicular lines to the cuts you just made.

Carefully pour the maple syrup over the ham and coat evenly with a brush. Season the ham lightly all over with the rub. Then let the ham sit out on the counter for about 30 minutes.

Place the ham on the top rack of the cooker, and cook until the ham reaches an internal temperature of 155°F (68°C). This will probably take 1 to 1½ hours.

When the ham reaches the correct internal temperature, use a brush to apply a layer of glaze to the surface of the ham. Repeat the glazing every 15 minutes, until the ham reaches an internal temperature of 160°F (71°C), which should take 30 to 45 minutes.

When the ham reaches an internal temperature of 160°F (71°C), remove it from the cooker and let it rest, loosely tented with aluminum foil, for 20 to 30 minutes.

Slice the ham and serve it with the extra ham glaze.

SIMPLY DELICIOUS HAM GLAZE

What's a holiday ham without a glaze? I'm not talking about the little packet that comes with a previously cooked ham either. I'm talking about making your own, and I think you're going to love this glaze! There is no salt in this recipe. The glaze doesn't need any because of the salt content in the ham. What I like about this glaze is that the sweetness of the honey, the savory background flavor of the mustard and the subtle hint of heat from the chipotle all come together to make this a perfectly balanced glaze for your holiday ham.

COOK TIME:
10 minutes

YIELD:
about 2 cups (480 ml)

In a medium-sized saucepan, heat up the vinegar to a boil and then add the brown sugar, stirring until the sugar is dissolved.

Remove the pan from the heat. Add the honey, pineapple juice, mustard and chipotle powder. Mix it well.

Return the pan to a medium-low heat and simmer for about 15 minutes.

1 cup (240 ml) cider vinegar

½ lb (227 g) dark brown sugar

½ cup (120 ml) honey

¼ cup (60 ml) pineapple juice

2 tbsp (30 ml) Dijon mustard

¼ tsp chipotle powder

HAM PIE

I think the first time I had this unbelievable masterpiece was in 2015 at the Triple Threat BBQ contest in Harrington, Delaware. Mike Sadgwar from Pigheaded BBQ had made a couple of these ham pies and asked if I wanted some. Of course I said yes . . . and OH MY GOD! It was ridiculously delicious! The buttery crust and the saltiness of the meats, along with the nuttiness of the Parmesan and other creamy, melted cheeses atop the pie, took me on a flavor ride you have to experience for yourself. So, a big thank you goes to Mike for allowing me to share his recipe with all of you!

COOK TIME:
1 to 1½ hours

YIELD:
8 servings

Use a nonstick 9-inch (23-cm) springform pan, commonly used for baking. If you are not using a nonstick pan, spray the pan with cooking spray.

For the crust, in a large mixing bowl, sift together the flour, salt and garlic powder. Mix in the Parmesan and Italian seasoning. Add the butter and mix the dough with your hands until it becomes crumbly. Gradually add the water until the dough forms a ball.

Take a handful of the dough and roll it out in a large round piece, large enough to fit into the springform pan, fitted all around the bottom, up the sides and with about a ½ inch (1.3 cm) overlapping the top of the pan.

Starting with the mozzarella and provolone, arrange the cheeses in one layer over the dough at the bottom of the pan. Then arrange the prosciutto, capicola and salami in one layer on top of the cheese.

Roll out another thin layer of dough. This layer will cover all the meats and cheeses. Stop at the side of the pan; do not overlap the sides.

Add another layer of cheeses and meats, and then another layer of dough. Repeat this, creating layers to fill up the pan. There should be at least three layers of meats and cheeses when you are finished.

Top it off with a thin layer of dough, this time with a little extra on the sides to meet the overlapping dough from the base piece. Pinch the dough together and roll it over to form an even crust all around the edge. Press the crust with a fork all around the edges.

Brush the top of the crust with a light layer of olive oil, Parmesan cheese and parsley.

Cook the pie at 350°F (177°C) for 1 to 1½ hours or until the Parmesan cheese on top is browned. Start checking for doneness after 1 hour.

Rest the pie for 10 minutes.

CRUST (YOU WILL HAVE EXTRA LEFT OVER)

6 cups (750 g) all-purpose flour

2 tsp (12 g) salt

3 tsp (8 g) garlic powder

1 cup (100 g) grated Parmesan cheese

2 tsp (1 g) Italian seasoning

2 cups (454 g) butter, softened

7–8 tbsp (105–120 ml) water

DELI CHEESES AND MEATS

1 lb (454 g) mozzarella, sliced thin

1 lb (454 g) provolone, sliced thin

1 lb (454 g) prosciutto, sliced thin

1 lb (454 g) capicola, sliced thin

1 lb (454 g) Genoa salami, sliced thin

TOPPING

Olive oil, to coat the dough

Parmesan cheese

1 tsp parsley

3

HOT SMOKED BEEF *and* LAMB

Compared to most other proteins, I think beef handles the high-heat cooking process best. Using the hot-and-fast cooking method, you're able to form a flavorful and crunchy crust on the surface of the meat—more so than when you cook at lower temperatures.

I think beef pairs best with a nut wood, such as hickory, oak or pecan. Beef has a robust taste that works well with a seasoning mix as simple as salt, pepper and garlic. Beef also handles salt well. With the exception of brisket and chuck roast, I prefer to cook beef medium-rare to medium. If you overcook steak—or worse, prime rib—to anything past medium, then I think you're doing the protein an injustice.

I enjoy beef with a hearty root vegetable, like potato, and my favorite meal just might be prime rib with red bliss garlic mashed potatoes and green beans. I also like that I can cook the entire meal in about an hour. After you work your way through the recipes in this chapter, I have a hunch you'll be able to cook your favorite beef dish, just the way you like it, in an hour or so too.

SIDE NOTE: **The FDA recommends that beef or lamb is cooked to an internal temperature of 145°F (63°C) and ground meat to 165°F (74°C).**

FINISHED RESULT	TEMPERATURE
Rare	120–125°F (49–52°C)
Medium-Rare	130–135°F (54–57°C)
Medium	140–145°F (60–63°C)
Medium-Well	150–155°F (66–68°C)
Well-Done	160–165°F (71–74°C)

TEXAS-STYLE S&P BRISKET IN 4½ HOURS

When I first started cooking at barbecue contests, I learned how to cook brisket using the hot-and-fast cooking method. I had cooked a couple of the briskets using the traditional low-and-slow method, but I couldn't quite get the consistency I liked until I started using the hot-and-fast method. This is a great method for cooking briskets, not only because it takes less time, but also because the end results are moist and fantastic each and every time.

COOK TIME:
4 to 4½ hours. Brisket normally takes 12 to 14 hours when cooking with the traditional low-and-slow method.

YIELD:
10 to 12 servings

For the brisket rub, in a small bowl, mix together the salt, pepper and garlic powder.

For the brisket, cut off all the loose fat over the flat surface, and trim the fat all around the point down to about ¼ inch (6 mm) in thickness. Here's how to do that:

Start by trimming a long, thin section off each side to square off your brisket. Flip the brisket over, and you will see the entire fat cap. There will be a big chunk of fat on the point. Cut that off. Using a sharp knife, start from the top and lift up while you slide your knife in between the brisket and the fat. Work your knife back and forth while simultaneously lifting the fat piece with your hand. Now, use your knife to remove any of that thick, shiny-looking skin, known as silver skin, as well as any remaining large fatty pieces.

Apply the brisket rub liberally all over the brisket. Place the brisket in the fridge for 2 hours up to overnight. Remove the brisket from the fridge 15 to 30 minutes before you put it on the cooker.

Set up your cooker for the hot-and-fast cooking method at 350°F (177°C). You will need one fully lit chimney of charcoal and two unlit chimneys. Dump one of the unlit chimneys into the center of the charcoal ring, add the fully lit chimney and then add the second unlit chimney on top of that. Let it sit for 10 to 15 minutes, and then reassemble the WSM.

Place the oak wood on top of the charcoal, and then put the brisket on the top rack of the WSM with the fat cap pointing down. Cook for 2 to 2½ hours, or until the brisket reaches an internal temperature of 170°F (77°C).

Lay out two pieces of butcher paper, one atop the other, and make certain each piece is large enough to completely wrap the brisket. When the desired internal temperature of the brisket is reached, remove the brisket from the cooker and place it on top of the butcher paper. Tightly wrap the brisket in the first piece of butcher paper. Rotate the wrapped brisket 90 degrees, and tightly wrap the brisket using the second piece of butcher paper. Rotating the brisket helps provide a better seal along the edges.

(continued)

BRISKET RUB
¼ cup (72 g) kosher salt

¼ cup (25 g) coarse black pepper

¼ cup (34 g) garlic powder

BRISKET
1 (10–12-lb [4.5–5.4-kg]) brisket (see Notes)

2 fist-sized chunks oak wood

Butcher paper, for wrapping

Once wrapped, place the brisket back on the cooker, fat cap down, and cook for an additional 1½ to 2½ hours until the internal temperature reaches 200°F (93°C) in the flat part and 205 to 210°F (96 to 99°C) in the point. The probe should easily go into the brisket like a knife cutting through warm butter. When that happens, the brisket is done.

Remove the brisket from the cooker. Open the butcher paper and steam down—letting the steam escape—for 10 minutes. This will allow the brisket to stop cooking.

Wrap the brisket back up in the same butcher paper. Place it in an empty cooler, cover it with old but clean towels and rest the brisket for 1 hour. By using the cooler this way, it acts as an insulator and the brisket remains hot.

One of my favorite parts of this process is that some of the slices will have both the flat and the point parts. The flat is leaner, and the point is a little fattier and juicer.

Remove the brisket from the cooler. Unwrap and slice the entire brisket into ¼- to ½-inch (6-mm to 1.3-cm) slices.

Serve the brisket slices with any side of your choice. I like cornbread and beans! Or you could make delicious sandwiches served on a bulky roll with a little slaw and BBQ sauce.

NOTES: If you are using a larger brisket, extend the cooking time.

Catching the grease drippings greatly helps with cleanup when you are done. Line the water pan with some heavy-duty aluminum foil, or you can wrap the bottom grate with foil and place an empty disposable pan on top of the foiled grate.

When cooking at a higher temperature, you are able to bring the meat's internal temperature higher without fear of overcooking. Collagen needs time to break down to form gelatin, which is what creates a nice, tender brisket when cooking low and slow. Cooking at a higher temperature allows you to bring the meat to a higher internal temperature because the brisket can't "sweat" itself cool. The higher temperature will break down collagen faster than a lower temperature would.

The great thing about cooking hot-and-fast brisket is that you can start it at noon and have it ready for dinner.

CHUCK ROAST STREET TACOS

If you want an absolute flavor bomb and a renewed vision on street tacos, then look no further, mis amigos y amigas! These tacos are going to take you on the flavor trip of your dreams! The flavors from the rub mixed with subtle smoke and the super-rich sauce are balanced out by the onion, cilantro, cheese and lime, making for a true flavor ride you won't want to stop!

COOK TIME:
3½ hours. Typical low and slow is at least 6 hours.

YIELD:
12 tacos

For the rub, in a small bowl, mix together the salt, chili powder, paprika, pepper, garlic powder and cumin. Set it aside. Save 2 tablespoons (20 g) for the braise.

For the braise, in a medium bowl, mix together the beef stock, tomato paste, chipotles, adobo sauce and 2 tablespoons (20 g) of the rub.

Coat the outside of the chuck roast with olive oil, season it with the rub and let it sit for 30 minutes.

In the meantime, fire up the WSM to 350°F (177°C) using a foil-lined water pan. You will need one full chimney of lit charcoal and one full chimney of unlit charcoal. Dump the lit charcoal into the fire ring and top it off with the unlit charcoal. Let it sit for 10 minutes, and then reassemble the WSM.

Place the roast in a disposable aluminum half pan, then place the pan on the top cooking rack. Add the smoke wood on top of the lit charcoal.

Cook the roast until it reaches an internal temperature of 170 to 175°F (77 to 79°C), about 2 hours.

Remove the chuck roast from the smoker. Cut it into four smaller chunks, and place them back in the pan with the braising liquid. Cover the pan with heavy-duty aluminum foil, and cook it to an internal temperature of 210°F (99°C), about 1½ hours.

(continued)

RUB
2 tbsp (36 g) kosher salt

2 tbsp (15 g) chili powder

2 tbsp (14 g) smoked paprika

1 tbsp (6 g) coarse black pepper

1 tbsp (8 g) garlic powder

1 tbsp (6 g) cumin

BRAISE
1½ cups (360 ml) beef stock

1 (6-oz [170-g]) can tomato paste

1–2 chipotles, finely diced (if you like it spicy, use two)

2 tbsp (30 ml) adobo sauce, from canned chipotles

ROAST
3 lb (1.4 kg) chuck roast

Olive oil

Disposable aluminum half pan

2 chunks apple wood

Heavy-duty aluminum foil

12 (4" [10-cm]) soft corn tortillas

1 large sweet onion, diced

1 bunch cilantro, chopped

8 oz (227 g) Cotija cheese or feta, crumbled

3–4 limes, cut into wedges

CHUCK ROAST STREET TACOS (CONTINUED)

Once the meat reaches the correct internal temperature, remove it from the cooker. Let it rest for 20 minutes.

Shred the beef, and mix in half of the braising liquid from the pan.

With the remaining half of the liquid, brush one side of the tortillas and place them on the cooker for 5 minutes.

Remove the tortillas from the cooker. Assemble the tacos with the shredded beef and garnish with onion, cilantro, Cotija cheese, a squeeze of lime and a drizzle of the extra sauce. *Disfruten del paseo de comida, mis amigos y amigas!*

NOTES: Cooking the chuck roast in a pan allows you to retain all the meat juices. This will be important later on as we add those juices back into the shredded beef.

As mentioned in other recipes, when cooking low and slow the internal temperature you're trying to achieve is lower. When cooking hot and fast, you are able to bring the internal temperature of the meat higher without fear of overcooking the meat. Collagen needs time to break down to form gelatin, which is what creates a nice, tender brisket when cooking low and slow. Cooking at a higher temperature allows you to bring the internal temperature higher because the brisket can't "sweat" itself cool, and the higher temperature will break down that collagen faster than a lower temperature would.

MONSTER BEEF SHORT RIBS

Delicious, incredibly rich and tasty smoked beef ribs are a pretty hot item these days in most BBQ joints. The short ribs, also called plate ribs, aren't really so short. It's kind of an oxymoron, like jumbo shrimp! They come from the short plate of the cow. They have a lot of meat on them, as well as a ton of marbling, meaning they will be very juicy and tender when cooked right. These would take upward of 8 to 9 hours to cook using the traditional low-and-slow method, but I'm going to speed this up for you and have them done in half the time and just as tasty!

COOK TIME:
approximately 4 hours

YIELD:
4 bones, enough for four hungry people or eight normal people, LOL!

Set up your WSM cooker for hot-and-fast cooking at 350°F (177°C). You will need one fully lit chimney of charcoal and two unlit chimneys. Dump one of the unlit chimneys into the center of the charcoal ring, add the fully lit chimney and then add the second unlit chimney on top of that. Let it sit for 10 to 15 minutes, and then reassemble the WSM.

For the seasoning, in a small bowl, mix together the salt, pepper, garlic powder and chili powder.

Brush the meat side of the short ribs with olive oil and generously season with the seasoning. Place the short ribs on the top cooking grate, add your smoke wood and cook until the internal temperature reaches 165 to 170°F (74 to 77°C), about 2½ hours.

Lay out three sheets of butcher paper, each one big enough to wrap the short ribs. Once the internal temperature has been reached, remove the short ribs from the WSM and wrap them in the three sheets of butcher paper, one sheet at a time.

Place the short ribs back on the top cooking grate and cook them until the internal temperature reaches 200°F (93°F), about 1½ hours.

Remove the short ribs, and allow them to rest for about 15 minutes.

NOTE: You know they are tender if you can probe them and it feels like the probe is going into soft butter.

SEASONING

2 tbsp (36 g) kosher salt

2 tbsp (13 g) coarse black pepper

2 tbsp (17 g) garlic powder

2 tbsp (15 g) chili powder

1 (4-rib, 6-lb [2.7-kg]) rack beef plate short ribs

¼ cup (60 ml) olive oil

3 chunks hickory wood

Butcher paper, for wrapping

SMOKED BEEF BRACIOLE ROLL

A classic homestyle Italian dish, the braciole roll is a thinly pounded-out flank steak that's stuffed with cheeses, breadcrumbs and Italian herbs. Then, it's seared off and set to braise in tomato sauce for hours, creating a rich, hearty and delicious meal. Well, here I am going to put a little BBQ twist on this traditional dish and introduce a little smoke flavor, just a little something I know you will like.

COOK TIME:
1½ hours

YIELD:
4 servings

For the stuffing, in a medium bowl, mix together the Pecorino Romano, breadcrumbs, Parmesan, provolone, basil, parsley, garlic and ½ cup (120 ml) of olive oil. Set it aside.

For the tomato sauce, in a medium bowl, mix together the tomatoes, salt and pepper, oregano, basil and garlic. Set it aside. Also set out a disposable aluminum pan.

Place the flank steak between two pieces of plastic wrap, and, with a meat mallet, pound the steak until it's about ¼ inch (6 mm) thick.

Brush some of the remaining olive oil on one side of the pounded flank steak and season with salt and pepper. Lay the prosciutto on the seasoned flank steak.

Spread the stuffing on top of the prosciutto, making sure it's completely covered.

Starting at one end, carefully roll the flank steak into a log, making sure to tuck in the ends and tie it up with butcher's string every 1 to 2 inches (2.5 to 5 cm).

Brush the outside of the rolled steak with the remaining olive oil and season the outside with salt and pepper. Set it aside until you are ready to put it on the smoker.

Fire up the WSM to 350 to 375°F (177 to 191°C) using a foil-lined water pan. Start with one fully lit chimney in the charcoal ring, then top it off with one-half of an unlit chimney. Let it sit for 10 minutes, and then reassemble the WSM.

Pour the tomato sauce in the disposable aluminum pan, and place it on the bottom cooking grate. Place the rolled flank steak on the top grate, and cook to an internal temperature of 145°F (63°C) for about 1 hour.

Once the desired internal temperature is reached, remove the rolled steak from the top cooking grate, and place it in the pan with the sauce. Cover the pan with heavy-duty foil, place it on the top grate and cook for 30 minutes.

Remove the pan from the smoker and let it sit for 10 minutes.

Slice the braciole into ½-inch (1.3-cm) pieces, and serve with the pasta, sauce and some extra cheese.

STUFFING

¼ cup (25 g) shredded Pecorino Romano cheese, plus more for serving

¼ cup (27 g) breadcrumbs

¼ cup (25 g) grated Parmesan cheese

¼ cup (33 g) shredded provolone cheese

1 tbsp (3 g) fresh basil, chopped

1 tbsp (4 g) fresh Italian parsley, chopped

4 cloves garlic, minced

¾ cup (180 ml) olive oil, divided

TOMATO SAUCE

1 (28-oz [794-g]) can crushed tomatoes

Salt and pepper, to taste

1 tbsp (3 g) dried oregano

8 basil leaves, finely chopped

2 cloves garlic, minced

Disposable aluminum half pan

STEAK

1 (2-lb [908-g]) flank steak

Plastic wrap

Kosher salt

Freshly ground black pepper

4 to 6 slices prosciutto, thin

Butcher's string

Heavy-duty aluminum foil

1 lb (454 g) cooked spaghetti

KOREAN SHORT RIBS

I remember the first time I had Korean short ribs. They were so tender and exploded with flavor. I was like "Woah . . . What just happened?" Seriously, I could not stop eating them! It became a quest to try to replicate them. I think this is darn close, if not better, in my opinion. I hope you think so too!

COOK TIME:
15 minutes

YIELD:
8 servings

For the marinade, in a medium bowl, combine the soy sauce, brown sugar, sesame oil, rice wine vinegar, ginger paste, garlic, garlic paste and red pepper flakes. Mix it well, and then pour it into a gallon-sized (3.8-L) resealable plastic bag. Add the short ribs, seal the bag and allow the ribs to marinate in the fridge for at least 4 hours, but overnight is best, making sure to flip the bag often.

Fire up your WSM to 400°F (204°C), using one fully lit chimney of charcoal. Remove the water pan from the smoker. For this recipe, you will cook on the bottom cooking grate.

Remove the short ribs from the bag. Place them on the lower cooking grate and cook the ribs for 7½ minutes. Flip the short ribs, and cook for 7½ minutes.

Remove the short ribs from the smoker. Sprinkle them with sesame seeds, then garnish them with chopped green onions and serve with white rice.

NOTES: Flanken is a short cut, usually about ½ inch (1.3 cm) thick. The cut goes across the short ribs, and each slice of meat contains a few pieces of bone.

You are looking to form a little char on the ribs. Start checking the ribs after 7 minutes and leave on longer if needed.

You can save the marinating liquid and use it as a sauce too. Per the FDA, you will need to boil the liquid and bring it to 165°F (74°C) to kill off any of the bacteria from the raw meat.

MARINADE

1 cup (240 ml) soy sauce

1 cup (220 g) brown sugar

¼ cup (60 ml) sesame oil

½ cup (120 ml) rice wine vinegar

¼ cup (66 g) ginger paste

4 cloves garlic, minced

1 tbsp (15 g) chili garlic paste

1 tsp red pepper flakes

4 lb (1.8 kg) flanken short ribs (see Notes)

Sesame seeds, for garnish

Green onions, for garnish

White rice, cooked, to serve

TRI-TIP SANDWICH

Out here on the East Coast, especially in the Boston area, we have some of the best roast beef sandwiches in the country. These sandwiches are usually made up of thinly sliced beef served on a big, delicious onion roll with sauce and cheese. I'm telling you, when you are here you have to try one! For this recipe, I want to take that sandwich and use tri-tip. Some people may not have had tri-tip, and if you haven't, you are missing out. Tri-tip is a triangular cut of meat from the bottom sirloin. It looks like a steak, slices like brisket and has the flavor and tender chew of sirloin. Thinly sliced, tri-tip makes for a phenomenal sandwich, especially one with sautéed onions and melted cheese!

COOK TIME:
approximately 45 minutes

YIELD:
6 servings

For the paste, in a small bowl, mix together the olive oil, salt, pepper, garlic powder, onion powder, paprika and rosemary. It will form a paste. Store it in the fridge until you are ready to use it. This can be made the day before you cook.

For the Garlic Aioli, in a medium bowl, mix together the garlic paste, olive oil, mayo, lemon juice, Worcestershire sauce, chili powder, salt and pepper. Store it in the fridge until you are ready to use it.

Fire up the WSM for high-heat cooking to 375°F (191°C). You won't be using the water pan, so you can leave it out. One fully lit chimney of hot coals will be sufficient for this recipe.

About an hour before you are ready to cook, remove the tri-tip from the fridge and cover it with the paste. Wrap the tri-tip in plastic wrap, and let it sit on the counter for 1 hour.

Remove the tri-tip from the plastic wrap, place it on the bottom rack of the WSM for 5 minutes and then flip it over and cook it for 5 minutes. Place the tri-tip on the top rack and continue cooking it until the desired doneness: 120 to 125°F (49 to 52°C) for rare, 130 to 135°F (54 to 57°C) for medium rare. This should take approximately 30 minutes, depending on the thickness of the tri-tip and how you like it cooked.

When the meat reaches the correct internal temperature, remove it from the smoker and allow it to rest for about 10 minutes.

While the meat is resting, slice the rolls in half, butter each half and place them on the bottom grate for 3 to 4 minutes, until they are nice and toasty. Remove them from the WSM and set aside.

It's time to assemble the sandwich.

Slice the tri-tip very thinly, about ⅛ inch (3 mm) thick. Spread the Garlic Aioli on both halves of the toasted rolls, then lay four to six slices of tri-tip on one side of each sandwich, making sure each sandwich gets the same amount of meat. Add ¼ cup (70 g) of the sautéed onions on one side of each sandwich, and top it with two slices of cheese. Place the "loaded" half of the sandwiches on the top cooking grate, and cook for 3 to 5 minutes to melt the cheese. Remove them and place the top of the roll onto each sandwich.

PASTE

2 tbsp (30 ml) olive oil

1 tbsp (18 g) kosher salt

1 tbsp (6 g) coarse black pepper

1½ tsp (4 g) garlic powder

1½ tsp (4 g) onion powder

2 tsp (4 g) smoked paprika

2 tsp (1 g) finely chopped fresh rosemary

GARLIC AIOLI

¼ cup (66 g) garlic paste

2 tsp (10 ml) olive oil

½ cup (120 ml) mayo

Juice from half a lemon

1 tsp Worcestershire sauce

½ tsp chili powder

Salt and pepper, to taste

1 (2-lb [908-g]) tri-tip roast

6 onion rolls, toasted

1 stick (½ cup [114 g]) softened butter

2 cups (420 g) sautéed sweet red onion

12 slices sharp cheddar cheese

BEEF TENDERLOIN WITH FRESH HORSERADISH

COOK TIME:
35 to 45 minutes

YIELD:
9 to 12 servings, about ⅓ lb (151 g) per person

Tenderloin is probably everyone's favorite cut of beef because it is so tender and melts in your mouth when properly cooked. This is a popular dish to serve around the holidays as well, but this time we're kicking it up a little: We are coating the entire outside with fresh horseradish. I can see all you horseradish lovers out there salivating over this, and I assure you, this dish will not disappoint.

1 cup (240 ml) good red wine

For the red wine reduction, in a small saucepan, add 1 cup (240 ml) of a good red wine that you would drink. Heat on medium-high until it reduces to about ½ cup (120 ml). This should take approximately 15 minutes. Set it aside.

For the Horseradish Rub, in a small bowl, combine the horseradish, black pepper, garlic and salt. Set it aside.

For the Red Wine Sauce, in a small bowl, mix together the Worcestershire sauce and the red wine reduction. Set it aside.

Fire up your WSM to 400°F (204°C). Remove the water pan and place an empty disposable aluminum half pan on the bottom grate. You will need about one fully lit chimney and about a half of an unlit chimney of charcoal. Dump the lit coal into the fire ring and add the unlit charcoal to it. Let sit for about 15 minutes, and then reassemble the WSM. All the vents should be fully open.

Rub the Dijon mustard onto the tenderloin. Press the Horseradish Rub mixture all over the mustard-covered tenderloin. You may have to roll the tenderloin a couple times to get it all to stick.

Roast the tenderloin for 35 to 40 minutes for rare, which is 120 to 125°F (49 to 52°C) on an instant-read thermometer. For medium-rare, roast the tenderloin for 40 to 45 minutes, which is 130 to 135°F (54 to 57°C) on an instant-read thermometer.

Remove the tenderloin from the WSM and allow it to rest for 15 minutes before slicing. Drizzle the slices with the Red Wine Sauce.

HORSERADISH RUB

½ lb (227 g) fresh horseradish, peeled and grated, about 1½ cups

1½ tsp (3 g) finely ground black pepper

2 tbsp (17 g) chopped garlic

1 tbsp (18 g) coarse salt

RED WINE SAUCE

½ cup (120 ml) Worcestershire sauce

½ cup (120 ml) red wine reduction

Disposable aluminum half pan

¼ cup (60 ml) Dijon mustard

1 (3–4-lb [1.4–1.8-kg]) beef tenderloin, trimmed

> **NOTE:** Fresh horseradish is available in most supermarkets, usually in the produce section. To prepare the horseradish, peel the outer skin using a vegetable peeler. Shred it using the coarse side of a box grater, and then pulse it in a food processor just to break it up a little more. Be careful, because your eyes are definitely going to tear up from the potency of the fresh horseradish.

PRIME RIB, "CLOSED OVEN" METHOD

For me, prime rib is the ultimate holiday meal. The tender meat, the buttery fat and all those drippings turn into a rich brown gravy to dunk each piece into! Oh yeah, how I love that holiday heaven! For this recipe, I am going to show you the "closed oven" method of cooking a prime rib. What's nice about this method is that it's faster than the traditional way and just as delicious. Welcome to beef heaven!

For the Herb Butter, in a small bowl, mix together the butter, parsley, garlic, oregano and pepper. Store it in the fridge until you are ready to use it.

Fire up the WSM to 450°F (232°C). You will most likely need about two fully lit chimneys to achieve this. Remove the water pan and place a disposable half pan on the bottom cooking grate.

Remove the prime rib from the fridge about 1 hour before you want to cook it. The reason is if your roast is cold in the center, it will make it hard to cook evenly. Place the ribeye in the disposable half pan, and then cover the entire roast with the Herb Butter. Season the prime rib liberally with kosher salt, and let it sit on the counter until you are ready to put it on the smoker.

Place a temperature probe into the center of the prime rib. Place the prime rib on the top cooking grate, and follow the "closed oven" method below.

"CLOSED-OVEN" METHOD

Basically, you'll be cooking at around 450°F (232°C) for 5 minutes per pound (454 g) for the weight of the roast. In this case, the prime rib weighs 8 pounds (3.6 kg), so at 5 minutes per pound (454 g) we are looking at a 40-minute cook time with the vents open. After the 40 minutes, shut all four vents and let the roast sit there until it reaches a temperature of 130°F (54°C). This could take anywhere from 1 to 2 hours. When the prime rib reaches 130°F (54°C), remove it from the smoker. Allow it to rest for 30 minutes, loosely tented with foil. After the 30 minutes, your roast should be down to 125°F (52°C). It's then ready to slice.

> NOTE: If you're looking for more of a medium finished temperature, bring the meat to 135°F (57°C).

COOK TIME:
1 to 3 hours, depending on the size of your prime rib

YIELD:
8 to 10 servings

HERB BUTTER
1 cup (227 g) softened butter, such as Land O' Lakes butter spread

¼ cup (15 g) fresh chopped parsley

2 tbsp (17 g) minced garlic

1 tbsp (15 g) fresh chopped oregano

1 tsp black pepper

ROAST
Disposable aluminum half pan

1 (8-lb [3.6-kg]) ribeye roast, boneless

Kosher salt

MEATLOAF WITH CRUSHED PORK RINDS

Meatloaf is a fantastic and delicious dish cooked on the smoker, and even more so using crushed pork rinds instead of crackers or breadcrumbs. That salty pork flavor is going to make you wish you had been cooking meatloaf this way all along!

COOK TIME:
approximately
75 minutes

YIELD:
6 servings

Grease a 9 x 5-inch (23 x 13-cm) loaf pan.

For the meatloaf, in a large bowl, mix together the ground beef, ground pork, eggs, milk, onion, garlic, pork rinds, salt and pepper. Place the meat mixture in the prepared loaf pan.

Heat up the WSM to 375°F (191°C) with an empty, foil-lined water pan for easy cleanup. Use a full chimney of lit charcoal and dump the hot coals into the charcoal ring. Dump another half chimney of unlit charcoal over the lit coals. Wait 10 minutes, then reassemble the cooker.

For the meatloaf glaze, in a small bowl mix together the ketchup, brown sugar, chili powder, Worcestershire sauce, salt and garlic. Spread the glaze on top of the meatloaf and place it on the top rack of the WSM. Cook the meatloaf until the internal temperature reaches 135°F (57°C), about 60 minutes. At this point, cover the meatloaf with the foil and cook until it reaches 150°F (65°C), about 15 minutes.

Remove the meatloaf from the WSM and allow it to rest for about 15 minutes before carefully removing it from the pan.

> **NOTE:** The FDA recommends cooking ground beef to 160°F (71°C); however, this recipe only takes it to a 150°F (65°C) internal temperature. I feel any higher than that and you run the risk of drying it out. If you feel safer bringing it to 160°F (71°C), then by all means do so, but don't say I didn't warn you about dry meatloaf.

MEATLOAF

1½ lb (681 g) ground beef, 85/15 meat-to-fat ratio

1½ lb (681 g) ground pork

2 eggs

¼ cup (60 ml) milk

¼ cup (40 g) chopped onion

3 cloves garlic, minced

1 cup (85 g) crushed pork rinds

1 tbsp (18 g) kosher salt

½ tsp black pepper

MEATLOAF GLAZE

½ cup (120 ml) ketchup

¼ cup (55 g) light brown sugar

1 tbsp (8 g) chili powder

1 tbsp (15 ml) Worcestershire sauce

1 tsp kosher salt

1 tsp granulated garlic

Heavy-duty aluminum foil

MEDITERRANEAN MARINATED RACK OF LAMB

COOK TIME:
30 to 45 minutes

YIELD:
4 servings

Lamb is a great dish to serve around the Easter holiday, along with other favorites, such as glazed ham and roast pork. Lamb is a very lean meat, and I recommend not cooking it past medium, 135°F (57°C). This will ensure you get juicy, tender lamb every time. This recipe has bold flavors, such as garlic, rosemary and thyme, to help cut through the gaminess of lamb.

In a medium bowl, mix together the olive oil, lemon juice, orange juice, Worcestershire sauce, garlic, oregano, rosemary, thyme, salt and pepper. Pour the mixture into the resealable plastic bag. Place the rack of lamb in the bag. Remove all the air from the bag, seal it and place it in the fridge for at least 4 hours; overnight is best.

Heat up your WSM to approximately 375°F (191°C), using an empty water pan, lined with heavy-duty aluminum foil for easy cleanup. One fully lit chimney of charcoal will do the trick for this cook. Just dump it right in the center of the charcoal ring, and reassemble the cooker.

Remove the lamb from the fridge 20 to 30 minutes before cooking.

Place the lamb on the top cooking grate. Cook it until the internal temperature reaches 135°F (57°C), 30 to 45 minutes. Remember, lamb is delicate, and you don't want it to overcook. Start checking the internal temperature of the meat at the 30-minute mark.

When the meat reaches the internal temperature, remove it from the cooker and allow it to rest for 10 minutes.

½ cup (120 ml) olive oil

¼ cup (60 ml) lemon juice

¼ cup (60 ml) orange juice

¼ cup (60 ml) Worcestershire sauce

4 cloves garlic, minced

1 tbsp (1 g) finely chopped fresh oregano

1 tbsp (2 g) finely chopped fresh rosemary

1 tbsp (2 g) finely chopped fresh thyme

2 tsp (12 g) kosher salt

1 tsp coarse black pepper

1 (1-gallon [3.8-L]) resealable plastic bag

1 rack of lamb, 8 bones, trimmed (see Note)

> NOTE: "Trimmed" means the ends of the bones are clean. They usually come packaged this way. If not, your butcher can do this for you.

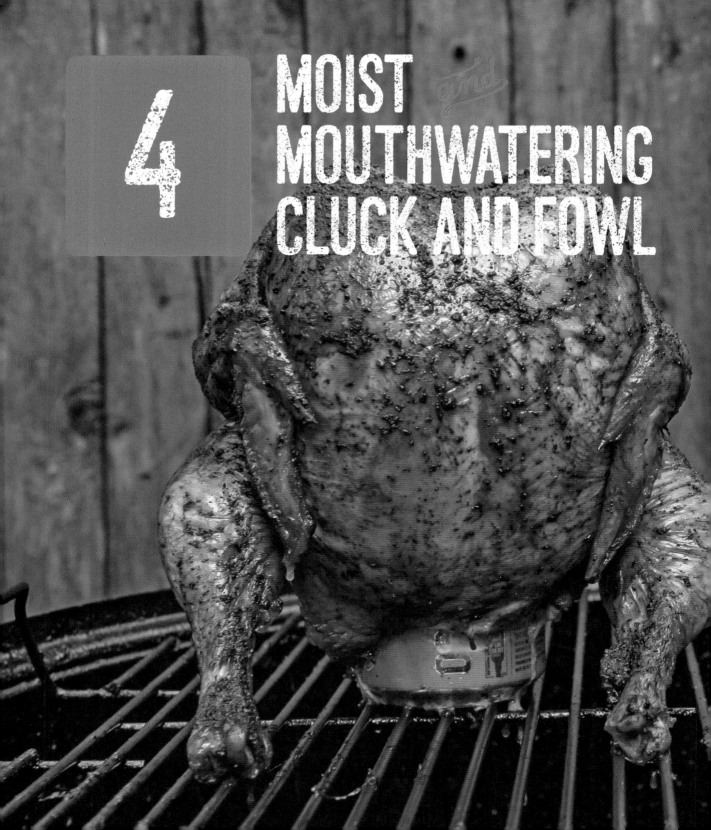

4

MOIST MOUTHWATERING CLUCK AND FOWL

Chicken is a versatile protein that handles the hot-and-fast cooking method well. It's somewhat bland, which makes it a joyful playground for experimenting with flavor. From fresh lemon and herbs in the bird's cavity as it cooks to mole, teriyaki or a sticky sweet barbecue glaze, you can play all kinds of games with the rubs, sauces and seasonings you use on chicken.

In contrast, turkey has a stronger, more distinct flavor. It's richer in flavor, even in the white meat areas of the bird. Turkey works well with a simple smoke wood and a light coating of a savory rub. When I think of turkey, I think of the holidays. You can feed more people with turkey, whereas chicken is better suited for smaller gatherings.

Cooking hot and fast is similar to cooking in your indoor oven. When you cook poultry hot and fast, you'll get a nice crispy skin, and the meat has a texture that's similar to what's produced when cooked in the oven. The hot-and-fast cooking method is my preferred method for cooking chicken wings. Take a bite of that crispy skin and I think you'll understand why!

SIDE NOTE: The FDA recommends that poultry (ground, parts or whole) is cooked to an internal temperature of 165°F (74°C).

WINGS

I love serving chicken wings at parties and tailgates. I also love ordering them out when watching football games and other sporting events. To me, chicken wings are the perfect party food, and when you wash them down with a cold beer, there's nothing better! There are so many different flavors to choose from that it can be really hard to pick just one. I don't want you to suffer with making this choice, so I am going to show you how to make a couple of my favorites: Buffalo-style and dry seasoned. I am also going to show you how to cook these so they come out crispy crunchy each and every time!

COOK TIME:
45 to 60 minutes. Traditional low-and-slow cooking can take upward of 2 to 2½ hours.

YIELD:
4 to 6 people

Set up your cooker for 375°F (177°C), removing the water pan. You will need one fully lit chimney. Dump it right in the center of the charcoal ring, and reassemble the cooker.

Set out a sheet pan large enough to hold the wings and line it with foil. Lay out the raw chicken wings and apply a light coating of salt and pepper to both sides of the wings. Place the wings in the fridge, uncovered, to set up. If you opt to leave the wings in the fridge overnight, then cover them with plastic wrap. Remove the wings from the fridge about 15 minutes before cooking.

Place the apple and peach wood on top of the charcoal. Cook the wings on the top section of the smoker. They will be high enough from the coal so that flare-ups won't be a problem.

Cook the wings until an internal temperature of 180°F (82°C) is reached. Start checking for the internal temperature after 45 minutes. Keep them on longer only if needed; just make sure the wings reach this internal temperature.

Set out a large bowl. When the wings are done, take them off the smoker and immediately place them in the bowl. Toss the wings with either the Hot Wing Sauce or the Dry Seasoning.

Serve the wings with ranch or blue cheese dressing, or if you are like me, eat them straight up.

(continued)

4 lb (1.8 kg) chicken wings, cut into flats and drumettes

Salt and pepper

1 chunk each apple and peach wood

Hot Wing Sauce (page 66) or Dry Seasoning (page 66)

NOTES: I like to use apple and peach wood when cooking wings because it provides a really nice sweet and mild smoke flavor on the wings.

One of the reasons I like cooking chicken wings this way is that I love the flavor that the fat dripping into the charcoal gives to the wings; it's really close to that grilled flavor. If you prefer not to cook this way because you do not like the flavor, then place an empty disposable aluminum pan on the bottom cooking grate to catch the drippings.

HOT WING SAUCE

I don't know about you but I get bored with the same old hot wing sauce, which is why I came up with this one. It's loaded with flavor, from the butter to the spices in the Italian dressing to the chili powder, plus that little extra kick from the chipotle to make you feel all warm inside. You're gonna want to put this on everything, not just wings!

YIELD:
1¾ cups (415 ml)

½ stick (57 g) of butter

1 cup (240 ml) Frank's hot sauce

1 clove garlic, minced

¼ cup (60 ml) Italian dressing

¼ cup (60 ml) honey

1 tbsp (8 g) chili powder

½ tsp chipotle powder

Salt and pepper, to taste

In a small saucepan, melt the butter on medium heat. Then stir in the hot sauce, garlic, Italian dressing, honey, chili powder and chipotle powder. Simmer the sauce for 5 minutes, and then add the salt and pepper.

DRY SEASONING

Every now and again I want a nice, well-balanced dry-seasoned wing, something with a little salt, a little sweet and a little savory: With this dry seasoning you get all three. The key to getting maximum flavor is to add the seasoning as soon as the wings come off the smoker. The heat from the freshly cooked wings will allow the seasoning to stick better, giving you the ultimate flavor.

YIELD:
¾ cup (175 g)

¼ cup (72 g) kosher salt

2 tbsp (30 g) granulated sugar

2 tbsp (28 g) brown sugar

1 tsp garlic powder

1 tsp onion powder

2 tsp (4 g) paprika

2 tsp (5 g) chili powder

In a small bowl, mix together the salt, granulated sugar, brown sugar, garlic powder, onion powder, paprika and chili powder. Store it in an airtight container until you're ready to use it.

FAST AND CRISPY CHICKEN QUARTERS

I can remember having chicken quarters when I was a kid. My mom would bake them in the oven, sometimes basically plain with just a little salt and pepper, and other times with the premade Shake 'n Bake seasoning mix. I personally loved chicken quarters with just salt and pepper. I remember as a kid I would peer through the oven window and watch the chicken quarters brown as they cooked. That brown, crispy skin was my favorite part! Who doesn't love crispy chicken skin? When you cook this chicken recipe using the hot-and-fast cooking method and bite into that nice crispy skin, for one brief moment you'll embrace a small part of my childhood.

COOK TIME:
approximately 1½ hours. These would take over 2½ hours if you used the low-and-slow method.

YIELD:
6 servings

6 chicken quarters, skin on

2 (1-gallon [3.8-L]) resealable bags

2 qt (1.9 L) Delicious All-Purpose Chicken Brine (page 68), divided

Coarse black pepper

1 fist-sized chunk apple wood

Sticky Sweet BBQ Sauce (page 121)

Using a sharp knife, trim any loose or hanging fat or skin from the chicken quarters. Place three chicken quarters into a plastic resealable bag and add 1 quart (960 ml) of the Delicious All-Purpose Chicken Brine. Using your hands, squeeze out all of the air from the bag, and seal it closed. Repeat this process for the three remaining chicken quarters. Place both bags in a pan, in case the bags leak, and place the pan in the fridge for 4 hours.

Prepare the WSM for 325 to 350°F (163 to 177°C). About one fully lit chimney and half of an unlit chimney should be enough charcoal. Dump the fully lit chimney into the charcoal ring, and then add the half chimney of unlit coals on top of the lit coals. Give this about 10 minutes for the unlit charcoal to catch, and then reassemble the WSM.

Remove the plastic bags from the fridge, and take out the chicken quarters. Discard the brine remaining in the bags and rinse off the chicken. Pat the chicken dry with a paper towel.

Season the chicken quarters lightly on both sides with pepper, and place them on the top rack of the WSM. Add the smoke wood to the hot charcoal. Cook the chicken until it reaches an internal temperature of 180°F (82°C).

(continued)

FAST AND CRISPY CHICKEN QUARTERS (CONTINUED)

In a medium saucepan over medium heat, heat the barbecue sauce to a low simmer. Remove it from the heat and cover. Do this about 10 minutes before you're ready to dunk the chicken.

Remove the quarters from the smoker. Using tongs or gloved hands, submerge each chicken quarter into the warm sauce. Shake off the excess sauce, and place the leg quarters back on the smoker, directly on the grill grate. Cook them until the sauce is caramelized, about 10 minutes.

Remove the leg quarters from the smoker, and let them rest for 5 minutes.

> **NOTES:** The USDA says to cook chicken to 165°F (74°C), which is fine for the white meat, but I like to take the dark meat—that is, legs and thighs—to 180 to 185°F (82 to 85°C). I do this because it allows the chicken fat to render, and it creates a more tender and juicy piece of meat.
>
> Instead of tongs, I wear cotton gloves and put nitrile gloves over them. This will help protect your hands from the heat of the sauce and hot food.

DELICIOUS ALL-PURPOSE CHICKEN BRINE

Brine is a salty liquid solution that helps add flavor and keeps meat tender and moist. When placing meat into a brine, the salty solution is drawn into the meat along with any other flavors the brine contains. Brined meat is loaded with extra moisture, and it will remain that way as it cooks, making for a more delicious piece of meat. When you cook chicken on a smoker, either low and slow or hot and fast, you run the risk of it drying out, and nobody likes dried-out chicken. If you want perfect, juicy and tender chicken every time you cook, then I highly recommend brining the chicken. This recipe will do just that!

YIELD:
1¼ gallons (4.7 L)

1 cup (240 ml) water

¾ cup (216 g) coarse kosher salt

¾ cup (165 g) brown sugar

1 cup (240 ml) apple cider vinegar

½ gallon (1.9 L) cold water

½ gallon (1.9 L) apple cider

1 tbsp (6 g) cracked black peppercorns

Get a container large enough to hold more than a gallon of liquid. You may have to use two containers. Use containers you can cover and store in the fridge.

In a large stockpot, bring 1 cup (240 ml) of water to a boil. Dissolve the salt and brown sugar in the boiling water. Stir the mixture until it is incorporated. Stir in the apple cider vinegar, cold water, apple cider and peppercorns. Pour the mixture into the container(s) and store it covered in the fridge until you're ready to use it.

WHOLE CHICKEN, BEER CAN-STYLE

One of my favorite ways to cook chicken is beer can–style! The main reason is, it looks pretty badass, and it tastes pretty darn good, too! But seriously, what's great about this method is the skin gets all nice and caramelized from the rub, and the meat gets super tender and juicy.

COOK TIME:
1½ hours

YIELD:
4 servings

Set up your WSM for 350°F (177°C), using an empty water pan lined with foil for easier cleanup. About one fully lit chimney and half of an unlit chimney should be enough charcoal for this recipe. Dump the fully lit chimney into the charcoal ring, and then add the half chimney of the unlit coals on top of the lit coals. Give this about 15 minutes to catch and then reassemble the WSM.

Clean the chicken thoroughly, inside and out. Remove any unwanted parts.

Open the beer can and consume one-quarter of the beer. You certainly don't want to waste it, but you don't need the whole beer for this recipe. Add the garlic to the remaining beer.

Inject the butter injection into the breast meat, legs, thighs and wings.

Gently lower the chicken down onto the can of beer with the legs pointing down, so that the chicken is supported upright, as if it's on a tripod.

Generously apply the dry rub.

Place the apple wood on top of the charcoal, and then place the can with the chicken on the top cooking grate.

Cook the chicken until an instant-read thermometer inserted into the thickest part of the thigh registers 180°F (82°C) or 165°F (74°C) in the breast.

When the appropriate internal temperature is reached, remove the chicken from the cooker and let it rest for 15 minutes before carving.

(continued)

1 whole chicken

1 (12-oz [354-ml]) can of your favorite dark beer (see Notes)

3 cloves garlic, minced

1–1½ cups (240–360 ml) The Best Buttery Butter Injection (page 72)

¼ cup (25 g) Everyday/Everything Rub (page 120)

2 chunks apple wood

NOTES: For a dark beer, Harpoon Flannel Friday is in between a brown ale and a red IPA. Think fall in New England.

You can tell it's done when you see clear liquid coming out of where you probed it.

THE BEST BUTTERY BUTTER INJECTION

What better way to introduce flavor to your food than by using an injection? This injection is perfect for any cut of meat that has the chance of being dried out when cooked, like chicken breast or lean pork. Using this injection will ensure you get juicy, tender food every time.

In a small saucepan over medium heat, melt the butter. Then add in the broth, garlic powder, onion powder, pepper and thyme. Stir it well. Allow the mixture to cool enough to work with and then load the butter into a meat injector. Refrigerate the butter if you're not quite ready to use it, allowing it to warm up for about 30 minutes on the counter before using.

COOK TIME:
5 to 10 minutes

YIELD:
about 2½ cups (600 ml)

2 sticks (1 cup [227 g]) unsalted butter

2 cups (480 ml) chicken broth

2 tsp (6 g) garlic powder

2 tsp (5 g) onion powder

2 tsp (4 g) finely ground pepper

1 tsp ground thyme

TURKEY BREAST, HOTEL-STYLE

What is hotel-style turkey breast, and why do we only cook one on Thanksgiving? Okay, for the first question, most supermarkets will offer two different styles of whole bone-in turkey breast: regular and hotel. Regular bone-in turkey breast includes the whole bone-in breast with ribs, a portion of the wing meat and a portion of the back and neck skin. The hotel-style bone-in turkey breast is basically the same cut and comes with its whole wings, neck and giblets. For the second question, a whole turkey breast roasted with fresh rosemary, sage and thyme is a great weeknight dinner, and the leftovers make delicious sandwiches the next day. Roasting the turkey at 325 to 350°F (163 to 177°C) and then allowing it to rest for 15 minutes ensures that the finished product will be very moist.

COOK TIME:
1½ to 2 hours

YIELD:
4 to 8 servings

1 (6½–7-lb [3–3.2-kg]) whole, bone-in turkey breast

1 (2½-gallon [9.5-L]) resealable plastic bag

1 gallon (3.8 L) The Only Turkey Brine You'll Ever Need (page 74)

2 tbsp (30 ml) olive oil

1 tsp minced garlic

2 tsp (10 ml) freshly squeezed lemon juice

2 tsp (7 g) dry mustard

1 tbsp (2 g) chopped fresh rosemary leaves

1 tbsp (2 g) chopped fresh sage leaves

1 tsp chopped fresh thyme leaves

½ tsp freshly ground black pepper

Heavy-duty aluminum foil

Place the bone-in turkey breast into the resealable plastic bag and add the brine. Set the bag in a pan, and place the pan in the fridge for 12 hours.

Set up the WSM for 325 to 350°F (163 to 177°C), using a foil-lined water pan for easy cleanup. About one fully lit chimney and one unlit chimney should be enough. Dump the coal from the fully lit chimney into the charcoal ring, then add the coal from the unlit chimney on top of the lit coals. Give this about 15 minutes to catch and then reassemble the WSM.

Remove the plastic bag from the fridge. Discard the bag with the remaining brine, rinse off the turkey breast with water and pat it dry with a paper towel.

In a small bowl, combine the olive oil, garlic, lemon juice, mustard, rosemary, sage, thyme and pepper, forming a paste. Rub the paste evenly all over the skin of the turkey breast. You can also loosen the skin and spread half of the paste underneath, directly on the meat.

Place the turkey breast on the top cooking grate, skin side up.

Roast the turkey for 1½ to 2 hours, until the skin is golden brown and an instant-read meat thermometer registers 160°F (71°C) when inserted into the thickest and meatiest area of the breast. Check the breast after an hour or so. If the skin is overbrowning, cover it loosely with aluminum foil.

When the turkey reaches the desired internal temperature, remove it from the smoker, cover the pan with aluminum foil and allow the turkey to rest at room temperature for 15 minutes. Slice the turkey breast and serve warm with the pan juices.

(continued)

TURKEY BREAST, HOTEL-STYLE (CONTINUED)

THE ONLY TURKEY BRINE YOU'LL EVER NEED

One of the best things you can do to improve the flavor and moisture of a turkey or chicken is to brine it. Brining is basically soaking a turkey (or chicken) in a salty solution for an extended period of time, whereby the salt actually changes the molecular structure of the meat. Now, you might think the meat would be too salty, but instead, it creates the most tender and moist piece of meat you will ever have. You can buy premade brines, but where's the fun in that? Making your own brine is easy to do, and you get to pick the ingredients, so you know it'll be fresh and delicious. When selecting a turkey to brine, stay away from the ones that have already been injected with a solution. Those have basically already been brined, and brining it again will make the meat very salty. With that said, you should only select a fresh turkey if you are intending to brine it.

In a large stockpot, combine the apple cider, chicken stock, spring water, salt, brown sugar, apple cider vinegar, cinnamon stick, orange peels, garlic, peppercorns, rosemary and all-spice. Stir the mixture until the salt and sugar have dissolved. Bring the solution to a boil and then turn off the heat. Add the ice-cold water. Store the brine in the fridge until you are ready to use it.

COOK TIME:
about 15 minutes

YIELD:
about 1 gallon (3.8 L)

1 qt (960 ml) apple cider

2 cups (480 ml) chicken stock

2 cups (480 ml) spring water

½ cup (144 g) kosher salt

½ cup (110 g) light brown sugar, packed

½ cup (120 ml) apple cider vinegar

1 cinnamon stick

2 whole orange peels

4 cloves garlic, chopped

¼ cup (25 g) mixed peppercorns

3 tbsp (5 g) fresh rosemary leaves

1 tbsp (6 g) all-spice berries

½ gallon (1.9 L) heavily iced spring water

CHICKEN CORDON BLEU WRAPPED IN BACON

Typically, cordon bleu is chicken stuffed with ham and Swiss cheese, and then breaded and either baked or fried. We're going to do something a little different here; after all, this is a BBQ book! We are going to omit the breading and wrap the chicken in bacon. Oh, and instead of using ham we're using prosciutto! When you cut into this smoky succulent piece of goodness and discover melted Swiss cheese oozing out around the folds of prosciutto, you'll experience for yourself firsthand why I love this version of a chicken classic so much.

COOK TIME:
1 hour

YIELD:
4 servings

4 chicken breasts (1 per person)

1 (1-gallon [3.8-L]) resealable plastic bag or plastic wrap

Everyday/Everything Rub (page 120), to coat the chicken breasts

8 slices prosciutto, sliced thin

8 slices Swiss cheese

1 lb (454 g) bacon

1 chunk apple wood

Place the chicken breasts in the resealable plastic bag or between two pieces of plastic wrap. Using a meat mallet, lightly pound the chicken until it flattens to a thickness of ½ inch (1.3 cm).

Remove the chicken from the bag. Apply a light coating of the Everyday/Everything Rub to both sides of each chicken breast.

Lay two slices of prosciutto on top of each breast and then two slices of Swiss cheese on top of the prosciutto.

Roll up each chicken breast like a pinwheel. Lay out three to four slices of bacon next to each other, depending on the width of the rolled chicken. This will be for one chicken breast roll.

Place the seam side of the rolled chicken down, and roll the bacon around the chicken, making sure that when you are done the bacon seam is facing down. Repeat with the remaining chicken rolls. Season the outside of the bacon with more rub.

Go ahead and fire up the WSM to 350°F (177°C), using a foil-lined water pan for easy cleanup when you are done. You'll need one fully lit chimney and one-half of an unlit chimney. Fill the charcoal ring with the lit coal and add the unlit coal to the top of that. Give it about 10 minutes to catch and then reassemble the WSM.

Place each chicken roll on the top cooking grate, and make sure the bacon seam is facing down. Add your smoke wood on top of the charcoal. Cook the chicken until it reaches an internal temperature of 165°F (74°C), about 1 hour.

NOTES: When you cook the rolled chicken, it is very important to have the seam of the bacon facing down. Arranging the chicken this way will eliminate the need for using toothpicks to pin the bacon in place. The weight of the chicken will prevent the bacon from curling up.

I like to wrap each chicken roll, complete with the bacon and seasoning, in plastic wrap and place them in the fridge for about 1 hour. This helps set the bacon on the chicken.

SMOKY COUNTY FAIR TURKEY LEGS

I don't know about you, but when I think of smoked turkey legs it reminds me of all the festivals that happen in autumn. In my area, one in particular is King Richard's Faire, a Renaissance fair that opens on the first weekend in September and runs through the third weekend in October. While enjoying all that the fair has to offer, one of the biggest draws is the smoked turkey legs. People line up to get their hands and taste buds around one of those delicious meat sticks. Now you can make them right at home and turn any event you choose into a royal celebration!

COOK TIME:
1½ hours. Cooking low and slow would take almost 3 hours.

YIELD:
6 servings

Place three turkey legs and 3 cups (720 ml) of the turkey brine into each resealable plastic bag. Close the bags and put them in the fridge for 12 to 16 hours.

In a small bowl, mix together the brown sugar, paprika, garlic powder and pepper. Store it in an airtight container until you are ready to use it.

Set up the WSM for 350°F (177°C), using a foil-lined water pan for easy cleanup. About one fully lit chimney and a half chimney of unlit charcoal should be enough for this cook. Dump the fully lit chimney into the charcoal ring, and then add the half chimney of unlit charcoal on top of the lit coals. Give this about 15 minutes to catch, and then reassemble the WSM.

Remove the plastic bags from the fridge. Take the turkey legs out of the bags, and discard the remaining brine. Rinse the turkey legs under cold water and pat them dry with a paper towel.

Sprinkle the seasoning onto all six turkey legs.

Add the cherry wood on top of the charcoal, place the turkey legs on the top cooking grate and cook them until the turkey reaches an internal temperature of 180 to 185°F (82 to 85°C).

TURKEY
6 turkey legs

6 cups (1.4 L) The Only Turkey Brine You'll Ever Need (page 74)

2 (1-gallon [3.8-L]) resealable plastic bags

SEASONING
¼ cup (55 g) brown sugar

2 tbsp (14 g) sweet paprika

2 tbsp (14 g) garlic powder

2 tsp (4 g) black pepper

1 chunk cherry wood

NOTE: The reason there is no salt in this rub is because you will be brining the legs, and there is sufficient salt in the brine.

5

HOTTER *and* FASTER COMPETITION DISHES

The Kansas City Barbeque Society (KCBS) is the largest sanctioning body on the competition circuit, and there are hundreds of contests per year. Each contest has four categories: chicken, pork ribs, pork shoulder and beef brisket. Judges score the food entries according to three core criteria: appearance, taste and tenderness.

For appearance, color is key. The color of the food you're serving should be tantalizing and get people excited to eat. Taste is very subjective, and everyone's palate is different. For the most part, I like to aim for a balanced flavor, where ingredients complement the natural taste of the food. Tenderness can be the trickiest of the three criteria, but there are some simple things to take into consideration. Generally speaking, perfectly cooked meat should contain moisture and have a nice mouthfeel, or texture. The hot-and-fast cooking method creates a finished product that is still tender but has a little more structural integrity.

Another perk when using the hot-and-fast cooking method is you won't be up all night tending to the fire source in your smoker. You don't have to start cooking until about five in the morning, and as long as you get your big meats on by six in the morning, you'll be good for turn-in time.

I'm an experienced backyard cook, and my culinary knowledge was shaped by learning to cook food according to the judging criteria used on the competition circuit. I've spent many long hours learning to cook each contest category, and drawing from my experience on the circuit, I'm going to teach you how to cook for a contest as well. Just turn the

JUICY, TENDER BITE-THRU-SKIN CHICKEN THIGHS

I think chicken just might be the single most hated category in all of competition barbecue. At contests, it's not uncommon for contestants to turn in chicken thighs. The dark meat of the thighs has a higher fat content, which usually helps create a very moist finished product. A lot of time and effort goes into selecting and prepping chicken thighs, but when you do it, you turn them into little saucy pillows of barbecue joy! One of the biggest challenges with chicken thighs is the skin. Turn-in entries are served to judges in a Styrofoam box. Sometimes, the boxes can sit for 20 minutes before the judges access them. In my experience, it's nearly impossible to get and keep the skin crispy, particularly if the turn-in box isn't served to a judge right away. Ideally, the next best thing is creating a bite-through skin, where the skin holds securely in place except for the portion of the thigh you bite into. Yes, that is only part of the battle. The chicken has to be tender, juicy and taste good. In this recipe, I'll show you how to achieve all those results. Before you know it, we might just jump onto the competition chicken train together!

COOK TIME:
1 hour, 40 minutes

YIELD:
12 servings

12 bone-in, skin-on chicken thighs

1 bottle Smokin' Hoggz BBQ Rib Rub

1 bottle Smokin' Hoggz BBQ Smokin' Applewood Rub

2 disposable aluminum half pans

1 (16.9-oz [500-ml]) bottle spring water

¼ cup (60 ml) Butcher's Bird Booster, original flavor

1 stick (½ cup [114 g]) of butter/margarine, cut into 12 slices

1 bottle of spray butter, such as I Can't Believe It's Not Butter

Aluminum foil

1 (16-oz [480-ml]) bottle Smokin' Hoggz Pitmaster Blend BBQ Sauce

¼ cup (60 ml) white grape juice

Carefully remove the skin from the chicken thighs and it set it aside for reuse. Lay the thighs out flat and trim each one into uniform, trapezoid shapes, removing some of the excess fat.

Using a sharp fillet knife, gently fillet the high peaks of excess fat from the chicken skins.

Sprinkle a little of the Smokin' Hoggz BBQ Rib Rub and the Smokin' Hoggz BBQ Smokin' Applewood Rub onto the bare surface of the thighs. Wrap the skin back around each piece of chicken, and place the chicken in the disposable aluminum pans. Refrigerate the chicken for 4 hours, up to overnight.

Mix the bottle of water and the Butcher's Bird Booster. Using an injector, inject about ½ ounce (15 ml) of this chicken injection mix into the left and right side of each thigh. Sprinkle the back of each thigh with both rubs.

Place six slices of butter in each pan, then place a chicken thigh on top of each pat of butter. Season the top side of the chicken with both rubs. Spray the tops of the chicken with the spray butter. Place the pans in the fridge for 1 hour.

Fire up the WSM at 325°F (163°C), using a foil-lined water pan. You will need one fully lit chimney of charcoal and a half chimney of unlit charcoal. Dump the fully lit chimney into the charcoal ring, and then add the unlit charcoal on top. Wait 10 minutes and then reassemble the WSM.

(continued)

JUICY, TENDER BITE-THRU-SKIN CHICKEN THIGHS (CONTINUED)

Remove the pans from the fridge and spray the tops of the chicken thighs with spray butter. Place one pan on the bottom rack and one on the top rack of the WSM. Cook the chicken for 25 minutes. Spray the tops of each chicken thigh with the spray butter, and then cook for 25 minutes. After this additional 25 minutes, rotate the pans so that the one that was cooking on the top rack is moved to the bottom rack, and the one that was cooking on the bottom rack is now on top. This helps ensure a more uniform and even cook. When you rotate the pans, apply the spray butter, and cook the chicken for 25 minutes. After that, apply the spray butter again and cook for an additional 25 minutes.

During the last 25-minute interval, get out a cooling rack for the chicken thighs. Then, in a medium saucepan over medium heat, combine the Smokin' Hoggz Pitmaster Blend BBQ Sauce and white grape juice. Let it simmer for about 10 minutes.

Remove the pans of chicken from the smoker. At this point, your chicken thighs should be around 180°F (82°C). Using tongs or gloved hands, submerge each thigh into the warm sauce. Place the thighs on the cooling rack and select your best six pieces to turn in.

> **NOTES:** The skin should wrap around the thigh, fully covering the front, and each end should overlap on the back side. I also do this the day before turn-ins because letting the skin set overnight allows for better adhesion, meaning the skin will stick better to the meat.
>
> I don't like to use any extra wood while cooking competition chicken. I find that using extra wood causes the chicken to become too smoky and the skin to be rubbery, which is not good for competition. Remember, we're trying to get bite-thru skin.

Trimming chicken, removing skin completely

Trimming both ends of thigh

Trimming the sides of thigh, squaring up

Trimming the skin and removing excess fat

Laying thigh meat side down onto skin and wrapping skin around thigh

After wrapped, turning over so meat side is up

RIBS, HANGING

I have cooked a lot of ribs during my career in competition. In fact, ribs are the main reason I got into BBQ in the first place. I prefer to cook spareribs for competition. For one, they are meatier, and two, I think they are more flavorful because they are located right behind the belly, where all that delicious pork fat is—and who doesn't love some good ole pork fat? This style of cooking ribs I am about to show you is a pretty popular method in competition BBQ. We are going to be hanging the ribs directly over the hot coals—that's right, hanging them! They will cook a little faster, and they will taste amazing. The flavor will almost be as if you had grilled them, and that's because the fat will drip over those hot coals, creating that wonderful grill-like flavor. So, what do you say we "hang" around and cook some ribs?

I like to trim my ribs so that there are eleven bones in the rack. On one end of the rack of ribs there is usually a big hunk of meat. I like to leave this on because it helps protect the ribs on that end when you hang and cook them, because that end will be closest to the hot coals.

Lay out the ribs with the meat side facing down. Take one "S" hook and insert it into the rack of ribs about two ribs in, on the smaller end of the rack. Apply the Smokin' Hoggz BBQ Rib Rub to the back side of the ribs, and let it set up for about 20 minutes. Flip the racks over, apply the rub to the meat side and let it set up for 20 minutes.

Set your WSM for 325 to 350°F (163 to 177°C). Remove the water pan and the bottom cooking grate. You will need one fully lit chimney of charcoal and one unlit chimney. Dump the fully lit chimney to one side of the fire ring, and then dump the unlit chimney on top of the lit coals. Wait 10 minutes, then reassemble the WSM.

Take each rack of ribs and hang them from the top cooking grate. Rotate the cooking grate so that the ribs hang opposite of where the lit coals are stacked. Add the smoke wood on top of the hot charcoal. Cook for 2 hours.

(continued)

COOK TIME:
2½ to 2¾ hours

YIELD:
12 servings

3 racks of St. Louis spareribs, membrane removed

3 "S" hooks, for hanging ribs

1 bottle Smokin' Hoggz BBQ Rib Rub

2 chunks apple wood

3 pieces heavy-duty aluminum foil

1 bottle Smokin' Hoggz Pitmaster Blend BBQ Sauce

1½ cups (330 g) brown sugar, ½ cup (110 g) per rack

12 oz (354 ml) honey, 4 oz (118 ml) per rack

1½ sticks (168 g) butter, cut into 12 slices

RIBS, HANGING (CONTINUED)

Lay out three sheets of heavy-duty foil, making sure each sheet is longer than the rack of ribs.

Pour ¼ cup (60 ml) of Smokin' Hoggz Pitmaster Blend BBQ Sauce and ¼ cup (55 g) of brown sugar onto each foil piece. Place the rack of ribs on top of the sweeteners, meat side down. Then, pour another ¼ cup (60 ml) of BBQ sauce, ¼ cup (55 g) of brown sugar, 4 ounces (118 ml) of honey and four pieces of butter on top of the rack. Wrap the ribs tightly in the foil. Repeat this process for the other two racks.

Place the wrapped ribs back on the top grate. Cook them for 30 to 45 minutes.

To check if the ribs are done, look at the back side of the ribs. First, the meat will have shrunken from the bone ¼ to ½ inch (6 mm to 1.3 cm). Second, the bones will start to pop through on the back side.

If the ribs are done, remove them from the WSM and open the foil to let them vent for 5 to 10 minutes. This will stop them from cooking any further.

Cut the ribs and pick out your best six rib bones to present to the judges.

> NOTE: You will want to trim off any loose fat, square up the ribs—rectangular—as best as you can, and remove the membrane if it hasn't been removed. Squaring off the ribs allows them to cook more evenly, giving you a much better end product and hopefully that walk to the stage. Removing the membrane is pretty simple; you will want to turn the ribs over so the bones are facing up. Using a butter knife, insert it between the membrane and the bone. Gently lifting up, grab that membrane with a paper towel—this allows for getting a better grip—and gently pull off the membrane.

Trimming back side of ribs

Removing end bone

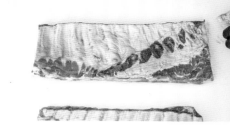

Removing other end bone

Removing membrane

Squaring up the ribs

Adding hooks to the thinner end of ribs

Seasoning ribs

Checking to see if ribs are done

Wrapping ribs meat side down

Adding butter and BBQ sauce to ribs

Adding brown sugar and honey to ribs

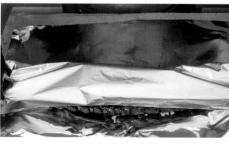

Wrapping ribs tightly in heavy-duty foil

5-HOUR COMPETITION PORK

Competition pork is a completely different animal than cooking a pork butt for friends and family. You are striving to cook certain muscles of the butt to perfection in the hope that if the judges like what you have presented, you'll receive a high score. We will be focusing on the muscles around the bone, known as the horn muscles, and the money muscle, known as the tiger muscle because of the lined striations of fat running through it. The money muscle is the giant muscle opposite the bone. I know you're probably asking, "Why do they call it the money muscle?" Well, the answer is pretty simple. If cooked perfectly, it will be as tender and delicious as pork tenderloin, and you will get to walk to the competition stage to collect your money!

COOK TIME:
5 hours. Typical low-and-slow cooking of a pork butt can take upward of 16 hours, depending on the size of the butt.

YIELD:
24 servings

The trimming of the pork will be fairly aggressive on this next step. This is an important step that helps when it's time to remove the money muscle and finish cooking the pork butt.

Locate the money muscle. It's opposite the bone and runs the width of the pork butt. Using a sharp knife, carefully cut along the back side of the money muscle; there is a fat line to follow. Go down about halfway through the pork butt, creating a nice valley from side to side. Then, round it off and form it so it will cook evenly (see page 93).

The next part of the trim focuses on the bone side of the pork butt. You will notice that there is another fat line that separates the meat from the bone and the middle of the pork butt. You will want to follow along that fat line with your knife, all the way almost to the bottom. You'll see that it goes down on an angle. Remove that bit of meat to expose the meat around the bone. What you'll notice is you have a butt that looks like three separate sections (see page 93).

Repeat the trimming process for the second pork butt.

For the injection, in a small bowl, mix the Butcher's Original Pork Injection with the bottle of spring water. You can do this the day before and keep it in the fridge until you're ready to use it.

Take half of the injection and, using a meat injector, start injecting the pork butt. Use about one cylinder's worth of injection liquid in the money muscle, and then inject the rest into the muscles around the bone.

Repeat the injection process for the second pork butt.

Once you are finished injecting, generously apply Smokin' Hoggz BBQ Rib Rub to both pork butts. Wrap both pork butts in plastic wrap and store them in the fridge until about 30 minutes before they go on the WSM.

Remove the pork butts from the refrigerator, remove the plastic wrap and apply another generous coating of rub. Let the rerubbed meat sit at room temperature until you're ready to put them on the WSM.

(continued)

2 (8-lb [3.6-kg]) Boston butts, bone-in

PORK INJECTION, ENOUGH FOR TWO BUTTS
¼ cup (60 ml) Butcher's Original Pork Injection

1 (16.9-oz [500-ml]) bottle spring water

1 bottle Smokin' Hoggz BBQ Rib Rub

Plastic wrap

1 chunk each apple and sugar maple wood

Heavy-duty aluminum foil

PORK BRAISE
2 bottles Stubb's Pork Marinade, strained

1 cup (240 ml) Smokin' Hoggz Pitmaster Blend BBQ Sauce, plus more for brushing onto the butts

5-HOUR COMPETITION PORK (CONTINUED)

Fire up the WSM to 350°F (177°C), using a foil-lined water pan. You will need one fully lit chimney of charcoal and two chimneys of unlit charcoal. Dump one of the unlit chimneys of charcoal into the charcoal ring, dump the fully lit chimney on top of the unlit charcoal, then the second unlit chimney on top of that. Wait 15 minutes, then reassemble the WSM.

Place the apple and sugar maple wood on top of the charcoal, and then put both butts on the top grate of the WSM, fat side down. Cook the butts until the money muscle reaches an internal temperature of 165°F (74°C), about 2½ hours.

Lay out four sheets of heavy-duty aluminum foil: two for the money muscle and two for the rest of the butt.

Once the internal temperature is reached, remove the butts from the WSM. Using a knife, carefully remove the money muscle from each one.

For the pork braise, in a medium bowl, mix together both bottles of the strained Stubb's Pork Marinade and the Smokin' Hoggz Pitmaster Blend BBQ Sauce.

Place the money muscle onto a sheet of foil. Place the rest of the pork butt, fat side down, on a separate sheet of foil. Pour ⅓ cup (80 ml) of the braising liquid onto the money muscle of each butt. Use the rest of the braise for the other part of each butt. Wrap each item tightly in the foil and place the wrapped meat back on the WSM. Cook them until the money muscle reaches an internal temperature of 185°F (85°C), 1½ to 2 hours, and the pork butt reaches 195 to 200°F (91 to 93°C), about 2½ hours.

Remove the pork butts from the WSM, open the foil, and allow the steam to dissipate for about 10 minutes to help stop the cooking process. During this time, apply a coating of BBQ sauce to the top surface of both parts of the butt. Close the foil and let the meat rest for a minimum of 1 hour.

Slice the money muscle into ½-inch (1.3-cm) slices. Brush the slices with BBQ sauce, and sprinkle a little rub on each slice.

For the other section of the butt, use your hands and pull off chunks about 1 inch (2.5 cm) long. Toss the chunks in the BBQ sauce, sprinkle them with a little more rub and then select your pieces for the judges.

> **NOTE:** We won't be using the center section as part of the turn-in entry, so I use it as a handle when moving the pork butt on and off the smoker. It is still good meat, so don't throw it out. Save it for yourself.

Trimming competition pork butt, removing loose fat

Side view of money muscle

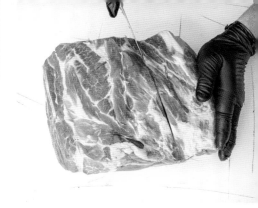

Partially separating money muscle

Finished partially separated money muscle

Finished trimmed competition butt

Seasoning trimmed butt

Removing cooked money muscle

Applying sauce to cooked money muscle

Applying sauce to rest of butt

COMPETITION BRISKET IN 4½ HOURS

COOK TIME:
4 to 4½ hours

YIELD:
8 servings

In my opinion, brisket is the hardest competition category to cook properly on a consistent basis. When perfectly cooked, beef brisket is the juiciest, most tender, flavorful piece of meat your mouth will ever know! There are two cuts of meat associated with a brisket: the flat and the point. The flat is just that, a flat rectangular piece of meat that makes up the majority of the brisket. It's the leaner of the two pieces and is what you will be cutting into slices. The point is the other part of the brisket. It lies across part of the flat and is a fattier piece of meat. You can also slice this section, but it's better for making chopped chunks of meat or for serving up a barbecue delicacy: velvety smooth burnt ends.

1 (15-lb [6.8-kg]) full packer brisket, containing both flat and point

BRISKET INJECTION
¼ cup (60 ml) Butcher's Original Beef Injection

1 (16.9-oz [500-ml]) bottle spring water

1 bottle Smokin' Guns BBQ Hot Rub

Plastic wrap

4 chunks hickory or oak wood

Heavy-duty aluminum foil

1 bottle Stubb's Beef Marinade

¼ cup (60 ml) Smokin' Hoggz Pitmaster Blend BBQ Sauce

Trim all the loose fat and silver skin from the flat side of the brisket. Flip the brisket over, so the flat is facing down, and trim most of the fat from the point. Leave a layer that's ¼ to ½ inch (6 mm to 1.3 cm) thick.

Just like the pork trim (page 93), the brisket trim will be equally aggressive. We are going to be separating the flat and the point and cooking them at the same time, just separately.

There is a fat line that runs through the brisket that separates the two muscles. With the brisket flat facing down and using a sharp knife starting at the point, slowly insert the knife and follow the fat line until it meets the flat and you are left with two pieces: the point and the flat. For now, you want to leave all the fat on the flat part of the brisket. We will trim this later.

Once you have two separate pieces, finish trimming up the point by squaring off the edges. Make sure the point is close to the same thickness from end to end.

Moving back to the flat, remove some of the heavy fat you left earlier. You want a ¼- to ½-inch (6-mm to 1.3-cm) thickness of fat.

Finish trimming the flat by squaring off the edges and making sure it's close to the same thickness from end to end.

For the brisket injection, in a small bowl, mix together the Butcher's Original Beef Injection and the bottle of water.

(continued)

Starting with the point, and going perpendicular to the grain of the meat, inject the mixture every 2 inches (5 cm), going in a checkerboard pattern. Then, do the same thing for the flat.

Generously season the two pieces of meat with the Smokin' Guns BBQ Hot Rub. Wrap each piece of meat in plastic wrap, and store them in the fridge. Remove them from the fridge about 30 minutes before cooking them on the WSM.

Fire up the WSM to 350°F (177°C), using a foil-lined water pan. You will need one fully lit chimney of charcoal and two chimneys of unlit charcoal. Dump one of the unlit chimneys of charcoal into the charcoal ring, dump the fully lit chimney of charcoal on top of the unlit charcoal, and then dump the second unlit chimney of charcoal on top of that. Wait 10 minutes and then reassemble the WSM.

Place the hickory wood on top of the charcoal. Put both pieces of brisket next to each other on the top rack of the WSM, fat side down, and cook them until the meat reaches an internal temperature of 170°F (77°C), 2 to 2½ hours.

Lay out two sheets of heavy-duty aluminum foil. Place each piece of meat on its own sheet of foil, fat side down. Pour half of the bottle of Stubb's Beef Marinade on the point and the other half on the flat. Wrap both pieces of the brisket tightly in foil, and put them on WSM. Cook the meat until it reaches an internal temperature of 195 to 200°F (91 to 93°C), about 2 hours, or until it's probe-tender.

Remove the meat from the WSM and vent the foil to release the steam for about 10 minutes to stop the cooking process. At this time, take some of the Smokin' Hoggz Pitmaster Blend BBQ Sauce and coat the surface of each piece of meat. Wrap the brisket back up and allow it to rest in a Cambro—an insulated holding box—or dry, empty cooler for a minimum of 1 hour, up to 4 hours.

Remove the meat from the holding container, and slice up the flat. You want the slices to be ¼ inch (6 mm) thick. Brush each slice with a little bit of the juices from the foil for a little added flavor. Slice the point into 1-inch (2.5-cm) cubes and glaze them with a little bit of the remaining BBQ sauce.

> **NOTES:** The heat source in the WSM is located beneath the cooking grates. By leaving a layer of fat on the bottom, you are protecting the meat from the heat coming up from the bottom of the smoker.
>
> You can make the injection mixture the day before and keep it in the fridge until you are ready to use it.
>
> Probe-tender means that when you push to insert the probe into the brisket, it offers the same resistance as a knife going through room-temperature butter.

Brisket trimming, removing loose fat

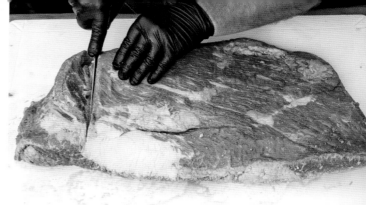

Squaring up the flat

Removing more fat from the side

Removing more fat from the other side

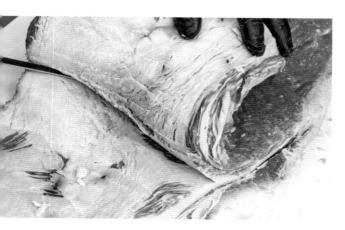

Separating the brisket into the two cuts: the flat and point

Finished trimmed brisket, the flat (right) and point (left)

PIZZA *with* PIZZAZZ *and* A SENSATIONAL STROMBOLI

Chicago claims to have the best pizza. So does New York. There are other regions across the country making similar boasts. I guess it all depends on where you live and what your personal preferences are. You know what? I like it all! I love the thin, crispy crust of New York–style pizza, the thick and inviting buttery crust of Chicago-style deep dish pizza, and every other type of pizza I've ever had. Variety is a gift, especially when it comes to eating delicious food!

Growing up in southeastern Massachusetts, meeting up with friends to watch sporting events always seemed to include pizza. In fact, this region of the state is known for South Shore bar pizzas, which are small, roughly 10-inch (25-cm) pizzas for one that are always made to order.

I like the fact that there isn't much of a crust on the South Shore bar pizzas. The sauce and cheese go right to the edge of the pizza, and the edge is nice and crispy. You usually have to order them well done, otherwise the crust will be a little soggy. A well-done pizza isn't burnt. There is a fine line between burnt and well done, especially with this style of pizza. If you're curious, just turn the page, and we'll get started making some perfect pizzas right on your WSM!

THICK CRUST, CHICAGO-STYLE DEEP DISH

The thick, buttery crust of a Chicago-style deep dish pizza brings me to a happy place. In this recipe, I'll show that it is absolutely possible to achieve that pizza crust using the WSM! Once you get this process down and realize you can cook pizza in less than 30 minutes, delivery is likely to become a thing of the past.

COOK TIME:
25 to 30 minutes

YIELD:
4 to 8 servings

Using cooking spray, lightly coat two round cake pans, 9 inches (23 cm) in diameter and 2 inches (5 cm) deep.

For the crust, in the bowl of your stand mixer fitted with the dough hook attachment, combine the flour, cornmeal, salt, sugar and yeast. If you do not own a mixer, you can do this all by hand; just combine the dry ingredients in a very large bowl. Give the ingredients a quick stir with your mixer on low or with a large wooden spoon, if mixing by hand. Add the warm water and the ¼ cup (60 ml) of melted butter. The warm water should be around 100°F (32°C). Make sure it is not very hot or it will kill the yeast. Also, make sure the butter isn't boiling hot. If you melt the butter in the microwave, let it sit for 5 minutes before adding it to the mixture. On low speed, beat the dough ingredients until everything begins to moisten. Continue on low speed, or remove from the bowl and knead by hand if you do not own a mixer, and beat the dough until it is soft, gently pulls away from the sides of the bowl and falls off the dough hook, 4 to 5 minutes. If the dough is too hard and feels too tough, beat in 1 teaspoon of warm water. Alternatively, if it feels too soft, beat in 1 tablespoon (8 g) of flour.

Lightly grease a large mixing bowl with olive oil. Remove the dough from the bowl, form it into a ball, and place it in the bowl. Roll the dough ball around so it's entirely coated with oil. Cover the bowl tightly with plastic wrap and place a towel over it. Allow the dough to rise in a warm environment for 1 to 2 hours, or until it doubles in size.

Once the dough is ready, lightly flour a large, flat work surface. Remove the dough from the bowl. Gently punch down the dough to remove any air bubbles, and roll the dough into a 15 x 12–inch (38 x 30.5–cm) rectangle. Spread ¼ cup (57 g) of the softened butter on top of the dough. Roll it up lengthwise, forming a log. Cut the dough log in half. Form the two pieces of dough into balls and place them into your greased bowl. Cover the dough balls with plastic wrap, and allow the dough to rise in the refrigerator for 1 hour, or until puffy.

For the sauce, in a medium bowl, combine the tomatoes, salt, oregano, pepper flakes and garlic. Set it aside.

(continued)

PIZZA DOUGH, MAKES TWO 9" (23-CM) CRUSTS

3¼ cups (406 g) all-purpose flour, plus more for dusting

½ cup (60 g) yellow cornmeal

1¼ tsp (8 g) salt

1 tbsp (15 g) sugar

2¼ tsp (10 g) yeast

1¼ cups (300 ml) slightly warm water

½ cup (114 g) unsalted butter, divided, ¼ cup (60 ml) melted, ¼ cup (57 g) softened to room temperature

SAUCE FOR BOTH PIZZAS

1 (28-oz [794-g]) can crushed tomatoes

¼ tsp salt

1 tsp dried oregano

½ tsp crushed red pepper flakes

3 cloves garlic, minced

Olive oil, for coating

4 cups (448 g) shredded mozzarella cheese

1 (6-oz [168-g]) package of sliced pepperoni

1 lb (454 g) cooked Italian sausage, crumbled

½ cup (50 g) grated Parmesan cheese

THICK CRUST, CHICAGO-STYLE DEEP DISH (CONTINUED)

Fire up your WSM to 400 to 425°F (204 to 218°C), removing the water pan. This recipe requires one fully lit chimney and half of an unlit chimney of charcoal. Dump the hot charcoal into the charcoal ring, and then add the half chimney of unlit on top. Wait 10 minutes and then reassemble the WSM.

To make the pizzas, keep one ball of dough in the refrigerator as you work with the first one. Roll out the dough ball on a lightly floured work surface, into a 12-inch (30.5-cm) circle. Place the flattened dough over the round cake pan. Press the dough into the cake pan. Make sure it fits nice and tight inside the pan. Trim any excess dough off the edges with a paring knife. Repeat this process for the second dough ball. Brush the top edges of the dough with a little olive oil, which helps give the crust a beautiful sheen. Fill each pizza with 2 cups (224 g) of the cheese. Split the pepperoni and sausage between the two pizzas. Pour about 1¼ cups (360 ml) of sauce on top of each pizza. Sprinkle each pizza with ¼ cup (25 g) of the grated Parmesan cheese.

Place the cake pans on the top grate and cook the pizzas for 25 to 30 minutes, or until the crust is golden brown. Remove the pizzas from the WSM, place them on a wire rack and allow them to cool for 10 minutes.

> **NOTE:** If you are using the 18-inch (46-cm) WSM, place one pan on the bottom rack and one pan on the top rack. After 15 minutes, rotate from top to bottom and bottom to top and cook for an additional 15 minutes. If you are using the 22-inch (56-cm) WSM, the pans will fit side by side on the top cooking grate.

SOUTH OF BOSTON BAR PIZZA

One thing the South Shore of Massachusetts is known for is our bar pizza, and it absolutely has a cult following! A bar pizza is a small 10-inch (25-cm) personal pizza cooked in a pan where the sauce and cheese go all the way out to the edges. As the pizza cooks, the cheese gets all nice and crispy, forming "laced edges," as we like to call them. The laced edge is a very fine detail that is essential if you want your South Shore bar pizza to be just right!

COOK TIME:
20 minutes

YIELD:
4 individual bar pizzas

Coat the interior of two to four 10-inch (25-cm) pans, on the bottom and sides, with 2 tablespoons (30 ml) corn oil each. You can also use 9½-inch (24-cm) cake pans if you don't have the special 10-inch (25-cm) pizza pans. Coating the pans with oil is a very important step. It helps create a nice, crispy, uniform crust.

In a small bowl, dissolve the yeast and sugar with the warm water and let it sit for 3 to 5 minutes until it's nice and foamy. The perfect temperature for the water is 110°F (43°C). Don't go hotter than that or you'll kill the yeast.

In the bowl of a stand mixer with the dough hook attachment, add the flour. If you don't have a mixer, just mix it by hand in a large bowl.

Pour the yeast mixture into the flour. Start mixing on speed #2. Then add ¼ cup (60 ml) of the corn oil, melted butter and salt. Mix with a bread hook until a ball forms, about 2 minutes. Do not overmix the dough, or the dough will become tight and can easily tear.

Add the remaining 2 tablespoons (30 ml) corn oil to oil a large mixing bowl. Set the dough in the oiled bowl and cover with plastic wrap and a towel. Leave the bowl out at room temperature for at least 6 hours.

While you are waiting for the dough to do its thing, you can prepare the sauce and grate the cheese.

For the sauce, strain the crushed tomatoes in a wire mesh strainer. In a medium bowl, combine the tomatoes, salt, garlic and oregano. Set this aside or store it in the fridge until you are ready to use it.

(continued)

8 tbsp (120 ml) corn oil, for coating

THE DOUGH

1 (2¼-tsp [9-g]) packet active yeast

2 tsp (8 g) granulated sugar

1 cup (240 ml) warm water

3 cups (375 g) all-purpose flour or bread flour

¼ cup + 2 tbsp (90 ml) corn oil, divided

2 tbsp (30 ml) melted butter

2 tsp (12 g) kosher salt

PIZZA SAUCE

1 (28-oz [794-g]) can crushed tomatoes, such as Tuttorosso crushed tomatoes

1½ tsp (9 g) sea salt

1¼ tsp (4 g) granulated garlic

1 tsp (2 g) dried oregano

CHEESE

1 lb (454 g) block white sharp cheddar cheese

1 lb (454 g) block whole milk, low-moisture mozzarella

SOUTH OF BOSTON BAR PIZZA (CONTINUED)

For the cheese, over a large bowl, grate the cheddar and mozzarella. Set it aside or store it in the fridge until you are ready to use it.

When the dough is finished rising, you should have a very light and fluffy dough that you can easily push to the sides of your pan. Cut the dough into four even pieces. You want roughly 6½-ounce (184-g) pieces of dough, about the size of a baseball.

Take a dough ball, place it into a pan, and start pushing it all the way to the edges of your pan. If the dough is tough to get to the edge, wait a couple of minutes for the dough to relax and then continue. If you want charred and laced edges, keep the dough nice and flat all the way to the edge of the pan. You do not need to pinch the crust against the edges.

With a fork, poke a few holes in the dough. This helps prevent bubbles from forming during the cooking process, and it's a very important step in preparing the pizza.

Spread one-fourth of the sauce all the way to the edge of each pan. Make sure the sauce touches the edge of the pan because this, along with the cheese, creates that laced edge.

Take one-fourth of the cheese blend and sprinkle it over each pizza, making sure to get cheese all the way to the edge of the pan.

Fire up your WSM to 450°F (232°C). Remove the water pan from the smoker. You will need two fully lit chimneys of charcoal for this recipe.

Place the pizzas on the WSM and cook them for about 10 minutes. Rotate the pizzas from top to bottom and bottom to top and cook for an additional 10 minutes.

Remove the pizzas from the WSM and let them sit for 5 minutes. Transfer the pizzas to a wooden cutting board before slicing.

NOTES: Go to your deli counter and ask for a 1-lb (454-g) chunk or look for the mozzarella cheese that says on the package that it's best for shredding.

When you are straining the sauce, you don't have to push it through the strainer; just let it sit in there. This process is only to allow the excess water to drain out. Here's the great thing about this sauce: You don't have to cook it because it will cook when the pizza cooks.

This recipe provides enough dough for four pizzas. If you have a 22-inch (56-cm) WSM, you can cook two pizzas side-by-side on the top rack and two pizzas side-by-side on the bottom rack. If you have the 18-inch (46-cm) WSM, you can cook one pizza on top and one pizza on the bottom. On the 18-inch (46-cm) WSM, while the second pizza is cooking, light up a half chimney of charcoal and dump it on top of the lit charcoal.

ITALIAN STROMBOLI

Here's a great dish to serve at your next party or get-together. It's easy to make and super tasty. The salty richness of the meats and creamy melted cheese balance the sweetness of the peppers to make for an experience that will leave your guests wanting more.

COOK TIME:
30 minutes

YIELD:
8 servings

Fire up your WSM to 375°F (191°C), using an empty foil-lined water pan. This recipe requires one fully lit chimney of charcoal and one half chimney of unlit charcoal. Dump the fully lit chimney into the charcoal ring, and then add the unlit charcoal on top. Wait 15 minutes and then reassemble the WSM with the vents fully open.

For the dough, lay out a 16-inch (41-cm) sheet of parchment paper on the counter and dust it with flour. Roll the dough ball out on the floured parchment paper and form a 14 x 11-inch (36 x 26–cm) rectangle.

For the filling, layer the salami on the dough to within ½ inch (1.3 cm) of the edges. Overlap the slices so that no dough shows beneath the salami. Continue the layers with the provolone, hot capicola, mozzarella, sweet capicola, roasted red peppers and 1 tablespoon (2 g) of the dried oregano.

Brush the edges of the dough with the egg. Using the parchment to help you, lift up one long end and start rolling to form a pinwheel-like form. Continue rolling until the seam on the log is on the bottom. Pinch the ends so they don't open, and tuck the dough under the roll.

Transfer the rolled dough to the foil-lined pan. Brush the dough all over with egg, and sprinkle with the Parmesan and the remaining 1 tablespoon (2 g) of oregano.

Cook the stromboli on the top rack of the WSM for about 30 minutes, or until the log is golden and the cheese is oozing at the slits.

Remove the stromboli from the WSM and let it rest for about 10 minutes. Cut it into 1-inch (2.5-cm) slices.

All-purpose flour, for dusting

1 prepared store-bought pizza dough ball

½ lb (227 g) thinly sliced Genoa salami

16 slices provolone

½ lb (227 g) hot capicola, sliced

1½ cups (168 g) shredded mozzarella

½ lb (227 g) sweet capicola, sliced

1 cup (150 g) roasted red peppers, drained

2 tbsp (3 g) dried oregano, divided

1 large egg, lightly beaten

¼ cup (25 g) finely shredded Parmesan, for sprinkling

> **NOTE:** When rolling the stromboli, make sure that it is tightly rolled so that there are no air pockets, which can cause blowouts in the dough.

7

SINFUL *and* SURE-FIRE SEAFOOD

From Gloucester to Cape Cod, and all the way out to Georges Bank, Massachusetts has a deep history tied to the fishing industry. I have fond childhood memories of family vacations at my aunt's cottage inside Myles Standish State Park, right near Cape Cod Bay. We'd usually go during the summer, and when I was a kid, I'd go fishing in the nearby ponds.

I also remember my father getting up early in the morning, just to take me on fishing trips. With a cup of night crawlers in my hand, I'd watch him row the boat for what seemed like an eternity, until we reached the center of the lake. We'd drop anchor, and about 20 minutes later I'd lose interest and want to go back to shore. Each time it happened, my father would row the boat all the way back to shore, only to turn around and head back out. He would fish for hours, and it seemed like my father always returned home with fish. Whatever he caught we'd cook for dinner.

It's probably no surprise to hear that I enjoy a variety of seafood. This chapter has my take on some classic seafood dishes, including a haddock dish. At one time, haddock was the preferred catch that the old New England fishermen kept for themselves. Ready to give it a try and see what you think?

SIDE NOTE: **The FDA recommends that seafood is cooked to an internal temperature of 145°F (63°C).**

THE BEST SALMON YOU'LL EVER EAT

COOK TIME:
15 to 25 minutes

YIELD:
4 servings

Salmon was the first category I ever won an award for when I first entered the world of competition cooking. In fact, it was the very first contest I entered. I received a fourth-place call on my grilled salmon, and I've been hooked on competition cooking ever since. It's fifteen years later, and I'm still at it! The FDA recommends that salmon be cooked to a 145°F (63°C) internal temperature; however, you run the risk of overcooking it at this temperature. No one really likes dry, overcooked salmon, so that's why I like to cook it to 130°F (54°C) and then give it 5 minutes to rest. Cooking salmon to this temperature ensures the fish is tender, moist and superbly flavorful. This recipe is simple, yet it just might provide the most perfectly cooked and delicious piece of salmon you've ever had!

½ cup (120 ml) pure maple syrup, not the fake stuff, divided

2 lb (908 g) salmon, cut into four ½-lb (227-g) portions (see Notes)

Everyday/Everything Rub (page 120)

1 chunk sugar maple wood

Brush half of the maple syrup all over each piece of salmon.

Sprinkle the dry rub on all three sides. Let the salmon sit in the fridge for about 30 minutes.

While you're waiting for the salmon to set up, fire up your WSM for 350°F (191°C), using an empty foil-lined water pan. This recipe requires one fully lit chimney of charcoal. Dump the fully lit chimney into the center of the charcoal ring, reassemble the cooker and let it come up to temperature.

Place the salmon on the top grate of the WSM, add your smoke wood and cook the salmon until it reaches an internal temperature of 130°F (54°C) for medium, 15 to 20 minutes. If you like your salmon cooked a little more, bring the internal temperature to 140°F (60°C), 20 to 25 minutes, but I wouldn't go higher than that or you run the risk of the salmon being overcooked and dry.

After about 10 minutes of cooking, brush the tops of each piece of salmon with the remaining maple syrup.

Once your desired temperature is reached, remove the salmon from the WSM and let it rest for 5 minutes before serving.

NOTES: You can ask your local fishmonger to cut the fish into the ½-lb (227-g) portions.

For salmon, I like to use a mild smoke wood because I want to be able to taste the flavors of the fish and the subtleties of the smoke. Too much smoke results in bitter tasting food.

SHRIMP AND ANDOUILLE SAUSAGE

I like shrimp, I like Andouille sausage and I certainly like butter. Put it all together with a little Cajun spice, and I'm a very happy person. Serve it with some nice crusty bread, and you have yourself a fantastic treat! Bon appétit!

COOK TIME:
20 to 25 minutes

YIELD:
4 to 8 servings

Set up your WSM for 375°F (191°C), and remove the water pan. We'll be cooking on the bottom grate for this recipe. You will need one full chimney of lit charcoal for this cook. Dump the charcoal into the fire ring and then reassemble the cooker.

Place the shrimp and sausage in the half pan. Add the garlic, shallot, ⅛ cup (8 g) of the parsley and ⅛ cup (13 g) of the Cajun seasoning. Mix everything well and then add the melted butter.

Place the half pan on the bottom cooking grate, and cook for 10 to 12 minutes. Stir the contents of the pan and cook for 10 to 12 minutes more.

Remove the pan from the smoker, and transfer the contents into a serving dish. Sprinkle it with the remaining ⅛ cup (13 g) of Cajun seasoning, and garnish with the remaining ⅛ cup (8 g) of parsley.

Serve with the crusty baguette.

> **NOTES:** French baguette bread is crusty on the outside and soft on the inside, making it the perfect bread for dipping.
>
> The andouille sausage is already cooked, so you are just heating it through.

1 lb (454 g) large shrimp, 16–20, peeled and deveined

1 lb (454 g) andouille sausage cut into ½-inch (1.3-cm)-thick slices

Disposable aluminum half pan

2 tbsp (17 g) minced garlic

1 shallot, finely diced

¼ cup (15 g) chopped fresh parsley, divided

¼ cup (25 g) Cajun seasoning, divided

2 sticks (1 cup [240 ml]) melted butter

1 loaf French baguette bread, cut into 1-inch (2.5-cm) slices, for dipping (see Notes)

CRAB-STUFFED HADDOCK

One of the things we have in New England is a lot of fresh seafood. It's some of the best in the world. More times than not, when you go to a seafood restaurant, they will have a stuffed haddock dish on the menu. The stuffing is good, but it can be very dense and bready. This recipe lightens the amount of bread in the stuffing by adding a delicious crabmeat filling. Trust me, the dish might be light on the breadcrumbs, but it didn't lose any of its great flavors!

COOK TIME:
20 to 30 minutes

YIELD:
4 servings

Set up your WSM for 350°F (177°C), using an empty foil-lined water pan. You will need one full chimney of lit charcoal for this cook. Dump the charcoal into the charcoal ring and then reassemble the cooker.

In a small bowl, add the crushed crackers, crab and melted butter. Mix it well.

Place the slices of butter in the half pan, two pieces of butter per fillet. Lay the haddock fillets on top of the butter slices, brush the fillets with lemon juice and season with salt and pepper.

Divide the crab mixture into four portions and top each fillet with the crab mixture.

Place the half pan on the top cooking grate and cook until the fish is done and flaky, 20 to 30 minutes.

One sleeve Ritz crackers, crushed

8 oz (227 g) lump crabmeat

2 sticks (1 cup [227 g]) butter, divided, ½ cup (120 ml) melted, ½ cup (114 g) cut into 8 slices

Disposable aluminum half pan

4 (6-oz [170-g]) haddock fillets

2 lemons, juiced

Salt and pepper

> **NOTE:** Start checking to see if the fish is flaky at the 20-minute mark. Let it cook longer if it is not.

CRAB CAKES WITH LEMON DILL AIOLI

This recipe takes the crab stuffing from the previous recipe plus a couple of extra ingredients and turns it into a mouthwatering, rich and decadent, full of crab . . . cake. I pair this with a lemon dill aioli because the lemon balances out the richness of the butter and crab, creating the perfect complement of flavors.

COOK TIME:
20 to 25 minutes

YIELD:
8 crab cakes

Set up your WSM for 425°F (220°C) and remove the water pan. We'll be cooking on the bottom grate for this recipe. You will need one full chimney of lit charcoal and one half chimney of unlit charcoal for this. Dump the lit charcoal into the fire ring and add the unlit charcoal to the top of it. Let it sit for 5 to 10 minutes and then reassemble the cooker.

For the Lemon Dill Aioli, in a small bowl, mix together the garlic, mayo, mustard, lemon juice, dill, paprika and salt. Cover and store in the fridge until you are ready to use it.

Place the cast-iron skillet on the bottom cooking grate and add the olive oil. While that is heating up, start making the crab cakes.

In a large mixing bowl, place the cracker crumbs and parsley. Add the melted butter and mix together until all the cracker crumbs are coated in butter. Add in the Worcestershire sauce, lemon juice, egg, mayo and Old Bay seasoning. Stir the mixture until it's all incorporated. Season with salt and pepper to taste. Gently fold in the lump crabmeat, until it's all coated.

Form the crab mixture into eight equal-sized cakes, roughly 3½ ounces (99 g) each. Once you have made the last one, add them to the heated cast-iron skillet and cook for about 10 minutes. Flip the crab cakes, and cook for 10 minutes.

You will most likely have to cook these in two batches, because you can only fit four in the pan at one time.

Remove the crab cakes from the pan, and place them on a paper towel to drain the oil. Let them sit for 5 minutes, while you start the next batch.

Serve with the Lemon Dill Aioli.

> **NOTE:** Don't overmix the crab with the bread mix. You want to keep the integrity of the crab together. By that I mean you want to keep the large pieces of crab intact. Crab is very delicate and crumbles easily.

LEMON DILL AIOLI
1 clove garlic, minced

¾ cup (180 ml) mayonnaise

1 tsp Dijon mustard

1 whole lemon, juiced

1 tsp finely chopped fresh dill

¼ tsp paprika

¼ tsp kosher salt

10" (25-cm) cast-iron skillet

¼ cup (60 ml) olive oil

CRAB CAKES
1 sleeve Ritz crackers, crumbled

2 tbsp (4 g) chopped fresh parsley

1 stick (½ cup [120 ml]) melted butter

1 tbsp (15 ml) Worcestershire sauce

Juice from half a lemon

1 egg

¼ cup (60 ml) mayo

1 tsp Old Bay seasoning

Kosher salt, to taste

Coarse black pepper, to taste

16 oz (454 g) lump crabmeat

8

QUICK APPS, SIDES, VEGGIES *and* THINGS

Growing up in my house, it seemed like every vegetable was boiled. Not just boiled, but boiled to the point where you've cooked the flavor out of everything. I think that's why my parents and grandparents salt-and-peppered the hell out of their vegetables—must be an Irish thing.

Preparing vegetables using the hot-and-fast cooking method is similar to roasting them. The natural aromatic flavors of the vegetables remain prominent, but you're getting that cooked-over-fire flavor. It's not overpowering; it's just a subtle hint of flavor that adds a little something extra to whatever you're cooking.

Crank up the happy and make parties more fun with grilled appetizers, finger foods and sides! This chapter features takes on jalapeño poppers, dips, grilled breads and roasted corn. And because no backyard gathering is complete without baked beans, I've included a quick and simple take on this old-fashioned New England dish.

EVERYDAY/EVERYTHING RUB

It's always a good idea to have a go-to rub you can use on anything you cook on the smoker. This rub is something I came up with years ago, and I think it will serve you well. I use it on everything from veggies to popcorn, pork chops to chicken, and pretty much everything else. The rub's well-balanced flavor is not overly hot or sweet, making it a versatile complement for many dishes and recipes.

YIELD:
about 2 cups (390 g)

¼ cup (72 g) kosher salt

½ cup (101 g) turbinado sugar (sugar in the raw)

½ cup (110 g) light brown sugar

¼ cup (30 g) Ancho chili powder

2 tbsp (14 g) onion powder

2 tbsp (17 g) garlic powder

2 tbsp (13 g) coarse black pepper

1 tbsp (5 g) cayenne pepper

1 tbsp (5 g) ground coriander

1 tbsp (6 g) ground cumin

2 tsp (4 g) allspice

2 tsp (5 g) cinnamon

2 tsp (4 g) celery seed

2 tsp (4 g) ginger

In a medium bowl, mix together the salt, turbinado sugar, brown sugar, chili powder, onion powder, garlic powder, coarse black pepper, cayenne pepper, coriander, cumin, allspice, cinnamon, celery seed and ginger. Store the mixture in an airtight container.

NOTE: You can apply rubs anywhere from an hour before cooking the meat to mere moments before the meat hits the smoker. As a general rule, you should try to apply a rub 1 hour before you cook.

STICKY SWEET BBQ SAUCE

BBQ sauce and meat cooked on a smoker is a perfect match. It's something worthy of a romance novel. I personally love the way the sugars of a good BBQ sauce caramelize and create another level of flavor. Plus, almost everyone loves BBQ sauce—one part sticky icky and one part great big smile. The key is that you want the barbecue sauce to complement the meat, not to overpower it. Ideally, you want to apply the sauce to your meat about 15 minutes before the meat comes off the cooker. When the meat is served, you can certainly provide a dipping sauce on the side. That's actually how I like to eat my ribs: dry rubbed, cooked, with sauce on the side. This is the perfect sauce for such a thing!

COOK TIME:
10 minutes

YIELDS:
about 2½ cups (600 ml)

In a medium saucepan on medium heat, add the ketchup, apple cider vinegar, molasses, Worcestershire sauce, brown sugar, chili powder, cayenne, salt, black pepper, garlic powder and onion powder. Mix all the ingredients together and simmer for about 10 minutes. Allow it to cool before storing it in a covered container in the fridge.

1½ cups (360 ml) ketchup

½ cup (120 ml) apple cider vinegar

¼ cup (60 ml) molasses

2 tbsp (30 ml) Worcestershire sauce

1 cup (220 g) packed light brown sugar

2 tbsp (15 g) chili powder

½ tsp cayenne powder

½ tbsp (9 g) kosher salt

2 tsp (4 g) coarse black pepper

1½ tsp (4 g) garlic powder

1 tsp onion powder

ATOMIC BUFFALO TURDS—ABTS

Don't let the name scare you away. Jalapeños stuffed with cream cheese that are wrapped in bacon, seasoned and lightly glazed with barbecue sauce deserve a crazy name, right? The first time I heard about this crazy idea, I said, "You had me at jalapeño." I swear I could eat 100 of these wonderful little treats. This is definitely my favorite app of all time. The subtle heat from the jalapeño and the creaminess of the cheese pair great with the savory bacon and sweet sauce. What's not to love? You're welcome!

COOK TIME:
1 hour. If you were cooking low and slow, these would take 2 to 2½ hours.

YIELD:
8 servings

2 cups (480 ml) water

8 jalapeños

8 oz (227 g) cream cheese

⅓ cup (105 g) peach preserves

16 slices bacon

Everyday/Everything Rub (page 120)

1 chunk each apple and sugar maple wood

Sticky Sweet BBQ Sauce (page 121)

Set up your cooker for 350°F (177°C). One full chimney of hot coal is all you'll need for this. Line your water pan with foil for easy cleanup and add the water.

Cut the jalapeños in half, lengthwise, and remove the seeds. Make sure to keep the stem intact.

Take ½ ounce (14 g) of the cream cheese and spread it in the cavity of each halved jalapeño.

Take 1 teaspoon of the peach preserves and spread it on top of the cream cheese layer of each pepper half.

Starting from the stem end of the pepper, wrap the bacon around the pepper in a spiral pattern. Make sure the end of the bacon is on the bottom of the pepper.

Generously sprinkle the rub all over the bacon-wrapped peppers.

Place the apple and sugar maple wood on top of the charcoal. Put the peppers on the top rack of the WSM and cook for approximately 45 minutes.

Using a basting brush, apply a light coating of barbecue sauce, and cook for 15 minutes.

Remove the peppers from the WSM, and let them sit for 10 minutes before serving.

NOTE: Adding a little bit of water to the water pan will help prevent the grease that drips off the bacon from burning.

INCREDIBLE BUFFALO CHICKEN DIP

Creamy, cheesy, spicy and downright delicious—that's what this recipe brings to the table! If you like buffalo chicken, then I promise that you're going to love this dip. I could eat the entire dish in one sitting, no lie, and it takes restraint not to do so. A nice buffalo chicken dip is perfect for just about any occasion. It holds well and can easily be assembled a day in advance. Are you ready to fire up that smoker and cook?

COOK TIME:
45 minutes

YIELD:
8 to 12 servings

Set the WSM for 350°F (177°C), using an empty water pan. You will only be using one fully lit chimney of hot coals, dumped right into the center of the charcoal ring. Reassemble the WSM and let it come up to temperature.

In a large bowl, place the chicken, cream cheese, ranch dressing, hot sauce, 1 cup (113 g) of the shredded cheese, blue cheese and half of the green onions. Stir the mixture until all the ingredients are incorporated.

Pour the dip mixture into the aluminum half pan, sprinkle it with the remaining ½ cup (57 g) of shredded cheese, remaining green onion and the crumbled crackers on top.

Place the pan on the top rack of the WSM, and cook for 45 minutes, or until the dip mixture starts to bubble on the edges.

Remove the dip and let it sit for 10 minutes.

Serve with the tortilla chips.

> **NOTE:** If you assemble this dip a day ahead of time, just heat it up at 350°F (177°C) for about 45 minutes.

1 (5–6-lb [2.3–2.7-kg]) whole rotisserie chicken, shredded and chopped

2 (8-oz [227-g]) packages cream cheese, softened, cut into ½-inch (1.3-cm) cubes

1 cup (240 ml) ranch dressing

¾ cup (180 ml) Frank's hot sauce

1½ cups (170 g) shredded cheddar cheese, divided

½ cup (68 g) crumbled blue cheese

2 green onions, diced, divided

Small disposable aluminum half pan

1 (8-oz [227-g]) box Chicken in a Biscuit crackers, crumbled

2 bags tortilla chips, for serving

MEXICAN STREET CORN DIP

This recipe is another one of my favorites. I fell in love with Mexican street corn the first time I ever had it. The sweetness of the corn, the saltiness of the Cotija cheese and the mild heat from the chili powder are what did it for me. I was a goner, hopelessly cast under a food spell of love. I longed for it again, and then as I sat and fondly remembered, I thought, *Hmmmm . . . these flavors would make an awesome dip.* Sure, there were a few less-than-ideal attempts, but then, I captured it. This is the final masterpiece, a passion of love—all the elements of Mexican street corn, perfectly served in a dip. *Como te amo, mi dulce!*

COOK TIME:
45 to 60 minutes

YIELD:
8 to 12 servings

8 ears of Roasted Corn (page 136), cut off the cob

1 jalapeño pepper, roasted, seeded and finely chopped

¼ cup (40 g) red onion, plus 2 tbsp (20 g) for garnish

¼ cup (60 ml) mayonnaise

¼ cup (60 ml) Mexican crema or sour cream

¾ cup (113 g) crumbled Cotija cheese, divided

2 tsp (5 g) chili powder

⅓ tsp cayenne pepper

¼ cup (4 g) chopped fresh cilantro, divided

1 tbsp (10 g) Everyday/ Everything Rub (page 120)

1 lime, cut into four wedges

Tortilla chips, for serving

Get out a 10-inch (25-cm) cast-iron skillet.

In a large bowl, add the corn, jalapeño, ¼ cup (40 g) of red onion, mayo, crema, ½ cup (75 g) of the Cotija cheese, chili powder, cayenne pepper and 2 tablespoons (2 g) of the cilantro. Stir the mixture well, and transfer it to the cast-iron skillet.

Set your WSM for 350°F (177°C), and use an empty water pan. You will need one chimney of fully lit charcoal. Dump the charcoal into the center of the charcoal ring and reassemble the WSM.

Place the cast-iron skillet on the top cooking grate and cook the mixture until the outer edges start to bubble, 30 to 45 minutes.

Once it starts to bubble, add the remaining 2 tablespoons (20 g) of red onion, the remaining ¼ cup (38 g) of Cotija cheese and the remaining 2 tablespoons (2 g) of cilantro. Sprinkle with Everyday/Everything Rub and cook for 15 minutes.

Remove the pan and let it sit for 10 minutes.

Squeeze lime wedges over the top, and serve the dip with the tortilla chips.

SMOKED QUESO DIP

Queso is a cheese dip usually made on the stovetop. It's good, and it works, but in my honest opinion it's missing a little something. That little something is a rich, smoky flavor you can only get from cooking outdoors on a smoker. This recipe features lots of bold flavors, like Mexican chorizo sausage, garlic, three different hot peppers, four different cheeses and, of course, that wonderful smoked flavor. Get ready to be appointed the Pope of Flavorville with this one!

COOK TIME:
45 to 60 minutes

YIELD:
8 servings

You will NOT be stirring the mixture in this first step. In a large cast-iron skillet, add the chorizo, taco seasoning, Monterey jack, pepper jack, Oaxaca cheese, Velveeta, cream of garlic soup, fire-roasted tomatoes, green chilies, onions, jalapeños and the poblano. Sprinkle the Everyday/Everything Rub on top.

Set your WSM for 350°F (177°C), and use an empty water pan. You will need one chimney of fully lit charcoal. Dump the charcoal into the center of the charcoal ring and reassemble the WSM.

Place the skillet on the top cooking grate of the WSM. Add the chunk of hickory. Let the dip cook for 15 minutes before stirring. Cook the dip, stirring every 15 minutes, until it is well mixed and bubbling on the sides.

Serve the dip with pork rinds and tortilla chips.

> **NOTE:** Oaxaca, also known as Queso Oaxaca, Asadero or Quesillo, is a Mexican name for a semi-soft, white, string-type, very good melting cheese. If you can't find this, any kind of string cheese will work, such as mozzarella.

½ lb (227 g) cooked chorizo, crumbled

1 tbsp (5 g) taco seasoning

8 oz (227 g) Monterey jack cheese, cut into ½-inch (1.3-cm) cubes

8 oz (227 g) pepper jack cheese, cut into ½-inch (1.3-cm) cubes

8 oz (227 g) shredded Oaxaca Mexican cheese (see Note)

8 oz (227 g) Velveeta cheese, cut into ½-inch (1.3-cm) cubes

1 (10.75-oz [305-g]) can cream of garlic soup

1 (14.5-oz [411-g]) can fire-roasted tomatoes

1 (4-oz [113-g]) can diced green chilies

½ cup (80 g) diced sweet onions

2 jalapeño peppers, roasted and chopped

1 poblano pepper, roasted and chopped

2 tbsp (20 g) Everyday/Everything Rub (page 120)

1 chunk hickory wood

Pork rinds and tortilla chips, to serve

BBQ PORK AND BEANS

One of my favorite side dishes when preparing barbecue, or having just about any grilled entree, is a simple BBQ bean dish. I love the rich, sweet flavor of the sauce, mixed with onions and a little bit of some good ole bacon fat, which in some circles is a type of aphrodisiac!

COOK TIME:
1½ hours

YIELD:
8 to 12 servings

Set your WSM for 350°F (177°C), using an empty water pan. You will need one fully lit chimney of charcoal and one half chimney of unlit charcoal. Add the fully lit chimney of charcoal, and then add the unlit charcoal on top of the lit charcoal. Wait about 10 minutes, and then reassemble the WSM.

In the disposable pan, combine the baked beans, BBQ sauce, sweet onion, bacon, bacon fat, pork, rub and jalapeño pepper. Place the pan on the top rack of the WSM.

Add the apple wood on top of the charcoal and cook for 30 minutes. Stir the beans to help mix in some of that great smoke flavor. Continue cooking for 30 minutes, and then stir the beans again. Cover the pan with the heavy-duty aluminum foil and cook for 30 minutes.

Remove the pan from the smoker and let it rest for about 10 minutes.

Disposable aluminum half pan

2 (28-oz [794-g]) cans baked beans, such as B&M or Bush's original flavor, drained

1½ cups (360 ml) Sticky Sweet BBQ Sauce (page 121)

½ sweet onion, diced

1 lb (454 g) bacon, cooked and diced, saving the fat

¼–½ cup (60–120 ml) bacon fat from rendered bacon, or whatever you are able to collect

1 lb (454 g) Hot and Fast Pulled Pork (page 23)

2 tbsp (20 g) Everyday/Everything Rub (page 120)

1 jalapeño pepper, seeded and finely chopped

1 chunk apple wood

Heavy-duty aluminum foil

HONEY-CHEDDAR CORNBREAD

There's a great debate on whether or not cornbread should be sweet. If you are from the north, then yes it should be sweet; if you are from the south, then no—the only sweetness is from the corn itself. Just think the Hatfields vs. the McCoys. Personally, I like them both. If you are like me, then you enjoy a nice slice of cornbread with your barbecue entrees. I like my cornbread crispy on the outside, and moist and dense on the inside, sort of a stick-to-your-ribs type of dense. In this recipe, I am showing you a sweet-and-savory version where I add a bit of honey for the sweet and some nice sharp cheddar cheese for the savory. Go on and give it a try. Serve this up with some ribs and a side of beans, and you'll have the perfect meal!

COOK TIME:
approximately
35 minutes

YIELD:
8 servings

2½ cups (305 g) yellow cornmeal, good-quality stone ground

½ cup (63 g) all-purpose flour

¼ cup (55 g) light brown sugar

1 tbsp (14 g) baking powder

1 tsp kosher salt

1 cup (240 ml) buttermilk

¼ cup (60 ml) honey, plus more for drizzling

1 cup (240 g) creamed corn

2 eggs

2 sticks (1 cup [227 g]) butter, 1 stick (½ cup [120 ml]) melted, the other cut into eight slices

8 oz (227 g) shredded sharp cheddar cheese

Grease a 10- to 12-inch (25- to 30.5-cm) cast-iron skillet with Crisco.

Set your WSM for 400°F (204°C), using an empty water pan. You will need one fully lit chimney of charcoal and a half chimney of unlit charcoal. Dump the fully lit chimney into the center of the charcoal ring, and then the unlit charcoal on top of that. Wait 10 minutes, and then reassemble the WSM.

In a large bowl, combine the cornmeal, flour, brown sugar, baking powder and salt. Set it aside.

In a medium bowl, whisk the buttermilk, honey, creamed corn and eggs.

Pour the buttermilk mixture into the bowl containing the flour mixture and stir. Then slowly add the melted butter until it's just combined. The batter will be slightly lumpy. Fold in the cheddar cheese and allow the batter to rest at room temperature for 10 minutes. Then pour the batter into the prepared skillet.

Place the skillet on the top rack of the WSM and cook until a toothpick inserted into the center comes out mostly clean and the edges are starting to look golden, approximately 35 minutes.

Remove the cornbread from the WSM. Let it rest in the pan for 10 minutes. Slice it into eight equal slices and serve each slice with a pat of butter and a drizzle of honey.

> **NOTE:** By *mostly clean*, I mean there will be some batter stuck to the toothpick, and that is quite all right. When you remove it from the WSM, it will continue to cook a little more.

FOCACCIA BREAD

When I go to a restaurant, I love it when they bring out bread before your meal, especially when it's focaccia bread and an olive oil dipping sauce. It's a nice change from the plain old boring dinner rolls. This recipe has a ton of great flavor with the garlic and caramelized onion. I guarantee you'll be making this a staple in your weekly meal plan!

COOK TIME:
25 to 30 minutes

YIELD:
8 to 10 servings

For the dough, in a large bowl, combine the yeast, water and sugar. Allow it to rest for about 5 minutes, or until the yeast starts to foam. Add the olive oil, flour and salt to the yeast mixture. Using an electric mixer with a dough hook, mix the dough on low speed until all the flour is incorporated. Mix and knead for 1 minute.

Form the dough into a ball and place it back into the mixing bowl. Cover the bowl with plastic wrap, and let it rise in a warm place for about 2 hours, or until it has doubled in size.

For the Herb Mix, in a medium bowl, combine the rosemary, thyme, pepper flakes, ½ cup (120 ml) of olive oil, parsley, garlic, salt and pepper. Take 2 to 3 tablespoons (30 to 45 ml) of the Herb Mix and coat the bottom of a 10 x 15–inch (25 x 38–cm) baking sheet. Once the dough ball has doubled in size, transfer it to the baking sheet.

Let the dough rest for about 15 minutes on the baking sheet. Spread out the dough into a rectangular shape. If the dough starts to spring back, let it rest for 10 minutes and then continue. Once you have the dough spread out, cover it with plastic wrap, and put it into the fridge for 1 hour.

Set your WSM for 400°F (204°C), and use an empty foil-lined water pan. You will need one fully lit chimney of charcoal and a half chimney of unlit charcoal. Add the fully lit chimney of charcoal to the center of the charcoal ring, spread out the coals and then top it with the unlit charcoal. Wait 15 minutes, and then reassemble the WSM.

Remove the dough from the fridge. Create dimples in the surface of the dough using your fingers, about 1 inch (2.5 cm) apart. Spread the Herb Mix evenly on the dough, and then top it with the caramelized onions.

Place the pan on the top cooking grate of the WSM, and cook for 25 minutes, or until it's golden brown. Remove the focaccia from the WSM and lightly brush the edges with the remaining 1 tablespoon (15 ml) of olive oil.

DOUGH

1 tsp active dry yeast

8 oz (237 ml) warm water (100°F [37.8°C])

1 tsp granulated sugar

2 tbsp (30 ml) extra-virgin olive oil

2½ cups (313 g) all-purpose flour

1 tsp sea salt

HERB MIX

1 tsp finely chopped fresh rosemary

1 tsp chopped fresh thyme

½ tsp red pepper flakes

½ cup (120 ml) extra-virgin olive oil, plus 1 tbsp (15 ml) for brushing

¼ cup (15 g) finely chopped Italian parsley

4 cloves garlic, minced

1 tsp kosher salt

½ tsp coarse black pepper

Plastic wrap

½ red onion, thinly sliced, cooked until caramelized

½ white sweet onion, thinly sliced, cooked until caramelized

NOTES: If you don't have a stand mixer with a dough hook attachment, you can do this by hand using a wooden spoon. Just stir until the dough is combined, and then remove the dough and place it on a floured surface. Knead it for about 1 minute.

If the dough is too sticky, lightly dust it with flour directly in the bowl for easy handling.

ROASTED CORN

Roasted corn is one of those foods I enjoy eating at an outdoor festival because you can hold it in one hand and eat it as you walk around. The other thing I like about it is how the flavor of the corn changes when it's roasted. The corn still has its sweetness, and it takes on a nuttiness from its sugars caramelizing during the cooking process. Roasted corn drenched in melted butter . . . you are in for a treat!

COOK TIME:
approximately
45 minutes

YIELD:
8 servings

Drizzle each ear of corn with olive oil, and dust each ear with chili powder, salt and pepper.

Set the WSM for 350°F (177°C), and remove the water pan completely. You will need one fully lit chimney of charcoal for this recipe. Dump the lit coals into the center of the charcoal ring and then reassemble the WSM.

Place the peach wood on top of the charcoal. Put the corn on the bottom cooking grate and cook for 20 minutes. Turn each piece 180 degrees and cook for 20 minutes.

Take four ears of corn and wrap them in foil with 1 stick (½ cup [114 g]) of butter. Repeat with the remaining four ears. Place each packet of wrapped corn on the smoker and cook for 5 minutes.

Remove the corn from the smoker, leave them wrapped and let them sit for 5 minutes before serving.

8 ears of corn, out of the husk

Olive oil, for drizzling

¼ cup (30 g) Ancho chili powder

Salt and pepper, to taste

1 chunk peach wood

Heavy-duty aluminum foil

2 sticks (1 cup [227 g]) butter

ROASTED POTATOES

The potato is probably my favorite root vegetable. No, it *is* my favorite root vegetable! I love potatoes mashed, baked, fried, roasted, served cold, hot, any which way, it's all good to me. One of the things I like to serve is roasted potatoes. I love how the outsides get a little crispy, and the insides are nice and soft. Pair that with some fresh herbs, a little garlic and BOOM, now we're talking! I know you are going to like this, and so are your friends and family!

COOK TIME:
45 to 50 minutes

YIELD:
6 to 8 servings

Get out a 9 x 13–inch (23 x 33–cm) baking dish.

Set your WSM for 350 to 375°F (177 to 191°C), and remove the water pan. You will need one fully lit chimney of charcoal for this recipe. Dump the fully lit chimney into the center of the charcoal ring, and then reassemble the WSM.

In a large bowl, place the halved potatoes, olive oil, minced garlic, rosemary, thyme, parsley, paprika, onion, salt and pepper. Stir the potatoes until everything is well incorporated.

Transfer the potatoes to the baking dish, and place the dish on the bottom cooking grate. Cook for 20 minutes. Give the potatoes a quick stir and cook until they are fork-tender, 23 to 30 minutes.

NOTE: If you cannot find small multicolored potatoes, then just use red potatoes cut into 1-inch (2.5-cm) cubes.

2 lb (907 g) small multicolored potatoes, cut in half (see Note)

¼ cup (60 ml) olive oil

4 cloves garlic, minced

1 tbsp (2 g) chopped fresh rosemary

1 tbsp (2 g) chopped fresh thyme

1 tbsp (4 g) chopped fresh parsley

1 tbsp (7 g) paprika

½ cup (80 g) diced sweet onion

Salt and pepper, to taste

BANGIN' BRUSSELS SPROUTS WITH BACON, ONION AND BALSAMIC GLAZE

COOK TIME:
45 to 60 minutes

YIELD:
4 servings

Here's another veggie I love to cook. Yeah, I know, there is a good chance you don't like them. Here's the thing though; I think a lot of people don't like Brussels sprouts because they've never had them cooked correctly. Don't boil them, and don't steam them. You need to cook them over high heat to bring out the nuttiness when they get all charred up—not burnt, just charred. Drizzle a little balsamic glaze over these bad Larrys, and I promise, all of a sudden, you'll like this green veggie!

¼ cup (60 ml) olive oil

½ cup (80 g) diced sweet onion

½ lb (227 g) bacon, diced

2 lb (908 g) fresh Brussels sprouts, cut in half

Salt and pepper, to taste

Balsamic glaze, for drizzling after sprouts are cooked

Get out a 9 x 13-inch (23 x 33-cm) roasting pan or a disposable aluminum pan.

Set your WSM for 350 to 375°F (177 to 191°C), and remove the water pan. You will need one fully lit chimney of charcoal for this recipe. Dump the fully lit chimney of charcoal into the center of the charcoal ring, and then reassemble the WSM.

Place the olive oil, onion and bacon in the pan, and place the pan on the top cooking grate of the WSM. Cook it for 15 to 20 minutes, or until the bacon starts to render.

Remove the pan from the cooker. Add the Brussels sprouts to the pan, season with salt and pepper and toss them to evenly coat.

Place the pan on the top grate of the WSM and cook until fork-tender, 30 to 40 minutes.

Remove the Brussels sprouts from the WSM, and let them sit for 5 minutes before drizzling with the balsamic glaze.

SMOKE-ROASTED BUTTERNUT SQUASH

COOK TIME:
1¼ to 1½ hours

YIELD:
4 to 6 servings

So gone are the days of boiled-to-death flavorless veggies. I can't tell you the last time I cooked veggies that way. If you like roasted veggies from your oven, you are going to love them even more smoke roasted in your WSM. My wife loves butternut squash, and I make sure it is an autumn staple in our household. We usually have it at least once a week. One of the things I love about smoke-roasting these is the mild flavor they pick up from the smoke wood and the natural sugars that take on a nutty flavor as you roast them. Go on and give it a try. I trust you'll be glad you did, and your guests will too!

1 large butternut squash, cut in half and seeds removed

¼ cup (60 ml) olive oil

Everyday/Everything Rub (page 120)

1 chunk each apple and pecan wood

2 tbsp (30 ml) pure maple syrup, not the fake stuff

4 tbsp (56 g) butter

Brush the cut sides of the squash with olive oil and lightly season with Everyday/Everything Rub.

Set your WSM to 350°F (177°C), removing the water pan. You will need one fully lit chimney of charcoal and a half chimney of unlit charcoal. Dump in the fully lit chimney, and then add the unlit charcoal on top of the lit charcoal. Wait about 10 minutes, and then reassemble the WSM.

Place the apple and pecan wood on top of the charcoal. Place the squash on the top cooking grate, cut side down, and cook for 45 minutes.

Flip the squash over and brush the inside with maple syrup, sprinkle on a little more rub, and place 2 tablespoons (28 g) of butter into each cavity. Cook the squash for 30 to 45 minutes, or until fork-tender.

Remove the squash from the WSM, and allow it to rest for 10 minutes.

NOTES: If you don't have pecan wood, you can use hickory.

Fork-tender is when you insert a fork into something and it goes in with no resistance.

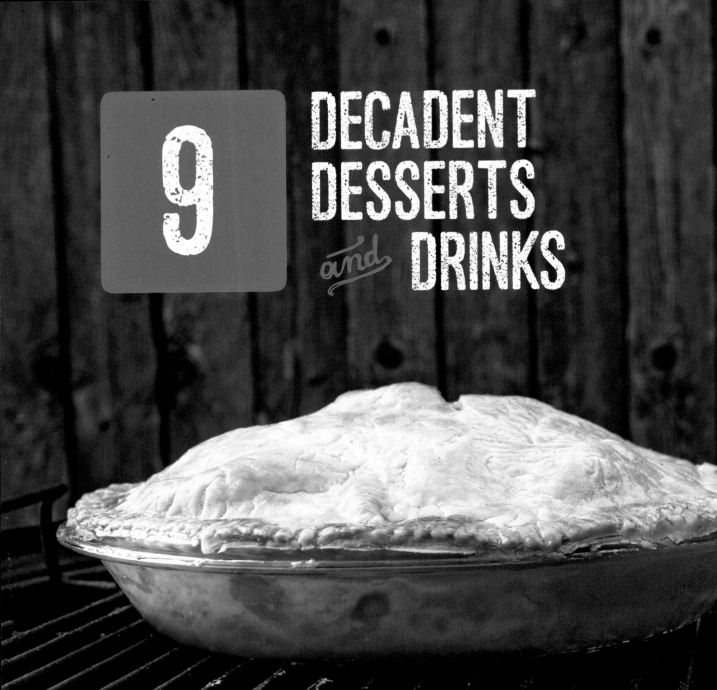

9

DECADENT DESSERTS and DRINKS

A little bit sweet and a lot a bit tempting, these delights are the perfect way to usher in the ending of a backyard gathering. The hot-and-fast cooking method helps caramelize the sugar, ensuring that the dessert delivers just a little more gratification. Whether it's chocolatey fudge brownies, a moist apple pie, decadent cheesecake or an adult-oriented elixir, these treats have a little something to offer just about everyone.

OOEY GOOEY BROWNIES

This is one of my nana's recipes I wanted to share with the world. These little flavor bombs of chocolatey gooey goodness are so addicting they have to be hidden before serving them because people have been known to eat the entire batch in one sitting. The key to getting them so ooey gooey good is that you want to cook them until they are almost done and then pull them off the cooker so the center stays soft.

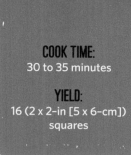

COOK TIME:
30 to 35 minutes

YIELD:
16 (2 x 2-in [5 x 6-cm])
squares

Using Crisco, grease an 8 x 8-inch (20 x 20-cm) baking pan.

Set your WSM to 350°F (177°C), using an empty water pan. You will need one fully lit chimney of charcoal plus one half chimney of unlit charcoal. Dump the fully lit chimney of charcoal into the center of the charcoal ring, and then put the unlit charcoal on top of that. Wait 10 minutes, and then reassemble the smoker.

Melt the semi-sweet chocolate chips in the microwave.

In a large mixing bowl, add the flour, cocoa powder, granulated sugar, brown sugar and salt. Mix it well. To the same bowl, add in the eggs, melted butter, vanilla and melted chocolate. Stir the mixture until it's all incorporated. Transfer the batter to the baking ban, and spread it evenly from edge to edge. Sprinkle the top of the batter with the milk chocolate chips.

Place the pan on the top rack of the WSM and cook for 30 to 35 minutes, or until a toothpick inserted in the middle still has a little batter sticking to it.

Remove the pan from the WSM and set it on the counter to come to room temperature, 45 to 60 minutes.

1 cup (170 g) semi-sweet chocolate chips

1¼ cups (156 g) all-purpose flour

½ cup (43 g) unsweetened cocoa powder

1¼ cups (250 g) granulated sugar

1 cup (220 g) light brown sugar

½ tsp kosher salt

3 eggs

1 cup (240 ml) melted butter

1 tbsp (15 ml) vanilla extract

½ cup (85 g) milk chocolate chips

NOTE: When testing for doneness with a toothpick, it will come out dirty, meaning some batter will remain on the toothpick for ooey gooey fudgy brownies like my nana used to make.

SWEET POTATO CHEESECAKE

Anyone who knows me knows I love sweet potatoes. At Thanksgiving, I am the one with half my plate full of candied sweet potatoes. I love them so much that my wife surprised me with this absolutely wonderful sweet potato cheesecake. I thought, *How can it get any better than this?* Honestly, it can't. My wife is the best! Not only that, the flavor of the sweet potato, the crunchy crust and the buttery pecan topping is sure to bring you to that happy and wonderful place known as food coma bliss!

COOKING TIME:
60 to 75 minutes

YIELD:
8 servings

Lightly grease a 9½-inch (24-cm) springform pan with cooking spray.

Set your WSM to 350°F (177°C), using an empty water pan. You will need one fully lit chimney of charcoal and a half chimney of unlit charcoal. Dump the fully lit chimney into the center of the charcoal ring, and add the unlit charcoal on top. Wait 10 to 15 minutes, and then reassemble the WSM.

For the crust, in a small bowl, mix together the graham crackers, melted butter and sugar. Press the mixture firmly along the bottom of the springform pan.

Place the pan on the top cooking grate of the WSM and cook for 10 minutes. Remove the pan and set it aside.

For the cheesecake filling, in a large bowl, mix together the cream cheese and sugar until smooth. Add the sour cream, heavy cream, mashed sweet potatoes, vanilla, cinnamon, nutmeg and cloves. Stir the filling well, and then add in one egg at a time, mixing until the eggs are incorporated.

Pour the filling into the crust and spread evenly.

Place the cheesecake on the top cooking grate of the WSM and cook it until a toothpick inserted into the middle comes out clean. Start checking it at the 1-hour mark.

When the cheesecake is done, remove it from the cooker and allow it to rest for 30 minutes.

For the topping, in a small saucepan over medium heat, combine the brown sugar and butter. Stir the mixture until the sugar dissolves. Add in the heavy cream and chopped pecans and mix it well. Remove it from the heat and let it sit for 5 minutes.

Pour the hot topping over the top of the cheesecake. Remove the outer ring portion of the springform pan.

NOTE: The center of the cheesecake should have sunken in a little bit while resting. This will be perfect for the topping to sit on.

CRUST

1¼ cups (125 g) crushed graham crackers

¼ cup (60 ml) melted butter

¼ cup (50 g) sugar

CHEESECAKE FILLING

3 (8-oz [227-g]) packages cream cheese, softened

¾ cup (150 g) plus 2 tbsp (30 g) granulated sugar

⅓ cup (80 ml) sour cream

¼ cup (60 ml) heavy whipping cream

2 lb (908 g) sweet potatoes, cooked, peeled and mashed

1 tsp vanilla extract

½ tsp ground cinnamon

¼ tsp ground nutmeg

¼ tsp ground cloves

3 large eggs

TOPPING

¾ cup (165 g) light brown sugar

½ stick (¼ cup [56 g]) butter

¼ cup (60 ml) heavy whipping cream

1 cup (109 g) chopped pecans

STUFFED FRENCH TOAST

French toast is always a great treat for breakfast, brunch or dessert, but French toast stuffed with cream cheese and raspberry jam and cooked on the WSM is an absolute dream come true. The only bread I use when making French toast is brioche. I prefer it because it is thick and will soak up the right amount of liquid, making it soft but not soft enough to turn soggy. This recipe is prepped the day/night before for two reasons: one, the bread will soak in all that great flavor from the custard, and two, all you have to do is cook in the morning or at night after dinner for a little twist on dessert.

COOK TIME:
30 minutes

YIELD:
6 servings

8 oz (227 g) cream cheese, softened

1 cup (320 g) raspberry jam, divided

1 loaf brioche bread, cut into 12 slices

7 large eggs

2 cups (480 ml) half and half

1 tsp vanilla extract

1 pinch salt

Plastic wrap

Maple syrup, to serve

Using Crisco, grease a 10 x 13-inch (25 x 33-cm) casserole dish. Set it aside.

In a small bowl, mix together the cream cheese and ½ cup (160 g) of the raspberry jam. Spread a thick layer of the cream cheese mixture on a slice of bread, and close it with a second slice to make a sandwich. Be sure to divide up the cream cheese mixture evenly among the slices. Place the sandwich in the casserole dish. Repeat with the remaining slices.

In a medium bowl, add the eggs, half and half, vanilla and salt. Stir the mixture until it is all incorporated.

Pour the egg mixture over the stuffed French toast. Allow it to soak for a couple of minutes, and then carefully flip each sandwich over. Cover the dish with plastic wrap, and place it in the refrigerator overnight.

In the morning, take the pan out of the fridge. Set your WSM to 350°F (177°C), and use an empty water pan. You will only need one full chimney of lit charcoal for this. Dump the fully lit chimney of charcoal into the center of the charcoal ring, and reassemble the WSM.

Place the pan of French toast on the top cooking grate of the WSM, and cook for 35 to 45 minutes, or until it's golden brown.

Let it rest for 5 minutes before serving with maple syrup and the remaining ½ cup (160 g) of raspberry jam.

> **NOTE:** Make sure your pan is large enough that you can place six pieces of bread next to each other on the bottom of the pan.

ROASTED-LIME MARGARITA

It's summertime, it's hot outside, and you're sitting out by the pool. What are you drinking? I don't know about you, but I'm drinking a nice cold margarita on the rocks. Not just any old margarita, no, no, no. I'm drinking a roasted lime margarita. "Roasted lime?" you say. Oh, yeah, roasted lime! This isn't kicking up the flavor dial, this is STOMPING on it. By roasting the limes, you are concentrating the lime flavor to create the best margarita you will ever drink!

COOK TIME:
20 to 25 minutes

YIELD:
4 to 6 servings

Get out a 1-gallon (3.8-L) pitcher.

Fire up your WSM to 425°F (218°C), and remove the water pan. You will need one fully lit chimney of charcoal for this recipe. Dump the lit charcoal into the center of the charcoal ring, and then reassemble the smoker.

For the limes, dip each of the halved limes into the sugar to coat.

Place each lime half on the bottom cooking grate directly over the hot coals. Cook for about 20 minutes.

While the limes are cooking, for the simple syrup, in a large saucepan, bring the water to a boil and add the sugar. Cook it until all the sugar is dissolved. Remove the syrup from the heat and let it sit for about 30 minutes.

When the limes are done, remove them from the WSM.

To assemble the margarita, squeeze the juice from the limes into the pitcher. Use a citrus squeezer if you have one. If you do not, use your hands to squeeze the limes, but try to get as much juice as you can. Reserve the lime skins. Add the cold water, simple syrup, about half of the grilled lime skins, the tequila, orange liqueur and ice. Stir thoroughly.

> **NOTE:** Adding sugar to the surface of the limes will cause the limes to caramelize and create a richer lime flavor.

LIMES
12 limes cut in half, crosswise

½ cup (100 g) granulated sugar

SIMPLE SYRUP
3 cups (720 ml) water

1½ cups (300 g) granulated sugar

MARGARITA
32 oz (960 ml) cold water

2 cups (480 ml) really good tequila, such as Patrón Silver

1 cup (240 ml) orange liqueur, such as Grand Marnier

4 cups (600 g) ice

NANA'S APPLE PIE

This is the one dessert I really look forward to the most around the holidays. My nana would make an apple pie for every holiday gathering. I fondly remember the flavors like it was yesterday. In the finished pie, the apples still had a tiny crunch to them, were not overly sweet so you could still taste the apple and had subtle flavors of cinnamon and nutmeg. For years I tried to replicate this, and for years I failed. I used variety after variety of different apples and could never get it quite right. So then one day I decided to ask my mom, just to see if she knew. And maybe I should have asked her right from the beginning because Mom told me that my nana used an equal mix of Cortland and Macintosh apples. So, the next pie I made was made with an equal mix of those apples. I went in for the first bite and voila! I had hit the jackpot! It tasted exactly as I remembered. So, this recipe is a tribute to my nana. I hope you enjoy it as much as I do!

COOK TIME:
45 to 60 minutes

YIELD:
8 servings

6 to 8 Cortland and Macintosh apples, cored and sliced, equal amounts of each variety (see Notes)

Juice of 1 lemon

½ cup (100 g) sugar

1 tbsp (8 g) cinnamon

1 tsp nutmeg

1 tsp vanilla extract

2 store-bought piecrusts, big enough for a 9-inch (23–cm) pie dish

½ stick (57 g) butter, cut into 8 pieces

1 extra large egg plus 1 tbsp (15 ml) water, beaten

Using Crisco, grease the bottoms and sides of a 9-inch (23-cm) pie dish.

Set your WSM to 350°F (177°C), using an empty water pan. You will need one chimney of fully lit charcoal and a half chimney of unlit charcoal. Dump the fully lit chimney into the center of the charcoal ring, and then add the unlit charcoal on top. Wait about 10 minutes, and then reassemble the WSM.

In a large mixing bowl, add the sliced apples and lemon juice. Mix them well.

To that bowl, add the sugar, cinnamon, nutmeg and vanilla, and mix until all the apples are coated.

Place one of the piecrusts in the bottom of the pie dish, making sure to press it against the bottom and sides to form the base of the pie.

Add the apple mixture to the bottom crust, and spread it around so it is the same height at the edges and mounds taller in the center. Place the butter slices on top of the apples.

Top the pie with the other piecrust. It will overlap with the bottom crust. With a fork, go around the edges and press down, pinching the bottom and top crusts together. Repeat all the way around the entire pie. With a sharp knife, make an "X" in the center of the top crust.

(continued)

NANA'S APPLE PIE (CONTINUED)

Brush the edges and top of the piecrust with the egg and water mixture. This will result in a beautiful golden color after the pie is cooked.

Place the pie on the top cooking grate, and cook it until the pie starts to bubble at the seams, 45 to 60 minutes. Start checking at 45 minutes, and watch for bubbles along the seams.

Remove the pie from the WSM and allow it to cool for about 1 hour.

NOTES: I have a piece of equipment that cores and slices the apple all in one step. It's definitely a time saver and makes processing the apples a lot easier; however, you certainly don't need one of these and can use a paring knife instead.

I prefer glass or Pyrex pie dishes.

The acid in the lemon juice prevents the apples from turning brown.

Creating that "X" in the top crust allows the pie to release pressure and for the steam to escape so that the piecrust doesn't break while it's cooking.

REFERENCES

AFTERMARKET PARTS AND USEFUL WEBSITES

In addition to Weber's product offerings, a variety of aftermarket parts are also available. If you explore the internet, you'll quickly realize that you can find just about any product modification or enhancement for the WSM. Common modifications, including a hinged lid, attachable handles to make moving the center section of the smoker easier or gasket kits to help seal the lid and side access door are easy to find, but this is just scraping the surface of the changes some hobbyists make to their products.

Here are some additional sites I like to use or have found interesting.

- **Fruitawood:** https://fruitawoodchunks.com/
- **Heritage Steel Cutlery:** https://www.heritagesteel.us/
- **Smokin' Hoggz BBQ Products:** https://www.smokinhoggzbbq.com/
- **Butcher's BBQ Products:** https://www.butcherbbq.com
- **Smokin' Guns BBQ Products:** https://www.smokingunsbbq.com
- **BBQ Spot:** https://bbqspot.com/
- **BBQ Guru:** https://bbqguru.com/
- **Thermapen:** https://www.thermoworks.com/Thermapens
- **Lavatools:** https://www.lavatools.co/
- **Hunsaker Smokers:** https://www.hunsakersmokers.com/collections/weber-modifications
- **Arborfab:** https://arborfab.com/grillcookeraccessories
- **Amazon.com** also provides access to numerous aftermarket WSM product offerings.

ACKNOWLEDGMENTS

My wife, Shaune Gillespie, for keeping me focused in life and for her continued support and believing in me throughout this BBQ journey.

My teammate and best friend, Alan Burke, for always being willing to drive the trailer anywhere, allowing me to save vacation time, always being there to help out, no questions asked and for being a constant source of a good time.

Tim O'Keefe, for willingly taking on another project (#4) with me and knowing how to translate my thoughts into words people can understand.

My publisher, Will Kiester, editor, Marissa Giambelluca, and the entire staff at Page Street Publishing for this opportunity to write a fourth book!

Photographer Ken Goodman for his extraordinary talent in making the food jump off the pages.

All my friends and family who came out to help with the photo shoot, whether it was helping with food prep or running to the store to get an ingredient, THANK YOU!!

ABOUT THE AUTHOR

BILL GILLESPIE is the founder and head pitmaster for the World Champion Smokin' Hoggz BBQ Team. The team consists of his wife, Shaune Gillespie, and longtime friend of over 35 years, Alan Burke. Bill spends his days working for the local utility company as a design engineer, but his true passion is grilling and cooking BBQ. For over 30 years, Bill has been perfecting his craft in BBQ cooking in his backyard for friends and family. In 2005, Bill joined the BBQ circuit and in 2008 formed Smokin' Hoggz BBQ.

Since then, they have competed in over 200 contests nationwide (20 states) including Canada and have gone on to win 35 Grand and 22 Reserve Grand Championships, over 140 overall top-ten finishes, over 430 category (chicken, ribs, pork and brisket) top-ten finishes and numerous other awards.

Here are some of the accomplishments Bill and his team have achieved:

- 2011 Jack Daniels World BBQ Championship
- 2014 American Royal Invitational World Series of BBQ

(These are two of the most prestigious BBQ competitions on the circuit.)

- Northeast BBQ Society (NEBS) Overall Team of the Year (TOY) in 2014 and 2015, NEBS Ribs TOY (2013, 2014, 2015 and 2016), NEBS Chicken TOY (2013), NEBS Pork TOY (2017), NEBS Brisket TOY (2013 and 2015)
- KCBS 2014 Team of the Year (15th overall)
- KCBS 2018 Team of the Year (9th overall, 10th in chicken, 5th in ribs)
- KCBS 2019 Team of the Year (5th in ribs)

He is also the author of three grilling and BBQ cookbooks: *The Secrets to Great Charcoal Grilling on the Weber*, *Secrets to Smoking on the Weber Smokey Mountain Cooker and Other Smokers* and *The Smoking Bacon & Hog Cookbook*. Bill has also created a line of award-winning dry rubs and BBQ sauces, such as Smokin' Applewood All-Purpose Rub and RibRub & Pitmaster Blend.

TIM O'KEEFE has lifetime membership in the Kansas City Barbeque Society and has been an active judge for fifteen years. His love of barbecue included three years on the barbecue circuit as part of the Can U Smell My Pits competition team. In addition to cowriting four cookbooks with pitmaster Bill Gillespie, he also assisted with *Operation BBQ*, a collection of 200 recipes from competition grand champions. Tim enjoys writing about barbecue and is always looking to expand his knowledge of this unique cuisine.

INDEX